Lecture Notes in Computer Science 9212

Commenced Publication in 1973
Founding and Former Series Editors:
Gerhard Goos, Juris Hartmanis, and Jan van Leeuwen

More information about this series at http://www.springer.com/series/7407

Andrzej Pelc · Alexander A. Schwarzmann (Eds.)

Stabilization, Safety, and Security of Distributed Systems

17th International Symposium, SSS 2015
Edmonton, AB, Canada, August 18–21, 2015
Proceedings

 Springer

Editors
Andrzej Pelc
Université du Québec en Outaouais
Gatineau, QC
Canada

Alexander A. Schwarzmann
University of Connecticut
Storrs, CT
USA

ISSN 0302-9743   ISSN 1611-3349   (electronic)
Lecture Notes in Computer Science
ISBN 978-3-319-21740-6   ISBN 978-3-319-21741-3   (eBook)
DOI 10.1007/978-3-319-21741-3

Library of Congress Control Number: 2015943848

LNCS Sublibrary: SL1 – Theoretical Computer Science and General Issues

Springer Cham Heidelberg New York Dordrecht London
© Springer International Publishing Switzerland 2015

Printed on acid-free paper

Springer International Publishing AG Switzerland is part of Springer Science+Business Media
(www.springer.com)

Preface

The International Symposium on Stabilization, Safety, and Security in Distributed Systems (SSS) is an international forum for researchers and practitioners working on the design and development of distributed systems that guarantee specific desired properties despite adversity, or that are able to restore the desired properties following adversarial perturbations in the computing medium building on the principles of self-stabilization. Research in distributed computing and distributed systems continues its vibrant development, marked by the importance of dynamic systems, such as peer-to-peer networks, large-scale wireless sensor networks, mobile ad hoc networks, mobile agent computing, opportunistic networks etc. Moreover, new applications such as grid and web services, banking and e-commerce, e-voting, e-health and robotics, aerospace and avionics, automotive, industrial process control, have joined the expanded landscape of distributed systems. It is becoming increasingly important to endow all such systems with built-in means for self-management, self-protection, and self-repair.

This volume contains the papers presented at the 17th International Symposium on Stabilization, Safety, and Security of Distributed Systems, held August 18–21, 2015 in Edmonton, Alberta, Canada.

This year the Program Committee was organized into several tracks reflecting most topics related to the conference interests. The tracks are: Self-Stabilization, Fault-tolerance and Dependability, Ad-hoc and Sensor Networks, Mobile Agents, System Security in Distributed Computing, and Formal Methods and Distributed Algorithms. We received 38 regular paper submissions. Each submission was reviewed by at least three Program Committee members with the help of external reviewers. Out of these 38 submissions, 16 papers were accepted for presentation at the symposium and publication in the proceedings as regular papers. The proceedings also include eight brief announcements.

Two regular papers received awards. The Best Paper Award was given to Colin Cooper, Anissa Lamani, Giovanni Viglietta, Masafumi Yamashita, and Yukiko Yamauchi for their paper "Constructing Self-Stabilizing Oscillators in Population Protocols," and the Best Student Paper Award was given to Lili Su (student) and Nitin Vaidya for their paper "Reaching Approximate Byzantine Consensus with Multi-hop Communication."

The program also included three distinguished keynote lectures by Sergio Rajsbaum (UNAM, Mexico), Roger Wattenhofer (ETH Zurich, Switzerland), and Philipp Woelfel (University of Calgary, Canada).

On behalf of the Program Committee, we thank all authors who submitted their work to SSS 2015. We gratefully acknowledge the substantial effort of the track chairs and the Program Committee members invested in paper selection. Thanks are also due to the external reviewers for their valuable and insightful comments. We also thank to the Steering Committee members for their valuable advice and guidance and to the

Organizing Committee members for their work in ensuring a successful and pleasant meeting.

Colocated with the symposium was the Summer School on Distributed Computing and Cryptography organized by Shlomi Dolev.

SSS 2015 acknowledges with gratitude the support of the Faculty of Science, University of Alberta, and EasyChair.org for the use of their system in handling submissions, managing the review process, and helping compile these proceedings.

August 2015   Andrzej Pelc
                                                          Alexander A. Schwarzmann

Organization

General Co-Chairs

Ted Herman   University of Iowa, USA
Jared Saia   University of New Mexico, USA

Program Committee Co-Chairs

Andrzej Pelc   Université du Québec en Outaouais, Canada
Alexander A. Schwarzmann   University of Connecticut, USA

Program Committee

Self-Stabilization Track

Joffroy Beauquier,   Université Paris-Sud, France
  Track Chair
Janna Burman   Université Paris-Sud, France
Ajoy Datta   University of Nevada Las Vegas, USA
Swan Dubois   Université Paris 6, France
Sukumar Ghosh   University of Iowa, USA
Shay Kutten   Technion, Israel
Christian Scheideler   University of Paderborn, Germany
Masafumi Yamashita   Kyushu University, Japan

Fault-tolerance and Dependability Track

Nitin Vaidya, *Track Chair*   University of Illinois at Urbana-Champaign, USA
Mostefaoui Achour   Université de Nantes, France
James Aspnes   Yale University, USA
Bernadette Charron-Bost   Ecole Polytechnique, France
Xavier Defago   Japan Advanced Institute of Science and Technology
Borzoo Bonakdarpour   McMaster University, Canada
Shlomi Dolev   Ben-Gurion University of the Negev, Israel
Maurice Herlihy   Brown University, USA
Vijay Garg   University of Texas at Austin, USA
Rachid Guerraoui   EPFL, Switzerland
Luis Rodrigues   Universidade de Lisboa, Portugal
Srikanth Sastry   Google, USA
Sebastien Tixeuil   Université Pierre et Marie Curie, France
Jennifer L. Welch   Texas A&M University, USA

Ad-hoc and Sensor Networks, Mobile Agents Track

Paola Flocchini, *Track Chair*	University of Ottawa, Canada
Jeremie Chalopin	CNRS/Aix-Marseille Université, France
Sandor Fekete	Technische Universität, Braunschweig, Germany
Magns M. Halldorsson	Reykjavik University, Iceland
Taisuke Izumi	Nagoya Institute of Technology, Japan
Adrian Kosowski	INRIA Bordeaux, France
Flaminia Luccio	University of Venice, Italy
Russ Martin	University of Liverpool, UK
Lata Narayanan	Concordia University, Canada
Calvin Newport	Georgetown University, USA
Koichi Wada	Hosei University, Japan

System Security in Distributed Computing Track

Alexander Russell, *Track Chair*	University of Connecticut, USA
Mohamed Gouda	University of Texas, Austin, USA
Aggelos Kiayias	University of Athens, Greece
Nicolas Nicolaou	IMDEA Networks Institute, Spain
Ravi Sundaram	Northeastern University, USA
Hong-Sheng Zhou	Virginia Commonwealth University, USA

Formal Methods and Distributed Algorithms Track

Helmut Veith, *Track Chair*	Vienna University of Technology, Austria
Parosh Abdullah	Uppsala University, Sweden
Borzoo Bonakdarpour	McMaster University, Canada
Sagar Chaki	Carnegie Mellon University, USA
Giorgio Delzanno	University of Genoa, Italy
Cezara Dragoi	INRIA, France
Pierre Ganty	IMDEA Software Institute, Spain
Swen Jacobs	Universitat des Saarlandes, Germany
Zachary Kincaid	University of Toronto, Canada
Igor Konnov	Vienna University of Technology, Austria
Ken McMillan	Microsoft Research, USA
Stefan Merz	INRIA Nancy/LORIA, France
Andreas Podelski	Universität Freiburg, Germany
Lenore D. Zuck	University of Illinois at Chicago, USA

Symposium Organization

Local Arrangements Chair

Ioanis Nikolaidis	University of Alberta, Canada

Finance Co-Chairs

Borzoo Bonakdarpour   McMaster University, Canada
H. James Hoover   University of Alberta, Canada

Publicity Chair

Maxwell Young   Drexel University, USA

Steering Committee

Anish Arora   Ohio State University, USA
Ajoy K. Datta   University of Nevada, USA
Shlomi Dolev, *Chair*   Ben-Gurion University of the Negev, Israel
Sukumar Ghosh   University of Iowa, USA
Mohamed Gouda   University of Texas at Austin, USA
Ted Herman   University of Iowa, USA
Toshimitsu Masuzawa   Osaka University, Japan
Vincent Villain   Université de Picardie Jules Verne (UPJV), France

External Reviewers

Andrew Berns   Fukuhito Ooshita
Stéphane Devismes   Franck Petit
Anaïs Durand   Maria Potop-Butucaru
Martina Eikel   Othmane Rezine
Chryssis Georgiou   Alexander Setzer
Yoshiaki Katayama   Devan Sohier
Shuji Kijima   Thim Strothmann
Andreas Koutsopoulos   Giovanni Viglietta
Anissa Lamani   Bingsheng Zhang
Hammurabi Mendes

Keynote Lectures

Distributed Runtime Verification

where combinatorics, fault-tolerance and formal methods meet

Sergio Rajsbaum

Instituto de Matemáticas, Universidad Nacional Autónoma de México,
D.F. 04510, Mexico

Abstract of Keynote Lecture

Runtime verification. RV techniques are concerned with monitoring software
and hardware system executions. They are complementary, and sometimes more
versatile than conventional testing, and more practical than exhaustive formal
verification, such as model checking and theorem proving, as well as incomplete
solutions such as testing and debugging. There is an international conference,
RV dedicated to these techniques.

Distributed runtime verification. This talk gives an overview of distributed
runtime verification (DRV). Building a decentralized runtime monitor for a
distributed system is an especially difficult task since it involves designing a
distributed algorithm that coordinates the monitors in order for them to reason
consistently about the temporal behavior of the system. DRV techniques are less
developed; they involve designing a distributed algorithm that monitors another
distributed algorithm.

In an asynchronous system where processes may crash, it is impossible for the
monitors to agree on the order of events in the system, due to the impossibility of
solving consensus. Thus, it is unavoidable that monitors emit different opinions
about the validity of the computation, that nevertheless, should be consistent
with each other. Lower and upper bounds on the number of opinions that may
have to be emitted, can be derived, as a function of the specification φ that is
being monitored.

At the crossroads where distributed algorithms and formal methods meet. An
overview of the different types of techniques used in DRV is presented, which
range from formal methods techniques related to LTL and multi-valued logics,
on the one hand, to algorithmic techniques related to computing snapshots in an
efficient manner to reason about temporal properties of a distributed system, on
the other hand, and passing through combinatorial and topological techniques.
RV is an exemplary area for interdisciplinary research opportunities, given that
logic and algorithmic techniques converge, and few papers explore the difficulties
introduced when failures and asynchrony can occur in the system.

Supported by a UNAM-PAPIIT Grant.

Acknowledgements. The results presented involve joint work with Borzoo Bonakdarpour, Pierre Fraigniaud, Matthieu Roy, David Rosenblueth and Corentin Travers. Some of them have been published in DISC'11, OPODIS'14, RV'14, and *Distributed Computing* (2013).

A Fast and Scalable Payment Network with Bitcoin Duplex Micropayment Channels

Christian Decker and Roger Wattenhofer

Distributed Computing Group, ETH Zurich
{cdecker,wattenhofer}@ethz.ch

Abstract. Bitcoin does not scale, because its synchronization mechanism, the blockchain, limits the maximum rate of transactions the network can process. However, using off-blockchain transactions it is possible to create long-lived channels over which an arbitrary number of transfers can be processed locally between two users, without any burden to the Bitcoin network. These channels may form a network of payment service providers (PSP) and payments can be routed between any two users in real time, without any confirmation delay. In this work we present a protocol for duplex micropayment channels, which guarantee end-to-end security and allow instant transfers, laying the foundation of the PSP network.

Correctness Conditions for Randomized Shared Memory Algorithms

Philipp Woelfel

Department of Computer Science, University of Calgary, Canada

Abstract of Keynote Lecture

In an asynchronous shared memory system, processes communicate by applying operations on shared *base* objects. From an algorithm designer's perspective it is ideal if the operations on these objects are *atomic*, meaning that each such operation happens instantaneously. However, objects provided by systems are typically not truly atomic, and neither are objects implemented from base objects. As a result, if multiple processes concurrently execute methods on such objects, the set of all possible outcomes is difficult to predict.

For almost two decades, *linearizability*, defined by Herlihy and Wing [4], has been the gold standard among correctness conditions for non-atomic objects. It guarantees that any possible result that can arise from an interleaving of processes using linearizable operations could arise if the operations were atomic. Hence, the worst-case behaviour of algorithms can be analyzed under the assumption that all operations are atomic, even when they are only linearizable. For that reason, the terms linearizability and atomicity have often been used interchangeably (see for example [5]).

Golab, Higham, and Woelfel [2] observed that linearizable implementations do not preserve the probability distribution of the possible results if we replace atomic objects used in a *randomized* algorithm with implemented ones. An *adversary*, which schedules process steps, can "stretch out" a method call that was originally an atomic operation, and inspect the outcome of other processes coin flips before allowing the method call to be completed. As a result, replacing an atomic object with a linearizable one in a randomized algorithm amounts to increasing the power of the adversary. In order to be able to employ the power of randomization in shared memory algorithms, we need to devise new correctness conditions that eliminate the deficiencies of linearizability. In this talk the state of the art [1–3] of finding such correctness conditions will be presented.

References

1. Denysyuk, O., Woelfel, P.: Wait-freedom is harder than lock-freedom under strong linearizability (2015, submitted)
2. Golab, W., Higham, L., Woelfel, P.: Linearizable implementations do not suffice for randomized distributed computation. In: Proceedings of 43rd ACM STOC, pp. 373–382 (2011)
3. Helmi, M., Higham, L., Woelfel, P.: Strongly linearizable implementations: possibilities and impossibilities. In: Proceedings of 31st PODC, pp. 385–394 (2012)

4. Herlihy, M., Wing, J.: Linearizability: a correctness condition for concurrent objects. ACM Trans. Prog. Lang. Syst. **12**, 463–492 (1990)
5. Lynch, N.: Distributed Algorithms. Morgan Kaufmann Publishers Inc. (1996)

Contents

Brief Announcements

Keynote Lecture

A Fast and Scalable Payment Network with Bitcoin Duplex Micropayment Channels

Christian Decker$^{(\boxtimes)}$ and Roger Wattenhofer

Distributed Computing Group, ETH Zürich, Zürich, Switzerland
{cdecker,wattenhofer}@ethz.ch

Abstract. Bitcoin does not scale, because its synchronization mechanism, the blockchain, limits the maximum rate of transactions the network can process. However, using off-blockchain transactions it is possible to create long-lived channels over which an arbitrary number of transfers can be processed locally between two users, without any burden to the Bitcoin network. These channels may form a network of payment service providers (PSPs). Payments can be routed between any two users in real time, without any confirmation delay. In this work we present a protocol for duplex micropayment channels, which guarantees end-to-end security and allow instant transfers, laying the foundation of the PSP network.

1 Introduction

Credit card companies process a growing number of transactions, currently more than 10,000 per second. In contrast, Bitcoin currently handles about one transaction per second. Bitcoin's turnover is growing, and ultimately Bitcoin may become a viable payment alternative. However, can Bitcoin scale to match the throughput of credit cards, or even an envisioned world of millions of micropayments per second?

The answer to this question is astonishingly negative. In order to verify whether a new transaction is valid, and in order to bootstrap new peers, every peer in the Bitcoin network stores every transaction ever. The size of an average transaction is 500 bytes, so with 1 transaction per second, every Bitcoin peer now needs almost 20 GB of additional storage each year. A turnover of 500 transactions per second would require 10 TB of additional disk space per year, which is at the limit for a consumer.

A bigger problem is processing power. Checking the signatures of each transaction (mostly because of disk seek time) takes about 5 ms, so with current machines we cannot hope to scale beyond 200 transactions per second.

Every node in the bitcoin network is informed about every transaction, multiple times because of the fault-tolerant gossip process. Assuming a common end-user bandwidth of 10 Mbit/s, then the rate peers can receive transactions is limited to approximately 1,000 transactions per second. Finally, while peers may individually be able to receive and process up to 200 transactions per second, the synchronization mechanism underlying Bitcoin is susceptible to latency, and does not work with transaction rates above 100 transactions per second [6].

© Springer International Publishing Switzerland 2015
A. Pelc and A.A. Schwarzmann (Eds.): SSS 2015, LNCS 9212, pp. 3–18, 2015.
DOI: 10.1007/978-3-319-21741-3_1

In summary, Bitcoin in its current form will have a hard time scaling beyond 100 transactions per second, because of storage, processing, latency, and bandwidth. The problem of Bitcoin is its reliance on a synchronized global state, the replicated *blockchain*.

In this paper, we propose to reduce the reliance on the blockchain to further decentralize the architecture of Bitcoin. We believe that the blockchain should only be used to establish long lived point-to-point channels between parties over which an arbitrary number of transfers can be performed. These transfers are no longer Bitcoin transactions that are committed to the blockchain, instead they rely on off-blockchain transactions that summarize any number of transfers between two parties. The blockchain is only involved during the setup and the closure of such a channel, while the vast majority of updates is never committed to the blockchain.

Towards this goal we present a duplex micropayment channel protocol. Duplex micropayment channels are established between *payment service providers* (PSPs). PSPs are the equivalent autonomous systems in the Internet, routing transfers between end users, possibly over multiple hops, guaranteeing end-to-end security and enabling real-time transfers. Unlike Bitcoin transactions, which take minutes to be confirmed, transfers over our duplex micropayment channels are final and can be accepted without further confirmations, enabling real-time payments, and a truly scalable future Bitcoin.

2   Bitcoin

In this section we give a short overview on the basic Bitcoin protocol. Specifics necessary for the duplex micropayment channel are discussed in detail later on. Bitcoin is a distributed system running on a homogeneous peer-to-peer network. Peers in the network collectively maintain a global state, known as the ledger, which tracks bitcoins and their associations. The fundamental data unit tracked by the network is the *output*, a tuple consisting of a value denominated in bitcoins and an output script. The output script sets up a claiming condition that has to be satisfied in order to claim the bitcoins associated with the output. The most common case is that a signature matching an address is required. Hence, the balance of an address is the sum of all outputs whose output scripts require that address' signature.

The only operation that may modify the global state is a *transaction*. A transaction claims one or more previously unclaimed outputs and creates new outputs. By providing inputs matching the output script, the creator of the transaction proves that she is allowed to claim the output. A transaction may redistribute the sum of values to new outputs and may set up arbitrary claiming conditions for the outputs.

In order to apply a transaction to the replicas of the ledger, the transaction is flooded in the network. When a node in the network receives a transaction the node first verifies the signatures of the transaction and, if valid, the transaction is applied to the local replica. For each input the script is executed with the input from the claiming transaction. If all scripts return true, the outputs were not claimed by a previous transaction, and the sum of new output values is smaller than the sum of claimed output values the transaction is valid. Due to the distributed nature of the system, the order in which transactions are applied is not identical across peers, and peers may disagree about the validity of a transaction, e.g., if two or more transactions attempt to claim the same output, the validity depends on the order they are seen by the peers.

Bitcoin eventually resolves inconsistencies by electing one peer as leader, which may then impose its changes to other peers, by sending a *block* containing all transactions it accepted since the last block. Each block contains a reference to its predecessor, incrementally building the *blockchain*, a shared history of all transactions that were applied. Transactions that are included in a block of the blockchain are said to be committed or confirmed. Leader election happens only rarely at random intervals; on expectation conflicts are resolved every 10 minutes. This is on purpose in order to minimize collisions in which multiple contradicting blocks are broadcast. However, it also introduces a long delay until a transaction is confirmed.

3 Building Blocks

In the following the concepts and sub-protocols used in this work are described in more detail.

3.1 Bitcoin Contracts

Off-blockchain transaction protocols are an example of *cryptocurrency contracts*. Contracts allow business logic to be encoded in Bitcoin transactions which mutually guarantee that an agreed upon action is performed. The blockchain acts as conflict mediator should a party fail to honor an agreement.

In this work we concentrate on off-blockchain transaction protocols. Furthermore we limit the description to two parties, A and B, i.e., the two ends of the duplex micropayment channel. We denote the effective balances in the protocols or sub-protocols as σ_A and σ_B. Since the balances may change we denote the balances after update i as $\sigma_{A,i}$ and $\sigma_{B,i}$.

The main concern with off-blockchain transactions is to ensure that no party may renege on the agreement, possibly stealing funds from the other party. While on-blockchain transactions ascertain that a transaction has been committed before starting the next trade, a contract may last a long time and all parties have to ensure that they cannot be defrauded. A protocol is required in order to achieve mutual assurance that the latest update to the agreement is the one that will eventually be committed, and thus to invalidate any previous agreements. That is, each update creates a new set of transactions that supersede the previous update. At any time only one set of transactions may be released to Bitcoin and will be confirmed.

The protocol has to be carefully designed to avoid any possibility for fraud. Fraudulent behavior of a party may result in funds being stolen and funds being inaccessible either temporarily or permanently. Our protocol guarantees that funds are eventually refunded.

We assume that a suitable solution for transaction malleability [7] has been implemented [1,15]. Since transactions refer to the outputs they spend by the hash of the transaction which created the output, any change causing the hash to change will unlink the transactions. The protocols in this work use chains of transactions with multiple signatures. Since ECDSA signatures are inherently malleable, anyone with the ability to re-sign a transaction may invalidate subsequent transactions. If deterministic and non-malleable signature schemes are used instead, all of our presented schemes can still be implemented securely, although they will become more complex. Most of the solutions aim to normalize transaction hashes by removing the signatures before hashing. This also enables the creation of transactions that spend outputs created by a transaction that is partially signed.

3.2   Timelocks and Invalidation

Bitcoin provides a mechanism to makes transactions invalid until some time in the future: *timelocks*. In addition to the validity conditions mentioned in the Section 2, a transaction may specify a locktime: the earliest time, expressed in either a Unix timestamp or a blockchain height, at which it may be included in a block and therefore be confirmed.

Peers in the network discard transactions with future timelocks. Any block including the transaction, that appears at a lower height or before the specified time, is deemed invalid. Timelocks can be used to replace or supersede transactions: a transaction with timelock T can be superseded by another transaction, spending some of the same outputs, with timelock $T' < T$ and ensuring that the superseding transaction is broadcast to the network before the superseded transaction becomes valid.

Timelocks are transitive, i.e., a transaction spending an output created by a timelocked transaction will only be valid once the timelocked transaction is committed. Hence a transaction spending timelocked outputs has an effective timelock matching the maximum timelock of any transaction it depends on.

In order to update the contract, e.g., to increase the value one party will receive in the end, it is necessary to invalidate or replace transactions during the execution, ensuring that only the latest update is valid. Throughout the protocol two invalidation techniques are used:

- *Replace by timelock*: both parties hold fully signed transactions, with different bitcoin allocations, of which only one may be committed. All transactions have a timelock in the future. Only the transaction with the smallest timelock will eventually be committed, i.e., it is released before any other transaction becomes valid.

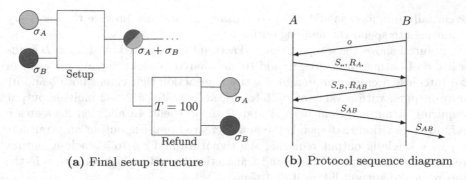

(a) Final setup structure   **(b)** Protocol sequence diagram

Fig. 1. Setup creating a multisig output of value $\sigma_A + \sigma_B$ from two outputs of value σ_A and σ_B. The refund transaction is timelocked and only valid after T=100. The sequence of transaction exchanges detailed on the right ensures the security of the setup. Subscripts represent the signatures by A and B or a . if a signature is missing.

- *Replace by incentive*: one party has multiple fully signed transactions, with different values transferred to it, of which only one may be committed. The party will commit the transaction transferring the highest amount to it.

In order to guarantee that replace by timelock is secure the difference between timelocks that supersede each other has to be at least ΔT. Due to the confirmation rate of Bitcoin we chose ΔT to be 1 hour. To simplify the notation we express timelocks as multiples of ΔT and use offsets such that the protocol starts at $T = 0$.

3.3   Shared Accounts

When an output can be claimed by providing a single signature it is called a *singlesig output*. In contrast the script of *multisig outputs* specifies a set of n public keys and requires m-of-n (with $m \leq n$) valid signatures from distinct matching public keys from that set in order to be valid.

In the 2-of-2 case two parties, A and B, have to sign transactions spending the output. This is akin to a shared account where any transaction spending the common funds must be signed off by both parties. If both A and B have supplied σ_A respectively σ_B bitcoins to a multisig output, the output's value is $\sigma_A + \sigma_B$. Of this total value we say that A effectively owns σ_A and B effectively owns σ_B, despite both signatures being required to spend the output.

Once a multisig output has been created and committed to the blockchain, A and B are guaranteed that the funds of the output may not be spent by either of the parties without both agreeing. As such the creation of a multisignature output is often used in order to setup a contract.

In order to securely create a shared account (multisig output) two transactions are needed: a *setup transaction* and a *refund transaction*. The setup transaction claims some funds from singlesig outputs owned by A and B, and creates the multisig output. The refund transaction ensures that the funds are eventually refunded should one party disappear and not provide the necessary signatures to spend the multisig output.

Figure 1 shows the setup of a shared account coordinated by A. First B sends a list o of outputs it desires to add to the shared account, for a total value of σ_B bitcoins. A creates an unsigned setup transaction that claims both o and its own outputs, with a value of σ_A bitcoins, and creates a 2-of-2 multisig output requiring signatures from both A and B to be spent. In addition it creates a refund transaction that spends the newly created multisig output and transfers σ_A to a singlesig output requiring A's signature and σ_B to a singlesig output requiring B's signature. The refund transaction has a timelock some time in the future, making it invalid until that time.

The protocol sequence diagram in Figure 1 shows the order in which messages are exchanged. A adds its signature to the refund transaction and sends both the refund transaction and the unsigned setup transaction to B. Upon receiving the transactions, B verifies that the refund transaction eventually returns its funds and adds its signature to both transactions. B now has a valid refund transaction and a partially signed setup transaction. Both transactions are returned to A which adds the missing signature to the setup transaction, making all transactions fully signed. The setup transaction is then released to the Bitcoin network and committed to the blockchain. This locks the funds until the refund returns them to the respective owners or until both parties agree on a different division of the funds, signing another transaction that supersedes the refund.

3.4   Simple Micropayment Channels

Simple micropayment channels, first introduced by Hearn and Spilman [9], are contracts that can be established between two parties, a sender and a receiver. Once a micropayment channel is established, the sender can send incremental micropayments to the receiver. The channel has a limit determined by the sender upon the channel's creation. Once the limit is consumed, i.e., transferred entirely to the receiver, the channel is closed.

The micropayment channel can be created by setting up a shared account, as described in the previous section, between the sender and the receiver. The sender A funds the channel with σ_A, whereas the receiver does not contribute, i.e., σ_B is 0. We denote $\sigma_{A,i}$ and $\sigma_{B,i}$ to be the owned amounts after the ith update by A and B respectively.

In order to perform an incremental micropayment of value δ at time $i + 1$, A creates a *micropayment update transaction* spending the multisig output and transferring $\sigma_{A,i+1} = \sigma_{A,i} - \delta$ and $\sigma_{B,i+1} = \sigma_{B,i} + \delta$ to A and B respectively.

The update transaction is signed by A and sent to the receiver B. At this point the receiver could add its own signature and broadcast it to the Bitcoin network, committing it to the blockchain. However, normally the transaction is not broadcast. Instead the receiver accepts new update transactions, which transfer a larger amount to it. Only one of the update transactions may be committed to the blockchain since they all spend the same output. The receiver

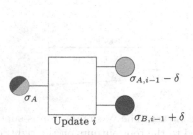

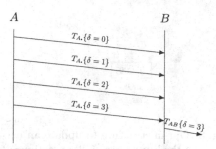

(a) Micropayment channel structure.   (b) Payment channel sequence.

Fig. 2. The structure of the payment channel consists of a single transaction splitting the value of a multisig output among the participants. In this case A funded the channel and may send to B and δ is the sum of increments.

is incentivized to only use the latest update as it is the one paying out the maximum amount.

Eventually (i) all the initial funds $\sigma_{A,0}$ are transferred to B, (ii) both parties agree on closing the channel, or (iii) the refund time from the setup is approaching, triggering B to close the channel. To close the channel, B broadcasts the last update transaction which supersedes the refund transaction.

Note that such a micropayment channel is intrinsically unidirectional, i.e., the amount that the receiver is assigned in update transactions must be strictly increasing, otherwise the receiver might release an earlier update, which pays out a higher amount.

3.5   Atomic Multiparty Opt-In

In the shared account setup protocol, great care had to be taken about the order in which signatures were added, to avoid situations where funds could be locked in indefinitely. *Atomic multiparty opt-in* is an off-blockchain protocol that enables multiple parties to negotiate the creation of a complex structure of transactions, built on top of existing multisig outputs, without having to worry about the order in which the signatures are added. The structure can be negotiated openly since parties activate, or opt in, only after it is secure.

The atomic multiparty opt-in protocol uses an *opt-in transaction O* which claims a multisig output and creates a new multisig output, called the *root output*. Subsequent transactions spend the root output and thus are valid only if the opt-in transaction is valid, i.e., when all parties sign the opt-in transaction. This also obviates any refund addresses attached to intermediate outputs, which would be needed if each subsequent transaction were negotiated independently.

One party creates an unsigned opt-in transaction which spends a multisig output, requiring signatures from all participants, and creates one or more root outputs. The participants then collaborate to create the updated version of the contract, openly sharing any necessary transactions and signatures. As soon

Fig. 3. Opt-in structure to update an existing contract. The version on top is super-seded by the lower version. Transactions attached to the root outputs on the right are negotiated openly, with the opt-in transaction determining validity.

as all parties are content with the contract they sign the opt-in transaction, making it valid. The fully signed opt-in transaction is then exchanged among all participants to ensure that all parties can enforce the decision.

The atomic multiparty opt-in can be used in two ways: (i) to initially set up a contract starting from a multisig output owned by the participants, or (ii) to update an existing contract by building a structure that spends the root output of an outdated contract. In the latter case, depicted in Figure 3, it is necessary to enforce that only the new version is valid by using a smaller timelock.

The protocol is off-blockchain as its transactions are only committed to the blockchain if one party defects. Notice that the party signing last may unilater-ally decide whether to sign and commit or not. It is therefore advisable to use the multiparty opt-in exclusively in idempotent updates, i.e., when the value that is paid out to the parties does not change depending on whether or not the opt-in is committed.

3.6   Hashed Timelock Contracts (HTLC)

Hashed Timelock Contracts, or HTLCs, are contracts that require the recipient of a payment to reveal a secret in order to claim an output before it is refunded to the sender. The ability of the recipient to claim the output is therefore con-ditioned on its ability to reveal the secret.

This can be used to enable end-to-end security in a multi-hop scenario, in which a single payment is forwarded through multiple parties. In this scenario, B requests a payment from A and specifies the hash $h(S)$ of a secret S, which will be used to unlock the payment. A creates an HTLC output from a shared account with the next hop on the path to B. The HTLC output sets up the claiming condition as shown in Figure 4: either the next hop provides S' s.t. $h(S) = h(S')$ and a valid signature from both parties, or both parties must sign the transaction spending the HTLC output. This procedure is repeated by each node on the path until B is reached. B then releases S to its previous node, claiming the HTLC output, and giving the previous node the ability to claim the previous HTLC output. This is repeated until the secret is revealed to A, thus completing the transfer.

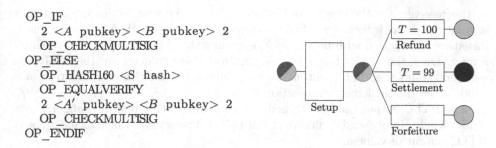

```
OP_IF
    2 <A pubkey> <B pubkey> 2
    OP_CHECKMULTISIG
OP_ELSE
    OP_HASH160 <S hash>
    OP_EQUALVERIFY
    2 <A' pubkey> <B pubkey> 2
    OP_CHECKMULTISIG
OP_ENDIF
```

Fig. 4. HTLC output script and structure. The first branch is a normal multisig script while the second branch requires a secret and both signatures.

For each hop there is a sender H_A and a receiver H_B and they share a multisig output that is used for the transfer. The HTLC output is created by an *HTLC setup transaction*, claiming the multisig output. During the execution of the protocol up to three transactions are created that may claim the HTLC output: a *refund transaction*, a *settlement transaction*, and a *forfeiture transaction*. The refund transaction is identical to the one from the shared account setup and ensures that H_A is refunded should H_B not cooperate. The settlement transaction performs the transfer from H_A to H_B if the latter reveals the secret. Finally, the forfeiture transaction is used to guarantee that H_A is refunded even if the secret is eventually revealed. The last scenario is used to remove the HTLC output before the refund becomes valid, i.e., when both parties agree to free the funds locked in the HTLC output without performing the transfer.

The sender creates the HTLC setup transaction and all three transactions spending the HTLC output and signs refund transaction, forfeiture transaction and settlement transaction. The settlement transaction uses the *else*-branch of the script, which uses a separate *HTLC signing key* for the sender. This is necessary since otherwise H_B could simply use the same signature in the *if*-branch, since signatures are valid for both branches. The partially signed refund, forfeiture and settlement transactions are then sent to the receiver which adds its signature to the refund and sends it back. The sender signs the HTLC setup transaction and sends it to the receiver, which may attempt to claim the HTLC output unilaterally by providing its signature and the secret to the settlement transaction.

The lifetime of the HTLC output is limited by the refund transaction's timelock, and should H_B want to claim it, it must release the settlement transaction before the refund is valid. While this protocol works when committing transactions directly to the blockchain, its main use is in off blockchain transactions.

In order to be usable in off-blockchain transactions, the timelock of the refund must be later than those in refund transactions attached to the root outputs, i.e., it must be guaranteed that H_B indeed has time to claim the HTLC output on the blockchain before the refund transaction becomes valid. Should the receiver disclose the secret S to the sender, then both parties can agree on removing the HTLC output and instead add its value to another output that directly transfers to the receiver. On the other hand, should H_B not be able to disclose S then it may decide to forfeit the HTLC output. In this case both parties sign the forfeiture transaction with no timelock, spending the HTLC output back to the sender. Once the sender has a fully signed forfeiture transaction, the receiver may not claim the HTLC output anymore since the forfeiture transaction is valid before the settlement transaction.

The HTLC output can be attached to an existing micropayment channel, the sender would simply send a micropayment update transaction which includes the HTLC output of value δ.

4   Duplex Micropayment Channel

The secure setup, the micropayment channel and the hashed timelock contract alone enable the use multi-hop micropayments with end-to-end security. However setting up two independent micropayment channels between two peers, one for each direction between, is fairly limited. Each channel is unidirectional and is limited by the amount of bitcoins locked in during the setup by the sender. Once the limit has been consumed, the channel has to be torn down and a new one created, incurring time delay and cost of committing several transactions to the blockchain.

While this cannot be avoided on connections at the edge of the network in which a majority of payments flows in one direction, connections in which payments flow in both directions may take advantage from resetting their channels once the limit is consumed. For example, consider the channels C_{AB} from A to B and C_{BA} in the opposite direction, each initially funded with 1 coin. The limit of C_{AB} may have been consumed, and C_{BA} has a residual of 0.5 bitcoins. No further transfer from A to B can be performed despite A having a non-zero balance on the C_{BA} channel, i.e., when considering both channels the balances are $\sigma_A = 0.5$ and $\sigma_B = 1.5$. In order to enable future transfers from A to B both parties could agree to reset the channel, i.e., new channels C'_{AB} and C'_{BA} are created and funded with 0.5 and 1.5 bitcoins respectively. Notice that in both the depleted case and the reset case A and B own the same amount of bitcoins, but the channel their share is bound to has changed.

In the following we describe the duplex micropayment channel protocol that enables atomically resetting a set of channels. By doing so we enable the initial funds to be transferred over the duplex channel an arbitrary number of times, and hence reduce the necessity to commit to the blockchain.

A duplex micropayment channel (DMC) is established between two parties A and B. The protocol establishes pairs of simple micropayment channels, one for each direction between the two parties. In order to reset the channels the protocol generates a sequence of pairs of unidirectional micropayment channels. We use $C_{AB,j}$ and $C_{BA,j}$ to indicate the simple micropayment channels in the jth pair of channels. Furthermore we define $\sigma_{X,j,i}$ to be the amount that the pair of micropayment channels would transfer to party $X \in \{A, B\}$ if they were committed to the blockchain after update i in the pair j.

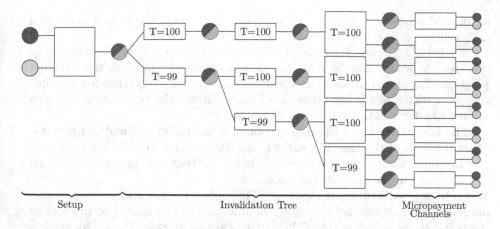

Fig. 5. A full example of the duplex micropayment channel with $n = 1$ and $d = 3$, allowing up to 4 resets

4.1 Structure

The fundamental structure of the DMC is the *invalidation tree*. The invalidation tree is a tree in which multisig outputs are the nodes of the tree, connected by transactions as edges. Each transaction in the tree is given a timelock, such that there is a unique minimal timelock among all sibling transactions, i.e., transactions sharing the same parent output. By the replace by timelock rule, only one path from the root of the tree is therefore first valid, i.e., the path with the minimal timelocks for each level in the tree. Hence as long as all timelocks are in the future, we can invalidate an entire subtree, by adding a new transaction spending that subtree's root output, with a smaller timelock than all existing transactions. We define two times T_{max} and T_{min} in terms of locktime. All refund transactions are set to have locktime T_{max}, forcing parties to commit the protocol's state to the blockchain before that time in order to avoid triggering the refunds. T_{min} is the minimum timelock that is going to be used in the invalidation tree to replace other transactions. The time from the channel creation to T_{min} is referred to as the channel's lifetime.

The number of replacement by timelock is limited by $n = (T_{max} - T_{min})/\Delta T$. Therefore each multisig output in the invalidation tree may have at most n outgoing transactions which replace each other. Furthermore, due to the transitivity of timelocks, the full range may not be available as adding a timelock that is lower than one of its parent transactions has no effect: all transactions with a lower timelock become valid simultaneously, resulting in a race condition. For simplicity we limit the depth of the tree to d. This limits the number of transactions that have to be committed to the blockchain should one party defect.

The depth d, the number of replacements in the tree n and time until funds are refunded T_{max} are parameters to the duplex micropayment channel and are negotiated before the channel is created. T_{min} can be derived from T_{max}, n and ΔT, which is a system parameter.

Furthermore, knowing n and d allows the enumeration of all branches in the tree. A branch can be represented as a string of length n, the alphabet $\{T_{min}, ..., T_{max}\}$ and the elements are increasing. Thus every branch has a unique successor that directly invalidates it. This facilitates the negotiation of which branch to select next.

The internal nodes of the invalidation tree are individual multisig outputs, while the leafs of the tree are pairs of multisig outputs. On the leaf outputs a pair of simple micropayment channels is built, one transferring from A to B and the other one in the opposite direction.

Multi-hop payment flows result in HTLC outputs being attached to the simple micropayment channel matching the direction of the flow. The timelock of the transactions spending the HTLC outputs are larger than T_{max}. This ensures that the micropayment channel creating the HTLC have been committed to the blockchain and replace by timelock can be performed. The period between T_{max} and the last HTLC output being claimed is referred to as *conflict resolution phase*.

4.2 Setup

The setup initiates the micropayment channel between two parties by locking in the initial funds into a shared account. The shared account creation subprotocol from Section 3.3 is used to create the multisig output. Both parties exchange a set of singlesig outputs they would like to contribute to the channel and create the setup transaction. The initial funds from A and B are denoted as $\sigma_{A,0,0}$ and $\sigma_{B,0,0}$ since there were no resets and no updates yet. The refund transaction has a timelock of T_{max}. It transfers the funds back to their owners if no other agreement is committed first. Since the setup transaction is committed in the blockchain it is safe to build upon the multisig output. Committing the transaction may take several minutes and the channel is not operational until it is committed.

4.3 Reset

The reset process takes care of building a new branch of the invalidation tree and setting up the micropayment channels. This includes the first branch starting from the shared account the setup created. A reset is triggered after the initial setup, as well as when the limit of one of the simple micropayment channels is depleted. Assuming that the limit of A's channel $C_{AB,j}$ is consumed and therefore requires a reset. A is said to coordinate the reset: it will no longer perform updates to its channel $C_{AB,j}$ and send a *reset request* to the B. Upon receiving the reset request, B stops performing updates to its channel $C_{BA,j}$ and sends a *reset response*. The reset response signals to A that B is willing to perform the reset and that no further updates to $C_{BA,j}$ will be performed and that the value transferred by the two simple micropayment channels $\sigma_{A,j,i}$ and $\sigma_{B,j,i}$ will not change.

Upon receiving the reset response, A can proceed to build the next branch ending in two multisig outputs. The values of the two multisig outputs are $\sigma_{A,j+1,0} = \sigma_{A,j,i}$ and $\sigma_{B,j+1,0} = \sigma_{B,j,i}$, i.e., each multisig output is virtually owned by one party and its value represents the share the owner would get if the current branch were to be committed. On top of the leaf multisig outputs two new simple micropayment channels $C_{AB,j+1}$ and $C_{BA,j+1}$ are built with respective refund transactions. The branch is negotiated as an instance of the atomic multiparty opt-in protocol, with the transaction spending the existing output from the previous branch as opt-in transaction and the remainder of the branch as subsequent structure. A may sign the entire branch where necessary, except the opt-in transaction, which may only be signed once B has signed the refund transactions for the simple micropayment channels, therefore assuring that funds will not be locked in indefinitely.

The atomic multiparty opt-in ensures that either both agree on switching to the new branch or the old branch remains active. In both cases the same amounts are transferred to the two parties and updates to the micropayment channels $C_{AB,j+1}$ and $C_{BA,j+1}$ resume only once both parties have a fully signed opt-in transaction.

4.4 Teardown and Commit

Eventually the duplex micropayment channel needs to be closed and the summary of the channel committed to the blockchain. The closure of the duplex micropayment channel can be triggered by agreement or by the end to the channel's lifetime. Either both parties agree on the summary, or they disagree and do not collaborate. In the first case they may simply create a *teardown transaction*, which transfers $\sigma_{A,j,i}$ to A and $\sigma_{B,j,i}$ to B, assuming update i is the latest update in the current round j. The teardown transaction is not timelocked and directly spends the multisig output created in the setup process, hence it can be committed to the blockchain immediately. The process simply involves one party creating the teardown transaction, both parties signing it and committing it to the blockchain. HTLC outputs which have not been removed by agreement can be copied over to the summary transaction such that the same timelocks and resolution rules apply.

In the case parties do not agree on the summary of the channel, they still have the latest branch of the invalidation tree that guarantees eventual conflict resolution. Before the refunds become valid the branch is submitted to the Bitcoin network and will be committed to the blockchain. Unlike the commit using a summary transaction, which requires just a single transaction to be committed, the resolution by tree branch requires up to $d + 2$ transactions, hence we limit on the depth of the tree.

4.5 Refresh

In the case two parties have an existing duplex micropayment channel its lifetime may be extended using the refresh process. Analogously to the reset sub-protocol, both parties stop updating the existing duplex micropayment channel by exchanging *refresh request* and *refresh response* messages, thus flushing pending changes. The parties agree on new parameters T_{max} and T_{min} determining the new channel's lifetime. One party creates an opt-in transaction creating a new root output and a refund transaction with a timelock of T_{max} transferring $\sigma_{A,j,i}$ and $\sigma_{B,j,i}$ to their respective owners. Both parties then perform the atomic multiparty opt-in protocol using the opt-in transaction and the refund as subsequent structure. The opt-in transaction is then published on the Bitcoin network and committed to the blockchain, invalidating the entire invalidation tree built on the old root output.

Special care has to be taken with HTLC outputs as these may time out during the new channel's lifetime. The HTLC outputs are copied over to the opt-in transaction, and their resolution is handled on the blockchain.

The refreshed duplex micropayment channel is operational immediately, since the opt-in transaction is guaranteed to be eventually confirmed, i.e., no party may double-spend the old root output.

In addition funds can be removed and added during the refresh process. Funds can be removed adding singlesig outputs to the opt-in transaction that pay out part of a party's balance to one of its addresses, that party's share of the channel is then reduced accordingly. In order to add funds to the channel, a multisig output owned by both parties has to be created ahead of time using the protocol in Section 3.3 so that during the refresh the outputs are committed to the blockchain. This multisig output is then also claimed by the opt-in.

5   Routing Payments

A channel between two payment service providers (PSPs) can be established once; it has a lifetime of hundreds of days before it is either torn down or refreshed. The setup requires a single transaction that is committed to the blockchain locking in the initial funds, while the teardown requires a single transaction committed to the blockchain. In the case the two parties do not collaborate to close the channel, at most d transactions from the invalidation tree and two micropayment updates have to be committed to the blockchain. The amount of bitcoins transferred is only limited by the number of resets and the initial funds parties contribute to the channel. A channel with $n = 46$ and $d = 11$ results in $1.48 \cdot 10^{11}$ resets. If such a channel is initially funded with 1 bitcoin, the channel can be used to transfer a total of 148 billion bitcoins, an equivalent of 35.3 trillion USD at today's exchange rate, twice the US national debt. Notice that both n and d can be chosen arbitrarily, further extending the amount transferable by a channel.

By adding HTLC outputs to the micropayment channels, instead of sending the increment directly, the payment can be end-to-end secured so that the recipient of a payment has to confirm reception. The final recipient communicates the secret out of band to the sender of the payment. Each hop along the route from the sender to the recipient will create HTLC outputs transferring the funds only upon receiving the secret, which is only released once the final recipient is assured that the total is transferred.

6   Related Work

Bitcoin was introduced by Nakamoto in 2008 [11] and has since enjoyed a rapid growth both in value as in transaction volume. However, the design of Bitcoin intrinsically limits the rate it can process transactions. Barber et al. [4] identified problems with data retention, which later were adopted to create the simplified payment verification, using filtering nodes for mobile clients. An analysis of the information propagation [6] showed that the probability of blockchain forks rapidly increases with increasing transaction rates and the eventually the network is no longer able to resolve conflicts. Eyal et al. [8] further show how miners may use the propagation delay in the network as a force multiplier.

The GHOST protocol [14] allows an increase of the block generation rate by reusing blocks that are not in the main blockchain. Although mainly aimed at enabling innovation, Back et al. [2] propose dividing the single Bitcoin network into smaller networks that can operate independently. Discoin and PeerCensus [5] decouple the confirmation of transactions from the block generation and guarantee strong consistency. The slow confirmation also prevents a number of real-life uses of Bitcoin, as fast payment can be double-spent and not be detected for some time [3,10,13]. Our proposal enables secure end-to-end payments that do not require being confirmation in the blockchain, hence enabling true micropayment that clear in real-time.

Simple micropayment channels were introduced by Hearn and Spilman [9]. Finally the Lightning Network by Poon and Dryja [12], also creates a duplex micropayment channel. However it requires exchanging keying material for each update in the channels, which results in either massive storage or computational requirements in order to invalidate previous transactions. In our proposal the two channels operate independently allowing fully asynchronous operation between resets. Lightning renews the whole transaction structure on every update, requiring synchronous updates and high bandwidth consumption. Furthermore the Lightning protocol cannot be decomposed into smaller units that can be analyzed in isolation, making the security analysis difficult and resulting in complex implementations.

7   Conclusion

Duplex micropayment channels solve a multitude of problems. For one they enable near-infinite scalability for digital payments based on Bitcoin. Bitcoin transactions are no longer used directly to transfer bitcoins from a sender to a recipient, instead they are used to setup micropayment channels and handle conflict resolution. The actual transfers are now handled at a higher level through a network of payment service providers. The payments are end-to-end secure thanks to the use of hashed timelock contracts, ensuring transfers between hops are only performed if the intended recipient receives its payment. Unlike Bitcoin, which requires a long confirmation process, transfers on a network of duplex micropayment channels are secure from being reverted. Thus a payment network using duplex micropayment channels is a far better fit for real-time scenarios, e.g., buying a coffee, since transfers can be performed at the same speed messages are passed in the Internet. With a network of payment service providers, Bitcoin can support true micropayments with minimal fees at unprecedented scale, and where the transfers clear in real-time.

References

1. Andrychowicz, M., Dziembowski, S., Malinowski, D., Mazurek, Ł.: How to deal with malleability of bitcoin transactions. arXiv preprint arXiv:1312.3230 (2013)
2. Back, A., Corallo, M., Dashjr, L., Friedenbach, M., Maxwell, G., Miller, A., Poelstra, A., Timón, J., Wuille, P.: Enabling blockchain innovations with pegged sidechains (2014)
3. Bamert, T., Decker, C., Elsen, L., Welten, S., Wattenhofer, R.: Have a snack, pay with bitcoin. In: IEEE International Conference on Peer-to-Peer Computing (P2P), Trento, Italy (2013)
4. Barber, S., Boyen, X., Shi, E., Uzun, E.: Bitter to better — how to make bitcoin a better currency. In: Keromytis, A.D. (ed.) FC 2012. LNCS, vol. 7397, pp. 399–414. Springer, Heidelberg (2012)
5. Decker, C., Seidel, J., Wattenhofer, R.: Bitcoin meets strong consistency. arXiv preprint arXiv:1412.7935 (2014)
6. Decker, C., Wattenhofer, R.: Information propagation in the bitcoin network. In: IEEE International Conference on Peer-to-Peer Computing (P2P), Trento, Italy, September 2013
7. Decker, C., Wattenhofer, R.: Bitcoin transaction malleability and MtGox. In: Kutyłowski, M., Vaidya, J. (eds.) ESORICS 2014, Part II. LNCS, vol. 8713, pp. 313–326. Springer, Heidelberg (2014)
8. Eyal, I., Sirer, E.G.: Majority is not enough: Bitcoin mining is vulnerable. arXiv preprint arXiv:1311.0243 (2013)
9. Hearn, M., Spilman, J.: Bitcoin contracts. https://en.bitcoin.it/wiki/Contracts (accessed: May 2015)
10. Karame, G.O., Androulaki, E., Capkun, S.: Two bitcoins at the price of one? double-spending attacks on fast payments in bitcoin. In: Proc. of Conference on Computer and Communication Security (2012)
11. Nakamoto, S.: Bitcoin: A peer-to-peer electronic cash system. https://bitcoin.org/bitcoin.pdf (accessed: March 26, 2014)
12. Poon, J., Dryja, T.: The bitcoin lightning network
13. Rosenfeld, M.: Analysis of hashrate-based double spending. arXiv preprint arXiv:1402.2009 (2014)
14. Sompolinsky, Y., Zohar, A.: Accelerating bitcoin's transaction processing
15. Wuille, P.: BIP 0062: Dealing with Malleability (2014). https://github.com/bitcoin/bips (accessed: March 10th, 2014)

Regular Papers

Reaching Approximate Byzantine Consensus with Multi-hop Communication

Lili Su$^{(\boxtimes)}$ and Nitin Vaidya

Department of Electrical and Computer Engineering,
University of Illinois at Urbana-Champaign, Urbana, USA
{lilisu3,nhv}@illinois.edu

Abstract. We address the problem of reaching approximate consensus
in the presence of Byzantine faults in a synchronous system. We analyze
iterative algorithms that maintain *minimal* state, and impose the constraint that in each iteration the nodes may only communicate with other
nodes that are up to l hops away. For a given l, we prove a necessary
and sufficient condition on the network structure for the existence of correct iterative algorithms that achieve *approximate* Byzantine consensus.
We prove sufficiency of the condition by designing a correct algorithm,
which uses a trim function based on a *minimal messages cover* property
introduced in this paper. Our necessary and sufficient condition gener-
alizes the tight condition identified in prior work for $l = 1$. For $l \geq l^*$,
where l^* is the length of a longest cycle-free path in the given network,
our condition is equivalent to the necessary and sufficient conditions for
exact consensus in undirected and directed networks both.

Keywords: Approximate byzantine consensus · Iterative algorithm ·
Synchronous system · Incomplete network · Bounded length communication paths

1 Introduction

The Byzantine fault-tolerance problem was first introduced in [9] by Pease,
Shostak and Lamport in 1980, and is one of the most fundamental problems
in distributed computing. Fisher, Lynch and Paterson [7] showed that the fault-
tolerant consensus problem cannot be solved in *asynchronous* system even in the
presence of only one crash failure. As one way to circumvent this impossibility
result, the notion of *approximate Byzantine consensus* was introduced by Dolev
et al. in [4] by requiring that the agents agree with each other only approximately.
The notion of approximate consensus is of interest in *synchronous* system as well
[4,8,14]. The discussion in this paper applies to synchronous system.

This research is supported in part by National Science Foundation awards NSF
1329681 and 1421918. Any opinions, findings, and conclusions or recommendations
expressed here are those of the authors and do not necessarily reflect the views of
the funding agencies or the U.S. government.

© Springer International Publishing Switzerland 2015
A. Pelc and A.A. Schwarzmann (Eds.): SSS 2015, LNCS 9212, pp. 21–35, 2015.
DOI: 10.1007/978-3-319-21741-3_2

Let n be the total number of nodes and f be the upper bound on the number of faulty nodes in the system. In networks with bidirectional links, approximate consensus is achievable if and only if the network node-connectivity is at least $2f + 1$ and less than one third of nodes can be faulty, i.e., $n \geq 3f + 1$ [6]. Relaxing the bidirectional communication assumption, a tight condition for directed graphs was presented in [11]. There has been increasing interest in designing iterative variants of approximate Byzantine consensus where only local knowledge of the network topology (and local communication) is needed, and agents carry minimal state across iterations [2,5,8,13,14]. Fekete [5] studied the convergence rate of approximate consensus algorithms over complete networks. [8,14] considered arbitrary directed networks and derived tight (necessary and sufficient) topological conditions on the communication network. While [14] investigated the Byzantine fault model, [8] considered a restricted fault model in which the faulty nodes are restricted to sending identical messages to their neighbors.

To the best of our knowledge, no attempts have been made on investigating the impact of each node's communication range on the network condition for a correct iterative approximate consensus algorithm to exist. In this paper, we model the network as a directed graph, and assume that in each iteration, any node may only communicate with nodes that are up to l hops away, by forwarding messages through intermediate nodes. The directed graph model is motivated by the presence of directed links in wireless networks. Our goal is to prove a necessary and sufficient condition on the network structure for the existence of correct iterative algorithms that achieve approximate Byzantine consensus for a given l with minimal memory (i.e., minimal amount of state carried across iterations).

Contributions: Our main contribution is to prove a necessary and sufficient condition on the network structure for a given l. Our sufficiency proof is shown by constructing a simple iterative algorithm, whose trim function is defined based on a *minimal messages cover* property that we introduce in this paper. The tight condition we found is consistent with the tight condition identified in [14] when only local communication is allowed, i.e., $l = 1$. For $l \geq l^*$, where l^* is the length of a longest cycle-free path in the given network, our condition is equivalent to the necessary and sufficient condition for consensus in undirected networks [6] as well as exact consensus in directed networks [12].

Organization: The rest of the paper is organized as follows. Section 2 presents our models and the structure of the iterative algorithms considered in our work. Our necessary condition is presented in Section 3, and its sufficiency is proved constructively in Section 4. The correspondence between our condition and the results in [4,6,12] is discussed in Section 5. Section 6 discusses possible relaxations of our fault model and concludes the paper.

2   System Model and Structure of Iterative Algorithms

Communication model: The system is assumed to be *synchronous*. The communication network is modeled as a simple *directed* graph G. Define $\mathcal{V}(G) = \{1, \ldots, n\}$ as the set of n nodes, where $n \geq 2$, and $\mathcal{E}(G)$ as the set of directed edges between nodes in $\mathcal{V}(G)$. Node i can send messages to node j if and only if there exists an i, j–path of length at most l in G, where l is a positive integer. In addition, we assume each node can send messages to itself as well, i.e., $(i, i) \in \mathcal{E}(G)$ for all $i \in \mathcal{V}(G)$. For each node i, let N_i^{l-} be the set of nodes that can reach node i via at most l hops. Similarly, denote the set of nodes that are reachable from node i via at most l hops by N_i^{l+}. Due to the existence of self-loops, $i \in N_i^{l-}$ and $i \in N_i^{l+}$. When $l = 1$, we write N_i^{1-} and N_i^{1+} as N_i^- and N_i^+, respectively, for simplicity. Each node i is assumed to be aware of the network topology within its l-hop neighborhood (i.e., node i knows all the paths of length at most l from the nodes in N_i^{l-}, and all the paths of length at most l to the nodes in N_i^{l+}). Node i may send a message to node j via different i, j–paths. To capture this distinction in transmission routes, we represent a message as a tuple $m = (w, P)$, where $w \in \mathbb{R}$ and P indicates the path via which message m should be transmitted. It is assumed that the network layer in the system delivers the messages along the specified paths. The intermediate nodes on the paths do not view the message values (i.e., the message values are not used by intermediate nodes in performing consensus). Four functions are defined over message m. For $m = (w, P)$, let function value be $\mathsf{value}(m) = w$ and let path be $\mathsf{path}(m) = P$, whose images are the first entry and the second entry, respectively, of message m. In addition, functions source and $\mathsf{destination}$ are defined by $\mathsf{source}(m) = i$ and $\mathsf{destination}(m) = j$ if P is an i, j–path, i.e., i and j are source and destination on path P. For a given path P, Let $\mathcal{V}(P)$ denote the set of nodes along the path, including the source and the destination.

Fault model: Let $\mathcal{F} \subseteq \mathcal{V}(G)$ be the collection of faulty nodes in the system. We consider the Byzantine fault model with up to f nodes becoming faulty, i.e., $|\mathcal{F}| \leq f$. A faulty node may tamper the message value arbitrarily. Possible misbehavior includes sending incorrect and mismatching (or inconsistent) messages to different neighbors. In addition, a faulty node $k \in \mathcal{F}$ may tamper message m if it is in the transmission path, i.e., $k \in \mathcal{V}(\mathsf{path}(m))$. However, faulty nodes may only tamper $\mathsf{value}(m)$, leaving $\mathsf{path}(m)$ unchanged. This constraint is placed for ease of exposition; later in Section 6 we relax this constraint. Faulty nodes are also assumed to have complete knowledge of the execution of the algorithm, including the states of all nodes, contents of messages that the other nodes send to each other, and the algorithm specification, so that they may potentially collaborate with each other adaptively.

Iterative approximate Byzantine consensus (IABC) algorithms: The iterative algorithms considered in this paper have the following structure: Each node i maintains state v_i, with $v_i[t]$ denoting the state of node i at the *end* of the t-th iteration of the algorithm. Initial state of node i, $v_i[0]$, is equal to the initial *input* provided to node i. At the *start* of the t-th iteration ($t > 0$), the state of node i is $v_i[t-1]$. The IABC algorithms of interest will require each node i to perform the following three steps in iteration t, where $t > 0$. Note that the faulty nodes may deviate from this specification.

1. *Transmit step:* Transmit messages of the form $(v_i[t-1], P)$ on each l–hop path P (including self-loops) to nodes in N_i^{l+}. As noted previously, the network layer of the system forwards each message to its destination along the path specified for the message.
2. *Receive step:* Receive messages from N_i^{l-} for which destination is i. When node i expects to receive a message from a path but does not receive the message, the message value is assumed to be equal to some default value. Let $\mathcal{M}_i[t]$ be the set of messages that node i received in this step.
3. *Update step:* Node i updates its state using a transition function Z_i, where Z_i is a part of the specification of the algorithm, and takes as input the set $\mathcal{M}_i[t]$.

$$v_i[t] = Z_i(\mathcal{M}_i[t]). \qquad (1)$$

Algorithms with similar structure are considered in prior work as well [8,11,14]. The evolution of state $v_i[t]$ is governed by the update function defined in (1). Note that $v_i[t]$ only depends on $\mathcal{M}_i[t]$–the messages collected by node i at iteration t (which includes $v_i[t-1]$). No information collected/obtained during previous iterations will affect the update step in iteration t. Intuitively speaking, fault-free node i is assumed to have no memory across iterations other than its most recent state $v_i[t-1]$.

Let $U[t]$ be the largest state among the fault-free nodes at the end of the t-th iteration, i.e., $U[t] = \max_{i \in \mathcal{V}-\mathcal{F}} v_i[t]$. Since the initial state of each node is equal to its input, $U[0]$ is equal to the maximum value of the initial input of the fault-free nodes. Similarly, we define $\mu[t]$ to be the smallest state at the end of the t–th iteration and $\mu[0]$ to be the smallest initial input. For an IABC algorithm to be correct, the following two conditions must be satisfied:

– *Validity:* $\forall t > 0,\ \mu[t] \geq \mu[0]$ and $U[t] \leq U[0]$
– *Convergence:* $\lim_{t \to \infty} U[t] - \mu[t] = 0$

Our goal is to identify a necessary and sufficient condition on graph G for the existence of a *correct* IABC algorithm (i.e., an algorithm satisfying the above validity and convergence conditions) for a given l.

3   Necessary Condition

For a correct IABC algorithm to exist, the underlying network G must satisfy the condition presented in this section. First, we introduce some definitions.

Definition 1. *Suppose $W \subseteq \mathcal{V}(G)$ and $x \in \mathcal{V}(G)$ such that $x \notin W$. A W, x–path is a path from some vertex $w \in W$ to vertex x. A set $S_l \subseteq \mathcal{V}(G)$ with $x \notin S_l$ is an*

l–restricted vertex cut *if the deletion of S_l disconnects all W, x–paths of length at most l. The l–restricted W, x–connectivity, denoted by $\kappa_l(W, x)$, is defined by*

$$\kappa_l(W, x) = \min_{S_l : S_l \text{ is an } l-\text{restricted } W, x-\text{cut}} |S_l|.$$

A set of vertices S is a W, x–vertex cut if the removal of set S disconnects all W, x–paths. The W, x–connectivity, denoted by $\kappa(W, x)$, is defined by

$$\kappa(W, x) = \min_{S : S \text{ is a } W, x-cut} |S|.$$

The second part of the above definition is the classic definition of node connectivity in graph theory [15], which is a global notion. In our communication model, we assume that each fault-free node only knows the local network topology up to its l–th hop neighborhood. Thus, we adapt node connectivity to our model by restricting the path length of interest. Note that $\kappa_l(W, x) = \kappa(W, x)$ for all $l \geq l^*$, and that $\kappa_1(W, x) = |W \cap N_x^-|$.

In general, $\kappa_l(W, x) \neq \kappa(W, x)$ and $\kappa_l(W, x) \leq \kappa_{l+1}(W, x)$ for all l. For instance for the system depicted in Figure 1, via enumeration it can be seen that

$$\kappa(\{p_2, p_3\}, p_1) = 2 \geq 1 = \kappa_1(\{p_2, p_3\}, p_1).$$

Intuitively speaking, the stronger the communication capability of each node is (the larger l is), the harder it is to prevent one node from being influenced by other nodes.

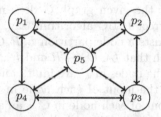

Fig. 1. In this system, there are five nodes p_1, p_2, p_3, p_4 and p_5; all communication links are bi-directional; and at most one node can be adversarial, i.e., $f = 1$

Definition 2. *For non-empty disjoint sets of nodes A and B in G, we say $A \Rightarrow_l B$ if and only if there exists a node $i \in B$ such that $\kappa_l(A, i) \geq f + 1$; $A \nRightarrow_l B$ otherwise.*

Informally speaking, the relation $A \Rightarrow_l B$ captures the existence of a node $i \in B$ that can be influenced by fault-free nodes in A despite the presence of Byzantine nodes.

Let $F \subseteq \mathcal{V}(G)$ be a set of vertices in G. Denote the subgraph of G induced by vertex set $\mathcal{V}(G) - F$ by G_F.[1] We describe a necessary and sufficient condition

---

[1] Subgraph of G induced by vertex set $S \subseteq \mathcal{V}(G)$ is the subgraph H with vertex set S such that $\mathcal{E}(H) = \{(u, v) \in \mathcal{E}(G) : u, v \in S\}$. Recall that $\mathcal{V}(\cdot)$ and $\mathcal{E}(\cdot)$ are the vertex set and edge set, respectively, of a given graph.

below, whose necessity is proved in Theorem 1 and sufficiency is shown constructively in Section 4. For ease of future reference, we termed the condition as *Condition NC*.

Condition NC: For any node partition L, C, R, F of G such that $L \neq \emptyset, R \neq \emptyset$ and $|F| \leq f$, in G_F, at least one of the two conditions below must be true: (i) $R \cup C \Rightarrow_l L$; (ii) $L \cup C \Rightarrow_l R$.

Intuitively, Condition NC requires that, for any node partition L, C, R, F, either the nodes in $R \cup C$ are able to collectively influence a node in L in G_F or vice versa. Note that when $l = 1$, Condition NC is equivalent to the following condition, which is shown to be both necessary and sufficient without message relay, i.e., $l = 1$, in [14].

" *For any node partition L, C, R, F of G such that $L \neq \emptyset, R \neq \emptyset$ and $|F| \leq f$, in the induced subgraph G_F, at least one of the two conditions below must be true: (i) there exists a node $i \in L$ such that $\left|(R \cup C) \cap N_i^-\right| \geq f + 1$; (ii) there exists a node $j \in R$ such that $\left|(L \cup C) \cap N_j^-\right| \geq f + 1$.*"

Theorem 1. *Suppose that a correct IABC algorithm exists over G. Then G satisfies Condition NC.*

Our proof shares the structure of the proof of Theorem 1 in [14]. The basic idea is as follows: Suppose that the given graph G does not satisfy Condition NC and that there exists a correct IABC algorithm, say $\mathcal{A}$. Since G does not satisfy Condition NC, there exists a node partition L, R, C, F, where L, R are both non-empty and $|F| \leq f$ such that $L \cup C \not\Rightarrow_l R$ and $R \cup C \not\Rightarrow_l L$ in G_F. Consider the execution in which all the nodes in F are faulty and all the remaining nodes are fault-free. In addition, the input of each node in L is 0, the input of each node in R is 2ϵ, and the input of each node in C is an arbitrary value within the interval $[0, 2\epsilon]$. The faulty nodes in F can behave in such a way that each node $i \in L$ cannot determine whether nodes in F are faulty or nodes in the minimum l–restricted $(R \cup C, i)$–cut are faulty. This is possible, since $\kappa_l(R \cup C, i) \leq f$. Thus, to guarantee validity, node i will update its state $v_i[t] = 0$ for all t. Since i is an arbitrary node in L, we have $v_i[t] = 0$ for all $i \in L$ and all t. Similarly, we can show that $v_j[t] = 2\epsilon$ for all $j \in R$ and all t. Thus $|v_i[t] - v_j[t]| = 2\epsilon$ for all t, where $i \in L$ and $j \in R$, contradicting the assumption that $\mathcal{A}$ is a correct IABC algorithm. A formal proof of Theorem 1 can be found in the full version of the paper [10].

The above necessary condition is in general weaker than the necessary condition derived under single-hop message transmission model in [14], i.e., when $l = 1$. Consider the system depicted in Figure 1. The topology of this system does not satisfy the necessary condition derived in [14] for $l = 1$. Since in the node partition $L = \{p_1, p_4\}, R = \{p_2, p_3\}, C = \emptyset$ and $F = \{p_5\}$, neither $L \cup C \Rightarrow_l R$ in G_F nor $R \cup C \Rightarrow_l L$ in G_F holds for $l = 1$ and $f = 1$. However, via enumeration it can be seen that the graph, depicted in Figure 1, satisfies Condition NC for $l \geq 2$ and $f = 1$.

It follows from the definition of Condition NC that if a graph G satisfies Condition NC for $l \in \{1, \ldots, n - 1\}$, then G also satisfies Condition NC for all $l' \geq l$. Let l_0 be the smallest integer for which G satisfies Condition NC. In particular, if G does not satisfy Condition NC for any $l \in \{1, \ldots, n - 1\}$, define $l_0 \triangleq n$ by convention. We observe that in general given a graph G, the diameter of G can be arbitrarily smaller than l_0. For instance, the diameter of the graph depicted in Figure 2 is 2. However, for the depicted graph, $l_0 \geq \frac{n+1}{4}$ when $n = 4k + 3$, where k is a positive integer. So l_0 is much larger than 2 for large n. To see $l_0 \geq \frac{n+1}{4}$, consider the node partition $F = \{p_1\}, C = \varnothing, L = \{p_2, \ldots, p_{\frac{n+1}{2}}\}$ and $R = \{p_{\frac{n+3}{2}}, \ldots, p_n\}$. For $f = 1$, in order to have $L \cup C \Rightarrow_l R$ or $R \cup C \Rightarrow_l L$ hold in G_F for this particular node partition, it must be hold that $l \geq \frac{n+1}{4}$. Thus $l_0 \geq \frac{n+1}{4}$.

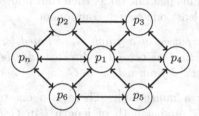

Fig. 2. In this system, there are n nodes $p_1, \ldots, p_n$; all communication links are bidirectional; and at most one node can be adversarial, i.e., $f = 1$. Nodes $p_2, \ldots, p_n$ form a cycle of length $n - 1$ and these nodes are all connected to node p_1.

Similar to [14], as stated in our next corollary, our Condition NC for general l also implies a lower bound on n and a lower bound on each node's incoming degree. Moreover, these lower bounds are independent of l.

Corollary 1. *For $f > 0$, if G satisfies Condition NC, then n must be at least $3f + 1$, and each node must have at least $2f + 1$ incoming neighbors other than itself, i.e., $|N_i^- - \{i\}| \geq 2f + 1$.*

The proof of Corollary 1 is similar to the proof in [14], and can be found in [10]. Note that Corollary 1 also characterizes a lower bound on the density of G, that is $|\mathcal{E}(G)| \geq n(2f + 2)$, including self-loops, which is independent of the communication range l as well.

3.1   Equivalent Characterization of Condition NC

Informally speaking, Condition NC describes the information propagation property in terms of four set partitions. In this subsection, an equivalent condition of Condition NC is proposed, which is based on characterizing the structure of a family of special subgraphs, termed as *reduced graphs*, of the power graph G^l. The new condition suggests that all fault-free nodes will be influenced by a collection of common fault-free nodes.

Definition 3. Meta-graph of SCCs: *Let $K_1, K_2, \ldots, K_k$ be the strongly connected components (i.e., SCCs) of G. The graph of SCCs of G, denoted by G^{SCC}, is defined as follows:*
(i) Nodes in G^{SCC} are $K_1, K_2, \ldots, K_k$; and
(ii) there is an edge (K_i, K_j) in G^{SCC} if there is some $u \in K_i$ and $v \in K_j$ such that (u, v) is an edge in G.
Strongly connected component K_h is said to be a source component *if the corresponding node in G^{SCC} is* not *reachable from any other node in G^{SCC}.*

It is known that the G^{SCC} is a directed acyclic graph, i.e., DAG [3]. It can be easily checked that due to the absence of directed cycles and finiteness, there exists at least one node in G^{SCC} that is not reachable from any other node. In particular, if G^{SCC} contains just one node, then that node is trivially the source. Thus, a graph G has at least one source component.

Definition 4. *The l–th power of a graph G, denoted by G^l, is a multigraph[2] with the same set of vertices as G and a directed edge between vertices u, v is defined by a path of length[3] l from u to v in G.*

The power graph G^l is a multigraph. There is a one-to-one correspondence between an edge e in G^l and a path of length l in G (including self-loops). A path of length 1 between vertices u and v in G exists if (u, v) is an edge in G. A path of length 2 between vertices u and v in G exists for every vertex w such that (u, w) and (w, v) are edges in G. Then for a given graph G with self-loop at each node, the $(u, v)^{th}$ element in the square of the adjacency matrix of G counts the number of paths of length at most 2 in G. Similarly, the $(u, v)^{th}$ element in the l–th power of the adjacency matrix of G gives the number of paths of length l between vertices u and v in G.

Let e be an edge in G^l, and let $P(e)$ be the corresponding path in G, we say an edge e in G^l is covered by node set S, if $\mathcal{V}(P(e)) \cap S \neq \emptyset$, i.e., path $P(e)$ passes through a node in S–recalling that $\mathcal{V}(P(e))$ is the vertex set of path $P(e)$.

Definition 5. *For a given graph G and $F \subseteq \mathcal{V}(G)$, let*

$$E = \{e \in \mathcal{E}(G^l) : \ \mathcal{V}(P(e)) \cap F \neq \emptyset\}$$

be the set of edges in G^l that are covered by node set F. For each node $i \in \mathcal{V}(G) - F$, choose $C_i \subseteq N_i^{l-} - \{i\}$ such that $|C_i| \leq f$. Let

$$E_i = \{e \in \mathcal{E}(G^l) : e \text{ is an incoming edge of node } i \text{ in } G^l \ \text{ and } \mathcal{V}(P(e)) \cap C_i \neq \emptyset\}$$

---

[2] A multigraph (or pseudograph) is a graph which is permitted to have multiple edges between each vertex pair, that is, edges that have the same end nodes. Thus two vertices may be connected by more than one edge.
[3] Recall that we assume that each node in G has a self-loop.

be the set of incoming edges of node i in G^l that are covered by node set C_i. A reduced graph of G^l, denoted by $\widetilde{G^l}_F$, is a subgraph of G^l whose node set and edge set are defined by (i) $\mathcal{V}(\widetilde{G^l_F}) = \mathcal{V}(G) - F$; and (ii) $\mathcal{E}(\widetilde{G^l_F}) = \mathcal{E}(G^l) - E - \cup_{i \in \mathcal{V}(G) - F} E_i$, respectively.

Note that for a given G and a given F, multiple reduced graphs may exist. Let us define set R_F to be the collection of all reduced graph of G^l for a given F, i.e.,

$$R_F = \{\widetilde{G^l}_F : \ \widetilde{G^l}_F \text{ is a reduced graph of } G^l\}. \tag{2}$$

G^l_F, the l-th power of the induced subgraph G_F, itself is a reduced graph of G^l, where we choose $C_i = \emptyset$ for each $i \in \mathcal{V}(G) - F$. Thus R_F is non-empty. In addition, $|R_F|$ is finite since the graph G is finite,

Theorem 2. *Graph G satisfies Condition NC if and only if every reduced graph $\widetilde{G^l}_F$ obtained as per Definition 5 contains exactly one source component.*

The proof of Theorem 2 is based on analogous proofs in [13,14], which can be found in [10].

4   Sufficiency: Algorithm 1

In this section we propose an algorithm, termed Algorithm 1 and show its correctness. First we introduce the definition of message cover that will be used frequently in this section.

Definition 6. *For a communication graph G, let $\mathcal{M}$ be a set of messages, and let $\mathcal{P}(\mathcal{M})$ be the set of paths corresponding to all the messages in $\mathcal{M}$, i.e., $\mathcal{P}(\mathcal{M}) = \{\mathsf{path}(m)|m \in \mathcal{M}\}$. A message cover of $\mathcal{M}$ is a set of nodes $\mathcal{T}(\mathcal{M}) \subseteq \mathcal{V}(G)$, such that for each path $P \in \mathcal{P}$, we have $\mathcal{V}(P) \cap \mathcal{T}(\mathcal{M}) \neq \emptyset$, i.e., each path P is covered by a node in $\mathcal{T}(\mathcal{M})$. In particular, a minimum message cover is defined by*

$$\mathcal{T}^*(\mathcal{M}) \in \arg \min_{\mathcal{T}(\mathcal{M}) \subseteq \mathcal{V}(G): \mathcal{T}(\mathcal{M}) \text{ is a cover of } \mathcal{M}} |\mathcal{T}(\mathcal{M})|.$$

Conversely, given a set of messages $\mathcal{M}_0$ and a set of nodes $\mathcal{T} \subseteq \mathcal{V}(G)$, a maximal set of messages $\mathcal{M} \subseteq \mathcal{M}_0$ that are covered by $\mathcal{T}$ is defined by,

$$\mathcal{M}^* \in \arg \max_{\mathcal{M} \subseteq \mathcal{M}_0: \mathcal{T} \text{ is a cover of } \mathcal{M}} |\mathcal{M}|.$$

Recall that $\mathcal{M}_i[t]$ is the collection of messages received by node i at iteration t. Let $\mathcal{M}'_i[t] = \mathcal{M}_i[t] - \{(v_i[t-1], (i,i))\}$. Sort messages in $\mathcal{M}'_i[t]$ in an increasing order, according to their message values, i.e., $\mathsf{value}(m)$ for $m \in \mathcal{M}'_i[t]$. Let $\mathcal{M}_{is}[t]$ be the largest sized subset of $\mathcal{M}'_i[t]$ such that (i) for all $m \in \mathcal{M}'_i[t] - \mathcal{M}_{is}[t]$ and $m' \in \mathcal{M}_{is}[t]$ we have $\mathsf{value}(m) \geq \mathsf{value}(m')$, and (ii) the cardinality of a minimum cover of $\mathcal{M}_{is}[t]$ is exactly f, i.e., $|\mathcal{T}^*(\mathcal{M}_{is}[t])| = f$. Similarly, we define $\mathcal{M}_{il}[t]$ to be the largest sized subset of $\mathcal{M}'_i[t]$ as follows: (i) for all $m \in \mathcal{M}'_i[t] - \mathcal{M}_{il}[t]$ and $m'' \in \mathcal{M}_{il}[t]$ we have $\mathsf{value}(m) \leq \mathsf{value}(m'')$, and (ii) the cardinality of a minimum cover of $\mathcal{M}_{il}[t]$ is exactly f, i.e., $|\mathcal{T}^*(\mathcal{M}_{il}[t])| = f$. In addition, define $\mathcal{M}_i^*[t] = \mathcal{M}'_i[t] - \mathcal{M}_{is}[t] - \mathcal{M}_{il}[t]$.

Theorem 3. *Suppose that graph G satisfies Condition NC, then the sets of messages $\mathcal{M}_{is}[t]$, $\mathcal{M}_{il}[t]$ are well-defined and $\mathcal{M}_i^*[t]$ is non-empty for $f > 0$.*

This theorem is proved by construction, i.e., an algorithm is constructed to find the sets $\mathcal{M}_{is}[t]$, $\mathcal{M}_{il}[t]$ for a given $\mathcal{M}'_i[t]$. Details of the algorithm and its correctness proof can be found in [10]. We will prove that there exists an IABC algorithm – particularly *Algorithm 1* below – that satisfies the *validity* and *convergence* conditions provided that the graph G satisfies Condition NC. This implies that Condition NC is also sufficient. *Algorithm 1* has the three-step structure described in Section 2. With the exception of the update step (3) below, the algorithm is similar to the consensus algorithms in [8,14].

Algorithm 1

---

1. *Transmit step:* Transmit messages of the form $(v_i[t-1], P)$ on each l–hop path P (including self-loops) to nodes in N_i^{l+}. If node i is an intermediate node on path P for some message of the form $(\cdot, P)$, then node i forwards that to the next node on path P.
2. *Receive step:* Receive messages from N_i^{l-} for which destination is i. When node i expects to receive a message from a path but does not receive the message, the message value is assumed to be equal to some default value.[4]
3. *Update step:*
   Define

$$v_i[t] = Z_i(\mathcal{M}_i[t]) = a_i v_i[t-1] + \sum_{m \in \mathcal{M}_i^*[t]} a_i w_m. \qquad (3)$$

   where $w_m = \mathsf{value}(m)$ and $a_i = \frac{1}{|\mathcal{M}_i^*[t]|+1}$.

Note that in Step 3, only messages in $\mathcal{M}_i^*[t]$ and the value $v_i[t-1]$ are used in updating v_i in (3). Messages in both $\mathcal{M}_{is}[t]$ and $\mathcal{M}_{il}[t]$ are trimmed away. This trimming strategy is motivated by the observation that the messages in $\mathcal{M}_{is}[t]$ (or $\mathcal{M}_{il}[t]$) may be tampered by nodes in $\mathcal{T}^*(\mathcal{M}_{is}[t])$ (or $\mathcal{T}^*(\mathcal{M}_{il}[t])$). These faulty behaviors are possible because of the fact that $|\mathcal{T}^*(\mathcal{M}_{is}[t])| = f$ and $|\mathcal{T}^*(\mathcal{M}_{il}[t])| = f$. Recall $\mathcal{M}_i^*[t] = \mathcal{M}'_i[t] - \mathcal{M}_{is}[t] - \mathcal{M}_{il}[t]$. The "weight"

---

[4] Note that node i does not read the message value if the message destination is not i.

of each term on the right-hand side of (3) is a_i, where $0 < a_i \leq 1$, and these weights add to 1. For future reference, let us define α, which is used in Theorem 4, as:

$$\alpha = \min_{i \in \mathcal{V} - \mathcal{F}} a_i. \tag{4}$$

In *Algorithm 1*, each fault-free node i's state, $v_i[t]$, is updated as a convex combination of all the *messages values* collected by node i at round t. In particular, for each message $m \in \mathcal{M}'[t]$, its coefficient is a_i if the message is in $\mathcal{M}_i^*[t]$ or the message is sent via self-loop of node i; otherwise, the coefficient of m is zero. The update step in *Algorithm 1* is a generalization of the update steps proposed in [8,13,14,16], where the update summation is over all the incoming neighbors of node i instead of over message routes. In [8,13,14,16], only single-hop communication is allowed, i.e., $l = 1$, and the fault-free node i can receive only one message from its incoming neighbor. With multi-hop communication, fault-free node can possibly receive messages from a node via multiple routes. Our trim function in *Algorithm 1* takes the possible multi-route messages into account.

4.1 Matrix Representation of Algorithm 1

With our trim function, the iterative update of the state of a fault-free node i admits a matrix representation of states evolution of fault-free nodes. We use boldface upper case letters to denote matrices, rows of matrices, and their entries. For instance, $\mathbf{A}$ denotes a matrix, $\mathbf{A}_i$ denotes the i-th row of matrix $\mathbf{A}$, and $\mathbf{A}_{ij}$ denotes the element at the intersection of the i-th row and the j-th column of matrix $\mathbf{A}$. Some useful concepts and theorems are reviewed briefly in [10].

Definition 7. *A vector is said to be* stochastic *if all the entries of the vector are non-negative, and the entries add up to 1. A matrix is said to be* row stochastic *if each row of the matrix is a stochastic vector.*

Recall that $\mathcal{F}$ is the set of faulty nodes. Let $|\mathcal{F}| = \phi$. Without loss of generality, suppose that nodes 1 through $(n - \phi)$ are fault-free, and if $\phi > 0$, nodes $(n - \phi + 1)$ through n are faulty. Denote by $\mathbf{v}[0] \in \mathbb{R}^{n-\phi}$ the column vector consisting of the initial states of all the *fault-free* nodes. Denote by $\mathbf{v}[t]$, where $t \geq 1$, the column vector consisting of the states of all the *fault-free* nodes at the end of the t-th iteration, $t \geq 1$, where the i-th element of vector $\mathbf{v}[t]$ is state $v_i[t]$.

Theorem 4. *We can express the iterative update of the state of a fault-free node i $(1 \leq i \leq n - \phi)$ performed in (3) using the matrix form in (5) below, where $\mathbf{M}_i[t]$ satisfies the four conditions listed below. In addition to t, the row vector $\mathbf{M}_i[t]$ may depend on the state vector $\mathbf{v}[t-1]$ as well as the behavior of the faulty nodes in $\mathcal{F}$. For simplicity, the notation $\mathbf{M}_i[t]$ does not explicitly represent this dependence.*

$$v_i[t] = \mathbf{M}_i[t]\, \mathbf{v}[t-1] \tag{5}$$

1. $\mathbf{M}_i[t]$ *is a stochastic row vector of size* $(n - \phi)$*. Thus,* $\mathbf{M}_{ij}[t] \geq 0$*, where* $1 \leq j \leq n - \phi$*, and*

$$\sum_{1 \leq j \leq n - \phi} \mathbf{M}_{ij}[t] = 1$$

2. $\mathbf{M}_{ii}[t] \geq a_i \geq \alpha$*.*
3. $\mathbf{M}_{ij}[t]$ *is non-zero only if there exists a message* $m \in \mathcal{M}_i[t]$ *such that* source$(m) = j$ *and* destination$(m) = i$*.*
4. *For any* $t \geq 1$*, there exists a reduced graph* $\widetilde{G^l}_{\mathcal{F}} \in R_{\mathcal{F}}$ *with adjacent matrix* $\mathbf{H}[t]$ *such that* $\beta\,\mathbf{H}[t] \leq \mathbf{M}[t]$*, where* $\beta = \frac{1}{16n^{2t}}$*.*

In the full version of the paper [10], we prove the correctness of Theorem 4 by constructing $\mathbf{M}_i[t]$ for $1 \leq i \leq n - \phi$. Our proof follows the same line of analysis as in the proof of Claim 2 in [13]. Due to the complexity (in particular, the dependency of message covers) brought up by messages relay, we divide the universe into six cases to consider.

Theorem 5. Algorithm 1 *satisfies the validity and the convergence conditions.*

From the code of *Algorithm 1*, we know that

$$v_i[t] = a_i v_i[t - 1] + \sum_{m \in \mathcal{M}_i^*[t]} a_i w_m, \tag{6}$$

where $a_i = \frac{1}{|\mathcal{M}_i^*[t]| + 1}$. Theorem 4 states that we can rewrite (6) as

$$\sum_{j \in \mathcal{V} - \mathcal{F}} \mathbf{M}_{ij}[t] v_j[t - 1],$$

where $\mathbf{M}_{ij}[t]$s together satisfy the preceding four conditions. By "stacking" (5) for different i, $1 \leq i \leq n - \phi$, we can represent the state update for all the fault-free nodes together using (7) below, where $\mathbf{M}[t]$ is a $(n - \phi) \times (n - \phi)$ row stochastic matrix, with its i-th row being equal to $\mathbf{M}_i[t]$ in (5).

$$\mathbf{v}[t] = \mathbf{M}[t]\,\mathbf{v}[t - 1]. \tag{7}$$

By repeated application of (7), we obtain:

$$\mathbf{v}[t] = \left(\Pi_{\tau=1}^{t} \mathbf{M}[\tau] \right) \mathbf{v}[0].$$

As the backward product $\Pi_{\tau=1}^{t} \mathbf{M}[\tau]$ is a row-stochastic matrix, it holds that $\mu[0] \leq v_i[t] \leq U[0]$ for all $i = 1, \ldots, n - \phi$ and all t. Thus Algorithm 1 satisfies validity condition.

The convergence of $v_i[t]$ depends on the convergence of the backward product $\Pi_{\tau=1}^{t} \mathbf{M}[\tau]$. As a result of this, our convergence proof uses toolkit of weak-ergodic theory that is also adopted in prior work (e.g., [1,2,8,14]). The last condition in Theorem 4 plays an important role in the proof of Theorem 5. A formal proof of Theorem 5 is presented in [10].

5   Unbounded Path Length

In this section, we show that Condition NC is equivalent to some existing results for undirected graphs and directed graphs when path lengths are not constrained.

5.1   Undirected Graph with Unbounded Path Length

If G is undirected, it has been shown in [6], that $n \geq 3f+1$ and node-connectivity $2f + 1$ are both necessary and sufficient for achieving Byzantine approximate consensus. Recall that l^* is the length of a longest cycle-free path in G. We will show that when $l \geq l^*$, our Condition NC is equivalent to the above conditions.

Theorem 6. *When $l \geq l^*$, if G is undirected, then $n \geq 3f + 1$ and node-connectivity of G is at least $2f + 1$ if and only if G satisfies Condition NC.*

Informally, if the node-connectivity of G, denoted by $\kappa(G)$, is at most $2f$, then we are able to show that there exists a node partition L, R, C, F, where L, R are both non-empty and $|F| \leq f$, such that, in G_F, neither $L \cup C \Rightarrow_l R$ nor $R \cup C \Rightarrow_l L$ holds. Conversely, if $n \geq 3f+1$ and $\kappa(G) \geq 2f+1$, using Expansion Lemma [15] we are able to show Condition NC holds. Formal proof is given in [10].

5.2   Directed Graph with Unbounded Path Length

Synchronous exact Byzantine consensus is considered in [12].

Definition 8. *[12] Given disjoint subsets A, B, where B is non-empty:*
(i) We say $A \to B$ if and only if set A contains at least $f + 1$ distinct incoming neighbors of B. That is, $|\{i \mid (i, j) \in \mathcal{E}, i \in A, j \in B\}| > f$.
(ii) We say $A \not\to B$ iff $A \to B$ is not true.

The following necessary and sufficient condition is obtained in [12].

Theorem 7. *[12] Given a graph G, exact Byzantine consensus is solvable if and only if for any partition L, C, R, F of G, such that both L and R are non-empty, and $|F| \leq f$, either $L \cup C \to R$ in G_F, or $R \cup C \to L$ in G_F.*

We term this condition as Condition 1. Note that in order for $A \to B$ to hold, we only require that there are at least $f + 1$ incoming neighbors of set B in set A. As a result of this observation, our Condition NC with $l = 1$ is, in general, strictly stronger than Condition 1. However, we prove the following result in [10].

Theorem 8. *Condition NC is equivalent to Condition 1 when $l \geq l^*$.*

6   Summary and Discussion

In this paper, we assume that each node knows the topology within its l–hop neighborhood, and in each iteration it can send messages to nodes that are up to l hops away, where $l \geq 1$. We prove a necessary and sufficient condition for the existence of *iterative* algorithms that achieve *approximate Byzantine consensus* in directed graphs, while maintaining minimal memory across iterations. The class of iterative algorithms considered in this paper ensures that, after each iteration of the algorithm, the state of each fault-free node remains within the range (or convex hull) of the initial inputs at the fault-free nodes.

Throughout the paper so far, we assumed that faulty nodes are only able to tamper message values, leaving message paths unchanged. However, this restriction of faulty behaviors of Byzantine nodes is not necessary. In fact, the above results still hold when both message value tampering and message path tampering are allowed, provided that (i) the number of faked messages is finite and there exists a constant C such that $\mathcal{M}_i[t] \leq C$ for all t (i.e., each faulty node $k \in \mathcal{F}$ cannot create too many non-existing messages), and that (ii) for each message m tampered/faked by a faulty node k, $\mathsf{path}(m)$ must satisfy $k \in \mathcal{V}(\mathsf{path}(m))$ (i.e., the faulty node k cannot conceal itself from the message path). The constraints (i) and (ii) can be implemented as follows. Recall that each fault-free node knows the network topology in its l–hop neighborhood. In each iteration, a fault-free node should accept any one message of the form (w, P) for any particular l–hop path P that is known to exist – if more than one such message is received, discard all but one such message (or discard all, and replace by a default value). Also, if node i receives the message (w, P) where path P is not known to exist, then node i should discard the message. These rules implement constraint (i) above. Suppose node i receives or relays a message $m = (w, P)$ from node j containing a path that does not have the form $\ldots ji \ldots$ then i will discard the message. This way, on any given l–hop path P, at least the very last faulty node will have to remain on the path (it may delete the earlier nodes on the path, but not itself). Thus the constraint (ii) is imposed. The necessity of Condition NC can be easily verified for the above behavior as well. It can also be seen that Algorithm 1 works under this relaxed model, proving the sufficiency of Condition NC.

Acknowledgements. The authors thank the referees and Lewis Tseng for providing constructive comments on the paper.

References

1. Ali, J., Jie, L., Morse, A.S.: Coordination of groups of mobile autonomous agents using nearest neighbor rules. IEEE Transactions on Automatic Control **48**(6), 988–1001 (2003)

2. Bnzit, F., Blondel, V., Thiran, P., Tsitsiklis, J., Vetterli, M.: Weighted gossip:Distributed averaging using non-doubly stochastic matrices. In: 2010 IEEE International Symposium on Information Theory Proceedings (ISIT), pp. 1753–1757, June 2010
3. Cormen, T.H., Leiserson, C.E., Rivest, R.L., Stein, C., et al.: Introduction toalgorithms, vol. 2. MIT Press Cambridge (2001)
4. Dolev, D., Lynch, N.A., Pinter, S.S., Stark, E.W., Weihl, W.E.: Reaching approximate agreement in the presence of faults. J. ACM **33**(3), 499–516 (1986)
5. Fekete, A.D.: Asymptotically optimal algorithms for approximate agreement. Distributed Computing 4(1), 9–29 (1990)
6. Fischer, M.J., Lynch, N.A., Merritt, M.: Easy impossibility proofs for distributed consensus problems. In: Proceedings of the Fourth Annual ACM Symposium on Principles of Distributed Computing, PODC 1985, pp. 59–70. ACM, New York (1985)
7. Fischer, M.J., Lynch, N.A., Paterson, M.S.: Impossibility of distributed consensus with one faulty process. J. ACM **32**, 374–382 (1985)
8. LeBlanc, H.J., Zhang, H., Sundaram, S., Koutsoukos, X.: Consensus of multi-agent networks in the presence of adversaries using only local information. In: Proceedings of the 1st International Conference on High Confidence Networked Systems, HiCoNS 2012, pp. 1–10. ACM, New York (2012)
9. Pease, M., Shostak, R., Lamport, L.: Reaching agreement in the presence of faults. J. ACM **27**(2), 228–234 (1980)
10. Su, L., Vaidya, N.: Reaching approximate byzantine consensus with multi-hop communication (2014). arXiv preprint arXiv:1411.5282
11. Tseng, L., Vaidya, N.: Iterative approximate consensus in the presence of byzantine link failures. In: Noubir, G., Raynal, M. (eds.) NETYS 2014. LNCS, vol. 8593, pp. 84–98. Springer, Heidelberg (2014)
12. Tseng, L., Vaidya, N.H.: Fault-tolerant consensus in directed graphs. In: Proceedings of the 2015 ACM Symposium on Principles of Distributed Computing. ACM (to appear, 2015)
13. Vaidya, N.H.: Matrix representation of iterative approximate byzantine consensus in directed graphs. CoRR, arXiv:1203.1888 (2012)
14. Vaidya, N.H., Tseng, L., Liang, G.: Iterative approximate byzantine consensus in arbitrary directed graphs. In: Proceedings of the 2012 ACM Symposium on Principles of Distributed Computing, pp. 365–374. ACM (2012)
15. West, D.B., et al.: Introduction to graph theory, vol. 2. Prentice Hall, Upper Saddle River (2001)
16. Zhang, H., Sundaram, S.: Robustness of information diffusion algorithms to locally bounded adversaries. In: American Control Conference (ACC 2012), pp. 5855–5861 (2012)

The Complexity of Data Aggregation in Static and Dynamic Wireless Sensor Networks

Quentin Bramas[1]([✉]) and Sébastien Tixeuil[1,2]

[1] Sorbonne Universités, UPMC Univ Paris 06, UMR 7606, F-75005 Paris, France
[2] Institut Universitaire de France, Paris, France
quentin.bramas@lip6.fr

Abstract. The key feature of wireless sensor networks is to aggregate data collected by individual sensors in an energy efficient manner. We consider two techniques to save energy. The first one is to avoid collisions due to simultaneous transmissions among neighboring nodes. Second, when a node receives data from multiple neighbors, it aggregates these with its own data. Then, one transmission is sufficient to transmit all consolidated data to another neighbor. If the overall delay has to be kept as low as possible, scheduling sensors to avoid collisions while aggregating data becomes challenging.

The contribution of this paper is threefold. First, we give tight bounds for the complexity of data aggregation in static networks. In more details, we show that the problem remains NP-complete when the graph is of degree at most three. As it is trivial to solve the problem in static graphs of degree at most two, our result implies that the problem is intrinsically difficult for any practical setting. Second, we investigate the complexity of the same problem in a dynamic network, that is, a network whose topology can evolve through time. In the case of dynamic networks, we show that the problem is NP-complete even in the case where the graph is of degree at most two (and it is trivial to solve the problem when the graph is of degree at most one). Third, we give the first lower and upper bounds for the minimum data aggregation time in a dynamic graph.

We observe that even in a well-connected evolving graphs, the optimal solution cannot be found by a distributed algorithm or by a centralized algorithm that does not know the future. Thus we finally give the first approximation algorithm (centralized that knows the future) whose approximation factor is $T(n-1)$ if there exists a bound T such that there is a journey (a path in a dynamic graph) for all pairs of nodes in every time interval $[t, t + T]$.

Keywords: Data aggregation · Dynamic graphs · Complexity

This work was performed within the Labex SMART supported by French state funds managed by the ANR within the Investissements d'Avenir programme under reference ANR-11-IDEX-0004-02.

A. Pelc and A.A. Schwarzmann (Eds.): SSS 2015, LNCS 9212, pp. 36–50, 2015.
DOI: 10.1007/978-3-319-21741-3_3

1 Introduction

The growing number of sensor nodes with sensing, computing and communication capabilities, was made possible by recent technological advances. This growth was encouraged by a variety of applications and contributes to the widespread interest in practical and theoretical aspects of wireless sensor networks. Sensor nodes should be inexpensive, small and sustainable in order to be easily deployed in a dangerous area, inside a human body or in vehicles, generally for monitoring applications. They generate data that have to be retrieved by an end-user or a base station. However, the environment and the lack of networking infrastructure does not permit direct transmission to the end user, but only transmissions between sensors that are close to one another. This raises various challenges, such as energy (sensors are battery powered) and delay efficiency (information is relevant for a short period of time only).

In a wireless sensor network (WSN), sensor nodes can communicate through a wireless ad hoc network. Then, there exists a communication link between two nodes if the Euclidean distance between them is smaller than their communication range. Since we assume all sensors to be identical, they have the same communication range and the communication graph can be modeled as a unit-disk graph[1] [8]. Sensor nodes typically generate data from their environment, such as temperature, number of vehicles on a road, or number of passenger in a bus. The end-user, called *sink node*, wants to extract this information. To do so, a node can send its data directly to the sink node if it is located within its communication range, or, if it is far from the sink, can use intermediate nodes to relay the data to the sink node.

In this paper we investigate the problem of retrieving data from a WSN whose data transmissions are constrained by two rules: avoiding collisions, and allowing data aggregation. In more details, the time is discretized and, at each time slot, a node is able to send its data to all of its neighbors (*i.e.*, all nodes within its communication range). Now, if two or more nodes send their data in the same time slot, their common neighbors do not receive any data, due to interference. Whenever a node successfully receives data, it aggregates the data with its own and stores the result as its new data. This process ensures energy-efficiency of the protocol. Indeed, n transmissions are sufficient to retrieve the data from n sensors to the sink node (compared to possibly $\Omega(n^2)$ without the capability to aggregate data). The problem of aggregating data from all nodes in the network in a minimum amount of time slots (delay-efficiency), assuming that a node sends its data at most once (energy-efficiency) is known as the *minimum data aggregation time* (MDAT) problem [7]. A solution to this problem consists of a transmission schedule, meeting the communication constraints, with minimum duration.

In this paper we also introduce the dynamic version of the MDAT problem, where individual sensors are now mobile entities. This could model cars

---

[1] We suppose here that the area is a two dimensional plane, but our results naturally extend to greater dimensions.

evolving in a smart city, medical devices in a body area network, or mobile devices monitoring an area. A WSN whose topology evolves with time is modeled as a *dynamic unit-disk graph, i.e.*, a sequence of static unit-disk graphs. In this setting, the communication constraints hold at each time slot, and a solution of the MDAT problem consists of a transmission schedule with minimum duration.

When sensor nodes have fixed positions, the maximum distance (in hops) from the sink node to any other node is a lower bound for the minimum data aggregation time [7]. Indeed, if no collision occurs, the data from the farthest node can be sent through a shortest path. Each avoided collision increases the duration of the schedule by one time slot. However, if we suppose the nodes are moving, avoiding collisions can intuitively have a much greater impact. Indeed, if a collision occurs and we delay the transmission of a node by one time slot, the node may not be able to transmit again (maybe the node remains isolated thereafter). In other terms, the existence of a journey (a path in a dynamic graph) from every node to the sink node is not sufficient to guarantee the existence of a collision-free schedule.

Related Work. The data aggregation problem we consider here was first studied by Anamalai *et. al.* [2]. The authors assume that a fixed number of channels is available for a transmission, and a collision occurs at a receiver whenever two of its neighbors transmit on the same channel at the same time. The authors propose an algorithm that constructs a collision free convergecast tree that can also be used for broadcasting. Also, in-network aggregation [10] proposes an orthogonal approach and assumes that collisions are handled by the MAC layer and aims to find routes that minimize the delay, which differ significantely from the MDAT problem. Then, Chen *et. al.* [7] present a well-defined model for the study of the MDAT problem in wireless sensor networks. They prove that the problem is NP-complete, even in graphs of degree at most four (more precisely they restricted the problem to networks whose topology is a sub-graph of the grid). They also gave a $(\Delta - 1)$-approximation algorithm (where Δ is the maximum node degree of the graph).

After the work of Chen *et. al.* [7], a variety of papers proposed centralized and distributed approximation algorithms using geometric aspect of the MDAT problem to improve the data aggregation delay. Yu et. al. [16] give a distributed algorithm with an upper bound at $24D + 6\Delta + 16$ (where D is the diameter, and Δ the maximum degree of the graph). Xu et. al., in [15] and Ren et. al. in [14] propose centralized algorithms with upper bounds at $16R + \Delta - 14$ and $16R + \Delta - 11$ respectively (where R is the radius of the graph). The best known bound is due to Nguyen *et. al.* in [13], where they give a centralized algorithm that takes at most $12R + \Delta - 11$ time slots to aggregate all data.

On the other hand, dynamic graphs have received a lot of interest recently and efforts have been done in order to standardize the underlying model [3,6,11]. Various problems have been studied in a distributed setting, such as computing foremost, fastest and shortest broadcast [4,5]. For each problem, sufficient and necessary conditions on the (dynamic) graph are given. Most related to our concern are two previous attempts that consider data aggregation in dynamic networks [1,9], however they use a much more powerful communication model where no collision occurs (in more details, continuous aggregation [1] assumes that data have to be aggregated and disseminated such that there is a consensus among the nodes, and aggregation in dynamic networks [9] aims to minimize the number of nodes that owns data assuming *unicast* communication). In short, no previous works considers the data aggregation problem in dynamic networks taking into account the possibility of collisions.

Our Contribution. The contribution of this paper is threefold. First, in order to compare the complexity of the data aggregation in static and dynamic WSN, we give a tight bound for the complexity of the MDAT problem in static WSN. In more details, we show that, in a *static* WSN, the problem remains NP-complete when the graph is of degree at most three. As it is trivial to solve the problem in static graph of degree at most two, our result implies that the problem is intrinsically difficult for any practical setting. This result closes the complexity gap in the static case.

Second, we introduce an extension of MDAT problem in dynamic WSNs, and we prove that the dynamic MDAT is NP-complete in a *dynamic* WSN of degree at most two (and it is trivial to solve the problem if the graph is of degree at most one).

Third, we give the first lower and upper bounds for the dynamic MDAT problem. More precisely, we define the notion of the foremost journey tree to the sink node as a rooted tree whose branches are foremost journeys (journeys with the earliest arrival time) to the sink node. Then, the minimum time to aggregate all data in a dynamic network is greater than the duration of a foremost journey tree (this is valid in *any* graph, and for any degree Δ there exists a dynamic graph such that the bound is attained) and is smaller than the duration of $(n-1)$ independent foremost journey trees (this later bound is valid for any graph, but actually obtained for dynamic graphs of degree $n-1$). If we restrain the class of dynamic graphs to those of degree smaller than $n-1$, we prove that the upper bound is greater or equal to the duration of l independent foremost journey trees (with $l = (\Delta - 1)\log_\Delta (n(\Delta - 1) + 1) - \Delta + 2)$, which prevents previous approximation in the static case to be extended in the dynamic case. Finally, we observe that, even in periodic graphs, optimal solutions cannot be computed by an algorithm that is unaware of the future of the graph or by a distributed algorithm (even if each node knows its own future). This motivates our simple approximate algorithm presented in section 6 to be centralized with full knowledge. The approximation factor is $T(n-1)$ if there exists a bound T such that there is a journey between every two nodes in every time interval $[t, t+T]$.

2   Model and Preliminaries

Wireless sensor networks (WSNs) containing n nodes with transmission range normalized to 1, are modeled by unit disk graphs [8] *i.e.*, intersection graphs of n equal-sized circles. Each vertex corresponds to a circle of radius $1/2$, and an edge exists between two vertices when the corresponding circles intersect (tangent circles are assumed to intersect).

We model a *dynamic WSN* as a *discrete-time-varying* graph [6]. According to this model, we consider a discrete lifetime $T = \mathbb{N}$ with a constant *latency* function ρ that equals one for every edge at any time (messages can travel at most one hop at a given time). Under those assumptions, a dynamic graph is seen as an *evolving* graph *i.e.*, a sequence of *footprints*, where each footprint is a static graph that represents the evolving graph at a given time $t \in \mathbb{N}$. The maximum node degree of a dynamic graph, denoted Δ, is the maximum node degree among all its footprints. We recall that in dynamic graph, an edge is a couple $((u, v), t)$ where u and v are two nodes connected at time t.

Definition 1. *A dynamic wireless sensor network G is a dynamic graph $(V, (E_t)_{t \in \mathbb{N}})$ where V is the set of vertices and $(E_t)_{t \in \mathbb{N}}$ a sequence that represents the edges of the graph over the time, such that for each t, (V, E_t) is a unit-disk graph.*

Data Aggregation Schedule. The time is discrete and at each time round, called *time slot*, communications are constrained by the following rule. Sensor nodes can send or receive data, but cannot do both at the same time. Moreover, if two nodes send their data simultaneously, all their common neighbors do not receive anything, due to interference (see figure 1). A node can aggregate a received data with its own data, according to a given aggregation function (simple examples of aggregation functions include maximum and addition). The aggregation is supposed atomic, and the resulting data can be sent like the original data *i.e.*, in one time slot.

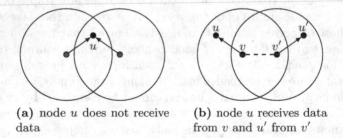

| (a) node u does not receive data | (b) node u receives data from v and u' from v' |

Fig. 1. Communication constraints

Let $G = (V, (E_t)_{t \in \mathbb{N}})$, $A \subseteq V$, and $B \subseteq A$. We say that *data is aggregated from A to B at time t*, denoted by $(G, A, t) \to (G, B, t + 1)$, if nodes in $A \backslash B$ transmit their data simultaneously and all the data is received by at least one node in B. Formally if:

$$\forall u \in A \backslash B, \ \exists v \in B, \ \forall u' \in A \backslash B - \{u\} :$$
$$(u, v) \in E_t \wedge (u', v) \notin E_t$$

A *dynamic data aggregation schedule* to s of duration l is a decreasing sequence of sets $V = R_0 \supseteq R_1 \supseteq \ldots \supseteq R_l = \{s\}$ satisfying the following condition:

$$\forall 0 \le i < l, \quad (G, R_i, i) \rightarrow (G, R_{i+1}, i+1)$$

Dynamic Minimum Data Aggregation Time Problem. An instance of the dynamic MDAT problem is a couple (G, s) in which $G = (V, (E_t)_{t \in \mathbb{N}})$ models a dynamic WSN and $s \in V$ the sink node. A solution of an instance (G, s) is a dynamic data aggregation schedule to s with minimum duration. The minimum duration is denoted by $MDAT_{Opt}(G, s)$.

Remark 1. This problem may have no solution, even in a dynamic WSN G connected over time (*i.e.*, if for all $u, v \in V$, there exists a journey from u to v). Indeed if the set of edges is defined as follow: $E_0 = V \times V$ and $\forall i \neq 0$, $E_i = \emptyset$, the graph is connected, but only one node can send its data to the sink node at time 0, and the other nodes are never able to send their data. A simple sufficient assumption (but not necessary) in order to ensure the existence of a solution, is that the graph is recurrent connected (see our algorithm GDAS in the sequel).

3 NP-Hardness

3.1 Static Grid Graphs of Degree at Most Three

A grid graph is a unit disk graph where all disks have centers with integer coordinates and radius $1/2$ *i.e.*, an induced sub-graph of the grid. However, a sub-graph of the grid (not necessarily induced, called partial grid) is not necessarily a grid graph.

Chen *et. al.* prove in [7] that finding the minimum data aggregation time is NP-hard, even when the network is restricted to partial grid (with maximum degree $\Delta = 4$). On the other side, if the maximum degree of a static graph is $\Delta = 2$, the graph is either a line or a cycle and the minimum data aggregation time is easy to compute. Let ε be the eccentricity of the sink node and n the number of nodes. If n is odd and $\varepsilon = (n-1)/2$ (the graph is either a cycle or a line with the sink node in the middle) then the MDAT is $\varepsilon + 1$. Otherwise the MDAT is ε.

In this section we close the complexity gap of the MDAT problem in static networks by proving that the MDAT is NP-hard, even when restricted to grid graphs with maximum degree $\Delta = 3$.

We use a construction that is similar to that of Chen *et al.* [7] with some improvements about the topology (grid graph instead of partial grid) and about the maximum node degree (3 instead of 4). We first state a lemma slightly different from their lemma 2 [7], and follow with our first theorem.

Lemma 1. *Let H be a planar graph with $n > 6$ nodes and maximum degree $\Delta \le 4$, there exist an orthogonal planar embedding of H such that each edge has the same length. This embedding can be computed in time polynomial in n.*

Theorem 1. *The MDAT problem restricted to grid graphs of degree at most three is NP-complete.*

The proof of the theorem is by reduction from restricted planar 3−SAT [12]. Let φ be a 3−SAT formula composed by a set C of m clauses $c_1, \ldots, c_m$ over a set V of n variables $v_1, \ldots, v_n$. We define the corresponding formula graph $G_\varphi = (V \cup C, E_1 \cup E_2)$, where $E_1 = \{(x_i, c_j) : x_i \in c_j \text{ or } \bar{x}_i \in c_j\}$ and $E_2 = \{(x_i, x_{i+1}) : 1 \leq i \leq n-1\} \cup \{(x_n, x_1)\}$. φ is said to be *planar* if the formula graph G_φ is planar. φ is said to be *restricted* if *(i)* each variable appears in at most three clauses, *(ii)* both negated and unnegated forms of each variable appears at least once, and *(iii)* clauses drawn on the same side of the cycle E_2 must share the same literal if they share the same variable (*i.e.*, at a variable vertex in G_φ, incident edges from one side correspond to the same literal). It is known that restricted planar 3-SAT is NP-complete [12].

Proof. Let φ be an instance of the restricted planar 3 − SAT on n variables and m clauses. From the planar formula graph G_φ, we construct a planar graph G with maximum degree $\Delta = 3$. The idea behind the construction is that, in order to have a fast data aggregation, the schedule must "choose" between two sides (*i.e.*, the data are aggregated along one of two possible paths) representing the true or false instantiation of a variable. The aggregation is fast if all clauses are connected to the correct side of at least one variable. First we construct the sub-graph X_i that represents the variable x_i (see figure 2).

X_i is composed of a cycle of nodes $e_i, l_i, r_i, s_i, o_i, \bar{s}_i, \bar{r}_i, \bar{l}_i$. Then, we connect to l_i (resp. $\bar{l}_i$) a path L_i (resp. $\bar{L}_i$) of length $5i - 3$. Thus l_i cannot sends its data before aggregating data from L_i *i.e.*, before $5i - 3$ timeslots. For $1 \leq i < n$ we connect o_i to e_{i+1} and we connect to e_1 a new node e_0.

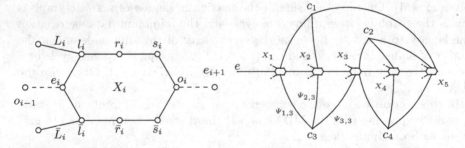

Fig. 2. sub-graphs X_i, L_i and $\bar{L}_i$

Fig. 3. example for $\varphi = (x_1 \vee x_2 \vee \bar{x}_5) \wedge (x_3 \vee \bar{x}_4 \vee \bar{x}_5) \wedge (\bar{x}_1 \vee \bar{x}_2 \vee \bar{x}_3) \wedge (\bar{x}_3 \vee x_4 \vee x_5)$

Each clause c_j is represented by a single node and for each variable x_i (resp. negation $\bar{x}_i$) in clause c_j, we connect c_j to r_i or s_i (resp. $\bar{r}_i$ or $\bar{s}_i$) by a path

$\Psi_{i,j}$ of length $(5i - 2)$ to r_i (resp. $\bar{r}_i$) or $(5i - 1)$ to s_i (resp. $\bar{s}_i$). Let $G = \bigcup_{1 \le i \le n}^{1 \le j \le m} (X_i \cup L_i \cup \bar{L}_i \cup \Psi_{i,j})$ (see figure 2 and 3).

In order to use the previous lemma we need to be able to change the distance between nodes. So we define G_T obtained from G by replacing every edge by a path of length T , i.e., by adding $T - 1$ nodes between two connected nodes, and by adding a pending node e connected to e_0.

Lemma 2. *For all $T \ge 1$, the minimum time to aggregate data from G_T to o_n is $5nT + 1$ if and only if φ is satisfiable.*

End of the proof of theorem 1: We now have to show that there exists a T such that G_T is a grid graph. From lemma 1 we deduce that G has an orthogonal embedding such that every edge has the same length $l \ge 1$ in a grid of size s. We divide the unit by 4 so that the embedding is in a grid of size $4s$ and every edge has length $4l$ (every vertex has their coordinates multiplied by 4). Then, we replace, in its embedding, each node by a disk of radius $1/2$, and every edge by a chain of $4l - 1$ disk of radius $1/2$, centered at integer coordinates along the edge. Finally, we add a disk of radius $1/2$, centered at integer coordinates, at distance 1 from e_0 and at distance greater than 1 from other disks. The corresponding unit disk graph (that is also a grid graph) is exactly G_{4l}.

So we have obtained a reduction from the restricted planar 3−SAT to the MDAT problem in a grid graph, with maximum degree $\Delta = 3$. The theorem follows from the NP-completeness of restricted planar 3−SAT [12].   □

3.2   Dynamic Graphs of Degree at Most Two

In a dynamic network we prove that, even when the maximum degree is two, the dynamic MDAT problems is NP-hard. This result is optimal since the problem is easy to solve in a graph of degree at most one (where no collision occurs).

Theorem 2. *The dynamic MDAT problem is NP-complete even in a dynamic wireless sensor network of degree at most two.*

Proof. The proof is by reduction from 3-SAT. Given any 3-SAT instance φ of n variables $v_1, \ldots, v_n$ and m clauses $c_1, \ldots, c_m$, we construct the dynamic grid graph $G_\varphi(V, E)$ as follow:

Nodes are composed of one sink node, literals, clauses, and copy of clauses:

$$V = \{s\} \bigcup_{1 \le i \le n} \{v_i\} \cup \{\bar{v}_i\} \bigcup_{1 \le i \le m} \{c_i\} \cup \{c_i'\}$$

Let $t_f = 3n + 2m$. We decompose the time interval $[1, t_f]$ in three periods T_1, T_2 and T_3 (see figure 4):

- During $T_1 = [1, 2n]$, we have for all $i \in [1, n]$:

$$E_{2i-1} = \{(v_i, s)\}, \quad E_{2i} = \{(\bar{v}_i, s)\}$$

- During $T_2 = [2n+1, 2n+2m]$ we have for all $j \in [1, m]$:

  with $\{a, b, c\} = c_j$, $E_{2n+2j-1} = \{(c_i, c'_i)\}$, $E_{2n+2j} = \{(c'_j, a), (c_j, b), (c_j, c)\}$

- During $T_3 = [2n+2m+1, 2n+2m+n]$ we have for all $i \in [1, n-1]$:

$$E_{2n+2m+i} = \{(v_i, v_{i+1}), (\bar{v}_i, v_{i+1}), (v_i, \bar{v}_{i+1}), (\bar{v}_i, \bar{v}_{i+1})\}$$

and

$$E_{2n+2m+n} = \{(v_i, s), (\bar{v}_i, s)\}$$

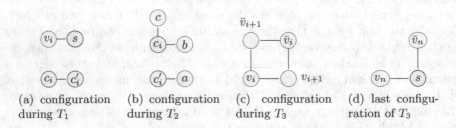

(a) configuration during T_1 (b) configuration during T_2 (c) configuration during T_3 (d) last configuration of T_3

Fig. 4. Node Configurations (clauses are blue and literals are red)

During T_3, either a variable or its negation can send its data to the sink node s, but not both, so that the set of literals that send data can be seen as an interpretation of a truth-functional propositional calculus.

During T_1, variables that does not send their data during T_3 can send their data directly to the sink node.

During T_2, there is a link between a clause c_i and its copy c'_i so that either c_i or c'_i can send both data. Since all clauses can send their data only once to all the literals it contains, the data is successfully sent to the sink node if and only if at least one literals it contains sends its data in T_3 *i.e.*, is *true*.

Thus, if the interpretation chosen in T_3 satisfies the formula φ, then each clause contains a literal that sends during T_3, and the minimum data aggregation time is exactly t_f. Otherwise, some clauses must send their data before $t = 1$, and the minimum data aggregation time is greater than t_f.

So that the 3-SAT instance φ is satisfiable if and only if the minimum data aggregation time ending before t_f is t_f.   □

4   Upper and Lower Bounds

In this section, we introduce the notion of foremost journey trees. Then we propose the first upper and lower bounds for the dynamic MDAT problem, given in terms of foremost journey tree duration.

A journey from a node u to node a v is a sequence of edges $((e_1, t_1), (e_2, t_2), \ldots, (e_r, t_r))$ such that $(e_1, e_2, \ldots, e_r)$ is a path from u to v in the static graph $(V, \cup_{i \in \mathbb{N}} E_i)$ and

$$\forall i \in [1..r-1], \; t_i < t_{i+1} \qquad \forall i \in [1..r], \; e_i \in E_{t_i}$$

For a journey J, we denote by $departure(J)$ the starting time t_1 and by $arrival(J)$ the arrival time $t_r + 1$ of the journey. The arrival time corresponds to the time of the existence of the last edge plus the latency to travel along the last edge. Then, $duration(J) = arrival(J) - departure(J)$ denotes the duration of the journey. We denote by $\mathcal{J}_{(u,v)}$ the set of journeys from u to v and by $\mathcal{J}_{(u,v)}^{[t_s,t_e]}$ the subset of journeys that start and end between t_s and t_e. We denote by $\mathcal{J}_{(u,v)}^{t_s \rightarrow}$ the set of *foremost* journeys starting after time t_s:

$$\mathcal{J}_{(u,v)}^{t_s \rightarrow} = \mathcal{J}_{(u,v)}^{[t_s, t_{\min}]} \quad \text{with} \quad t_{\min} = \min_t \left\{ t \mid \mathcal{J}_{(u,v)}^{[t_s,t]} \neq \emptyset \right\}$$

As a shortest path in a static WSN, a foremost journey is used in a dynamic WSN to transmit data from a node to another with a minimum delay. To define foremost journey trees, which is the equivalent of a shortest path tree in a dynamic WSN, we first need to define a journey tree.

Definition 2. *Let $G(V, E)$ be a dynamic graph. A journey tree to node s is a couple (T, c) where $T(V, T_{edges})$ is a tree rooted at s and c is a function $c : T_{edges} \mapsto \mathbb{N}$ that verifies:*

i) if $e \in T_{edges}$, then $e \in E_{c(e)}$.

ii) if u is the parent of v and v the parent of w in T, then $c(w, v) < c(v, u)$ i.e., if $(e_1, e_2, \ldots, e_r)$ is a path from a node u to the node s in T, then

$$((e_1, c(e_1)), (e_2, c(e_2)) \ldots, (e_r, c(e_r)))$$

is a journey in G called the journey from u to s induced by T.

The departure, *respectively the* arrival *of the journey tree is the departure of the first journey in T, respectively the arrival of the last journey in T:*

$$departure(T, c) = \min_{e \in T_{edges}} c(e) \qquad and \qquad arrival(T, c) = \max_{e \in T_{edges}} c(e) + 1$$

Definition 3. *Let $G(V, E)$ be a dynamic graph. A foremost journey tree (abbreviated as FJT) to node s starting at time t_s is journey tree (T, c) to s such that for each leaf node u in T, the journey from u to s induced by T is a foremost journey starting after time t_s. Its duration is $duration(T, c) = arrival(T, c) - t_s$.*

$FJT(G, s, t_s)$ denotes the set of foremost journey trees of G to node s starting after time t_s. The common duration of foremost journey trees starting after t_s is denoted $FJTD(G, s, t_s)$.

In dynamic WSNs, a foremost journey tree plays the same role as a shortest path tree in static WSNs. Indeed it gives the same lower bound as in the static version of the problem. Figure 5 shows an example of the unique foremost journey tree to the sink node s starting at time 0 of a simple dynamic graph (for the sake of simplicity, the position of the nodes do not change with time).

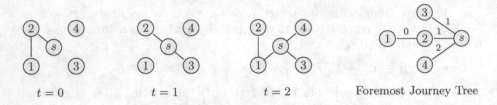

$t = 0$ $t = 1$ $t = 2$ Foremost Journey Tree

Fig. 5. An example of foremost journey tree

Lemma 3. *Let G be a dynamic graph, we have:*

$$MDAT_{Opt}(G, s) \geq FJTD(G, s, 0)$$

In a static WSN, the same shortest path tree can be used to avoid collisions. But in a dynamic WSN, a FJT T_1 that exits at a given time may not exists thereafter. If we delay the transmission of a node, to avoid a collision, another FJT T_2 will be used to retry a transmission. In order to be sure that T_2 can be used by all delayed nodes, it has to start after the end of T_1. In this case we say that (T_1, T_2) is a 2-time-independent FJT.

Definition 4. *A l-time-independent FJT of G to s starting at time t_s is a sequence of l foremost journey trees of G to s $((T_1, c_1), \ldots, (T_l, c_l))$ such that:*

- (T_1, c_1) *is a FJT starting at t_s.*
- *for all $1 < i \leq l$, (T_i, c_i) is a FJT starting at $arrival(T_{i-1}, c_{i-1})$.*

Its duration is the sum duration of all FJT in the sequence and also equals to $tarrival(T_1, c_1) - t_s$. The set of l-time-independent FJT of G to s starting at t_s is denoted $FJT^l(G, s, t_s)$. The common duration of all l-time-independent LTJs in $FJT^l(G, s, t_s)$ is denoted $LTJD^l(G, s, t_s)$.

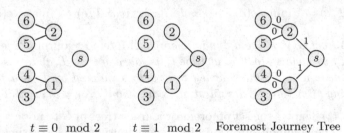

$t \equiv 0 \mod 2$ $t \equiv 1 \mod 2$ Foremost Journey Tree

Fig. 6. Creation of a perfect binary FJT

Theorem 3. *Let G be a dynamic graph with n nodes. We have:*

$$FJTD^{n-1}(G, s, 0) \geq MDAT_{Opt}(G, s) \geq FJTD(G, s, 0)$$

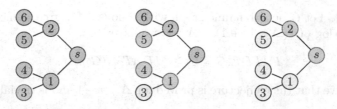

Fig. 7. Optimal data aggregation schedule when FJTs are complete binary trees

The lower bound and the upper bound are tight in the sense that there exists a graph that reaches the lower bound (any graph of degree at most one) and a graph that reaches the upper bound (for instance a graph whose sink node is of degree $n - 1$ at each time).

If we consider only graphs with a given maximum node degree Δ, the lower bound is still tight, but the upper bound is no longer tight. The following lemma gives a graph with a minimum data aggregation time that lowers the upper bound, for an arbitrary maximum node degree Δ. We conjecture that it also gives the worst data aggregation duration *i.e.*, that it also give an upper bound that remains tight for an arbitrary maximum node degree.

Lemma 4. *Let* $n \in \mathbb{N}^*$ *and* $\Delta \leq n$, *there exist a dynamic graph G with n nodes of degree at most Δ such that:*

$$FJTD^m(G, s, 0) = MDAT_{Opt}(G, s) < +\infty$$

with $m = (\Delta - 1)\log_\Delta(n(\Delta - 1) + 1) - \Delta + 2$

Proof. Let $\Delta \geq 2$. We consider the dynamic graph $G(V, E)$. For the sake of simplicity, we suppose that there exists $h \in \mathbb{N}$ such that $|V| = n = \frac{\Delta^{h+1}-1}{\Delta-1}$. One can construct G such that, there is a perfect $\Delta-$ary tree T (of height h) such that, for all $t \equiv 0 \mod h$, $FJT(G, s, t) = \{(T, c_t)\}$ and (T, c_t) is of duration h (and thus with collision appearing between every nodes having the same parent). See for instance figure 6 with $\Delta = 2$ and $h = 3$.

After time $d_1 = departure(T, c_0)$, we can only aggregate data along an unique path, from a leaf of T to s. Since all the path have the same length, we can choose an arbitrary path without loss of generality. This path contains one direct child of s. We need $\Delta - 1$ time-independent FJTs ending before d_1 to aggregate data from the other direct children. Let s' be the first direct child of s that transmits, and $T(s')$ the sub-tree of T rooted at s'. $T(s')$ is a perfect $\Delta-$ary tree of height $h - 1$. When s' transmits, its data have to contain the data of its direct children. Again, we need another $\Delta - 1$ time-independent FJTs to aggregate data from all direct children of s'.

Recursively, we need at least $(\Delta-1)h+1$ time-independent FJT to aggregate all the data from G. One can show that this is also sufficient (see figure 7). Since $h = log_\Delta(n(\Delta - 1) + 1) - 1$, the theorem is proved. □

Conjecture 1. Let G be a dynamic graph with n nodes of degree at most Δ. Let $m = (\Delta - 1) \log_\Delta (n (\Delta - 1) + 1) - \Delta + 2$, we have:

$$FJTD^m(G, s, 0) \geq MDAT_{Opt}(G, s)$$

We observe that the conjecture is proved for $\Delta = n-1$ and is trivial if $\Delta = 1$.

5 Impossibility Results

In this section we present several classes of dynamic graphs wherein only a centralized algorithm that knows the future can compute optimal and "good" approximate solutions. These impossibility results justify that our first approximation algorithm given in the next section is centralized and knows the future of the graph.

A hierarchy of classes of dynamic graphs has been identify in previous work [6]. Here we present only the few we are interested in.

– $\mathcal{RC}$ *(Recurrent connectivity)*: $\forall u, v \in V$, $\forall t \in \mathbb{N}$:

$$\mathcal{J}_{(u,v)}^{[t,+\infty)} \neq \emptyset$$

– $\mathcal{BRC}$ *(Time-bounded recurrent connectivity)*: There exists a bound T such that, $\forall u, v \in V$, $\forall t \in \mathbb{N}$:

$$\mathcal{J}_{(u,v)}^{[t,t+T]} \neq \emptyset$$

– $\mathcal{P}$ *(Periodic)*: the graph is connected and there exists $T \in \mathbb{N}$ such that:

$$(\exists t, \ (u, v) \in E_t) \Rightarrow (\forall k \in \mathbb{N}, \ (u, v) \in E_{t+kT})$$

Observation 1. *In* $\mathcal{P}$, *the dynamic MDAT problem does not have a distributed optimal algorithm, even if each node knows its own future.*

Moreover, one can show that every approximate solution can take as much time as the duration of $n - 1$ foremost journey trees.

Observation 2. *In* $\mathcal{P}$, *the dynamic MDAT problem does not have a centralized optimal algorithm, without the knowledge of future.*

One can remark that a sufficient assumption for the problem to be solvable by a centralized algorithm that does not know the future is to suppose the periodic graph is either *complete*, or if T is known.

6 Approximation Algorithm

In this section we give a simple and intuitive approximation algorithm. The maximum duration of a solution given by this algorithm reach the theoretical upper bound given in section 4. This solution is found in a backward manner as follow. The currentTime is set to a time t_f *i.e.*, the time when we try to finish the data aggregation. The set remainingNodes contains the nodes that have to transmit before the current time. Then, while remainingNodes is not empty, we decrement the current time and we remove from remainingNodes a node that can transmit without collision. If the current time reaches zero and there remain nodes the algorithm try again with a greater t_f.

One can define the procedure $canTransmit(n, S, t)$ that returns true if and only if the node n can transmit its data to a node in S_{t+1} at time t without interfering with other nodes in $S_t \setminus S_{t+1}$.

Algorithm GDAS. Greedy Data Aggregation Schedule

Input: MDAT Instance (G, s)

for $t_f = 1, 2 \ldots$ **do**

    $S_{t_f} \leftarrow \{s\}$,   currentTime $\leftarrow t_f$,   remainingNodes $\leftarrow G - \{s\}$

    while remainingNodes $\neq \emptyset$ **do**

        currentTime $\leftarrow$ currentTime -1

        $S_{\text{currentTime}} \leftarrow S_{\text{currentTime}} + 1$

        forall the node $\in$ remainingNodes **do**

            if $canTransmit$(node, S, currentTime) **then**

                remainingNodes $\leftarrow$ remainingNodes $-\{$node$\}$

                $S_{\text{currentTime}} \leftarrow S_{\text{currentTime}} \cup \{$node$\}$

    if remainingNodes $= \emptyset$ **then**

        return S;

Theorem 4. *If a graph G is in $\mathcal{RC}$, algorithm GDAS finds a valid dynamic data aggregation schedule such that*

$$duration(GDAS(G, s)) \leq LTJD^{n-1}(G, s, 0)$$

If the graph is T-time-bounded recurrent connected, then a FJT duration is smaller than T. Thus, we can derive the following approximation factor for the foremost data aggregation problem.

Corollary 1. *Algorithm GDAS is an approximation of factor $T(n-1)$, for the dynamic MDAT problem, in $\mathcal{BRC}$ with bound T.*

7   Conclusion

We studied the complexity of minimum data aggregation time problem in wireless sensor networks. We proved that the problem is NP-complete in a static WSN of degree at most three, and NP-complete in a dynamic WSN of degree at most two. The degree constraint is crucial, as a smaller one induces a trivial solution in both cases. Then we gave tight lower and upper bounds for the minimum data aggregation time problem in dynamic networks and the first approximation scheme for the problem. Also, in a dynamic graph with n nodes of degree at most

Δ, we conjecture a more accurate upper bound of l time-independent foremost journey trees (with $l = (\Delta - 1) \log_\Delta (n (\Delta - 1) + 1) - \Delta + 2)$.

Finally we observed that only a centralized algorithm that has full knowledge can compute the optimal solution of the problem. Thus, we gave a simple approximate algorithm giving a solution whose time match the theoretical upper bound.

References

1. Abshoff, S., Meyer auf der Heide, F.: Continuous aggregation in dynamic ad-hoc networks. In: Halldórsson, M.M. (ed.) SIROCCO 2014. LNCS, vol. 8576, pp. 194–209. Springer, Heidelberg (2014)
2. Annamalai, V., Gupta, S.K.S., Schwiebert, L.: On tree-based convergecasting in wireless sensor networks. In: 2003 IEEE Wireless Communications and Networking, 2003. WCNC 2003 , vol. 3, pp. 1942–1947. IEEE (2003)
3. Casteigts, A., Chaumette, S., Ferreira, A.: Characterizing topological assumptions of distributed algorithms in dynamic networks. In: Kutten, S., Žerovnik, J. (eds.) SIROCCO 2009. LNCS, vol. 5869, pp. 126–140. Springer, Heidelberg (2010)
4. Casteigts, A., Flocchini, P., Mans, B., Santoro, N.: Building fastest broadcast trees in periodically-varying graphs (2012). arXiv preprint arXiv:1204.3058
5. Casteigts, A., Flocchini, P., Mans, B., Santoro, N.: Shortest, fastest, and foremost broadcast in dynamic networks (2012). arXiv preprint arXiv:1210.3277
6. Casteigts, A., Flocchini, P., Quattrociocchi, W., Santoro, N.: Time-varying graphs and dynamic networks. In: Frey, H., Li, X., Ruehrup, S. (eds.) ADHOC-NOW 2011. LNCS, vol. 6811, pp. 346–359. Springer, Heidelberg (2011)
7. Chen, X., Hu, X., Zhu, J.: Minimum data aggregation time problem in wireless sensor networks. In: Jia, X., Wu, J., He, Y. (eds.) MSN 2005. LNCS, vol. 3794, pp. 133–142. Springer, Heidelberg (2005)
8. Clark, B.N., Colbourn, C.J., Johnson, D.S.: Unit disk graphs. Discrete Mathematics 86(13), 165–177 (1990)
9. Cornejo, A., Gilbert, S., Newport, C.: Aggregation in dynamic networks. In: Proceedings of the 2012 ACM Symposium on Principles of Distributed Computing, pp. 195–204. ACM (2012)
10. Fasolo, E., Rossi, M., Widmer, J., Zorzi, M.: In-network aggregation techniques for wireless sensor networks: a survey. IEEE, Wireless Communications 14(2), 70–87 (2007)
11. Kuhn, F., Oshman, R.: Dynamic networks: Models and algorithms. SIGACT News 42(1), 82–96 (2011)
12. Lichtenstein, D.: Planar formulae and their uses. SIAM Journal on Computing 11(2), 329–343 (1982)
13. Nguyen, T.D., Zalyubovskiy, V., Choo, H.: Efficient time latency of data aggregation based on neighboring dominators in wsns. In: 2011 IEEE Global Telecommunications Conference (GLOBECOM 2011), pp. 1–6. IEEE (2011)
14. Ren, M., Guo, L., Li, J.: A new scheduling algorithm for reducing data aggregation latency in wireless sensor networks. International Journal of Communications, Network & System Sciences 3(8) (2010)
15. XiaoHua, X., Li, M., Mao, X.F., Tang, S., Wang, S.G.: A delay-efficient algorithm for data aggregation in multihop wireless sensor networks. IEEE Transactions on Parallel and Distributed Systems 22(1), 163–175 (2011)
16. Yu, B., Li, J., Li, Y.: Distributed data aggregation scheduling in wireless sensor networks. In: IEEE INFOCOM 2009, pp. 2159–2167. IEEE (2009)

Enabling Minimal Dominating Set in Highly Dynamic Distributed Systems

Swan Dubois[✉], Mohamed-Hamza Kaaouachi, and Franck Petit

Sorbonne Universités, UPMC Univ Paris 06, CNRS, INRIA, LIP6 UMR 7606,
Paris Cedex 5, France
swan.dubois@lip6.fr

Abstract. We address the problem of computing a Minimal Dominating Set in highly dynamic distributed systems. We assume weak connectivity, *i.e.,* the network may be disconnected at each time instant and topological changes are unpredictable. We make only weak assumptions on the communication: every process is infinitely often able to communicate with other processes (not necessarily directly).

Our contribution is threefold. First, we propose a new definition of minimal dominating set suitable for the context of time-varying graphs that seems more relevant than existing ones. Next, we provide a necessary and sufficient topological condition for the existence of a deterministic algorithm for minimal dominating set construction in our settings. Finally, we propose a new measure of time complexity in time-varying graph in order to allow fair comparison between algorithms. Indeed, this measure takes account of communication delays attributable to dynamicity of the graph and not to the algorithms.

1 Introduction

In modern networks, items (users, links, equipments, *etc.*) may join, leave, or move inside the network at unforeseeable times. A common feature of these networks is their *high dynamic*, meaning that their topology keeps continuously changing over time. Classically, distributed systems are modeled by a static undirected connected graph where vertices are processes (nodes, servers, processors, etc.) and edges represent bidirectional communication links. Clearly, such modeling is not suitable for high dynamic networks. Numerous models taking into account topological changes over time have been proposed since several decades, *e.g.,* [1–4]. Some works aim at unifying most of the above approaches. For instance, in [5], the authors introduced the *evolving graphs*. They proposed modeling the time as a sequence of discrete time instants and the system dynamic by a sequence of static graphs, one for each time instant. More recently, another graph formalism, called *Time-Varying Graphs* (TVG), has been provided in [6].

This work was performed within the Labex SMART, supported by French state funds managed by the ANR within the "Investissements d'Avenir" programme under reference ANR-11-LABX-65.

© Springer International Publishing Switzerland 2015
A. Pelc and A.A. Schwarzmann (Eds.): SSS 2015, LNCS 9212, pp. 51–66, 2015.
DOI: 10.1007/978-3-319-21741-3_4

In contrast with evolving graphs, TVGs allow systems evolving within continuous time. Also in [6], TVGs are gathered and ordered into classes depending mainly on two main features: the quality of connectivity among the participating nodes and the possibility/impossibility to perform tasks.

In this paper, we focus on the *Minimal Dominating Set* (MDS) problem. A dominating set is a subset of vertices of a graph such as each vertex of this graph is either in the dominating set or neighbor of a vertex in the dominating set. A *minimal* dominating set is such that none of its proper subsets is also a dominating set of the graph. Like many distributed covering structure (such as trees, coloring, matching, *etc.*), Minimal Dominating Set is a key building block for numerous network protocols, *e.g.,* hierarchical routing and clustering, multicast, topology control, media access coordination, to name only a few.

Minimal Dominating Set and some of related problems (such as Maximal Independent Set and Connected Dominating Set) receive some attention in the context of dynamic networks, *e.g.,* [7–9]. The difficulty to define covering structures in dynamic networks (including MDS) is pointed out in [10]. Indeed, the authors show that the definition of such structures may become ambiguous, incorrect, or even irrelevant when applied in dynamic systems. As an example, if the dynamicity of the graph is modeled as a sequence of static graphs and a new MDS is computed at each topological change as in [7], the stability of the MDS fully depends on the dynamic rate of the network (*i.e.,* the relative speed of appearance/disappearance of edges). This natural definition may hence lead to a high instability (or even impossibility of use) of the MDS. We discuss more precisely this issue in Section 4.

This paper aims at proposing a new approach suitable for Minimal Dominating Set construction in time-varying graph with weak connectivity, *i.e.,* the graph may be disconnected at each time instant and topological changes are unpredictable. The only assumption on communications is that every process is infinitely often able to communicate with other processes (not necessarily directly). In this context, our contribution is threefold. First, we propose a new definition of MDS for time-varying graphs that increases stability of this structure. More precisely, we require each dominated node to be infinitely often neighbor of at least one dominating node. Next, we provide a necessary and sufficient topological condition for the existence of a deterministic algorithm for MDS construction in our settings. Finally, we propose a new measure of time complexity in time-varying graphs. This measure takes account of communication delays attributable to the dynamicity of the graph and not to the algorithm in order to allow fair comparison between algorithms.

The paper is organized as follows. Section 2 presents formally the time-varying graph model and our new measure of time complexity. We devote the Section 3 to some preliminaries necessary to our main results on MDS presented in Section 4. Finally, Section 5 concludes the paper.

2 Time-Varying Graph: Model and Complexity

2.1 Model

Let us first borrow the formalism introduced in [6] in order to describe the distributed systems prone to high dynamic. We consider *distributed systems* made of n *processes*. A process has a local memory, a local sequential and deterministic algorithm, and message exchange capabilities. We assume that each proccess has a unique identifier. Moreover, given two distinct processes p and q identified respectively by id_p and id_q, either $id_p < id_q$ or $id_q < id_p$. All these processes are gathered in a set V. Let E be a set of edges (or relations) between pairwise processes, that describes interactions between processes, namely communication exchange. The presence of an edge between two processes p and q at a given time t means that each process among $\{p, q\}$ is able to send a message to the other at t. For any given (static) graph g, we denote by $diam(g)$ the diameter of g (that is, the longest distance between two processes of g).

The interactions between processes are assumed to take place over a time span $T \subseteq \mathbb{T}$ called the *lifetime* of the system. The temporal domain $\mathbb{T}$ is generally assumed to be either $\mathbb{N}$ (discrete-time systems) or $\mathbb{R}^+$ (continuous-time systems).

Definition 1 (Time-varying graph [6]). *A time-varying graph (TVG for short) g is a tuple $(V, E, T, \rho, \zeta, \phi)$ where V is a (static) set of processes $\{v_1, \ldots, v_n\}$, E a (static) set of edges between these processes $E \subseteq V \times V$, $\rho : E \times T \rightarrow \{0, 1\}$ (called presence function) that indicates whether a given edge is available (i.e. present) at a given time, $\zeta : E \times T \rightarrow \mathbb{T}$ (called edge latency function) indicates the time it takes to cross a given edge if starting at a given date, and $\phi : V \times T \rightarrow \mathbb{T}$ (called process latency function) indicates the time an internal action of a process takes at a given date.*

Given a TVG g, let T_g be the subset of T for which a topological event (appearance/disappearance of an edge) occurs in g. The evolution of g during its lifetime T can be described as the sequence of graphs $S_g = g_1, g_2, \ldots$, where $g_i = (V, E_i)$ corresponds to the static *snapshot* of g at time $t_i \in T_g$, i.e. $e \in E_i$ if and only if $\forall t \in [t_i, t_{i+1}[, \rho(e, t) = 1$. Note that $g_i \neq g_{i+1}$ for any i.

We consider *asynchronous* distributed systems, *i.e.* no pair of processes has access to any kind of shared device that could allow to synchronize their execution rate. Furthermore, at any time, no process has access to the output of ζ, *i.e.* none of them can (*a priori*) predict a bound on the message delay. Note that the ability to send a message to another process at a given time does not mean that this message will be delivered. Indeed, the dynamicity of the communication graph implies that the edge between the two processes may disappear before the delivery of this message leading to the lost of messages in transit.

The presences and absences of an edge are instantly detected by its two adjacent processes. We assume that our system provides to each process a non-blocking communication primitive named **Send_retry** that ensures the following property. When a process p invokes **Send_retry**(m, q) (where m is an arbitrary message and q another process of V) at time t, this primitive delivers m to

q in a finite time provided that there exists a time $t' \geq t$ such that the edge $\{p,q\}$ is present at time t' during at least $\zeta(\{p,q\},t')$ units of time. In other words, the delivery of the message is ensured if there is, after the invocation of the primitive, an availability of the edge that is sufficient to overcome the communication delay of the edge at this time. Note that this primitive may never deliver a message (*e.g.* if the considered edge never appears after invocation). Details of the implementation of this primitive are not considered here but it typically consists in resending m at each apparition of the edge $\{p,q\}$ until its reception by q. This primitive allows us to abstract from topology changes and asynchronous communication and to write high-level algorithms.

Configurations and Executions. The *state* of a process is defined by the values of its variables. Given a TVG g, a *configuration* of g is a vector of $n+2$ components $(g_i, M_i, p_1, p_2, \ldots, p_n)$ such that g_i is a static snapshot of g (*i.e.* $g_i \in S_g$), M_i is the set of messages carried by each edge of E_i (one multi-set of messages per edge), and p_1 to p_n represent the state of the n processes in V. We say that a process p outputs a value v in a configuration γ if one of its variable (called an output variable) has the value v in γ. An *execution* of the distributed system modeled by g is a sequence of configurations $e = \gamma_0, \ldots, \gamma_k$, $\gamma_{k+1}, \ldots$, such that for each $k \geq 0$, during an execution step (γ_k, γ_{k+1}), one of the following event occurs: (i) $g_k \neq g_{k+1}$, or (ii) at least one process receives a message, sends a message, or executes some internal actions changing its state. The *algorithm* executed by g describes the set of all allowed internal actions of processes (in function of their current state or external events as message receptions or time-out expirations) during an execution of g. We assume that during any configuration step (γ_k, γ_{k+1}) of an execution, if $g_k \neq g_{k+1}$, then for each edge e such that $e \in E_k$ and $e \notin E_{k+1}$ (*i.e.* e disappears during the step (γ_k, γ_{k+1})), none of the messages carried by e belongs to M_{k+1}. Also, for each edge e such that $e \in E_{k+1}$ and $e \notin E_k$ (*i.e.* e appears during the step (γ_k, γ_{k+1})), e contains no message in configuration γ_{k+1}.

Connected over Time TVGs. A key concept of time-varying graphs has been identified in [6]. The authors shows that the classical notion of path in static graphs in meaningless in TVGs. Indeed, some processes may communicate even if there is no (static) path between them at each time. To perform communication between two processes, the existence of a *temporal path* (*a.k.a. journey*) between them is sufficient. They define such a temporal path of a TVG g as a sequence of ordered pairs $\{(p_1,t_1), (p_2,t_2), \ldots, (p_{k-1},t_{k-1}), (p_k,t_k)\}$ such that $p_1, p_2, \ldots, p_{k-1}, p_k$ is a (static) path of (V, E) and, for every $i \in \{1, \ldots, k-1\}$, $\rho(\{p_i, p_{i+1}\}, t_i) = 1$ and $t_{i+1} \geq t_i + \zeta(\{p_i, p_{i+1}\}, t_i) + \phi(p_{t+1}, t_i + \zeta(\{p_i, p_{i+1}\}, t_i))$. In other words, a temporal path from process p to process q is a sequence of adjacent edges from p to q such that availability and latency of edges and processes allow the sending of a message from p to q using the **Send_retry** primitive at each intermediate process (refer to [6] for a formal definition). Note that the existence of a temporal path is a non symmetric relation between two processes, even though the graph may be undirected. Based on various assumptions made about journeys (*e.g.* recurrence, periodicity, symmetry, and so on), [6] proposes a relevant hierarchy of TVG classes. In this paper, we choose to make minimal assumptions on the dynamicity of our system since we restrict ourselves on *connected-over-time* TVGs defined as follows:

Definition 2 (Connected-over-time TVG [6]). *A TVG $(V, E, \mathcal{T}, \rho, \varsigma, \phi)$ is connected-over-time if, for any time $t \in \mathcal{T}$ and for any pair of processes p and q of V, there exists a journey from p to q after time t. The class of connected-over-time TVGs is denoted by $\mathcal{COT}^1$.*

Note that the lifetime of a connected-over-time TVG is necessarily infinite by definition. The class $\mathcal{COT}$ allows us to capture highly dynamic systems since we only require that any process will be always able to communicate with any other one without any extra assumption on this communication (such as delay, periodicity, or used route). In particular, note that a connected-over-time TVG may be disconnected at each time and that the presence of an edge at a given time does not preclude that this edge will appear again after this time. Define an *eventual missing edge* as en edge that appears only a finite number of time during the lifetime of the TVG. The main difficulty encountered in the design of distributed algorithms in $\mathcal{COT}$ is to deal with such eventual missing edges because no process is able to predict if a given adjacent edge is an eventual missing edge or not. Note that the time of the last presence of such an eventual missing edge cannot even be bounded.

Definition 3 ((Eventual) Underlying Graph). *Given a TVG $g = (V, E, \mathcal{T}, \rho, \varsigma, \phi)$, the underlying graph of a g is the (static) graph $U_g = (V, E)$. The eventual underlying graph of g is the (static) subgraph $U_g^\omega = (V, E_g^\omega)$ with $E_g^\omega = E \setminus M_g$, where M_g is the set of eventual missing edges of g.*

Intuitively, the underlying graph (sometimes referred to as *footprint*) of a TVG g gathers all edges that appear at least once during the lifetime of g, whereas the eventual underlying graph of g gathers all edges that are infinitely often present during the lifetime of g. Note that, for any TVG of $\mathcal{COT}$, both underlying graph and eventual underlying graph are connected by definition. Let us define the *neighborhood* $\mathcal{N}_p$ of a process p is the set of processes with which p shares an edge in the underlying graph.

Induced Subclasses. In the following, we focus on specific subclasses of the class $\mathcal{COT}$ to establish our impossibility result. Informally, we focus on subclasses that gather all TVGs whose underlying graph belongs to a given set. The intuition behind this restriction is the following. In practice, some technical reasons may restrict or prevent the communication between some processes, that induces a given underlying graph for the TVG that models our system. In contrast, we cannot predict in general the availabilities of communication edges, that leads us to consider all TVGs sharing this underlying graph.

Definition 4 (Induced subclass). *Given a set of (static) graphs $\mathcal{F}$ and a class of TVGs C, the subclass of C induced by $\mathcal{F}$ (denoted by $C|_\mathcal{F}$) is the set of all TVGs of C whose underlying graph belongs to $\mathcal{F}$.*

---

[1] Authors of [6] refer to this class as C5 in their hierarchy of TVG classes.

2.2   Complexity Measures

To our knowledge, there exists no time complexity measure that is suitable for any class of TVGs. Some previous works deal with complexity measure in the TVG model but restrict themselves to synchronous systems (see *e.g.* [11,12]), to message complexity (see *e.g.* [13]), or to specific class of TVGs in which an existing notion of complexity naturally makes sense (*e.g.* [13,14]).

The first contribution of this paper is to propose a definition of a time complexity measure suitable for our model. To ease the reading of the formal definition (Definition 5), we first informally describe our approach. Let us first provide a definition that captures the "quality" of an algorithm independent of delays introduced by asynchronous communications but also by topological changes. A typical example of such a delay is the waiting after the next apparition of an incident edge to a disconnected process that may introduce a long delay that is not imputable to the algorithm but only to the dynamicity of the system. To perform our goal, we propose to extend the classical notion of time complexity commonly adopted in asynchronous message passing (static) systems.

The classical way to deal with communication delays in time complexity measure in asynchronous message passing models is to consider as the unit of time of an execution the worst delay between the sending and the reception of a message during this execution (see [15] for example). Using this time measure, we can bound the termination time of any execution of an algorithm independently of communication delays in this execution. This leads to a time complexity measure (the worst termination time over all possible executions of the algorithm) that induces a fair comparison between algorithms. Our proposal is to extend this idea to dynamic environments by including delays introduced by the dynamicity in this definition. In other words, we will consider as the unit of time of an execution the worst delay between the invocation of the **Send_retry** primitive and the delivery of the message by this primitive during this execution.

This natural extension of the definition of time complexity measure of asynchronous message passing systems is not sufficient. Indeed, the dynamicity of the system may introduce another possibly arbitrarily long delay that we call initial delay. As an example, consider a problem that requires each process to propagate an initial value (think about consensus-like problems). An easy way to delay the termination of any algorithm for this problem is to disconnect one process for an arbitrary long (but bounded) time that leads all other processes to wait after its first apparition. Such delay is not due to the algorithm but to the dynamicity of the system and our complexity measure have to ignore such initial delay. To deal with this issue, we propose to define for each problem a starting time as follows. Informally, it is the smallest time of an execution where the dynamicity of the system "shows" to processes the minimal topological information to solve the problem. Note that this starting time depends only of the problem (*e.g.* first connexion of the last process for consensus-like problems) and that, in a static system, the starting time and the initial time are identical (since the system cannot delay apparition of any topological information).

Then, we propose to measure the complexity of an algorithm by the worst time (expressed in the time unit described above) between the starting time and the termination of the algorithm over all its possible executions. We believe that this time complexity measure allows us to fairly compare algorithms designed in our model based on TVGs since it exhibits their intrinsic communication costs and does not take into account delays introducing by asynchronous communications and topological changes.

We now formally state the complexity measure. In the following, we first restrict to *fixed point computation problems* on a TVG class $\mathcal{C}$, *i.e.* problems that admit a specification of the following form: it is required that the execution $e = \gamma_0, \gamma_1, \ldots$ on every TVG of $\mathcal{C}$ reaches in a finite time a suffix $e_i = \gamma_i, \gamma_{i+1}, \ldots$ where each process outputs constantly a given value. The required value depends on the considered problem and is not necessarily the same at each process. Using this definition, leader election or spanning structure construction are fixed point computation problems whereas mutual exclusion or broadcast are not.

We consider now a (deterministic) distributed algorithm $\mathcal{A}$ that satisfies the specification of a fixed point computation problem $\mathcal{P}$ on a TVG class $\mathcal{C}$. Let e be the execution of $\mathcal{A}$ on a given TVG of class $\mathcal{C}$. For any message m sent during e, we call *delay* (of m) the time between the invocation of the **Send_retry** primitive by the sender of m and the delivery of m to its destination. Now, we call *communication step* (or simply step) of e the worst delay over the set of messages that are actually delivered during e (note that we do not consider messages that are never delivered in e).

We associate to $\mathcal{P}$ a function $NPS_{\mathcal{P}}$, called the *necessary presence sets function* of $\mathcal{P}$, that returns, for any TVG $(V, E, \mathcal{T}, \rho, \zeta, \phi)$ of $\mathcal{C}$, a set of subsets of E. Note that the actual definition of this function depends on the problem itself and not of a TVG nor an execution. Each element of $NPS_{\mathcal{P}}(g)$ describes one of the set of edges whose apparition is necessary and sufficient to start the effective solving the problem (independently of the used algorithm). We give some examples in the following. For the underlying graph computation problem $\mathcal{UG}$, we have $NPS_{\mathcal{UG}}(g) = \{E\}$ since each edge of E must appear in the output of any process. For a broadcast problem $\mathcal{B}$, we have $NPS_{\mathcal{B}}(g) = \{\{(p,q)\}|q \in \mathcal{N}_p\}$ (where process p is the initiator) since the apparition of any edge adjacent to p (that is, the first connexion of p to the system) is necessary and sufficient to begin the broadcast of a message by p.

We define the *starting time* of the execution e of $\mathcal{A}$ over a TVG g as the smallest time $t \in \mathcal{T}$ such that each edges of at least one element of $NPS_{\mathcal{P}}(g)$ are present at least once before t in this execution. Note that, in a static distributed system, the initial time and the starting time are always identical since all edges of all elements of $NPS_{\mathcal{P}}(g)$ are present in the initial configuration whatever the definition of $NPS_{\mathcal{P}}$ is. Finally, the *convergence time* of $\mathcal{A}$ on g is the time (expressed in communication steps of e) between the starting time of e and the smallest time in e where the specification of $\mathcal{P}$ is satisfied.

Definition 5 (Time complexity on a TVG class). *The time complexity of a distributed algorithm $\mathcal{A}$ that satisfies the specification of a fixed point* *computation problem* $\mathcal{P}$ *on a TVG class* $\mathcal{C}$ *is the worst convergence time of* $\mathcal{A}$ *on all TVGs of* $\mathcal{C}$.

Note that this definition may be naturally extended to so-called *service problems* in the following way. First, we consider as starting time the maximum between the starting time defined above and the time of request of a service (*e.g.* the sending of a message for a broadcast algorithm, the request of critical section for a mutual exclusion algorithm). Second, we substitute the convergence time of the algorithm by the time of achievement of the required service by the algorithm (*e.g.* the delivery of a message to its destinations for a broadcast algorithm, the starting of critical section for a mutual exclusion algorithm).

3 Underlying Graph Computation

In this section, we present an underlying graph computation algorithm (see Section 3.1) and proves its time optimality with respect to our new measure (see Section 3.2). This algorithm is used as a building block in the next section for our minimal dominating set construction algorithm. Before presenting our algorithm, we need to specify the underlying graph computation problem.

Specification 1 (Underlying graph). *An algorithm* $\mathcal{A}$ *satisfies the underlying graph specification for a class of TVGs* $\mathcal{C}$ *if the execution* $e = \gamma_0, \gamma_1, \ldots$ *of* $\mathcal{A}$ *on every TVG* g *of* $\mathcal{C}$ *has a suffix* $e_i = \gamma_i, \gamma_{i+1}, \ldots$ *for a given* $i \in \mathbb{N}$ *such that each process outputs the underlying graph of* g *in any configuration of* e_i.

3.1 Algorithm

Our underlying graph computation algorithm is presented in Algorithm 1. The intuition behind this algorithm is simple. Each process stores locally a graph, initially empty, that eventually gathers all edges of the underlying graph. At the first appearance of an edge, the two adjacent processes add this edge to their graph. Then, they try to propagate the last version of their graph to all processes that they have as neighbor at least once since the beginning of the execution. When a process receives such a message (that contains the current underlying graph of another process), it add to its own underlying graph every edge it does not already know. If its underlying graph grows during this operation, then the process propagates again its underlying graph to all processes that it has as neighbor at least once since the beginning of the execution.

This algorithm ensures that, upon the first apparition of the last edge of the underlying graph, this edge is added to the output of adjacent processes and then propagated (at least) to their neighbors in the eventual underlying graph in one step, and so on (note that we have no guarantees for neighbors in the underlying graph in general since some eventual missing edges may exist). Hence, in any execution, after at most $diam(U_g^\omega)$ steps, this edge (and all others) appears in the output graph of any process. In other words, we have the following result:

Theorem 1. *Algorithm 1 satisfies the underlying graph specification for* $\mathcal{COT}$. *Moreover, its convergence time on any TVG* g *of* $\mathcal{COT}$ *is* $diam(U_g^\omega)$ *steps.*

Algorithm 1. Underlying graph computation for process p

Variables:	**foreach** $r \in \mathcal{N}_p$ **do**
$\quad g_p = (V_p, E_p)$ initially $(\{p\}, \emptyset)$	$\quad\quad$ **Send_retry**$(add(g_p), r)$
$\quad \mathcal{N}_p$ initially $\emptyset$	**On reception of** $add(g_q)$ **from** q:
Upon appearance of an edge $\{p, q\}$:	$\quad$ **if** $E_q \setminus E_p \neq \emptyset$ **then**
$\quad$ **if** $\{p, q\} \notin E_p$ **then**	$\quad\quad g_p := (V_p \cup V_q, E_p \cup E_q)$
$\quad\quad \mathcal{N}_p := \mathcal{N}_p \cup \{q\}$	$\quad\quad$ **foreach** $r \in \mathcal{N}_p \setminus \{q\}$ **do**
$\quad\quad g_p := (V_p \cup \{q\}, E_p \cup \{\{p, q\}\})$	$\quad\quad\quad$ **Send_retry**$(add(g_p), r)$

3.2   Time Optimality

In this section, we interest in a lower bound result on the time complexity of underlying graph computation. We restrict ourselves to greedy algorithms that are the most natural ones for this problem. We define a *greedy algorithm* for the underlying graph computation as an algorithm that satisfies the following property. The initial output of any process is an empty graph and the graph outputted by a process can only grow (in the sense of inclusion) over time. In other words, such an algorithm ensures that, once a process start to output a given edge or process, this latter always appears in the output of this process afterwards. Note that Algorithm 1 falls in this category.

In the following, we prove that no greedy algorithm for underlying graph computation on $\mathcal{COT}$ can exhibit a better time complexity than our algorithm. Indeed, we prove that there exists, for any greedy algorithm, a TVG g in $\mathcal{COT}$ such that this algorithm needs $diam(U_g^\omega)$ steps to compute the underlying graph of g. Note that the complexity of the underlying graph computation depends surprisingly of a parameter of the *eventual* underlying graph. Before proving this result, we need a technical lemma for the proof of this optimality result.

Lemma 1. *For any greedy algorithm $\mathcal{A}$ that satisfies the underlying computation graph, for any TVG $g = (V, E, \mathcal{T}, \rho, \zeta, \phi)$ in $\mathcal{COT}$, for any edge $e \in E$ that is not a cut-edge of U_g^ω, for any process $p \in V$, for any $t \in \mathcal{T}$, e cannot belong to the graph outputted by p in the execution of $\mathcal{A}$ on g at time t if there exists no temporal path from one extremity of e to p that starts after the first appearance of e in g and ends before t.*

Theorem 2. *For any greedy algorithm $\mathcal{A}$ that satisfies the underlying graph specification on $\mathcal{COT}$, there exists a TVG g of $\mathcal{COT}$ such that the convergence time of $\mathcal{A}$ is at least $diam(U_g^\omega)$ steps.*

Proof. Let $\mathcal{A}$ be a greedy algorithm that satisfies the underlying graph specification on $\mathcal{COT}$. let us define the family of TVGs $(g_k)_{k \in \mathbb{N}^*}$ described by Figure 1. Note that, for any $k \in \mathbb{N}^*$, we have $diam(U_{g_k}^\omega) = 2k$ (and $diam(U_{g_k}) < diam(U_{g_k}^\omega)$ since $diam(U_{g_k}) = k + 1$). As this graph is connected, g_k belongs to $\mathcal{COT}$. By construction of g_k, the starting time of the execution of $\mathcal{A}$ on g_k is 1 for any $k \in \mathbb{N}^*$ (recall that $NPS_{\mathcal{UG}}(g) = \{E\}$). Note that, due to the choice of the latency function, any communication step of the execution of $\mathcal{A}$ on g_k takes exactly one time unit.

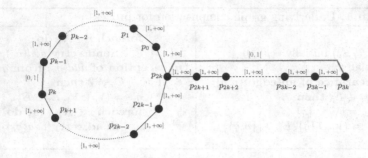

Fig. 1. An illustration of the TVGs family in the proof of Theorem 2

Consider e_k the execution of $\mathcal{A}$ on g_k for any $k \in \mathbb{N}^*$. From Lemma 1, we know that the edge $\{p_{k-1}, p_k\}$ cannot appear in the graph outputted by p_{3k} in e_k before there exists at least one temporal path from p_{k-1} or p_k to p_{3k}. Note that the construction of g_k implies that such a temporal path (after time 1) needs at least $2k$ steps (the length of the path from p_{k-1} or p_k to p_{3k} since g_k is static after time 1). As the edge $\{p_{k-1}, p_k\}$ must eventually appear in the output of any process in e_k by assumption on $\mathcal{A}$, we obtain that the convergence time of $\mathcal{A}$ is at least $diam(U_{g_k}^\omega)$ steps, that ends the proof.   □

4   Minimal Dominating Set Construction

Minimal dominating set construction is a classical problem in distributed computing since this spanning structure have interesting properties for a lot of practical problems as clustering. Recall that, in a static distributed system, a dominating set D is a subset of processes of the system such that each process that does not belong to D have at least one neighbor in D. Such a dominating set is minimal when it has is no strict subset that is also a dominating set.

Regarding dynamic distributed systems, two different approaches have been proposed to handle minimal dominating set problem. We survey them quickly here and show that these definitions seem not relevant in our context, that motivates the need of our new definition presented in this section.

The most natural way to extend minimal dominating set definition in the context of dynamic systems is presented in [7]. In this work, the dynamic graph is seen as a sequence of static graphs and a new minimal dominating set is computed at each topological change. This approach is not suitable in the case of highly dynamic systems since the system may be always in computation phase (the computation of the new dominating set at each topological change is not instantaneous). In this case, the dominating set may be never stable and is then useless for the application that required it.

The second approach, proposed by [10], consists in computing a stable dominating set on the underlying graph of the TVG. This approach is interesting since the outputted dominating set is stable in spite of the dynamicity of the system but is still not suitable for our purpose. Indeed, as the dominating set is computed on the underlying graph that may contain eventual missing edges, it is possible for a process to be dominated only through such edges. In other words, a dominated process may have eventually only dominated neighbors, that is counter-intuitive for a minimal dominating set and makes sense only in TVGs where there is no eventual missing edges.

To overcome flaws of precedent definitions in our context of highly dynamic distributed systems (captured by the class of TVGs $\mathcal{COT}$), we propose a third definition in which we require the outputted minimal dominating set to be stable and each dominated process to be infinitely often neighbor of at least one dominating process. In other words, we want to compute a minimal dominating set on the *eventual* underlying graph. Note that this definition is exactly the same as the one of [10] in TVGs where there is no eventual missing edges. We specify the minimal dominating set construction problem over TVGs as follows.

Definition 6 (Minimal dominating set over time). *A set of processes M is a minimal dominating set over time (MDST for short) of a TVG g if M is a minimal dominating set of U_g^{ω}.*

Specification 2 (Minimal dominating set). *An algorithm $\mathcal{A}$ satisfies the minimal dominating set specification for a class of TVGs $\mathcal{C}$ if the execution $e = \gamma_0, \gamma_1, \dots$ of $\mathcal{A}$ on every TVG g of $\mathcal{C}$ has a suffix $e_i = \gamma_i, \gamma_{i+1}, \dots$ for a given $i \in \mathbb{N}$ such that each process outputs constantly a boolean value in any configuration of e_i and that the set of processes outputting true is a minimal dominating set over time of g.*

4.1 Preliminaries

In this section, we present some preliminary results that are needed in the following. First, we introduce the definition of a strong minimal dominating set of a graph as a dominated set of any connected spanning subgraph of this graph. In Section 4.2, we prove that the existence of such a set in the underlying graph of a TVG is necessary to the existence of an algorithm to construct a minimal dominating set over time of this TVG. We claim in Section 4.3 that this condition is also sufficient. To prove this result, we use the following characterization of graphs that admit a strong minimal dominating set.

Definition 7 (Strong minimal dominating set). *A strong minimal dominating set (SMDS for short) of a (static) graph g is a subset of processes of g that is a minimal dominating set of every connected spanning subgraph of g.*

The following lemma follows directly from definitions and legitimates our interest for strong minimal dominating sets.

Lemma 2. *If the underlying graph of a TVG $g \in \mathcal{COT}$ admits a strong minimal dominating set M then M is a minimal dominating set over time of g.*

The next result provides us a characterization of (static) graphs that admits a SMDS. We use this characterization in our minimal dominating set construction algorithm. The quite simple proof of this lemma is delegated to the appendix.

Lemma 3. *For any (static) graph g and any minimal dominating set M of g, M is a strong minimal dominating set of g if and only if the set of edges $\{\{p,q\}|q \in M \cap \mathcal{N}_p\}$ is a cut-set in g for every process $p \in V \setminus M$.*

4.2 Impossibility Result

The proof of our impossibility result presented in Theorem 4 makes use of a generic framework we proposed in another work. We recall here the minimal definitions and results to understand our proof. Due to the lack of space, the interested reader is referred to [16] for more details.

Summary of [16]. For a given time domain $\mathbb{T}$, a given static graph (V,E) and a given latency function ζ, let us consider the set $\mathcal{G}_{(V,E),\mathbb{T},\zeta}$ of all TVGs over $\mathbb{T}$ that admit (V,E) as underlying graph and ζ as latency function. For the sake of clarity, we will omit the subscript $(V,E),\mathbb{T},\zeta$ and simply denote this set by $\mathcal{G}$. Remark that two distinct TVGs of $\mathcal{G}$ can be distinguished only by their presence function. For any TVG g in $\mathcal{G}$, let us denote its presence function by ρ_g. We define now the following metric $d_{\mathcal{G}}$ over $\mathcal{G}$. If $g = g'$, then $d_{\mathcal{G}}(g,g') = 0$. Otherwise, $d_{\mathcal{G}}(g,g') = 2^{-\lambda}$ with $\lambda = \mathrm{Sup}\ \{t \in \mathbb{T}|\forall t' \leq t, \forall e \in E, \rho_g(e,t') = \rho_{g'}(e,t')\}$.

For a given algorithm $\mathcal{A}$ and a given TVG g, let us define the $(\mathcal{A},g)$-output as the function that associate to any time $t \in \mathbb{T}$ the state of g at time t when it executes $\mathcal{A}$. We say that g is the supporting TVG of this output. Let us consider the set $\mathcal{O}_{\mathcal{A},\mathcal{G}}$ of all $(\mathcal{A},g)$-outputs over all TVGs g of $\mathcal{G}$. For the sake of clarity, we will omit the subscript $\mathcal{A},\mathcal{G}$ and simply denote this set by $\mathcal{O}$. Remark that two distinct output of $\mathcal{O}$ can be distinguished only by their supporting TVG. For any output o in $\mathcal{O}$, let us denote its supporting TVG by g_o. We define now the following metric $d_{\mathcal{O}}$ over $\mathcal{O}$. If $o = o'$, then $d_{\mathcal{O}}(o,o') = 0$. Otherwise, $d_{\mathcal{O}}(o,o') = 2^{-\lambda}$ with $\lambda = \mathrm{Sup}\ \{t \in \mathbb{T}|\forall t' \leq t, o(t') = o'(t')\}$.

Once we have observed that the metric spaces $(\mathcal{G},d_{\mathcal{G}})$ and $(\mathcal{O},d_{\mathcal{O}})$ are complete, we are now able to recall the main result of [16]. Intuitively, this theorem ensures that, if we take a sequence of TVGs with ever-growing common prefixes, then the sequence of corresponding outputs also converges. Moreover, we are able to describe the output to which it converges as the output that corresponds to the TVG that shares all commons prefixes of our TVGs sequence. This result is useful since it allows us to construct counter-example in the context of impossibility results. Indeed, it is sufficient to construct a TVG sequence (with ever-growing common prefixes) and to prove that their corresponding outputs violates the specification of the problem for ever-growing time to exhibit an execution that violates infinitely often the specification of the problem.

Theorem 3. *For any deterministic algorithm $\mathcal{A}$, if a sequence $(g_n)_{n \in \mathbb{N}}$ of $\mathcal{G}$ converges to a given $g_\omega \in \mathcal{G}$, then the sequence $(o_n)_{n \in \mathbb{N}}$ of the $(\mathcal{A},g_n)$-outputs converges to $o_\omega \in \mathcal{O}$. Moreover, o_ω is the $(\mathcal{A},g_\omega)$-output.*

Application to Minimal Dominating Set. We are now in measure to prove our impossibility result. This result states that there exists no deterministic algorithm that satisfies the minimal dominating set specification on a TVG of

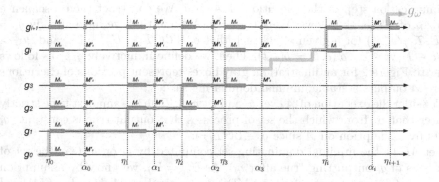

Fig. 2. An illustration of the sequence $(g_n)_{n \in \mathbb{N}}$ used in the proof of Theorem 4

$\mathcal{COT}$ as soon as the underlying graph of the considered TVG does not admit a strong minimal dominating set. Intuitively, this impossibility comes from the following fact. As no process is able to detect eventual missing edges, the minimal dominated set computed by any algorithm must be a minimal dominated set of any possible eventual underlying graph, that is of any connected subgraph of the underlying graph. In other words, the computed minimal dominated set is a strong minimal dominating set. The existence of such a set is then a necessary condition to the existence of an algorithm to compute a minimal dominating set over time. The main difficulty of the formal proof of this result lies in the construction of the TVGs sequence that allows us to apply Theorem 3.

Theorem 4. *For any set of (static) graphs $\mathcal{F}$ containing at least one graph that does not admit a strong minimal dominating set, there exists no deterministic algorithm that satisfies the minimal dominating set specification for $\mathcal{COT}|_{\mathcal{F}}$.*

Proof. Let us introduce some notation first. We define, for any TVG $g = (V, E, \mathcal{T}, \rho, \varsigma, \phi)$, the TVG $g \odot \{(E_i, \mathcal{T}_i) | i \in I\}$ (with $I \subseteq \mathbb{N}$ and for any $i \in I$, $E_i \subseteq E$ and $\mathcal{T}_i \subseteq \mathcal{T}$) as the TVG $(V, E, \mathcal{T}, \rho', \varsigma, \phi)$ with:

$$\rho'(e, t) = \begin{cases} 0 \text{ if } \exists i \in I, e \in E_i \text{ and } t \in \mathcal{T}_i \\ 1 \text{ if } \exists i \in I, e \in E \setminus E_i \text{ and } t \in \mathcal{T}_i \\ \rho(e, t) \text{ otherwise} \end{cases}$$

By contradiction, assume that there exists a set of (static) graphs $\mathcal{F}$ containing at least one graph that does not admit a strong minimal dominating set and that there exists a deterministic algorithm $\mathcal{A}$ that satisfies the minimal dominating set specification for $\mathcal{COT}|_{\mathcal{F}}$. In consequence, any process that executes $\mathcal{A}$ outputs a boolean value at any time.

Let $g = (V, E, \mathcal{T}, \rho, \varsigma, \phi)$ be a TVG of $\mathcal{COT}|_{\mathcal{F}}$ such that U_g does not admit a strong minimal dominating set and that all edges of U_g are present during the first communication step of the execution of $\mathcal{A}$ on g (g exists by construction of $\mathcal{F}$ and by definition of $\mathcal{COT}|_{\mathcal{F}}$). Let t_0 be the time of completion of the first communication step of the execution of $\mathcal{A}$ on g. We construct then a sequence $(g_n)_{n \in \mathbb{N}}$ of TVGs as follows. We set $g_0 = g$. Assume that we have already $g_i = (V, E, \mathcal{T}, \rho', \zeta, \phi)$ for a given $i \in \mathbb{N}$ such that $g_i \in \mathcal{COT}|_{\mathcal{F}}$, $U_{g_i} = U_g$, and $\exists \alpha_i > t_0, \forall e \in E, \forall t \leq \alpha_i, \rho'(e, t) = \rho(e, t)$. Then, we define inductively g_{i+1} as follows (refer to Figure 2 for an illustration, gray boxes represent portions of executions where $\mathcal{A}$ outputs a stable minimal dominating set):

1. Consider the execution of $\mathcal{A}$ over g_i and let $\eta_i \in \mathcal{T}$ be the smallest time strictly greater than α_i from which the set of processes that output true is constant (η_i exists by assumption on $\mathcal{A}$ since $g_i \in \mathcal{COT}|_{\mathcal{F}}$);

2. Let M_i be the minimal dominating set computed by $\mathcal{A}$ on g_i (i.e. the set of processes of g_i outputting true after η_i). As $U_{g_i} = U_g$, we know by assumption on U_g that U_{g_i} does not admit a SMDS. In particular, M_i is not a SMDS of U_{g_i}. Hence, there exists a process p_i of $V \setminus M_i$ such that the set of edges $E_i = \{\{p_i, q\} | q \in M_i \cap \mathcal{N}_{p_i}\}$ is not a cut-set of U_{g_i};

3. Let $g_i' = g_i \odot \{(E_i, \mathcal{T} \cap]\eta_i, +\infty[)\}$.

4. Remark that $U_{g_i'} = U_{g_i} = U_g$ (by construction of g_i' since $\eta_i > t_0$) and that $U_{g_i'}^\omega$ is connected (since $E(U_{g_i'}^\omega) = E(U_g) \setminus E_i$ by construction[2] and E_i is not a cut-set of U_g). Hence, $g_i' \in \mathcal{COT}|_{\mathcal{F}}$ and we can consider the execution of $\mathcal{A}$ over g_i'. Let $\alpha_i \in \mathcal{T}$ be the smallest time strictly greater than η_i from which the set of processes that output true is constant. Let M_i' be the minimal dominating set computed by $\mathcal{A}$ on g_i' (i.e. the set of processes of g_i' outputting true after α_i). Note that $M_i' \neq M_i$ since M_i is not a minimal dominating set of $U_{g_i'}^\omega$ (recall that, in $U_{g_i'}^\omega$, p_i has no neighbor in M_i);

5. Let $g_{i+1} = g_i \odot \{(E_i, \mathcal{T} \cap]\eta_i, \alpha_i])\}$.

It is straightforward to check that this construction ensures that, if there exists $g_i = (V, E, \mathcal{T}, \rho', \zeta, \phi)$ for a given $i \in \mathbb{N}$ such that $g_i \in \mathcal{COT}|_{\mathcal{F}}$, $U_{g_i} = U_g$, and $\exists \alpha_i > t_0, \forall e \in E, \forall t \leq \alpha_i, \rho'(e, t) = \rho(e, t)$, then g_{i+1} satisfies the same property. Moreover, as $g_0 = g$, this property is naturally satisfied for $i = 0$ with any $\alpha_0 > t_0$. Hence, the sequence $(g_n)_{n \in \mathbb{N}}$ is well-defined. Note that, for any $i \in \mathbb{N}$, $\eta_i < \alpha_i$ and $\alpha_i < \eta_{i+1}$ (by construction).

That allows us to define the following TVG: $g_\omega = g \odot \{(E_i, \mathcal{T} \cap]\eta_i, \alpha_i]) | i \in \mathbb{N}\}$. Note that $U_{g_\omega} = U_g$ and then that g_ω belongs to $\mathcal{COT}|_{\mathcal{F}}$. Observe that, for any $k \in \mathbb{N}^*$, we have $d_{\mathcal{G}}(g_k, g_\omega) = 2^{-\eta_k}$ by construction of $(g_n)_{n \in \mathbb{N}}$ and g_ω. Thus, $(g_n)_{n \in \mathbb{N}}$ converges in $\mathcal{COT}|_{\mathcal{F}}$ to g_ω.

We are now in measure to apply the Theorem 3 that states that the $(\mathcal{A}, g_\omega)$-output is the limit of the sequence of the $(\mathcal{A}, g_n)$-outputs. In other words, the $(\mathcal{A}, g_\omega)$-output shares a prefix of length η_i with the $(\mathcal{A}, g_i)$-output for any $i \in \mathbb{N}$ (recall that the sequence of the $(\mathcal{A}, g_n)$-outputs is Cauchy since it converges). That means that, for any $i \in \mathbb{N}^*$, the set of processes that output true in g_ω at η_i is M_i and the set of processes that output true in g_ω at α_i is M_i'. As we know that $M_i \neq M_i'$ for any $i \in \mathbb{N}$, we obtain that the set of processes that output true in g_ω never converges, that contradicts the fact that $\mathcal{A}$ satisfies the minimal dominating set specification for $\mathcal{COT}|_{\mathcal{F}}$ and ends the proof. □

---

[2] where $E(g)$ denotes the set of edges of g.

4.3 Algorithm

We are now able to prove the sufficiency of the existence of a strong minimal dominating set on the underlying graph for the construction of a minimal dominating set over time of any TVG of COT. This result is proved by presenting an algorithm based on our underlying graph computation algorithm presented in Section 3. This algorithm works as follows. Once a process has computed the underlying graph, it is easy to decide if this process belongs to the outputted minimal dominating set: the process enumerates (locally and in a deterministic order based *e.g.* on process identities) all minimal dominating sets of the underlying graph (it is sufficient to enumerate all subsets of processes and to keep only minimal dominating sets) and chooses the first one that satisfies Lemma 3. This latter is then a strong minimal dominating set of the underlying graph and hence a minimal dominating set over time of the TVG by Lemma 2. In order to avoid the use of an algorithm of termination detection (for the underlying graph computation), each process repeats the local computation of its output at each update of its local copy of the underlying graph by the algorithm of Section 3.

Theorem 5. *For any set of (static) graphs $\mathcal{F}$ containing only graphs that admit a strong minimal dominating set, there exists a deterministic algorithm that satisfies the minimal dominating set specification for $COT|_{\mathcal{F}}$.*

5 Conclusion

This paper addressed the construction of a minimal dominating set over time (MDST) in highly dynamic distributed systems. We considered the weakest connectivity assumption in the hierarchy of time-varying graphs: the graph may be disconnected at each time, topological changes are unpredictable but we know that any process is able to communicate with any other infinitely often using so-called temporal paths. We proposed a new definition of minimal dominating set increasing the stability of the computed MDST. Next, we provided a necessary and sufficient topological condition for the existence of a deterministic MDST algorithm. We then proposed a new measure of time complexity that takes into account the communication delays due to network dynamic.

The above results used the construction of an underlying graph. We showed the time optimality of our algorithm with respect to our measure. Note that our result (Theorem 2) is valid for greedy algorithms only. We conjecture that all distributed underlying graph algorithms are greedy. This would lead to generalize our result of optimality. Also, we would like to extend our approach to other related overlay constructions.

References

1. Anagnostopoulos, A., Kumar, R., Mahdian, M., Upfal, E., Vandin, F.: Algorithms on evolving graphs. In: ITCS, pp. 149–160 (2012)
2. Awerbuch, B., Even, S.: Efficient and reliable broadcast is achievable in an eventually connected network. In: PODC, pp. 278–281 (1984)

3. Ferreira, A.: Building a reference combinatorial model for manets. Network **18**(5), 24–29 (2004)
4. Schneider, J., Wattenhofer, R.: Coloring unstructured wireless multi-hop networks. In: PODC, pp. 210–219 (2009)
5. Xuan, B., Ferreira, A., Jarry, A.: Computing shortest, fastest, and foremost journeys in dynamic networks. IJFCS **14**(02), 267–285 (2003)
6. Casteigts, A., Flocchini, P., Quattrociocchi, W., Santoro, N.: Time-varying graphs and dynamic networks. IJPEDS **27**(5), 387–408 (2012)
7. Whitbeck, J., Dias de Amorim, M., Conan, V., Guillaume, J.L.: Temporal reachability graphs. In: MobiCom, pp. 377–388 (2012)
8. Schneider, J., Wattenhofer, R.: An optimal maximal independent set algorithm for bounded-independence graphs. Distributed Computing **22**(5–6), 349–361 (2010)
9. Casteigts, A., Mans, B., Mathieson, L.: On the feasibility of maintenance algorithms in dynamic graphs. Technical report, arXiv - abs/1107.2722 (2011)
10. Casteigts, A., Flocchini, P.: Deterministic algorithms in dynamic networks: Problems, analysis, and algorithmic tools. Technical report, DRDC 2013-020 (2013)
11. Kuhn, F., Moses, Y., Oshman, R.: Coordinated consensus in dynamic networks. In: PODC, pp. 1–10 (2011)
12. Kuhn, F., Lynch, N.A., Oshman, R.: Distributed computation in dynamic networks. In: STOC, pp. 513–522 (2010)
13. Casteigts, A., Flocchini, P., Mans, B., Santoro, N.: Deterministic computations in time-varying graphs: Broadcasting under unstructured mobility. In: ICTCS, pp. 111–124 (2010)
14. Ilcinkas, D., Klasing, R., Wade, A.M.: Exploration of constantly connected dynamic graphs based on cactuses. In: Halldórsson, M.M. (ed.) SIROCCO 2014. LNCS, vol. 8576, pp. 250–262. Springer, Heidelberg (2014)
15. Attiya, H., Welch, J.: Distributed Computing: Fundamentals, Simulations and Advanced Topics, 2nd edn. John Wiley Interscience (2004)
16. Braud-Santoni, N., Dubois, S., Kaaouachi, M.H., Petit, F.: A generic framework for impossibility results in time-varying graphs. In: APDCM (to appear, 2015)

The Match-Maker: Constant-Space Distributed Majority via Random Walks

Leszek Gąsieniec[1], David D. Hamilton[1(✉)],
Russell Martin[1], and Paul G. Spirakis[1,2]

[1] Department of Computer Science, University of Liverpool, Liverpool, UK
{l.a.gasieniec,d.d.hamilton,russell.martin,p.spirakis}@liverpool.ac.uk
[2] Computer Technology Institute and Press "Diophantus", Rion, Patras, Greece

Abstract. We propose and analyze here a simple protocol for consensus on the majority color in networks whose nodes are initially one of two colors. Our protocol guarantees that, if a majority exists, then eventually each node learns of the majority color. Our protocol requires only 2 bits of memory per node and uses a simple token message, of also 2 bits size, that performs random walks. We show correctness of our protocol for any connected graph (even unknown to the nodes) and even for a natural class of dynamic graphs. We show upper and lower bounds on the convergence time of our protocol. We discuss termination and we also provide a variant of our protocol which the token uses a counter that can count only up to $\sqrt{n} \log n$, where n is the number of network nodes. Our basic (memoryless) protocol takes only $\mathcal{O}(n \log n)$ expected time on the clique which surprisingly does not deviate from the cover time of the random walk, and $\mathcal{O}(n^2 m)$ time on any connected undirected network of m edges and this bound is met from below by an argument on the line. Finally, we also consider random walks that can count the difference of colors and we show upper bounds on the counter value by using coupling arguments.

1 Introduction

1.1 The Problem, Model and Motivation

Consider an undirected and connected graph $G = (V, E)$ of $|V| = n$ vertices (nodes) and $|E| = m$ edges. Initially, each node is colored either blue (BLUE) or red (RED). In the sequel we use $\overline{X}$ for $X = BLUE$ (resp. RED) to denote RED (resp. $BLUE$), i.e. if X is a color then $\overline{X}$ is its "complement". No node can store more than a fixed number of bits, in fact, not more than 2 bits. The main problem is to devise a correct and efficient distributed procedure executed by the network nodes which can communicate with neighbors via constant-size messages. Eventually, all nodes must agree on the initial majority color (if such a majority exists). We call this the *Majority Color Problem (MCP)*. The purpose of this paper is to propose and analyze a specific algorithmic procedure which solves the Majority Color Problem, with only $\mathcal{O}(1)$ bits per node and $\mathcal{O}(1)$ bits per message.

This work is partially supported by the Liverpool EEE/CS School NeST Initiative.

A. Pelc and A.A. Schwarzmann (Eds.): SSS 2015, LNCS 9212, pp. 67–80, 2015.
DOI: 10.1007/978-3-319-21741-3_5

We assume that the network is synchronous. We consider here networks that are unknown to the nodes, where each node knows only the links (edges) to its neighbors. We also consider dynamic networks in which neighbors may change from round to round. Because of the above, we allow any node to select a random link incident to it and send a message via that link. In other words, we allow nodes to initiate and maintain a random walk in the unknown graph.

Random walks have been extensively studied in distributed computing in the context of problems like exploration and information dissemination. In this paper we show that random walks are suitable, in particular they are very efficient in time and space, to solve the MCP. The random walk acts here like the match-maker person (in olden times) in several countries, going from village to village and trying to match boys (blue) with girls (red). Upon encountering a boy, the match-maker gets his "color" and places him in a "matched" condition and then proceeds to find a corresponding girl via the random walk in the network. Hence, we call our proposed protocol The Match-Making Algorithm.

Correct majority protocols with messages only a few bits in size, that only perform random walks, are very useful from a security point of view since:

(a) The origin of a random walk cannot be traced back.
(b) An eavesdropper that intercepts a token (of a few bits), doing a random walk, cannot infer anything about the vote of a particular person (neither about the result of the voting).

As we shall see, our proposed solution satisfies (a) and (b), and can be used in unknown (and even dynamic) networks, without the need of votes moving around or stored in any central place.

One of the important measures of performance of a random walk is the cover time:

Definition 1. *(Cover Time) Consider a random walk on an undirected, connected graph, starting at vertex v. Let t_v be the minimum time for the walk to visit all of G's vertices at least once. Let $\mathbb{E}(t_v)$ be the expected value of t_v. The maximum (over all vertices v) of $\mathbb{E}(t_v)$ is called the (expected) Cover Time of the graph.*

In this work we also consider dynamic networks i.e. graphs where the neighbors of every node change in an adversarial way in each round of the global clock. We however assume that our dynamic networks change due to a benign adversary that satisfies two properties:

Definition 2. *(Benign adversaries) An adversary that changes the graph structure per round is* benign *if and only if*

1. *The adversary is oblivious to any random choices made by our protocol.*
2. *For any two nodes u,v and any time t_0, the edge $\{u, v\}$ shall (re)appear in time (round) $t_0 + t_1$ with t_1 bounded above by some finite bound β (which may depend on the number of nodes, n in the graph).*
3. *The adversary maintains the nodes of the graph (no node deletions or insertions).*

We call β the tolerance time *of the dynamic graph.*

1.2 Our Results

We provide here a simple distributed algorithm called BASIC that uses only (1) 2 bits of memory per node, (2) a single token of 2 bits long, and (3) always converts the color of all nodes in the graph to the initial majority color, if such a color exists. Our algorithm, in its basic form, does not terminate but converts all colors to the majority color in finite time, even in unknown or dynamic graphs. One can equip the system with a global clock readable by all nodes allowing termination of our process with high probability (w.h.p)[1] if the value of n is known by the vertices. We provide a lower bound of the convergence time of BASIC, for any given initial placement of node colors. If there is no majority, the problem has no solution and there will remain an arbitrary division between two colors in the network.

We show that BASIC converts all nodes to the majority color in expected $\mathcal{O}(n \log n)$ time for the clique graph and in at worst $\mathcal{O}(n^2 m)$ time for any connected graph. Our bound for the clique matches the cover time of the random walk. Our bound for arbitrary graphs is tight on the line. Finally, we consider random walks that can count the difference in the number of colors visited, and show non-trivial upper bounds on the counter value in order for such procedures to work correctly.

1.3 Previous Work

Our proposed method is inspired by the work in [10] where a similar protocol was used in the context of population protocols. Here we convert the ideas of [10] into a message passing protocol that employs random walks and we prove its correctness for unknown static networks and for a certain natural class of dynamic networks. For the clique and for general graphs we show expected convergence time of $\mathcal{O}(n \log n)$ and $\mathcal{O}(n^2 m)$ respectively, while the corresponding times in [10] were $\mathcal{O}\left(\frac{n^2 \log n}{|majority| - |minority|}\right)$ and $\mathcal{O}(n^6)$.

Avin et al [4] have proved that random walks can cover all the vertices of dynamic graphs (in finite, possibly exponential, time) when the dynamic graphs either evolve in a Markovian way or they are always connected. Our model of dynamic graphs is not covered by those models because our dynamic graph can evolve in an adversarial way and may also not be connected at any (or all) rounds during the execution of the BASIC algorithm. Because of the finite expected cover time of the model of Avin et al, it can be easily shown that our protocol is also correct for those dynamic graphs.

Other works on distributed majority include [3, 6, 11] which show how to reduce multivalued consensus to binary consensus. However, such protocols assume either a stronger network with broadcast [11] or randomization [6].

The notion of using a *charge* was first proposed by Birk et al [5] to solve a similar problem, in which they combine an efficient spanning forest algorithm with a

---

[1] "With high probability" means with probability at least $1 - \frac{c}{n}$ for some constant c, where n is the number of nodes in the graph.

"charge fusion" algorithm. The paper proposes a stronger model to solve a more general problem, which has more requirements and enables direct access to neighbors. Also, their solution relies on larger memory and additional computation.

In contrast, our method requires only a single token of 2 bits able to perform a random walk in the network, and is always correct in the sense that if an initial color majority exists, then eventually all nodes agree on the majority color. Our method performs no artihmetic calculations and instead represents a finite state machine. The topology of the graph is unknown to the vertices and vertices are anonymous. For basic notations on probability, martingales and random walks, see [2, 8, 12].

2   Our Proposed Method: The Match-Making Algorithm

Our proposed method presumes the existence of a single token message, initially in some arbitrary node. The token is only keeping one of three values {RED, BLUE, UNCOLORED}. Each node maintains a pair of states {color, importance}. The color of a node is always RED or BLUE. The importance of a node is either HIGH or LOW. Initially all nodes have HIGH importance and the token is UNCOLORED.

Here is the description of the BASIC protocol, i.e., The Match-Making Algorithm to solve the MCP.

Protocol BASIC
Initially the token t is placed at an arbitrary vertex. Each vertex v executes the following protocol, in each round on receipt of t. Note that in the following cases, $X \in \{RED, BLUE\}$.
case 1: If $value(t) = UNCOLORED$ and $importance(v) = LOW$, then
    (a) v forwards t to a random neighbor (including, possibly, itself).
case 2: If $value(t) = UNCOLORED$ and $importance(v) = HIGH$, then
    (a) $value(t) \leftarrow color(v)$
    (b) $importance(v) \leftarrow LOW$
    (c) v forwards t to a random neighbor (including, possibly, itself).
case 3: If $value(t) = X$ and $importance(v) = LOW$, then
    (a) $color(v) \leftarrow X$
    (b) t is forwarded to a random neighbor (including, possibly, v).
case 4: If $value(t) = X$ and $color(v) = X$ and $importance(v) = HIGH$, then
    (a) v forwards t to a random neighbor (including, possibly, itself).
case 5: If $value(t) = X$ and $color(v) = \overline{X}$ and $importance(v) = HIGH$, then
    (a) $value(t) \leftarrow UNCOLORED$
    (b) $importance(v) \leftarrow LOW$
    (c) v forwards t to a random neighbor (including, possibly, itself).
"end of BASIC"

Note that the random walks defined here for the token are "extended" in the sense that the token may choose to stay at the same node (of degree d_t at round t)

with probability $\frac{1}{d_t+1}$. Also note that, in each round only one node executes the protocol because there is a single token in the network.

Theorem 3. *(Correctness) In any static undirected, connected, finite graph $G = (V, E)$, protocol BASIC eventually turns the color of every node to the initial majority color, even if the graph and its size are unknown to the nodes.*

Proof. The token matches each node of color X and high importance (i.e. as all nodes are initially) to a node of color $\overline{X}$ of high importance, and both X, $\overline{X}$ turn to low importance. Thus, the initial (high importance) nodes are paired in red-blue pairs. If a majority color X initially exists, then eventually the token will find it (by visiting all nodes), and then it will walk in the graph converting all nodes (of low importance) to the color X. For every color matching that needs to be made, the token's random walk needs time at most equal to the cover time of G. Finally it needs only the cover time of G in order to convert the color of all nodes to the first majority color having no match. So, the token needs, at worst, n cover times to convert all colors to the initial majority color (if there was an initial majority). We also know that the expected cover time of any finite G is finite with probability 1. By linearity of expectation, and since the walks are one after the other, the total time to convergence to the initial majority is finite with probability 1. $\square$

Corollary 4. *The BASIC protocol needs an expected number of rounds at most equal to $(n+1) \cdot \mathbb{E}(CoverTime(G))$ until convergence. For any connected graph, BASIC converges in expected time $\mathcal{O}(n^2 m)$.*

Proof. BASIC needs at most $\frac{n}{2}$ cover times to match appropriate colors of high significance and at most $\frac{n}{2}$ cover times to find a new color of high significance every time. Then it needs a final cover time to convert all node colors to the majority color. Finally, we use the fact that $\mathbb{E}(CoverTime(G)) \in \mathcal{O}(nm)$ for any connected graph G [1]. $\square$

3 The BASIC Protocol in Dynamic Graphs

We consider now the execution of the BASIC protocol in dynamic graphs with benign adversaries with tolerance β.

Lemma 5. *For any two nodes u,v, for any time t_1, with the token being at node u at time t_1, the probability that the token will visit node v at time at most $t_1 + \beta$ is at least $\left(\frac{1}{n}\right)^\beta$.*

Proof. Suppose the token is at node u at round t_1. Consider that the edge uv appears again in round $t_1 + \beta'$, where $\beta' \leq \beta$. The event $A_{u,v}$ = "the token stays at u for $\beta' - 1$ times and then chooses edge $\{u, v\}$ which then exists" has probability

$$\varphi = \prod_{i=1}^{\beta'} (\frac{1}{d_i+1})$$

where d_i is the degree of node u at round $t_1 + i$. But then $\varphi \geq (\frac{1}{n})^\beta$, since $(\beta' \leq \beta)$ and $n - 1 \geq d_i \geq 0 \ \forall i$ (so $n \geq d_i + 1 \geq 1$).   □

Lemma 5 allows us to conclude that BASIC works correctly on dynamic graphs.

Corollary 6. *The BASIC protocol converts all node colors to the initial majority color (if any) in any dynamic graph, with a benign adversary, in finite time with probability 1.*

Proof. The events A_{uv} are each a geometric stochastic process of a bounded variance. They are also independent of each other. Thus the (total) variance of the cover time of each walk is bounded.   □

Then we also have the following result:

Theorem 7. *The BASIC protocol converts all node colors to the initial majority color (if any) in expected time at most $n^{\beta+2}$ in any dynamic graph with a benign adversary with tolerance β.*

Proof. The token needs at most n cover times to match all possible color-pairs. The cover times (each time) is at least the cover time due to the repetition of the event $A_{u,v}$ n times. The expected time to visit all nodes is then at most $n^2 \cdot A_{u_i, u_{i+1}}$ where $u_0, \ldots, u_{n-1}$ is any permutation of the vertices, i.e. at most $n^2 \cdot \frac{1}{\varphi} = n^{\beta+2}$.   □

4   A Lower Bound for the Time Needed by BASIC for Static Graphs

4.1   The Match-Making Process Defines a Weighted Bipartite Graph

Let G be a static graph with some initial (arbitrary) distribution of node colors and with an initial majority color. Consider $B = u_1, \ldots, u_\kappa$, the set of all nodes $u_i \in V$ with blue color, and $R = v_1, \ldots, v_\lambda$ $(\lambda + \kappa = n)$, the set of all nodes $v_i \in V$ with red color. Let w_{ij} = the length of a shortest path between u_i and v_j in G.

Consider now the bipartite graph $U = (B, R)$ with node sets B, R and edges e_{ij} of weights $w(e_{ij}) = w_{ij}$. Consider any particular sequence of random walks of the token in protocol BASIC that matches all the red-blue pairs. Let the token start (say) in u_1 and match it with v_1. Then the token departs uncolored from v_1 till it meets a blue node, say u_2, again. Note that (1) each u_i is matched to a "new" v_i (not in $\{v_1, \ldots, v_{i-1}\}$), and (2) from each v_i the token seeks for a "new" u_i (not matched yet). Thus, the total time until convergence is at least the sum of the weights of two matchings in G, (a) the matching $\{u_i, v_i\}$, call it M_1, and (b) the matching $\{u_i, v_{i+1}\}$, call it M_2 (until all minority color nodes (say B) are matched). Let T be the time until convergence. In time T, the random walk process must hit the edges of the two matchings defined.

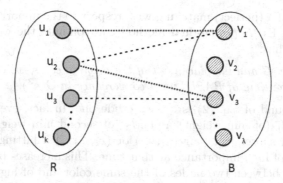

Fig. 1. Bipartite Matching

Thus,
$$T \geq (weight(M_1) + weight(M_2)) \cdot h$$
where h is the minimum time to hit a subsequent node on the other side, which implies
$$\mathbb{E}(T) \geq (weight(M) + weight(M')) \cdot h_{min} \qquad (1)$$
where M = the minimum weight matching in $U(B,R)$, M' = the second minimum weight matching in $U(B,R)$, and where $h_{min} \overset{def}{=}$ the minimum hitting time of G = the minimum (over all u, v) of the expected time for a random walk starting at u to reach v for the first time. The proof of Eq. (1) is done using linearity of expectation. Thus,
$$E(T) \geq 2 \cdot weight(M) \cdot h_{min}. \qquad (2)$$

If we know the initial placement of colors, then we can compute $weight(M)$ (and $weight(M')$) via a variation of the well-known Hungarian method [9] via the relaxed integer program Π.

$$\Pi: \quad minimize \sum_{i,j} w_{i,j} x_{i,j}$$

subject to
$$\sum_j x_{i,j} = 1 \quad \forall i \in B$$

$$\sum_i x_{i,j} = 1 \quad \forall j \in R$$

$$\sum_{i,j} x_{i,j} = \text{ the number of vertices of the minority color}$$

$$x_{i,j} \geq 0, \quad \forall i \in R, j \in B.$$

The Hungarian method (see [9]) shows that this is an integral relaxation in the sense that any extreme point of the polytope of Π's constraints is the incidence vector of a (perfect) matching with respect to the minority's color (see also [13], exercise E). A primal-dual method can compute the weight of M in time $\mathcal{O}(n^3)$ [9]. Thus,

Lemma 8. *Given G and the placement of the original color, we can compute a lower bound on the time of BASIC until convergence in $\mathcal{O}(n^3)$.*

Note that the bound of Eq. (2) is a very crude one. In fact, even if we know the matchings M_1 (of min weight) and M_2 (of second min weight), the walk requires, for each subsequent pair (u_i, v_i) or (v_i, u_{i+1}) a hitting time on the remaining colors of high importance at that time. This increases by at least the smallest distance between two nodes of the same color and of high importance every time.

Definition 9. *A k RED-BLUE line (on n nodes) is a path which consists of a red path of k nodes, joined to a blue path of $n - k$ nodes.*

Lemma 10. *The lower bound on the time of BASIC on a $\lfloor \frac{n}{2} \rfloor$ RED-BLUE line (with n odd) is $\Theta(n^3)$.*

Proof. The weight of each edge on the bipartite graph U is the square of the shortest distance between the particular red/blue pair because of the random walk, and more than $n/4$ such edges have weight which is $\Theta(n)$.   □

5   The Expected Convergence Time of BASIC on the Clique

Let $G = K_n =$ the clique of n nodes. Assume that one of the colors is a majority at the start of the BASIC protocol. Let b_t, r_t be the number of blue and red nodes, respectively, at round t (initially $b_1 + r_1 = n$) and assume, w.l.o.g., the time, T, of BASIC until convergence is the sum of times T_1, T_2, T_3, where $T_1 =$ the sum of all the times for the token to match two high-importance nodes of the same color, $T_2 =$ the sum of all times for the token to discover the next color of high importance to match, and $T_3 =$ the final cover time to convert all colors to the majority.

At round r, the initial probability that the random walk finds a matching node of the opposite color is $\frac{b_t}{n}$ (if it starts from a red node) or $\frac{r_t}{n}$ (if it starts from a blue node). Thus, the expected time till success is bounded above by $\frac{n}{b_t}$ ($\frac{n}{r_t}$) depending on the case, by the geometric process argument. Since the high importance colors are matched in pairs, we have (in each matching) $r_{t+2} = r_{t-1}$ and $b_{t+2} = b_{t-1}$. Let a be the time at which the minority color has only one node with that color. Thus both expectations of T_1, T_2 are bounded above by $\sum_{t=1}^{a+2} \frac{n}{b_t} + \sum_{t=1}^{a+2} \frac{n}{r_t}$ (to the convergence time) and each bound is $n(\frac{1}{b_1} + \frac{1}{b_{1-1}} + \cdots + 1)$ and $n(\frac{1}{r_1} + \frac{1}{r_{1-1}} + \cdots + 1)$, i.e., at worse $n \cdot H_n$ ($H_n =$ the nth harmonic number). Also, the expected cover time is $n \log n$ for the clique. Thus,

Lemma 11. *The expected convergence time of BASIC on the clique is $2nH_n + n \log n$, independently of the placement of the original colors. This matches the expected cover time of the clique, and thus is optimal.*

6   On Termination of the BASIC Process in Static Graphs

The BASIC process converges to the initial majority color (if any) in at most $n + 1$ cover times of the graph. This is because it needs at most $\frac{n}{2}$ walks of the token to match color pairs of high importance, at most $\frac{n}{2}$ walks to find the next candidate to match, and a final walk to convert all colors to the majority color. We can then supply BASIC with a termination criterion assuming:

1. The existence of a global clock, and
2. that each node v knows an upper bound $n' \geq n$ on the size of the graph.

Let T be the time (number of rounds) required for BASIC to converge. Then

$$\mathbb{E}(T) \leq (n + 1)\mathbb{E}(CoverTime(G)) \leq (n + 1)2mn \leq 2n^4. \qquad (3)$$

By Markov's inequality (see, e.g., [12]) we have

$$Prob(T \geq n\,\mathbb{E}(T)) \leq \frac{1}{n} \qquad (4)$$

implying that

$$Prob(T \geq 2n^5) \leq \frac{1}{n}. \qquad (5)$$

Therefore, BASIC can terminate (with probability of correctness at least $1 - \frac{1}{n}$) as follows:

Termination Criterion: Each node v reads the global clock. When the global clock shows $2n'^5$ elapsed rounds, then node v reports its current color as the majority color and stops executing BASIC.

7   Walks with Limited Counters in Graphs of Small Cover Time

One benefit of BASIC is the circulation of a single token in the net, having only 2 bits of memory. Suppose that we allow the token to be equipped with a counter. Then a single cover time of the graph clearly suffices for a randomly walking token to count the number of both colors in the graph and thus determine majority. Every time the token first encounters a color, it must mark the node as "visited" to avoid double-counting. This simple procedure requires a counter that can count up to n (the size of the graph). We describe here a modification of this procedure, with the benefit that the counter of the token can only count up to $\omega(\sqrt{n}\log n)$.

Basically, we equip the token with a counter (initially zero) and we start its random walk at an arbitrary node. The counter keeps the difference $\delta_t = b_t - r_t$ (b_t, r_t are the number of blue and red nodes that have been visited by time t) by setting $\delta_t \leftarrow \delta_t + 1$ when the token encounters an unvisited blue node, and $\delta_t \leftarrow \delta_t - 1$ when the token encounters an unvisited red node. Each time the token visits a node, if the status of the node is "unvisited" the token changes it to "visited" to avoid double-counting. After a time at least equal to a cover time, the token checks if the δ_t is positive or negative and then it performs another final walk to convert all nodes to the majority color (blue if $\delta_t > 0$, red if $\delta_t < 0$).

Clearly, if $|\delta_t| \leq g$ for all t until convergence (for some number g), then the counter will report correctly provided it can count up to some number g' strictly greater than g.

We show here that g is enough to be set to some value $\omega(\sqrt{n} \log n)$ for this procedure to correctly report majority with high probability. Our argument works under the following assumption.

Assumption A: Let p_t be the probability that the counter visits an unvisited majority color in the round t, and q_t be the probability that the counter visits an unvisited minority color in round t. We assume that $p_t \geq q_t$.

Assumption A is easily shown to hold when the colors are initially placed randomly in the vertices, and when the minimum degree of G is at least $\alpha \log n$ for some $\alpha \geq 2$.

Without loss of generality, assume that the initial majority color is blue. We consider a quite standard coupling process (δ_t, δ'_t) where $\delta_t = b_t - r_t$ and δ'_t is the current location of a simple random walk on (a subset of) the integers with a holding probability, i.e., a random walk on (a subset of) $\mathbb{Z}$ that can either increase or decrease by 1 with equal probablity, or remain stationary with (the remaining) positive probability. We give the details of this coupling below.

Let $\Delta(\delta_t) = \delta_{t+1} - \delta_t$, and $\Delta(\delta'_t) = \delta'_{t+1} - \delta'_t$ the corresponding increase or decrease in the random walk. There are nine cases to consider in the coupling, depending upon the values of $\Delta(\delta_t)$ and $\Delta(\delta'_t)$. The nine cases, together with the coupling probabilities are listed below. We need to define the coupling probabilities x_i for each of the cases.

$(\Delta(\delta_t), \Delta(\delta'_t))$	Coupling probability
$(0, 0)$	x_1
$(0, 1)$	x_2
$(0, -1)$	x_3
$(1, 0)$	x_4
$(1, 1)$	x_5
$(1, -1)$	x_6
$(-1, 0)$	x_7
$(-1, 1)$	x_8
$(-1, -1)$	x_9

First of all, we note that we want to couple the processes so that $\delta_t \geq \delta'_t$ for all t, so that if, for example, $\delta'_t = b_t$ then we guarantee that $\delta_t = b_t$ too. This immediately implies that we have $x_2 = x_7 = x_8 = 0$.

Secondly, to keep the coupling as tight as possible, we set $x_3 = x_4 = 0$.

We also have other conditions on the values x_i as follows:

$$x_1 + x_5 + x_6 + x_9 = 1 \text{ and } x_i \geq 0 \ \forall i \tag{6}$$

$$x_9 = q_t \tag{7}$$

$$x_5 + x_6 = p_t \tag{8}$$

$$x_5 = x_6 + x_9 \tag{9}$$

$$x_5 + x_6 + x_9 = p_t + q_t \tag{10}$$

Condition (6) come from the fact that the x_i form a probability distribution. (7) comes from the definition of the probability q_t, i.e., the chance of the token finding an unvisited minority color, and similarly (8) is from the defintion of p_t. Equation (9) is from the fact the the process $\Delta(\delta_t')$ is describing a simple random walk, i.e., $Pr(\Delta(\delta_t') = 1) = Pr(\Delta(\delta_t') = -1)$. We note that $p_t + q_t$ is the probability that the value of $\Delta(\delta_t)$ is non-zero.

Thus, solving for the values of x_i, we get the following coupling probabilities below (we show only the non-zero values):

$(\Delta(\delta_t), \Delta(\delta_t'))$	Coupling probability
$(0,0)$	$1 - p_t - q_t$
$(1,1)$	$\frac{1}{2}(p_t + q_t)$
$(1,-1)$	$\frac{1}{2}(p_t - q_t)$
$(-1,-1)$	q_t

With these probabilities, we have $\mathbb{E}(\Delta(\delta_t')) = 0$ and $|\Delta(\delta_t')| \leq 1$. We can apply the inequality of Azuma to the martingale $\Delta(\delta_t')$ with bounded difference. By Azuma's inequality then we have $|\delta_t'| = \mathcal{O}(\sqrt{n}\log n)$ through a period of a cover time $\Theta(n \log n)$.

Thus, the difference of colors counted will never exceed $c\sqrt{n}\log n$ in the minority direction (w.h.p.) and will end up with a correct value in the majority direction. Therefore:

Lemma 12. *For any static unknown graph G where (a) Assumption A holds and (b) $\mathbb{E}(CoverTime(G)) = \mathcal{O}(n \log n)$ the counter of the token needs to count only up to $\omega(\sqrt{n}\log n)$ in order to report the majority color w.h.p.*

8 Future Work

It would be interesting to study the Majority Color Problem on non-trivial special classes of graphs as complete graphs can be solved in $\mathcal{O}(n \log n)$ expected time and $\mathcal{O}(n^2 m)$ time on any connected undirected graph. Using Corollary 4, any upper bound on the expected cover time for a class of graphs immediately translates into an upper bound on the convergence time of BASIC. For example, it is known that the cover time for any regular graph on n vertices is at most $2n^2$, giving an upper bound of $\mathcal{O}(n^3)$ for convergence of BASIC on such graphs [7].

Appendix

This section demonstrates an example execution of the *BASIC* protocol on a graph where $n = 5$ and there exists a majority where $|RED| > |BLUE|$.

Table 1 traces the execution from the initialization step (step 0), when the token t is placed at an arbitrary vertex, to the state when all vertices have been converted to the majority color. Each row consists of the step number, the state of t (where $t = \{color, location\}$), the state of all the vertices (uppercase representing high influence and lowercase representing low influence of a color) and finally the case which should be executed given the current state of the graph.

Step	t	a	b	c	d	e	case
0	{U, a}	B	B	R	R	R	2
1	{B, b}	b	B	R	R	R	4
2	{B, a}	b	B	R	R	R	3
3	{B, c}	b	B	r	R	R	5
4	{U, e}	b	B	r	R	R	2
5	{R, b}	b	B	r	R	r	5
6	{U, e}	b	b	r	R	r	1
7	{U, d}	b	b	r	R	r	2
8	{R, b}	b	b	r	r	r	3
9	{R, a}	b	r	r	r	r	3
10	{R, b}	r	r	r	r	r	3

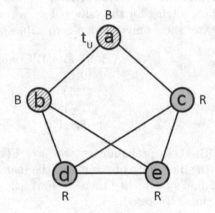

Table 1. Trace table for an execution of BASIC.

Initialization: t is randomly placed at vertex a.

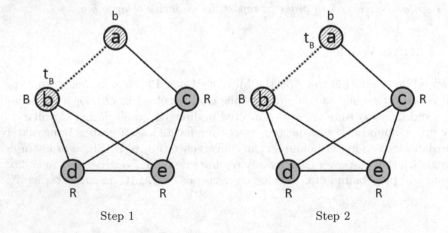

Step 1   Step 2

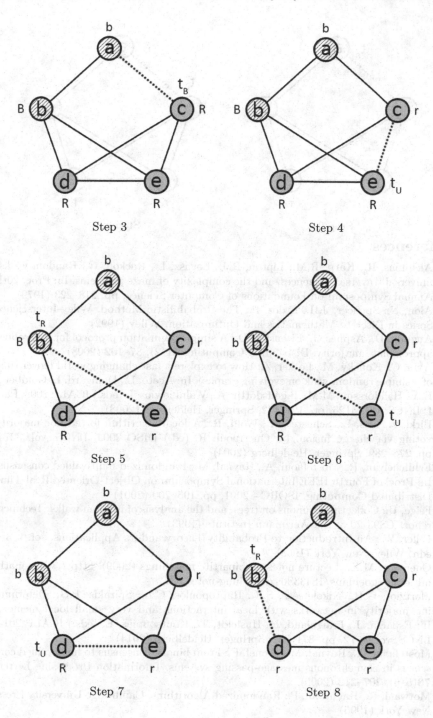

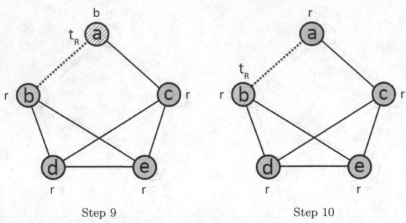

Step 9   Step 10

References

1. Aleliunas, R., Karp, R.M., Lipton, R.J., Lovász, L., Rackoff, C.: Random walks, universal traversal sequences, and the complexity of maze problems. In: Proc. 20th Annual Symposium on Foundations of Computer Science, pp. 218–223 (1979)
2. Alon, N., Spencer, J.H., Erdös, P.: The Probabilistic Method. Wiley-Interscience Series in Discrete Mathematics and Optimization. Wiley (1992)
3. Angluin, D., Aspnes, J., Eisenstat, D.: A simple population protocol for fast robust approximate majority. Distributed Computing **21**(2), 87–102 (2008)
4. Avin, C., Koucký, M., Lotker, Z.: How to explore a fast-changing world (cover time of a simple random walk on evolving graphs). In: Aceto, L., Damgård, I., Goldberg, L.A., Halldórsson, M.M., Ingólfsdóttir, A., Walukiewicz, I. (eds.) ICALP 2008, Part I. LNCS, vol. 5125, pp. 121–132. Springer, Heidelberg (2008)
5. Birk, Y., Liss, L., Schuster, A., Wolff, R.: A local algorithm for ad hoc majority voting via charge fusion. In: Guerraoui, R. (ed.) DISC 2004. LNCS, vol. 3274, pp. 275–289. Springer, Heidelberg (2004)
6. Ezhilchelvan, P., Mostefaoui, A., Raynal, M.: Randomized multivalued consensus. In: Proc. of Fourth IEEE International Symposium on Object-Oriented Real-Time Distributed Computing, ISORC - 2001, pp. 195–200 (2001)
7. Feige, U.: Collecting coupons on trees, and the analysis of random walks. Technical report CS93-20 of the Weizmann Institute (1993)
8. Feller, W.: An Introduction to Probability Theory and its Applications, vol. 1, 3rd edn. Wiley, New York (1968)
9. Goemans, M.X.: Lecture notes on bipartite matchings (2009). http://www-math.mit.edu/~goemans/18433S09/matching-notes.pdf
10. Mertzios, G.B., Nikoletseas, S.E., Raptopoulos, C.L., Spirakis, P.G.: Determining majority in networks with local interactions and very small local memory. In: Esparza, J., Fraigniaud, P., Husfeldt, T., Koutsoupias, E. (eds.) ICALP 2014. LNCS, vol. 8572, pp. 871–882. Springer, Heidelberg (2014)
11. Mostefaoui, A., Raynal, M., Tronel, F.: From binary consensus to multivalued consensus in asynchronous message-passing systems. Information Processing Letters **73**(5-6), 207–212 (2000)
12. Motwani, R., Raghavan, P.: Randomized Algorithms. Cambridge University Press, New York (1995)
13. Papadimitriou, C.H., Steiglitz, K.: Combinatorial Optimization: Algorithms and Complexity. Ch 11, exercise 5(c). Prentice-Hall, Inc., NJ (1982)

The k-Observer Problem on d-regular Graphs

Benjamin Ries[✉], Bernhard Schamberg, and Walter Unger

Department of Computer Science I, RWTH Aachen University, Aachen, Germany
ries@cs.rwth-aachen.de

Abstract. We consider the problem of observing every path of fixed length k in a given graph with a minimum number of nodes. This problem is known as the k-Observe problem, or as the k-path vertex cover problem respectively. It is a generalization of the well known vertex cover problem. The nodes of a solution to the k-Observer problem i.e. can be used to monitor the traffic of a given network or can provide data integrity in a (distributed) sensor network. In this work we focus on undirected d-regular graphs, where every node has a maximal constant degree of d. First we show for the case $k = 2$ a $(1 + \frac{1}{2d-2})$-approximation for bipartite d-regular graphs. Then we present a $(2 - o(1))$-approximation, again for $k = 2$. This slightly improves the results of [TZ11], which provides a 2-approximation. Moreover our approach can be generalized for $k \geq 2$ and leads to a 3-approximation for $k \leq \frac{d+2}{2}$. Furthermore this is the first algorithm with an better approximation factor than $k + 1$ for $k \geq 2$. Note also that this result can be extended to an α-approximation for $k \leq \frac{\alpha-2}{\alpha-1} d + 1$ for $\alpha \geq 3$.

1 Introduction and Motivation

We consider the problem of observing all paths of fixed length k in a undirected and unweighted graph $G = (V, E)$ with a minimum number of nodes. We focus on undirected and unweighted d-regular graphs without loops, where every node has a maximal degree of d. The length of a path P is denoted by the number of edges in P. Finding the minimum number of nodes that observe all paths of length k is known as the k-Observer problem and was first introduced in [ACBG12].

The authors in [ACBG12] present several applications for the k-Observer problem. For example a solution can be used in constructing optimal connectivity paths in wireless sensor networks. The nodes in the solution may be equipped with additional caches, and can serve nearby nodes in a content distribution network, so with a small number of nodes we can guarantee that every node has access to an nearby cache. Another application could be to use selected nodes to perform additional tasks in the network, i.e.: observing or collecting statistics in the network. Furthermore the nodes in a solution for the k-Observer problem may help to detect and prevent malicious attack to the network. The nodes in a solution for the k-Observer problem may help to decide where to place additional firewalls or filters.

© Springer International Publishing Switzerland 2015
A. Pelc and A.A. Schwarzmann (Eds.): SSS 2015, LNCS 9212, pp. 81–93, 2015.
DOI: 10.1007/978-3-319-21741-3_6

Beside the applications named in [ACBG12], our work is motivated by the so called k-generalized Canvas scheme [Nov10], which should provide data integrity in a sensor network. It combines the properties of cryptographic primitives and the network topology. This scheme aims to guarantees data integrity under the assumption that at least one node exists which is not captured on each path of length k in a communication network. In [Nov10] these nodes where called protected, and the authors point out, that on each path of length k there has to be a protected node.

1.1   Related Work

The problem of observing, or covering, all paths of a given length k was independently and at the same time examined by the author in [ACBG12] and in [BKKS11]. While the problem in [ACBG12] was named the k-Observer problem, the authors in [BKKS11] call it the k-path vertex cover, to point out that the problem is an natural generalization of the vertex cover problem. The 1-Observer problem, or the 1-path vertex cover problem, is equivalent to the well known vertex cover problem, where all edges have to be covered by a minimum number of nodes.

The NP-hardness of the k-Observer problem was shown in [ACBG12], as well as in [BKKS11]. Both proofs used a reduction from vertex cover, and implies that any c-approximation algorithm for the k-Observer problem, with polynomial running time, yields directly a c-approximation for the vertex cover problem, for $c \geq 1$. Together with the results of [KR08], this indicates that 2 can be seen as a lower bound for the approximation factor, not only for the vertex cover problem but also for the k-Observer problem. In both papers a centralized algorithm for tress is presented, that computes an optimal solution, however, the authors of [ACBG12] also presented a distributed version of their approach. Furthermore, algorithms for ring and grid graphs are also presented in [ACBG12].

In contrast to that, the authors in [BKKS11] focus on approximation algorithms. A simple approximation algorithm is the generalization of the well known 2-approximation of the vertex cover problem. Taking an arbitrary path P of length k and the $k+1$ nodes of P into the solution. Since the optimal solution has to take at least one of these $k + 1$ nodes, this leads to an $(k + 1)$-approximation only. In an additional work [BJK$^+$13] the authors present a lower and upper bound for the optimal solution in terms of the degree of the graph. Important for our work is the lower bound for an optimal solution of $\frac{d-k+1}{2d-k+1}|V|$.

To the best of our knowledge the only approximation factor better than $k + 1$ was shown in [TZ11], where an 2-approximation for the case $k = 2$ is presented. However, in contrast to our work, the algorithm can not be implemented in an distributed environment or extended to path lengths larger then k. Recently an optimal algorithm for the weighted version for tress was presented in [BKBSŠ14].

1.2   Outline

First, in Section 2, we concentrate on bipartite d-regular graphs. For the case $k = 2$ we present an algorithm with an approximation factor of $1 + \frac{1}{2d-2}$. In Section 3 we describe our algorithm on general for d-regular graphs. We start by presenting our analysis for the case $k = 2$, where we achieve an approximation factor of $2 - o(1)$ for d-regular graphs. For large graphs, if $|V| \gg d$, this factor becomes roughly $2 - \frac{1}{d}$. This is equal to the best known approximation factor for vertex cover [Hoc83]. We improve the results of [TZ11], where the authors show an 2-approximation for general graphs and $k = 2$. Additionally, in contrast to other results, our algorithm also works if $k > 2$. If $k \leq \frac{d+2}{2}$ we achieve an 3-approximation and, for $k \leq \frac{\alpha-2}{\alpha-1}d + 1$, we still obtain an α-approximation, for any $\alpha \geq 3$.

While the algorithm in Section 3 is still centralized, we present a distributed version in Section 4. Finally, in Section 5, we conclude this paper with some future work and open problems.

2   Bipartite d-regular Graphs

In this section we present our approximation algorithm for the 2-Observer problem on bipartite d-regular graphs. The algorithm simply takes one partition of the nodes. We show that this yields an approximation factor of $1 + \frac{1}{2d-2}$. The 2-Observer problem is equivalent to computing the dissociation number of a graph. A dissociation set D is a subset of the vertices of G, such that the subgraph induced by D has a maximum degree of 1. The dissociation number is the cardinality of the maximum dissociation set of a graph. Computing the dissociation number of a graph is the dual problem to the 2-Observer problem. Since computing the dissociation number of a bipartite graph with maximum degree 3 is NP-hard [BL01], the 2-Observer problem is also NP-hard. In contrast, an optimal vertex cover can be computed in polynomial time if the graph is bipartite.

Theorem 1. *There is a $(1 + \frac{1}{2d-2})$-approximation for the 2-Observer problem on bipartite d-regular graphs.*

Proof. Let $G = (V_1 \uplus V_2, E)$ be a bipartite d-regular graph, note that $|V_1| = |V_2|$. It is easy to see that a d-regular bipartite graph consists of d different perfect matchings. This can be shown, for example, by induction over d and make use of Halls theorem on matching. By choosing one partition of the bipartite graph, say V_1, as a solution for the 2-Observer problem, every matching edge is connected to one node of the cover. So there are no uncovered paths of length 2 are left in the graph, and we have a valid solution.

Now assume there is an optimal solution that uses less than half of the nodes. Hence there must be at least one pair of matched nodes where both of the nodes are not in this solution.

Let *opt* be the optimal solution. We consider a matched pair of nodes that is not in *opt*. Since *opt* needs to cover all paths of length 2, every neighbour of such a matched pair of nodes has to be chosen. Thus, there are at least $d - 1$ nodes on each half that have to be in the optimal solution.

In total, for each pair of matched nodes, which are not in opt, opt must choose $2(d - 1)$ nodes. Those $2(d - 1)$ nodes can be used by at most d many matching edges, which have d different perfect matchings. Combining these, we get that on each side for d nodes which are not in a solution, there have to be $d - 1$ other nodes in the solution. It follows that for every $2(d + d - 1)$ nodes in the graph we need at least $2(d - 1)$ nodes in an optimal solution. Hence opt is of size at least $\frac{2d-1}{2(d+d-1)}|V|$. Comparing the size of our solution with the size of the optimal solution we get:

$$\frac{V_1}{opt} \leq \frac{\frac{|V|}{2}}{\frac{2d-1}{2(d+d-1)}|V|} = \frac{(d + d - 1)}{2(d - 1)} = \frac{2d - 1}{2d - 2} = 1 + \frac{1}{2d - 2}$$

Note that, if there are less than d matching edges with two nodes, which are not in a solution, still $2(d-1)$ nodes in the solution are required. So the optimum can not be smaller than $2d - 2$.   □

In the next section we consider general d-regular graphs.

3   Approximation Algorithm for d-regular Graphs

In this section we present our approximation algorithm for d-regular graphs. We start with a short description of the algorithm, followed by it's analysis. The algorithm proceeds as follows: Starting a breadth-first search from an arbitrary node v, and stopping as soon as a cycle in the layered graph is detected. Let h be the level on which the cycle occurs and let $G' = (V', E')$ be the obtained subgraph. Let $C_k(G')$ be the solution for the subgraph G'. It consists of two parts:

(1) A set $S \subseteq V'$ with nodes of the lower level h, such that G' becomes a tree, i.e. G' has no cycle. Let T be this tree.
(2) The optimal solution for T.

An example is shown in Figure 1, where the first cycle occurs on level 4, and the black marked nodes are in the set S and have to be removed to delete all cycles.

After computing the set $C_k(G')$, delete the nodes from $C_k(G')$ in G and proceed with the remaining graph until no path of length k remain. Note that we only delete nodes in the solution $C_k(G')$, and not the complete subgraph G'. If we would delete all nodes in G' it could happen that the final solution does not cover all paths of length k. When we finished with the graph, we collect the nodes in the trees T, and recompute the optimal solution for the graph induced by this nodes. On the other hand, if we only take the union of these solutions, it could be that we take to many nodes. Recompute the optimal solution simplify the later analysis. Note that this graph is still a tree, and we can find the optimal

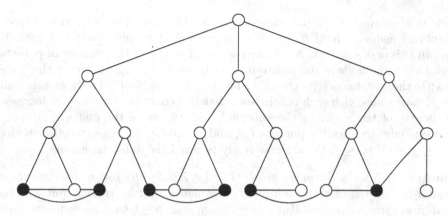

Fig. 1. Restricted to the lower level, we have to delete the marked nodes, to remove all cycles

solution in polynomial time [ACBG12]. The final solution for the complete graph G consists of the union of the computed sets S for all the subgraphs G' and the recomputed optimal solution for the trees.

To compute the optimal solution in (2) we can use either the algorithm proposed in [ACBG12] or the algorithm of [BKKS11]. Both algorithms runs in polynomial time and compute the optimal solution for a tree. The minimal set S in (1) may unfortunately not be found in polynomial time, since this would mean we have to solve a restricted version of the feedback vertex set problem, and this problem is NP-hard [ENZ96]. In Lemma 1 we give an upper bound on how many nodes we must remove in G' to cancel all cycles. We bound these number by the total number of nodes in G'. But before we make some adjustments to the graph, that will help in the later calculation. If a node v on level h during the breadth-first search causes an cycle, we distinguish between the following two cases:

(a) v is adjacent to an node u on the same level h
(b) v has two parent nodes on level $h - 1$.

Examples for both cases can be seen in Figure 1. Note that it is not possible that both cases occur on the same level during the breadth-first search, in contrast to the example in Figure 1. If we see both cases in the same iteration, case (a) happens on a level before case (b). Say we see case (a) on level $h - 1$, and case (b) on level h. Here we only consider the graph till level $h - 1$, the remaining graph is considered in a later iteration.

To simplify the subsequent analysis, we make the following adjustments. Our intention is, that we only have nodes of case (a) in G'. Hence we explain how to change a circle of case (b) to an circle of case (a), without increasing the degree of the nodes in the subgraph G'. As explained above, both cases can not occur on the same level, during the breath-first search, since we stop as soon as a circle is detected. For this purpose consider a node v on level h with two or more neighbour nodes on level $h - 1$, like the most right marked node in Figure 1. We call this nodes on level $h - 1$ the *parents* of v. Let p_v the number of parents of v. Delete the node v and create p_v new nodes $v_1, \ldots, v_{p_v}$. Connect the node v_i with the i-th former parent of v, for $1 \leq i \leq p_v \leq d$. Finally connect all the p_v new nodes with each other. Note that this construction does not increase the degree of the nodes in the subgraph G'. Any v_i of the nodes $v_1, \ldots, v_{p_v}$ have one edge to a former parent of v, and at most $d - 1$ edges to other nodes $v_j, 1 \leq j \neq i \leq p_v \leq d$. We are now ready to proof the following lemma:

Lemma 1. *Given a d-regular graph $G = (V, E)$. Starting at a node v with a breadth-first search to obtain a layered graph with height h. Assume that on level h the first cycle occurs and that two nodes on level $h - 1$ have no common child node on level h. Let $G' = (V', E')$ be this graph. On level h at most $\left\lceil |V'| \cdot \frac{d-2}{d} \right\rceil$ nodes have to be removed, to eliminate all cycles in G'.*

Proof. Since we restricting our attention to the lower level h, it is enough to compute a vertex cover for the subgraph induced by the nodes on this level. We know that each node on this level has a degree of at most $d - 1$, hence a vertex cover includes at most $\frac{d-1}{d}$ of the nodes. This comes from the fact that an independent set for these graphs contain at least $\frac{1}{d}$ of the nodes, since the graph is $d - 1$-regular.

Next we estimate how many nodes are on level h in G'. For that purpose we assume that in G' each node have at most $m = d - 1$ child nodes, except from the root node. Counting the numbers of nodes in V' we get $|V'| \leq 1 + (m + 1) \cdot \sum_{i=2}^{h} m^i$, since the root node may have $m + 1$ child nodes, and each of these have m child nodes themselves. The term can be simplified to $2 \cdot \frac{m^{h+1}+1}{m-1}$ and we get $|V'| \leq 2 \cdot \frac{m^{h+1}+1}{m-1}$. The number of nodes m^h on level h can now be estimated with $m^h \leq \frac{|V'|(m-1)+2}{m}$. It follows that we have to remove at most $\left\lfloor \frac{d-1}{d} m^h \right\rfloor$ nodes on the last level. This yields for the set S that we remove:

$$
|S| \leq \left\lfloor \frac{d-1}{d} m^h \right\rfloor \leq \left\lfloor \frac{d-1}{d} \cdot |V'| \cdot \frac{(m-1)+2}{m} \right\rfloor
$$

$$
\leq \left\lfloor |V'| \cdot \frac{d-2}{d} + \frac{2}{d} \right\rfloor \leq \left\lceil |V'| \cdot \frac{d-2}{d} \right\rceil
$$

The last estimation can be done because rounding up the term $|V'| \frac{d-2}{d}$ increases the value more than adding $\frac{2}{d}$ and rounding down to the lower integer. $\square$

Once a subgraph is completed, we remove the computed solution and proceed with the remaining graph, until no paths of length k are left. Note that all steps described above can be done in polynomial time, especially the set S can be determined by a simple greedy algorithm.

Dependent on k and d our algorithm yields different approximation factors. Nevertheless, the analysis of the approximation factor in each case is quite similar. First we present in Theorem 1.1 the analysis for the case $k = 2$. Here we achieve an $2 - o(1)$-approximation.

Theorem 1.1. *On d-regular graphs, with $d \geq 3$, the 2-Observer problem can be approximated with a factor of $2 - o(1)$.*

Proof. Let $G = (V, E)$ be a d-regular graph. We compare the size of the solution derived by our algorithm with the size of a optimal solution for G. Let $G' = (V', E')$ be a subgraph of G, obtained by the breadth-first search, as described above, and let $\mathcal{G}$ be the collection of all solutions for all of these subgraphs G'. Each of the single solution consists of two parts: First the set of vertices of the lower level S such that G' has no cycles, and second the vertices of the optimal solution for the remaining trees T. This is a valid solution for the subgraph G', since we solve the tree optimal all paths are covered there. The paths that are induced by the additional nodes in S are obviously covered. Since we only remove the nodes of the solution, and not all nodes of G', and the algorithm does not terminate until all paths of length 2 are covered, this is a valid solution.

Let $\mathcal{T}$ be the set of vertices of all optimal solutions of the trees T (that we have recomputed at the end), and $\mathcal{S}$ be the set of all nodes in the sets S. The number of nodes in $\mathcal{T}$ can be upper bounded by $\frac{|V| - |\mathcal{S}|}{3}$ [BKKS11]. Since the trees consists of $|V| - |\mathcal{S}|$ many nodes, and we have to take every third node to observe all paths of length 2. For the size of the optimal solution $\psi_2(G)$ we use the lower bound of $\frac{d-k+1}{2d-k+1} \cdot |V|$ provided in [BJK$^+$13] for d-regular graphs. If we now compare the size of our solution with the size of the optimal solution we get:

$$\frac{|\mathcal{T}| + |\mathcal{S}|}{\psi_2(G)} \leq \frac{\frac{|V| - |\mathcal{S}|}{3} + |\mathcal{S}|}{\psi_2(G)} \leq \frac{\frac{|V| - |\mathcal{S}|}{3} + |\mathcal{S}|}{\frac{d-1}{2d-1} \cdot |V|} \leq \frac{|V| + 2|\mathcal{S}|}{\frac{3d-3}{2d-1} \cdot |V|}.$$

To upper bound the size of the set $\mathcal{S}$ we use Lemma 1. In Lemma 1 we suppose that every node on the lower level has only one parent node in the level before. In general this does not hold. Nevertheless this is not a problem. If two or more vertices on level $h - 1$ have a common child node v in level h, we have to take v into our set $\mathcal{S}$, to cancel the circle. Since we do a worst case estimation in Lemma 1, our estimation for the size of S still holds. So we can $|\mathcal{S}|$ substitute by $\lceil |V| \cdot \frac{d-2}{d} \rceil$:

$$\frac{|V| + 2|\mathcal{S}|}{\frac{3d-3}{2d-1} \cdot |V|} \leq \frac{|V| + 2 \lceil |V| \cdot \frac{d-2}{d} \rceil}{\frac{3d-3}{2d-1} \cdot |V|}.$$

The Gaussian brackets can be removed by adding $\frac{d-1}{d}$, since this is the maximal value added by rounding up to the next integer.

$$\frac{|V| + 2 \lceil |V| \cdot \frac{d-2}{d} \rceil}{\frac{3d-3}{2d-1} \cdot |V|} \leq \frac{|V| + 2|V| \cdot \frac{d-2}{d} + \frac{2d-2}{d}}{\frac{3d-3}{2d-1} \cdot |V|}$$

Finally we do some rearrangements and get:

$$\frac{|V| + 2|V| \cdot \frac{d-2}{d} + \frac{2d-2}{d}}{\frac{3d-3}{2d-1} \cdot |V|} \leq 2 - \frac{1}{d} + \frac{4d-2}{3d|V|} = 2 - \frac{3|V| - 4d + 2}{3d|V|}$$

To show that the approximation factor is always smaller than 2, it remains to show that the second part is non-negative. If the subgraph has $|V| \geq \frac{4}{3}d - \frac{2}{3}$ nodes, this is obviously true.

On the other hand, if $\frac{3}{4}|V| + \frac{1}{2} \leq d$, the whole graph has a high regularity. In this case we can show that also the optimal solution needs more then $\frac{|V|}{2}$ nodes. In this case the input graph is at least $\lceil \frac{3}{4}|V| \rceil$-regular. Taking the whole set V into the solution leads automatically to an good approximation factor for dense graphs. For each node v that is not in the optimal solution, the optimal solution has to take at least $\lceil \frac{3}{4}|V| \rceil - 1$ of the neighbours of v. If the optimal solution omits more than one of the neighbours of v, there will be a path of length 2 that is not covered. Thus this will not happen. Hence taking the whole set V leads to an $\frac{4}{3}$-approximation.

Summing up we can conclude that:

$$2 - \frac{3|V| - 4d + 2}{3d|V|} < 2$$

So we get an approximation factor of $2 - o(1)$ for every d-regular graph. □

Note that for lager graphs, if $|V| \gg d$, the approximation factor is roughly $2 - \frac{1}{d}$. Our algorithm does even work for the vertex cover problem, i.e. $k = 1$, and achieves the same approximation factor as for $k = 2$, which is equal to the best known results for d-regular graphs [Hoc83].

The running time of our algorithm is dominated by the breadth-first search, hence the set S and the solution for the tree T can be found in linear time. A breath-first search can be done in time $O(|V|^2)$. Summing up we get a running time of $O(|V|^2)$, which is better as in [TZ11]. Though the approach in [TZ11] cannot be extended to an distributed algorithms, while, as we will see later, it is possible to extend our algorithm to an distributed algorithm.

The approximation factor can be improved even more, if we fix the degree of the input graph to $d = 3$. Doing the same calculation as above we get

Proposition 1. *The 2-Observer problem can be approximate with a factor of 1.389 + o(1) on 3-regular graphs.*

This factor is very close to the best achievable of 1.3606 [DS05] unless $P \neq NP$.

In contrast to previous approaches, our algorithm is also helpful when asking for coverings for longer path lengths than 2. We can use our algorithm any $k \leq \frac{d+2}{2}$. In this case, the analysis above does yield a 3-approximation instead of a 2-approximation.

Theorem 1.2. *The k-Observer problem can be approximated with a factor of 3 on d-regular graphs if $k \leq \frac{d+2}{2}$.*

Proof. Similar to the proof for Theorem 1.1 we compare the size of the optimal solution for the trees $\mathcal{T}$ and the size of the set $\mathcal{S}$ with the value of the optimal solution $\psi_k(G)$ for G. Again we can use the algorithm of [BKKS11] to compute the optimal solution for the trees in $\mathcal{T}$,

$$\frac{|\mathcal{T}| + |\mathcal{S}|}{\psi_k(G)} \leq \frac{\frac{|V| - |\mathcal{S}|}{k+1} + |\mathcal{S}|}{\psi_k(G)} \leq \frac{|V| + k|\mathcal{S}|}{(k+1)\psi_k(G)}.$$

The size of $\mathcal{S}$ can coarsely be estimated with $|V|$. This gives:

$$\frac{|V| + k|\mathcal{S}|}{(k+1)\psi_k(G)} \leq \frac{(k+1)|V|}{(k+1)\psi_k(G)}.$$

For $\psi_k(G)$ we can use again the lower bound of [BJK$^+$13], which holds for all $k \leq d$. We get:

$$\frac{|V|}{\psi_k(G)} \leq \frac{2d - k + 1}{d - k + 1}$$

Using this bound for our approximation ratio, we can figure out under which restrictions we can get a 3-approximation:

$$\frac{2d - k + 1}{d - k + 1} \leq 3$$

$$\Leftrightarrow \frac{d}{d - k + 1} + \frac{d - k + 1}{d - k + 1} \leq 3$$

$$\Leftrightarrow 1 + \frac{d}{d - k + 1} \leq 3$$

$$\Leftrightarrow \frac{d}{d - k + 1} \leq 2$$

Multiplying with $d - k + 1$, which is possible since $k \leq d$, yields:

$$d \leq 2d - 2k + 2$$

$$\Leftrightarrow 2k \leq d + 2$$

$$\Leftrightarrow k \leq \frac{d + 2}{2}$$

So for $k \leq \frac{d+2}{2}$ our algorithm gives a valid 3-approximation for the k-Observer problem on d-regular graphs. □

Unfortunately with our approach it is not possible to achieve an 2-approximation in this case. Some of the transformations from the proof of Theorem 1.1 only hold for the case $k \leq 2$.

The limitation that k is bounded by $\frac{d+2}{2}$ can be partially lifted up. If we replace the 3 in the approximation factor by an natural number $\alpha \geq 3$ in the calculation in Theorem 1.2 we achieve an α-approximation if $k \leq \frac{\alpha-2}{\alpha-1}d + 1$.

Proposition 2. *On d-regular graphs the k-Observer problem can be approximated with a factor of* α, *with* $\alpha \geq 3$, *if* $k \leq \frac{\alpha-2}{\alpha-1}d + 1$.

4 Distributed Algorithm

In the previous section we presented the idea and analysis of our (centralized) algorithm. In this section we show that this algorithm can also be executed in a distributed environment. Our algorithm for the k-Observer problem consists of three main parts:

1. A breath-first search,
2. determing the nodes in the set S on level h,
3. checking if there exists a path of length k in the remaining graph.

For each part we describe a distributed variant, and the interaction between the parts. We assume that the nodes in the network are equipped with an unique identifiers (UID), chosen from an totally ordered space of identifiers. Moreover, each node knows its neighbours and has the possibility to communicate with these. Also the number of nodes n in the network should be known to all nodes. In the beginning, the graph is strongly connected. After the first iteration it could be that by our virtual computation the graph decomposes in several connected components. In this case, the algorithm can proceed in parallel on each of these components.

At first, in each iteration a node must be chosen that begins with the breath-first search. This can be done, for example, by an simple leader election algorithm, like the one described in [Lyn96]. Once the starting node is fixed, a distributed breath-first search algorithm can be executed. An implementation is described, for example, in [Lyn96]. In this implementation the designated root node sends out a search message to all its neighbours. Once a node receives a search message, the node marked itself as marked. Then the nodes itself send a search message to all its neighbours and so on.

We use this algorithm to compute the subgraph G'. With the help of the search messages we can detect the circles. After a node receives a search message, the node can check whether there is an circle or not. If there is no circle detected, the node can report an *no circle* message back in the tree to the root node, otherwise it sends a *circle* message. There are two kind of circle messages, one for each case, we discussed above.

If the root node r receives no circle message, it sends a message that the node can continue with the breath-first search, otherwise its sends a stop message through the network. By this procedure we obtain a tree and discover it level by level.

If a node v receives two or more search messages at the same time, and have receive no one before, this node induced an circle of case (b). In this case v can mark itself as part of the solution for the k-Observer problem and report a circle message of case (b). The transformation before in Lemma 1 was only made to simplify the analysis of the algorithm.

On the other hand, if a node v receive at least one search message, and has already received one in a previous iteration, v reports a circle message of case (a) and its UID. The root node r collects all the circle messages and count the number of nodes that reports a circle of case (a).

This number is then reported to these nodes. These nodes can now use the algorithm proposed in [SJX13] to compute a maximal independent set among themselves (for this we need the number of nodes n in the network). Since the maximum degree of the subgraph induced by these nodes is bounded by $d - 1$, the computed maximal independent set is also an approximation to of the maximum independent set. This set is, because the subgraph has a bounded degree, an approximation of the vertex cover, with the desired size described in Lemma 1.

Once the set S is computed, the remaining nodes can proceed and compute the optimal solution for the tree T. Therefore the distributed algorithm presented in [ACBG12] can be used.

After this solution is computed, every node in G' knows if it is in the solution for G' or not. To start a new round, a message that a solution for a subgraph is computed, is broadcasted through the network. Again a leader for the breath-first search must be elected, but now only by the nodes that are not part of the solution at this point, or which are in a subgraph that have at least one path with length at least k. If a subgraph have a path of length k can be determining during the breath-first search.

At the end, every node is either part of the solution, or in a subgraph that only contains path of length smaller than k.

The running time of this procedure is again dominated by the running time of the breath-first search. The running time of the breath-first search increases from $O(|E|)$ up to $O(|E|^2)$, since we need to report after each step if a circle is detected or not. The distributed algorithm for computing the maximum independent set runs in $O(\log n)$, where n denotes the number of nodes.

To wait for the root node that the other nodes reports the circle message seems a little bit wasteful. The following approach can improve the running time: Once a node receives a search message, it wait one time step and then proceed with the breath-first search, if no circle is detected. Thus the breath-first search is delayed. Once a node detect a circle, say on level h, this message is reported without delay to the root node. To find the circle on level h it takes $2h$ time steps, and additional h steps are needed to report the circle to the root node. When the root node receive the circle message, its send a stop message without any delay, through the network. Note that during this, the remaining nodes proceed with the breath-first search. Since the nodes proceeds with the breath-first search only in every second time step, after at most $5h$ steps every node receives a stop message, and the breath-first search stops. This results in a total running time of $O(|E|)$ for the breath-first search.

5   Conclusion and Future Work

In this paper we presented approximation algorithms for the k-Observer problem on d-regular graphs. First we presented in Section 2 an approximation algorithm for bipartite d-regular graphs. In the case of $k = 2$ we achieved an $1 + \frac{1}{2d-2}$-approximation.

In Section 3 we considered d-regular graphs in general. We started by presenting our (centralized) idea of our algorithm. Our analysis shows that, in the case of $k = 2$, our algorithm achieves an $2 - o(1)$-approximation, that converges to $2 - \frac{1}{d}$, for large graphs when $|V| \gg d$. This improves the results of [TZ11], where the authors presented a 2-approximation. But our algorithm can also be executed in an distributed way, like described in Section 4. This approximation factor of $2 - \frac{1}{d}$ matches the best known approximation factor for vertex cover in d-regular graphs [Hoc83].

For longer path length, i.e. $k \geq 3$, our algorithm unfortunately only gives an 3-approximation, for the case $k \leq \frac{d+2}{2}$. The limitations in the path length can be partially lifted up, if it is not asked for an 3-approximation, but for an α-approximation instead, for $\alpha \geq 3$. For $k \leq \frac{\alpha-2}{\alpha-1}d + 1$ our algorithm achieves an α-approximation.

One open question is, weather there is some connection of the approximation factor between the k-Observer problem in regular graphs and in general graphs, like in [Fei03]. In [Fei03] the authors show that if the vertex cover problem on d-regular graphs can be approximated with ratio c, it can be approximated with the same ratio on every graph. A similar connection for the k-Observer problem would be exciting.

Up to now, the best known approximation factor for the problem in general graphs is $k+1$. There seems to be a lot room for improvement. Also a lower bound for the approximation factor in general graphs, like in [KR08] or [BFPS15], would be interesting.

In [ACBG12] the authors especially ask for solutions for Internet-like networks, like described in [CDZ97] and [FFF99]. Although the graphs are not regular in general, and our analysis only holds for regular or bounded degree graphs, it would be nice to see how our algorithm perform on these kind of networks. In [FFF99] those kind of networks where considered, and they discover that roughly 50% of the nodes are in trees. Since our algorithm solves trees optimal, it would be interesting how far away is our solution from the optimal in these networks.

References

[ACBG12] Acharya, H.B., Choi, T., Bazzi, R.A., Gouda, M.G.: The k-observer problem in computer networks Networking. Science **1**(1–5), 15–22 (2012)

[BFPS15] Bazzi, A., Fiorini, S., Pokutta, S., Svensson, O.: No Small Linear Program Approximates Vertex Cover within a Factor 2 - ϵ. ArXiv e-prints, March 2015

[BJK+13] Brešar, B., Jakovac, M., Katrenič, J., Semanišin, G., Taranenko, A.: On the vertex k-path cover. Discrete Applied Mathematics **161**(13), 1943–1949 (2013)

[BKBSŠ14] Brešar, B., Krivoš-Belluš, R., Semanišin, G., Šparl, P.: On the weighted k-path vertex cover problem. Discrete Applied Mathematics **177**, 14–18 (2014)

[BKKS11] Brešar, B., Kardoš, F., Katrenič, J., Semanišin, G.: Minimum k-path vertex cover. Discrete Applied Mathematics **159**(12), 1189–1195 (2011)

[BL01] Boliac, R., Lozin, V.V.: On computing the dissociation number of bipartite graphs (2001)

[CDZ97] Calvert, K.L., Doar, M.B., Zegura, E.W.: Modeling internet topology. IEEE Communications Magazine **35**(6), 160–163 (1997)

[DS05] Dinur, I., Safra, S.: On the hardness of approximating minimum vertex cover. Annals of Mathematics, pp. 439–485 (2005)

[ENZ96] Even, G., Naor, J., Zosin, L.: An 8-approximation algorithm for the subset feedback vertex set problem. In: Proceedings of the 37th Annual Symposium on Foundations of Computer Science, 1996, pp. 310–319. IEEE (1996)

[Fei03] Uriel, F.: Vertex cover is hardest to approximate on regular graphs. Technical report, Citeseer (2003)

[FFF99] Faloutsos, M., Faloutsos, P., Faloutsos, C.: On power-law relationships of the internet topology. In: ACM SIGCOMM Computer Communication Review, vol. 29, pp. 251–262. ACM (1999)

[Hoc83] Dorit, S.: Hochbaum. Efficient bounds for the stable set, vertex cover and set packing problems. Discrete Applied Mathematics **6**(3), 243–254 (1983)

[KR08] Khot, S., Regev, O.: Vertex cover might be hard to approximate to within 2- ε. Journal of Computer and System Sciences **74**(3), 335–349 (2008)

[Lyn96] Lynch, N.A.: Distributed algorithms. Morgan Kaufmann (1996)

[Nov10] Novotný, M.: Design and analysis of a generalized canvas protocol. In: Samarati, P., Tunstall, M., Posegga, J., Markantonakis, K., Sauveron, D. (eds.) WISTP 2010. LNCS, vol. 6033, pp. 106–121. Springer, Heidelberg (2010)

[SJX13] Scott, A., Jeavons, P., Xu, L.: Feedback from nature: an optimal distributed algorithm for maximal independent set selection. In: Proceedings of the 2013 ACM Symposium on Principles of Distributed Computing, pp. 147–156. ACM (2013)

[TZ11] Jianhua, T., Zhou, W.: A factor 2 approximation algorithm for the vertex cover p3 problem. Information Processing Letters **111**(14), 683–686 (2011)

Functional Encryption for Cascade Automata (Extended Abstract)

Dan Brownstein[1]([✉]), Shlomi Dolev[1], and Niv Gilboa[2]

[1] Department of Computer Science, Ben-Gurion University of the Negev,
Beersheba, Israel
{danbr,dolev}@cs.bgu.ac.il
[2] Department of Communication Systems Engineering,
Ben-Gurion University of the Negev, Beersheba, Israel
gilboan@bgu.ac.il

Abstract. We introduce a functional encryption scheme based on the security of bilinear maps for the class of languages accepted by extended automata. In such an automaton, n DFAs, each with at most q states, are linked in a cascade such that the first DFA receives the input to the system and a feedback symbol from the last DFA, and in each transition the i-th DFA, $i = 1, \ldots, n$, both performs its own transition and outputs a symbol that acts as the input for DFA number $i+1 \mod n$. The state of the whole system is an n-tuple consisting of the state of each component DFA.

Our work extends the work of Waters (Crypto'12) by replacing a single DFA with a cascade. Although both models accept all regular languages, a cascade automata reduces the number of states and therefore the key size for certain regular languages by an exponential factor. In both systems, a message m is encrypted with a word w and can be decrypted only by a key that is associated with an automaton that accepts w.

Our scheme has key size $O(nq^2)$ and all its other efficiency measures including the ciphertext length, encryption and decryption times are linear in the length of w. As an example of the additional power that a cascade provides, we show a construction of a cascade that accepts a word in a regular language only if it is accompanied by a standard public key signature on that word.

Our work improves on alternative approaches using functional encryption for general circuits or programs, by either being based on weaker assumptions, i.e. bilinear maps, or by being more efficient.

Keyword: Functional Encryption

Partially supported by the Rita Altura Trust Chair in Computer Sciences, Lynne and William Frankel Center for Computer Sciences, Israel Science Foundation (grant 428/11), the Israeli Internet Association, and the Ministry of Science and Technology, Infrastructure Research in the Field of Advanced Computing and Cyber Security.

A. Pelc and A.A. Schwarzmann (Eds.): SSS 2015, LNCS 9212, pp. 94–108, 2015.
DOI: 10.1007/978-3-319-21741-3_7

1   Introduction

Functional Encryption (FE) has emerged as a major generalization of traditional public key encryption. FE schemes enable a holder of a secret key to obtain a function of the plaintext and key as opposed to to either fully decrypting the plaintext or not learning any information on it.

One of the main directions of research on functional encryption has focused on extending the class of functions that can be used. The first notion that could be associated with functional encryption is that of Identity Based Encryption [2,7,19], in which the function is a comparison between the user's identity and its key. Progressing through functions expressed as formulas [13,18] and functions expressed as regular languages [20], recent breakthroughs [9–12] have enabled constructing FE schemes for general functions.

The latest constructions in this progression do not necessarily subsume some of the earlier schemes. While they enable a richer class of functions, they sometimes rely on less established cryptographic primitives and sometimes on less efficient constructions. As a result some of the earlier schemes are attractive for applications in which only a limited class of functions is required.

In this work we revisit and extend the scheme of Waters [20] which achieves FE for regular languages. More accurately, it is a functional encryption system in which a message m is encrypted with a word w and decryption is possible if and only only if the secret key is associated with a Deterministic Finite Automaton (DFA) that accepts w.

We extend the work in [20] by replacing acceptance by a DFA with acceptance by cascade automata. In this model, n DFAs are linked in a cascade such that the first DFA receives the input to the system and a feedback input from the last DFA, and in each transition the i-th DFA, $i = 1,\ldots,n$ both performs its own transition and outputs a symbol that acts as the input for DFA number $i+1 \mod n$. The state of the whole system is an n-tuple consisting of the state of each component DFA.

We are motivated in studying this question due to applications that cascade automata enable compared to standard DFA. Specifically, as we show in [5], there exists an efficiently sized cascade automaton that verifies standard public key signatures. We can therefore use this model to encrypt messages given words that are signed by different users. A user adding its signature to a word w, in a sense accepting that word, can allow any other user that has the appropriate key to decrypt, even long after the original encryption.

Alternatives to our approach are possible using constructions that achieve general functional encryption. However, these works either rely on stronger assumptions than the bilinear maps we use such as variations of multi linear maps [8–10] or use additional primitives such as fully homomorphic encryption [9,11], which implies much larger keys and longer encryption time compared to our solution.

Gorbunov et al. [12] present a novel scheme for attribute based encryption for circuits under the learning with errors assumption [17]. In their scheme, the noise grows exponentially with the depth of the circuit and the key size is linear in the size of the circuit. It is well known that every regular language is computable by NC^1 circuits of linear size. Thus, even though the noise grows exponentially with the depth of the circuit, their scheme can be used for our purposes. However the size of a secret key in Gorbunov et al. [12] construction is linear in the size of the circuit, i.e. in our terms the length of a word w, while our scheme has key size which is proportional to the representation size of the cascade automaton accepting the language.

In [3], Boneh et al. construct a scheme for arithmetic circuit ABE with secret keys of size $O(d)$ where d is the depth of the circuit. Even though this result is better than previous constructions, the depth of circuit for inputs of length $|w|$ is $O(\log |w|)$ since the fan-in of each gate in the circuit is fixed. In our case the length of w is arbitrary which leads to secret keys of arbitrary sizes. Moreover, the size of the public-key in their construction is proportional to $|w|$, which leads to a restriction of the public index space (the word w in our setting). In contrast, in our construction it has constant size.

Contributions. Our contribution is twofold. First, we show the first FE scheme for cascade automata that is (selectively) secure based on a q-type assumption on bilinear maps. The public parameters in our scheme are of size $O(1)$. A secret key associated with a cascade automata that is comprised of n DFAs, each with at most q states, has size $O(nq^2)$. Encrypting a message to a word w of length ℓ requires $O(\ell)$ group operations and produces a ciphertext of length $O(\ell)$ and decrypting such a message requires $O(n\ell)$ group operations.

Our second contribution shows the utility of cascade automata by describing an efficient construction of cascade automata that embeds a public key for standard public key signature algorithms such as Rabin or RSA and reaches an accepting state given a string $w, s(w)$ if and only if $s(w)$ is a signature on w.

Organization. In Section 2 we provide definitions and notation. Section 3 describes the main construction of a functional encryption scheme for cascade automata and states its security (security proof can be found in [5]) and section 4 includes the construction of a cascade automaton that verifies signatures.

2   Definitions and Notations

2.1   Finite Automata

A standard Deterministic Finite Automata (DFA) has a set of states, Q, an input alphabet, Σ and a transition function and a transition function We use Mealy's formalism [14] for an extension of a DFA in which each transition outputs a symbol. We then define a Cascaded Mealy Machine based Automata, which is a sequence of Mealy machines in which the output of every MMA is the input to the next MMA in the sequence.

Notation 1. *Let* $[1, n]$ *denote the set* $\{1, \ldots, n\}$ *for* $n \in \mathbb{N}$. *In state diagrams for finite automata we use Mealy machine state diagram conventions; each edge is labeled with* $j|k$ *where* j *is the input and* k *is the output.*

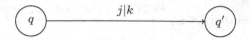

Fig. 1. Each edge is labeled with $j|k$ where j is the input and k is the output

Definition 1. *A Mealy Machine based Automata (MMA) $A = (Q, \Sigma, \delta, q_0, F)$ is a 5-tuple in which Q is a finite set of states, Σ is a finite set of symbols called the input and output alphabet and $\delta : Q \times \Sigma \to Q \times \Sigma$ is a transition and output function. The distinguished state $q_0 \in Q$ is called the start state and $F \subseteq Q$ is a set of accepting states. We say that a A accepts a string $w = (w_1, \ldots, w_\ell) \in \Sigma^*$ if there exists a sequence of states $r_0, \ldots, r_\ell \in Q$ s.t.*

1. *$r_0 = q_0$.*
2. *$\delta(r_i, w_i) = (r_{i+1}, \varphi_i)$, for $i \in [0, \ell - 1]$.*
3. *$r_\ell \in F$.*

Notation 2. *Given an MMA $A = (Q, \Sigma, \delta, q_0, F)$ we say that T_A is the set of transitions of A and define it by $T_A \overset{\triangle}{=} \{t = (x, y, \sigma, \varphi) | x, y \in Q, \sigma, \varphi \in \Sigma, \delta(x, \sigma) = (y, \varphi)\}$.*

In the following definition of CMMA, the set of states, the subset of accepting states and the initial states are all Cartesian products of the appropriate states in the component MMAs. The transition function links the input and output of the MMAs.

Definition 2. *A Cascade Mealy Machine based Automata (CMMA), CA, over a sequence of n MMAs $A1, \ldots, An$ s.t. $(A_j = (Q_j, \Sigma, \delta_j, q_{0j}, F_j))$ is a 5-tuple $(Q, \Sigma, \delta, q_0, F)$ in which $Q = Q_1 \times \ldots \times Q_n$, Σ is the input and output alphabet of all component MMAs and the transition (and output) function $\delta : Q \times \Sigma \to Q \times \Sigma$ is defined by $\delta(x, \sigma) = (y, \varphi_n)$ where $x = (x_1, \ldots, x_n) \in Q$, $\sigma \in \Sigma$, $y = (y_1, \ldots, y_n) \in Q$ and $\varphi_n \in \Sigma$, such that*

$$\sigma_1 = \sigma \text{ and } \delta_i(x_i, \sigma_i) = (y_i, \varphi_i) \text{ where } \varphi_i = \sigma_{i+1},$$

for every $i \in [1, n-1]$. The distinguished start state is $q_0 = q_{01}, \ldots, q_{0n}$ and the set of accepting states is $F = F_1 \times, \ldots, \times F_n$. We say that a ECMMA CA accepts a string $w = (w_1, \ldots, w_\ell) \in \Sigma^*$ if there exists a sequence of states $r_0, \ldots, r_\ell \in Q$ s.t.

1. *$r_0 = q_0$.*
2. *$\delta(r_i, w_i) = (r_{i+1}, \varphi_i)$, for $i \in [0, \ell - 1]$.*
3. *$r_\ell \subset F$.*

Fig. 2 illustrates the i'th transition of a CMMA.

Let CA be a CMMA over the sequence $(A_1, \ldots, A_n)$ of MMAs. A natural implementation using the representation of CA as n MMAs leads to storage that is the sum of the storage requirements for every A_j, $j \in [1, n]$. However, each

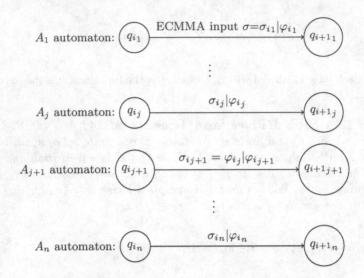

Fig. 2. Outputs of A_j are inputs of A_{j+1}

transition in CA requires n MMA transitions, one in each component. A different approach is to explicitly represent Q as $\Pi_{j=1}^{n}|Q_j|$. In such an implementation, each transition requires $O(1)$ time but the required storage is exponential in n.

The following definition of ECMMA expands the CMMA definition so it supports loops and feedback input. The transition function links the input and output of the MMAs. In addition, he transition function of the first MMA takes into consideration the output of the last MMA (feedback).

Definition 3. *An Expanded Cascade Mealy Machine based Automata (ECMMA), ECA, over a sequence of n MMAs $A1, \dots, An$ s.t. $A_1 = (Q_1, \Sigma \times \Sigma, \delta_1, q_{01}, F_1)$, $\forall j > 1$ $A_j = (Q_j, \Sigma, \delta_j, q_{0j}, F_j))$ is a 5-tuple $(Q, \Sigma, \delta, q_0, F)$ in which $Q = Q_1 \times \dots \times Q_n$, $\Sigma \times \Sigma$ is the input alphabet for the first component MMA, Σ is the output alphabet for the first component MMA and the input and output alphabet of all other component MMAs and the transition (and output) function $\delta : Q \times \Sigma \times \Sigma \to Q \times \Sigma$ is defined by $\delta(x, \sigma, \sigma') = (y, \varphi_n)$ where $x = (x_1, \dots, x_n) \in Q$, $\sigma, \sigma' \in \Sigma$, $y = (y_1, \dots, y_n) \in Q$ and $\varphi_n \in \Sigma$, such that*

$$\sigma_1 = \sigma \quad \sigma'_1 = \sigma_1$$
$$\delta_1(x_1, \sigma_1, \sigma'_1) = (y_1, \varphi_1)$$
$$\forall i \in [2, n] \ \delta_i(x_i, \sigma_i) = (y_i, \varphi_i) \text{ where } \sigma_i = \varphi_{i-1}$$

The distinguished start state is $q_0 = q_{01}, \dots, q_{0n}$ and the set of accepting states is $F = F_1 \times, \dots, \times F_n$. We say that a ECMMA ECA accepts the input $w = (w_1, \dots, w_\ell), w' = (w'_1, \dots, w'_\ell) \in \Sigma^* \times \Sigma^*$ if there exists a sequence of states $r_0, \dots, r_\ell \in Q$ s.t.

1. $r_0 = q_0$.
2. for $i \in [0, \ell - 1]$ $\delta(r_i, w_i, w_i') = (r_{i+1}, \varphi_i)$, s.t for $i \in [0, \ell - 2]$ $w_{i+1}' = \varphi_i$.
3. $r_\ell \in F$.

In our ECMMAs w_1' and $\varphi_{\ell-1}$ are insignificant in the sense that at the first transition the feedback w_1' is ignored and at the last transition the output $\varphi_{\ell-1}$ is not used in further steps. Since $\forall i > 1$ w_i' is defined by the transition function we will use only w as the input for our ECMMAs.

2.2 Functional Encryption for ECMMA

In this section we define a functional Encryption scheme for languages that areaccepted by a ECMMA. In our system, a ciphertext CT encrypts a message m and is associated with string w of arbitrary length. A secret key SK is associated with a ECMMA, ECA. A user is able to decrypt the ciphertext CT iff the ECMMA, ECA, associated with the user's private key, SK, accepts the string w. We use the terminology of [4] to define the system. By this terminology we devise a predicate encryption scheme with public index, since the string w is not hidden. The system consists of four algorithms: Setup, Encrypt, KeyGen and Decrypt described as follows:

Setup$(1^\kappa, \Sigma)$. The setup algorithm takes as input a security parameter κ and a description of a finite alphabet Σ. The alphabet is shared across the entire system. The algorithm outputs the public parameters PP and a master key MSK.

Encrypt(PP, w, m). The encryption algorithm takes as input the public parameters PP, an arbitrary length string $w \in \Sigma^*$ and a message m. It outputs a ciphertext CT.

Key Generation(MSK, ECA). The key generation algorithm takes as input the master key MSK and a ECMMA description $ECA = (A_1, \ldots, A_n)$. The description does not include the alphabet Σ since it is already determined by the setup algorithm.

Decrypt(SK, CT). The decryption algorithm takes as input a secret key SK and ciphertext CT. The algorithm attempts to decrypt and outputs a message m if successful. Otherwise, it outputs a special symbol $\perp$.

The scheme must satisfy the following correctness and security requirements.
Correctness. For any message m, string w and ECMMA ECA s.t. $Accept(ECA, w)$, If $Setup \rightarrow (PP, MSK)$, $Encrypt(PP, w, m) \rightarrow CT$ and $KeyGen(MSK, ECA) \rightarrow SK$, then $Decrypt(SK, CT) = m$.

Security. We describe a game based security definition for ECMMA-Based Functional Encryption.

setup: The challenger runs the setup algorithm, gives the public parameters, PP to the adversary and keeps the master secret key, MSK.

Phase 1: The adversary makes a polynomial number of private key queries for ECMMA of its choice. For any request ECA, the challenger returns $SK = KeyGen(MSK, ECA)$.

Challenge: The adversary submits two equal length messages m_0 and m_1. In addition, the adversary gives a challenge string w^* such that for all ECA requested in Phase 1, $Reject(ECA, w^*)$. Then, the challenger flips a coin $b \in \{0, 1\}$ and computes $Encrypt(PP, w^*, m_b) \to CT^*$. The challenge ciphertext CT^* is given to the adversary.

Phase 2: Phase 1 is repeated with the restriction that for all ECA requested $Reject(ECA, w^*)$.

Guess: The adversary outputs a guess $b' \in \{0, 1\}$.

The advantage of an adversary $\mathcal{A}$ in this game is defined as $|\Pr[b' = b] - \frac{1}{2}|$. A ECMMA-based Functional Encryption system is secure if all PPT adversaries have advantage less than κ^{-c} in the above game, for any constant $c > 0$.

In our security proof we use a weaker security model known as *selective security*. In this model we add an Init stage at the beginning of the game where the attacker must declare upfront what the challenge string w^* and the alphabet Σ will be, before seeing the public parameters.

2.3 Threshold-ℓ − $BDHE$ Assumption

We extend Waters' [20] decision ℓ-Expanded Bilinear Diffie-Hellman Exponent problem. Our extended problem is defined as follows. Let $\mathbb{G}, \mathbb{G}_T$ be two groups of prime order $p > 2^\kappa$ for a security parameter κ such that $e : \mathbb{G} \times \mathbb{G} \to \mathbb{G}_T$ is a bilinear mapping. Choose random $s, a, b_1, b', c_0, \ldots, c_{\ell+1}, d \in \mathbb{Z}_p^*$, a random $g \in \mathbb{G}$ and set $b = b_1 + b'$. Suppose an adversary is given $X =$

$$g^b$$

$$g, g^a, g^{ab_1/d}, g^{ab'/d}, g^{b_1/d}, g^{b'/d}$$

$$\forall_{i \in [0, 2\ell+1], i \neq \ell+1, e \in [0, \ell+1]} \ g^{a^i s}, g^{a^i b_1 s / c_e}$$

$$\forall_{i \in [0, 2\ell+1], e \in [0, \ell+1]} \ g^{a^i b' s / c_e}, g^{a^i b_1 d / c_e}, g^{a^i b' d / c_e}$$

$$\forall_{i \in [0, \ell+1]} \ g^{a^i b_1 / c_i}, g^{a^i b' / c_i}, g^{c_i}, g^{a^i d}, g^{ab_1 c_i / d}, g^{ab' c_i / d}, g^{b_1 c_i / d}, g^{b' c_i / d}$$

$$\forall_{i, e \in [0, \ell+1], i \neq e} \ g^{a^i b_1 c_e / c_i}, g^{a^i b' c_e / c_i}$$

then it must be hard to distinguish $e(g, g)^{a^{\ell+1} bs} \in \mathbb{G}_T$ from a random element $R \in \mathbb{G}_T$.

We say that an algorithm B that outputs $z \in \{0, 1\}$ has advantage ϵ in solving the threshold- ℓ − $BDHE$ problem in $\mathbb{G}$ if

$$\left| Pr\left[B(X, T = e(g, g)^{a^{\ell+1} bs}) = 1 \right] - Pr\left[B(X, T = R) = 1 \right] \right| \geq \epsilon$$

Definition 4. *We say that the Threshold ℓ-BDHE assumption holds if no poly-time algorithm has advantage κ^{-c} in solving the problem for some $c > 0$.*

3   ECMMA-Based Functional Encryption Scheme Construction

3.1   Intuition

Our scheme extends the work of Waters [20], which presented a system of functional encryption for regular languages. In this system a secret key is associated with a deterministic finite automaton (DFA) A. A ciphertext CT encrypts a message m and is associated with an arbitrary length string w. A user is able to decrypt the ciphertext CT if and only if the DFA A associated with his private key accepts the string w.

As we showed in section 2, an ECMMA ECA over a sequence $(A_1, \ldots, A_n)$ of MMAs can be implemented as an MMA A' by defining the set of states of A' as the product of the states of A_j $\forall j \in [1, n]$ and explicitly storing each such state. Theoretically this makes it possible to apply functional encryption using Waters' scheme on every ECMMA by converting it to an MMA and ignoring the output (which leaves us with a DFA). However, the algorithms in [20] depend on the size of the DFA which in this case grows exponentially with each n resulting in an infeasible scheme.

A different approach would be to use Waters' system for each of the MMAs A_j independently. In this scheme, the encryption algorithm divides m into n shares. Each share is associated with an MMA. By applying Waters' system on each MMA separately, the decryption algorithm retrieve the shares and reconstructs m. However, with this approach, during the decryption algorithm, it is impossible to assert that the outputs of A_j are indeed the inputs for A_{j+1}. Therefore, an attacker who has two keys associated with ECA_1 and ECA_2 such that ECA_1 includes $A_1, \ldots, A_j$ and ECA_2 includes $A_{j+1}, \ldots, A_n$ is able to decrypt a message, even though the word w is not accepted by either of its ECMMAs.

In Waters' system, when encrypting a ciphertext for a string w of ℓ symbols, the encrypting algorithm chooses $\ell + 1$ random exponents $s_0, s_1, \ldots, s_\ell \in \mathbb{Z}_p$ where p is the order of the group. A private key associated with an automaton $A = (Q, \Sigma, \delta, q_0, F)$ has $|Q|$ random group elements, $D_0, \ldots, D_{|Q|-1}$, from a bilinear group $\mathbb{G}$, where D_x is associated with state q_x. Suppose a decryption algorithm is applied to decrypt a ciphertext associated with string w with a secret key SK for automaton A. Throughout the process of decryption the algorithm can only compute $e(g, D_x)^{s_i}$ if A is in state q_x after reading i symbols of w. We can think of this as chaining between the state q_x that A lands on after reading i symbols of w and the computed value $e(g, D_x)^{s_i}$.

In our solution we add another level of chaining: the assertion that the outputs of A_j are used as the inputs of A_{j+1} for each MMA. In each transition of the MMA A_{j+1} with input of φ we use a random value R' to blind the value $e(g, D_x)^{s_i}$ by computing $R' \cdot e(g, D_x)^{s_i}$. In each transition of the MMA A_j with output of φ we blind the $e(g, D_x)^{s_i}$ value by computing $(R')^{-1} \cdot e(g, D_x)^{s_i}$. Values corresponding to inputs are reciprocals of values corresponding to outputs. Hence, multiplying decrypted values from consecutive MMAs will get rid of these blinding values iff the output-input property is satisfied.

102   D. Brownstein et al.

Efficiency. We now give an overview of the time/space complexity of our scheme. Given a message m, string w, and ECMMA ECA such that $Accept(ECA,w)$. If $Encrypt(PP,w,m) \to CT$ and $KeyGen(MSK,CA) \to SK$ where PP, MSK were generated from a call to *Setup* algorithm, where $|w|$ is the length of the string associated with the cypher-text, $|F_j|$ is the number of accept states of the $j'th$ MMA, A_j, $|T_j|$ is the number of transitions (x,y,σ,φ) in A_j and $|T_j'|$ is the number of transitions in A_{j+1} (x',y',σ',φ') s.t $\varphi = \sigma'$. The public parameters contain $6 + |\Sigma|$ group elements . The cypher-text contains $5 + 3|w|$ group elements. The encryption operation requires takes $5 + 4|w|$ exponentiations. A private key contains $\sum_{j=1}^{n} [2 + 2|F_j| + |T_j| * (2 + |T_j'|)]$ group elements. A successful decryption itself requires $n * (4 + 3|w|)$ bilinear pairing operations.

3.2 Algorithms

Setup$(1^\kappa, n, \Sigma)$. The setup algorithm takes as input the security parameter κ, the number of automata, n and alphabet Σ. It first chooses a prime $p > 2^\kappa$ and creates a bilinear group $\mathbb{G}$ of prime order p. It then chooses random group elements $g \in \mathbb{G}$ and for every $j \in [1,n]$ it chooses randomly and independently $h_{startj}, h_{endj}, z_j, H_j \in \mathbb{G}$. In addition, for every $\sigma \in \Sigma$ it chooses random $h_\sigma \in \mathbb{G}$. Finally, an exponent $\alpha \in \mathbb{Z}_p$ is randomly chosen. The public parameters PP are the description of the group $\mathbb{G}$ and the alphabet Σ along with : $e(g,g)^\alpha, g, \forall j \in [1,n]$ $h_{startj}, h_{endj}, z_j, H_j, \forall_{\sigma \in \Sigma} h_\sigma$. The Master Secret Key MSK is α along with the public parameters.

Encrypt$(PP, w = (w_1, \ldots, w_\ell), m)$. The encryption algorithm takes as input the public parameters PP, an arbitrary length string $w \in \Sigma^*$, and a message $m \in \mathbb{G}$. The encryption algorithm chooses $\ell + 1$ random numbers $s_0, \ldots, s_\ell \in \mathbb{Z}_p$. First, it sets:

$$C_m = m \cdot e(g,g)^{\alpha \cdot s_\ell}$$
$$C_{start1} = C_{0,1} = g^{s_0}, \quad \forall j \in [1,n] \; C_{start2j} = (h_{startj})^{s_0}$$

Then, for $i = 1$ to ℓ it sets:

$$C_{i,1} = g^{s_i}, \quad C_{i,2} = (h_{w_i})^{s_i}(z_1)^{s_{i-1}}, \quad \forall j \in [2,n] \; C_{i,3_j} = (H_j)^{s_i}(z_j)^{s_{i-1}}$$

Finally, it sets:

$$C_{end1} = C_{\ell,1} = g^{s_\ell}, \quad \forall j \in [1,n] \; C_{end2j} = (h_{endj})^{s_\ell}$$

The output ciphertext is:

$$CT = \Big(w, C_m, C_{start1}, \forall j \in [1,n] \; C_{start2j},$$
$$\forall i \in [1,\ell] \; (C_{i,1}, C_{i,2}, \forall j \in [2,n] \; C_{i,3_j}), \; C_{end1}, \forall j \in [2,n] \; C_{end2j} \Big)$$

$KeyGen(MSK, ECA = (A_1, \ldots, A_n))$. The key generation algorithm takes as input the master secret key and the description of a ECMMA, ECA. For each MMA $A_j \in ECA$ the description of A_j includes a set Q_j of states $q_{0j}, \ldots, q_{|Q_j|-1_j}$ and a set of transitions T_j where each transition $t_j \in T_j$ is a 4-tuple $(x_j, y_j, \sigma, \varphi) \in Q_j \times Q_j \times \Sigma \times \Sigma$. In addition, q_{0j} is designated as a unique start state and $F_j \subseteq Q_j$ is the set of accept states. For each MMA A_j the algorithm:

1. Chooses a random element $r_{start_j} \in \mathbb{Z}_p$, $|Q_j|$ random group elements $D_{0j}, \ldots, D_{|Q_j|-1_j} \in \mathbb{G}$ where D_{ij} is associated with the state q_{ij} and random elements $r_{t_j} \in \mathbb{Z}_p$ and $R_{t_j} \in \mathbb{G}$ for every $t_j = (x_j, y_j, \sigma, \varphi) \in T_j$. Then, it sets:

$$j = 1 \quad K_{start11} = \{D_{01}(h_{start1})^{r_{start1}} R_{t1} | \forall t_1 = (x_1, y_1, \sigma, \varphi) \text{ where } x_1 = q_{01}\}$$
$$\forall j \in [2, n] \quad K_{start1j} = D_{0j}(h_{startj})^{r_{startj}}$$
$$\forall j \quad K_{start2j} = g^{r_{startj}}$$

2. For every $t_j = (x_j, y_j, \sigma, \varphi) \in T_j$ the algorithm sets $K_{t_j,1}, K_{t_j,2}, K_{t_jt'}$. Let T'_{j+1} denote the set of all transitions in A_{j+1} that can be initiated by the transition t_j in A_j in a cyclic manner. Formally, $\forall j \in [1, n-1] \; T'_{j+1} = \{t_{j+1} = (x_{j+1}, y_{j+1}, \sigma', \varphi') \in T_{j+1} | \varphi = \sigma'\}$, for $j = n \; T'_{j+1} = \{t_1 = (x_1, y_1, \sigma', \varphi') \in T_1 | \varphi = \sigma'\}$. The second element, $K_{t_j,2}$, is set in the same way for all MMAs, $A_1, \ldots, A_n$:

$$K_{t_j,2} = g^{r_{t_j}}$$

The first element, $K_{t_j,1}$, has two different versions, one for A_1 and a second one for $A_2, \ldots, A_n$:

$$j = 1 \quad K_{t_1,1} = (D_{x1})^{-1} z_1{}^{r_{t1}} R_{t1}{}^{-1}$$
$$\forall j \in [2, n] \quad K_{t_j,1} = (D_{xj})^{-1} z_j{}^{r_{t_j}}$$

The third element, $K_{t_jt'}$, also has two different versions, one for A_1 and a second one for $A_2, \ldots, A_n$. KeyGen computes $K_{t_jt'}$ as follows:

$$j = 1 \quad K_{t_1t'} = \{D_{y_1}(h_\sigma)^{r_{t1}} R_{t2} | \forall t_2 \in T'_2\}$$
$$\forall j \in [2, n] \quad K_{t_jt'} = \{D_{y_j}(H_j)^{r_{t_j}} R_{t_j}{}^{-1} R_{t_{j+1}} | \forall t_{j+1} \in T'_{j+1}\}$$

3. The algorithm chooses $n - 1$ random exponents $\alpha_j \in \mathbb{Z}_p$ for $j = 1, \ldots, n-1$ and sets $\alpha_n = \alpha - \sum_{u=1}^{n-1} \alpha_u$. Then the algorithm chooses random $r_{end_xj} \in \mathbb{Z}_p$, for all $j = 1, \ldots, n$ and all $q_{xj} \in F_j$.

Finally, $\forall q_{xj} \in F_j$ the algorithm sets:

$$\forall j \in [1, n-1] \quad K_{end_x,1j} = g^{-\alpha_j} \cdot D_{xj}(h_{endj})^{r_{end_xj}}$$
$$j = n \quad K_{end_x,1n} = \{g^{-\alpha_n} \cdot D_{xn}(h_{endn})^{r_{end_xn}} R_{t1}{}^{-1} | \forall t_1 \in T'_{n+1}$$
$$\text{for each } t_n = (x_n, y_n, \sigma, \varphi) \text{ where } y_n = q_{xn}\}$$
$$\forall j \quad K_{end_x,2j} = g^{r_{end_xj}}$$

The output secret key is:

$$SK = \Big(ECA, \forall j \in [1,n] \; [K_{start1j}, K_{start2j}, \forall t_j \in T_j \; (K_{t_j,1}, K_{t_j,2}, K_{t_j t'}),$$

$$\forall q_{xj} \in F_j \; (K_{end_x,1j}, K_{end_x,2j})]\Big)$$

Decrypt(SK, CT). Let $SK = KeyGen(MSK, ECA)$ for some ECMMA, ECA, such that $Accept(ECA, w)$ and let $CT = Encrypt(PP, w, m)$. Then, for every A_j and for all $i = 1, \ldots, \ell$ there exists a sequence of $\ell+1$ states $r_{0j}, \ldots, r_{\ell j} \in Q_j$, $r_{0j} = q_{0j}$, and ℓ transitions $t_{1j}, \ldots, t_{\ell j} \in T_j$ such that $t_{ij} = (r_{ij}, r_{i+1j}, w_{ij}, w_{ij+1}) \in T_j$ where $w_{i1} = w_i$, the outputs of the last MMA used as feedback for the first MMA and $r_{\ell j} \in F_j$.

1. Let $K'_{start11}$ be the single element from $K_{start11}$ which corresponds to the transition t_{11}. The algorithm first computes:

$$B_{01} = e(C_{start1}, K'_{start11}) \cdot e(C_{start21}, K_{start21})^{-1} = e(g, D_{01})^{s_0} e(g, R_{t11})^{s_0}$$

$$\forall j \in [2,n] \; B_{0j} = e(C_{start1}, K_{start1j}) \cdot e(C_{start2j}, K_{start2j})^{-1} = e(g, D_{0j})^{s_0}$$

2. Then, for $i = 1$ to ℓ the algorithm iteratively computes:
   (a) Let $K_{t_{ij}}$ be the single element from $K_{t_j t'}$ where $t = t_{ij}$ and $t' = t_{ij+1}$.
   (b) For the first MMA A_1:

$$B_{i1} = B_{i-11} \cdot e(C_{(i-1),1}, K_{t_i,11}) \cdot e(C_{i,2}, K_{t_i,21})^{-1} \cdot e(C_{i,1}, K_{t_i1})$$

   (c) For all other MMAs $A_2, \ldots, A_n$:

$$B_{ij} = B_{i-1j} \cdot e(C_{(i-1),1}, K_{t_i,1j}) \cdot e(C_{i,3j}, K_{t_i,2j})^{-1} \cdot e(C_{i,1}, K_{t_{ij}})$$

3. Then, the algorithm computes:

$$B_\ell = \prod_{j=1}^{n} B_{\ell j} = e(g, R_{t\ell 1})^{s_\ell} \prod_{j=1}^{n} e(g, D_{r_\ell j})^{s_\ell}$$

4. Let $K'_{end_x,1_n}$ be the single element from $K_{end_x,1_n}$ which corresponds to the transition $t_{\ell n}$. Finally, the algorithm computes:

$$B_{end} = B_\ell \cdot e(C_{end1}, K'_{end_x,1_n})^{-1} \cdot e(C_{end2n}, K_{end_x,2n}) \cdot$$

$$\prod_{j=2}^{n} [e(C_{end1}, K_{end_x,1j})^{-1} \cdot e(C_{end2j}, K_{end_x,2j})]$$

$$= e(g,g)^{\alpha s_\ell}$$

Which can be used to retrieve the message m from C_m.

3.3 Main Theorem

We prove the following lemmas in [5].

Lemma 1. *Let $m \in \mathbb{Z}_p, w \in \{0,1\}^*$, ECA be a ECMMA with n MMAs such that Accept(ECA, w) and let $\kappa \in \mathbb{N}$ be a security parameter. If Encrypt(PP, w, m) $\rightarrow$ CT and KeyGen(MSK, ECA) $\rightarrow$ SK where Setup($1^\kappa, n, \Sigma$) $\rightarrow$ PP, MSK then Decrypt(SK, CT) = m.*

Lemma 2. *The threshold $\ell - BDHE$ Assumption is generically secure using the result of Boneh et. al [1] on generic bilinear groups.*

We prove security of our construction in the selective mode. We show a reduction algorithm $\mathcal{B}$, that given a successful attacker $\mathcal{A}$ against our system, will use it to break the threshold ℓ^*-BDHE assumption where ℓ^* is the length of w^*, the challenge ciphertext. The reduction simulates the Setup, Encryption and Key Generation algorithms.

Lemma 3. *If the threshold ℓ^*-BDHE assumption holds then no poly-time adversary can selectively break our ECMMA-based encryption system for n MMAs, each with at most q states, where the challenge string w^* is of length ℓ^* and n and q are polynomial in the security parameter κ.*

Theorem 1. *Our construction is a functional encryption system for ECMMA which is selectively secure under the threshold ℓ-BDHE assumption. For a ECMMA with n levels and at most q states in each level, the size of a public key in the construction is a constant number of group elements and the size of a secret key is $O(nq^2)$ group elements.*

The proof of theorem 1 is immediate from lemmas 1, 2, 3 and the construction.

4 Compact Signature Verification ECMMA

In the standard method of hash then sign, the inputs for a signature verification algorithm are an arbitrary length word w and a signature $sign(H(w))$, where H is a collision-resistant hash function and $sign$ is a digital signature algorithm. The output is 1 if $sign(H(w))$ is a valid signature of $H(w)$ and 0 otherwise. We can use Waters' scheme to construct an FE scheme for that functionality by constructing a DFA for the language of pairs $(w, sign(w))$ of an arbitrary length word w and a valid signature $sign(H(w))$. Intuitively, the size of a DFA for this language cannot be small, otherwise an adversary would be able to find a path between the start and accepting states and retrieve a valid pair $(w, sign(H(w))$ in time proportional to the DFA size.

We show an efficient ECMMA that accepts the language $w, sign(H(w))$, where H is the discrete-log based hash function proposed by Chaum et al [6] and $sign$ is the Rabin signature scheme [16]. Our methods readily extend to other signature schemes that require modular exponentiation such as RSA. In our construction each MMA computes a modular arithmetic operation. It takes as input the arguments for the operation and outputs the result of the operation on the inputs to the next MMA. We use the Montgomery reduction [15] for modular multiplication and exponentiation. We now show high level construction of an expanded cascade automaton that verifies signatures. In [5] we prove the following theorem:

Theorem 2. *Let M be a product of two prime numbers, let H denote the hash function of [6] over modulus $p, p < M$ and let sign denote the Rabin digital signature scheme with modulus M. Then, there exists a signature verification ECMMA of size $O(M^2)$ that takes as input an arbitrary length word w and a signature $sign(H(w))$ and accepts iff $sign(H(w))$ is a valid signature of $H(w)$.*

In order to prove theorem 2 we state several lemmas and give proof sketches for each of them. Detailed construction and proofs appear in [5]. In the following we regard an ECMMA as computing a function f, e.g. exponentiation or hash, in the sense that given an input x the output of the last MMA is $f(x)$.

Lemma 4. *Given a modular exponentiation ECMMA of size $O(M^2)$ and a modular multiplication ECMMA of size $O(M^2)$ there exists a hash ECMMA of size $O(M^2)$.*

Proof (sketch). Recall that the hash function of Chaum et al. [6] is defined as follows. Let p, q be two large primes such that $q | p - 1$. Let α and β be two random generators of a sub-group of $\mathbb{Z}_p^*$ of order q. The value $log_\alpha \beta$ is not public. The hash function $H : \{0, \ldots, q - 1\} \times \{0, \ldots, q - 1\} \to \mathbb{Z}_p \backslash \{0\}$ is defined as: $H(X_1, X_2) = \alpha^{X_1} \beta^{X_2} \mod p$. In order to calculate a hash function of arbitrary length inputs, we use Chaum's scheme as the internal block of the Merkle-Damgård construction.

The input to the ECMMA is $w = X_1, \ldots, X_n$ and the output is the hash value $h(w)$. Let i be the loop's iteration's index. At the first iteration, $i = 1$, the input (X_1) is echoed to the feedback input and the feedback input is ignored. At the second iteration, $i = 2$, the ECMMA uses the exponentiation ECMMA to compute $\alpha^{X_1} \mod p$, feeds this output together with X_2 to a second exponentiation ECMMA to compute $\beta^{X_2} \mod p$ and feeds both results to the multiplication ECMMA to compute their product. At each iteration $i > 2$, the input is X_i, the feedback input is $h(h(\ldots(h(X_1, X_2), \ldots), X_{i-1})$ and the output is $h(h(\ldots(h(X_1, X_2), \ldots), X_i)$. The final output of the last MMA is the hash value.

Lemma 5. *There exists a modular multiplication ECMMA of size $O(M^2)$ where M is the modulus.*

Montgomery Multiplication [15]. Let M be a positive integer and let R and T be integers such that $R > m, gcd(M, R) = 1$ and $0 \leq T < MR$. A Montgomery reduction of T modulo M with respect to R is a method to compute $TR^{-1} \mod M$. If M is presented as a base b integer of length len, then a typical choice for R is b^{len}. In this case, the condition that $gcd(M, R) = 1$ will hold only if $gcd(M, b) = 1$. In our case, M is odd and $b = 2$ so $R = b^{len}$ suffices.

Algorithm 1 uses the Montgomery reduction to compute the Montgomery product of two integers.

Algorithm 1. Montgomery Multiplication. $MMUL(X, Y)$

INPUT: n-bits integer M, integers X, Y s.t $(M > X, Y, M$ is odd$)$
OUTPUT: $XY2^{-n}$ mod M

1: $Z = 0$
2: **for** $i = 0$ to $n - 1$ **do**
3:    $Z = Z + X_i Y$
4:    **if** Z is odd **then**
5:       $Z = Z + M$
6:    **end if**
7:    $Z = Z/2$
8: **end for**
9: **if** $Z \geq M$ **then**
10:   $Z = Z - M$
11: **end if**
12: **return** Z

We prove this lemma by constructing an ECMMA for Montgomery Multiplication. Our ECMMA is made up of several CMMAs, which compute "basic" operations in the Montgomery multiplication algorithm such as addition modulo M or multiplication of a bit and an integer. Using similar techniques we construct an ECMMA for Montgomery modular exponentiation.

We can now prove (sketch) theorem 2:

Proof (Sketch Theorem 2). The ECMMA takes as input an arbitrary length word w and a signature of its hash value $sign(H(w))$. In Rabin's algorithm, verifying a signature $sign(w')$ of word w' is done simply by computing $sign(w')^2$ mod M and comparing this value with w'. First, the ECMMA calculates $H(w)$ using the construction from lemma 4. It then calculates $sign(H(w))^2$ using the construction from lemma 5 and then compares these values.

References

1. Boneh, D., Boyen, X., Goh, E.-J.: Hierarchical identity based encryption with constant size ciphertext. In: Cramer, R. (ed.) Advances in Cryptology EUROCRYPT 2005. LNCS, vol. 3494, pp. 440–456. Springer, Heidelberg (2005)
2. Boneh, D., Franklin, M.: Identity-based encryption from the weil pairing. In: Kilian, J. (ed.) Advances in Cryptology – CRYPTO 2001. LNCS, vol. 2139, pp. 213–229. Springer, Heidelberg (2001)

3. Boneh, D., Gentry, C., Gorbunov, S., Halevi, S., Nikolaenko, V., Segev, G., Vaikuntanathan, V., Vinayagamurthy, D.: Fully key-homomorphic encryption, arithmetic circuit ABE and compact garbled circuits. In: Nguyen, P.Q., Oswald, E. (eds.) Advances in Cryptology – EUROCRYPT 2014. LNCS, vol. 8441, pp. 533–556. Springer, Heidelberg (2014)
4. Boneh, D., Sahai, A., Waters, B.: Functional encryption: definitions and challenges. In: Ishai, Y. (ed.) Theory of Cryptography. LNCS, vol. 6597, pp. 253–273. Springer, Heidelberg (2011)
5. Brownstein, D., Dolev, S., gilboa, N.: Functional encryption for cascade automata. Technical report, Department of Computer science Ben-Gurion University of the Negev
6. Chaum, D., van Heijst, E., Pfitzmann, B.: Cryptographically strong undeniable signatures, unconditionally secure for the signer. In: Feigenbaum, J. (ed.) CRYPTO 1991. LNCS, vol. 576, pp. 470–484. Springer, Heidelberg (1992)
7. Cocks, C.: An identity based encryption scheme based on quadratic residues. In: Honary, B. (ed.) Cryptography and Coding 2001. LNCS, vol. 2260, pp. 360–363. Springer, Heidelberg (2001)
8. Garg, S., Gentry, C., Halevi, S.: Candidate multilinear maps from ideal lattices. In: Johansson, T., Nguyen, P.Q. (eds.) Advances in Cryptology – EUROCRYPT 2013. LNCS, vol. 7881, pp. 1–17. Springer, Heidelberg (2013)
9. Garg, S., Gentry, C., Halevi, S., Raykova, M., Sahai, A.,Waters, B.: Candidate indistinguishability obfuscation and functional encryption forall circuits. In: FOCS 2013, pp. 40–49
10. Garg, S., Gentry, C., Halevi, S., Sahai, A., Waters, B.: Attribute-based encryption for circuits from multilinear maps. In: Canetti, R., Garay, J.A. (eds.) Advances in Cryptology – CRYPTO 2013. LNCS, vol. 8043, pp. 479–499. Springer, Heidelberg (2013)
11. Goldwasser, S., Kalai, Y.T., Popa, R.A., Vaikuntanathan, V., Zeldovich, N.: Reusable garbled circuits and succinct functional encryption. In: STOC 2013, pp. 555–564
12. Gorbunov, S., Vaikuntanathan, V., Wee, H.: Attribute-based encryption for circuits. In: STOC 2013, pp. 545–554
13. Goyal, V., Pandey, O., Sahai, A., Waters, B.: Attribute-based encryption for fine-grained access control of encrypted data. In: CCS 2006, pp. 89–98
14. Mealy, G.H.: A method for synthesizing sequential circuits. Bell Systems Technical Journal
15. Montgomery, P.L.: Modular multiplication without trial division. In: Mathematics of Computation, vol. 44, pp. 519–521. American Mathematical Society (1985)
16. Rabin, M.O.: Digitalized signatures and public-key functions as intractable as factorization. Technical report, MIT
17. Regev, O.: On lattices, learning with errors, random linear codes, and cryptography. In: STOC 2005, pp. 84–93
18. Sahai, A., Waters, B.: Fuzzy identity-based encryption. In: Cramer, R. (ed.) Advances in Cryptology – EUROCRYPT 2005. LNCS, vol. 3494, pp. 457–473. Springer, Heidelberg (2005)
19. Shamir, A.: Identity-based cryptosystems and signature schemes. In: Blakely, G.R., Chaum, D. (eds.) CRYPTO 1984. LNCS, vol. 196, pp. 47–53. Springer, Heidelberg (1985)
20. Waters, B.: Functional encryption for regular languages. In: Safavi-Naini, R., Canetti, R. (eds.) Advances in Cryptology – CRYPTO 2012. LNCS, vol. 7417, pp. 218–235. Springer, Heidelberg (2012)

The Implication Problem of Computing Policies

Rezwana Reaz[1]([✉]), Muqeet Ali[1], Mohamed G. Gouda[1],
Marijn J.H. Heule[1], and Ehab S. Elmallah[2]

[1] University of Texas at Austin, Austin, TX 78712, USA
{rezwana,muqeet,gouda,marijn}@cs.utexas.edu
[2] University of Alberta, Edmonton, AB T6G 2R3, Canada
elmallah@ualberta.ca

Abstract. A computing policy is a sequence of rules, where each rule consists of a predicate and an action, and where each action is either "accept" or "reject". A policy P is said to accept (or reject, respectively) a request iff the action of the first rule in P, that is matched by the request is "accept" (or "reject", respectively). A pair of policies (P, Q) is called an *accept-implication* pair iff every request that is accepted by policy P is also accepted by policy Q. The *implication problem* of policies is to design an efficient algorithm that can take as input any policy pair (P, Q) and determine whether (P, Q) is an accept-implication pair. Such an algorithm can support step-wise refinement methods for designing policies. In this paper, we present a polynomial algorithm that can take any policy pair (P, Q) and determine whether (P, Q) is an accept-implication pair. The time complexity of this algorithm is $\mathcal{O}((m+n)^{t+2})$, where m is the number of rules in policy P, n is the number of rules in policy Q, and t is the number of attributes in P or in Q. This time complexity is polynomial when t is fixed, as is usually the case.

Keywords: Policy · Implication problem · Step-wise refinement · Firewalls · Access control · Routing

1 Introduction

A computing policy is a filter that is placed at the entry point of some resource. Each request to access the resource needs to be first examined against the policy to determine whether to accept or reject the request. The action of a policy to accept or reject a request depends on two factors:

1. The values of some attributes that are specified in the request
2. The sequence of rules in the policy that are specified by the policy designer

Examples of computing policies are firewalls in the Internet, routing policies and software-defined networks in the Internet, and access control policies [10]. Early methods for the logical analysis of computing policies have been reported in [6,7,11].

© Springer International Publishing Switzerland 2015
A. Pelc and A.A. Schwarzmann (Eds.): SSS 2015, LNCS 9212, pp. 109–123, 2015.
DOI: 10.1007/978-3-319-21741-3_8

A rule in a policy consists of a predicate and an action, which is either "accept" or "reject". To examine a request against a policy, the rules in the policy are considered one by one until the first rule, whose predicate satisfies the values of the attributes in the request, is identified. Then the action of the identified rule, whether "accept" or "reject", is applied to the request.

Note that there are three sets of requests that are associated with each policy P: (1) the set of requests that are accepted by P, (2) the set of requests that are rejected by P, and (3) the set of requests that are neither accepted nor rejected by P. (This third set is usually, but not always, empty.)

A pair of policies (P, Q) is called an accept-implication pair iff the set of requests accepted by policy P is a subset of the set of requests accepted by policy Q.

In this paper, we present an algorithm that can take as input any pair of policies (P, Q) and determine whether or not (P, Q) is an accept-implication pair. It turns out, as discussed in [5], that the problem of determining whether any given policy pair is an accept-implication pair is NP-hard in general. This means that the time complexity of any algorithm that solves this problem is very likely to be exponential in general. We show that the time complexity of our presented algorithm in this paper is polynomial in those cases where the number of attributes in policy P or Q is fixed, as is usually the case.

For convenience, we present next two examples of policy pairs, and show that one of these pairs is an accept-implication pair and the other is not.

Let u and v be two attributes whose integer values are taken from the interval [1,9]. A policy P_1 over these two attributes can be defined as follows:

$$((u \text{ in } [1, 4]) \wedge (v \text{ in } [8, 9])) \rightarrow \text{reject}$$
$$((u \text{ in } [2, 4]) \wedge (v \text{ in } [7, 9])) \rightarrow \text{accept}$$

Policy P_1 consists of two rules. The first rule states that each request (u, v), where the value of u is an integer in the interval [1, 4] and where the value of v is an integer in the interval [8, 9], is to be rejected. The second rule states that each request (u, v), that does not match the first rule and where the value of u is an integer in the interval [2, 4] and where the value of v is an integer in the interval [7, 9], is to be accepted. The set of requests that are accepted by policy P_1 is $\{(2, 7), (3, 7), (4, 7)\}$.

A second policy P_2 over attributes u and v can be defined as follows:

$$((u \text{ in } [1, 4]) \wedge (v \text{ in } [8,9])) \rightarrow \text{reject}$$
$$((u \text{ in } [2, 3]) \wedge (v \text{ in } [6,8])) \rightarrow \text{accept}$$

The set of requests that are accepted by policy P_2 is $\{(2, 6), (3, 6), (2, 7), (3, 7)\}$.

A third policy Q over attributes u and v can be defined as follows:

$$((u \text{ in } [2, 3]) \wedge (v \text{ in } [7, 7])) \rightarrow \text{accept}$$
$$((u \text{ in } [2, 4]) \wedge (v \text{ in } [7, 8])) \rightarrow \text{accept}$$

The set of requests that are accepted by Q is $\{(2, 7), (3, 7), (4, 7), (2, 8), (3, 8), (4, 8)\}$.

It follows that every request that is accepted by policy P_1 is also accepted by policy Q and so (P_1, Q) is an accept-implication pair. However, not every request that is accepted by policy P_2 is accepted by policy Q and so (P_2, Q) is not an accept-implication pair.

Our interest in designing an efficient algorithm that can take any policy pair (P, Q) and determine whether (P, Q) is an accept-implication pair is motivated by two observations.

First, this algorithm can be also used to determine whether any policy P or any policy pair (P, Q) satisfies other properties.

For example, to determine whether an accept rule ar in a given policy P is redundant, one can define a policy P' to be the same as policy P after removing rule ar from it, then use our algorithm to check whether the policy pair (P, P') is an accept-implication pair. If (P, P') is determined to be an accept-implication pair, then rule ar is redundant in policy P. Otherwise, rule ar is non-redundant in P.

As another example, to determine whether two policies P and Q accept the same set of requests [8], one can use our algorithm to check whether the two policy pairs (P, Q) and (Q, P) are accept-implication pairs. If both (P, Q) and (Q, P) are determined to be accept-implication pairs, then policies P and Q accept the same set of requests. Otherwise, P and Q do not accept the same set of requests.

Second, as discussed below, an efficient algorithm that can take any given policy pair (P, Q) and determine whether (P, Q) is an accept-implication pair can also support step-wise refinement methods for designing policies.

Note that determining whether (P, Q) is an accept-implication pair is trivial when the action of every rule in P is "reject". In this case, P accepts no request, and (P, Q) is an accept-implication pair for any policy Q. On the otherhand, determining whether (P, Q) is an accept-implication pair is not trivial when the "action" of at least one rule in P is "accept". Therefore, in this paper, we focus on determining whether (P, Q) is an accept-implication pair in those cases where P has at least one rule whose action is "accept".

2   Preliminaries about Policies

In this section, we formally introduce the main concepts related to computing policies, or policies for short. These concepts are: Intervals, Attributes, Requests, Predicates, Actions, Rules, and Policies. In the next section, we use these seven concepts to formally specify the policy implication problem. This is the problem which we solve in this paper.

2.1   Intervals

An interval is a finite and nonempty set of consecutive integers. An interval X can be denoted by a pair of integers $[y, z]$, where y is the smallest integer in X, and z is the largest integer in X. Note that an interval $[y, y]$ has only one integer y. Note also that any pair $[y, z]$, where $y > z$, is not an interval.

Two intervals $X = [y, z]$ and $X' = [y', z']$ are said to be overlapping iff one of the following two conditions holds: (1) $y \leq y'$ and $y' \leq z$, and (2) $y' \leq y$ and $y \leq z'$.

The intersection of two overlapping intervals $X = [y, z]$ and $X' = [y', z']$ is defined to be the interval $[max(y, y'), min(z, z')]$.

2.2 Attributes

An attribute is a "variable" that has a "name" and a "value". Throughout this paper, we assume that there are t attributes whose names are $a.1$, $a.2$, ..., and $a.t$. The value of each attribute $a.i$ is taken from an interval that is called the domain of attribute $a.i$ and is denoted $D.(a.i)$.

2.3 Requests

A request is a tuple $(v.1, ..., v.t)$ of t integers, where t is the number of attributes and each integer $v.i$ is taken from the domain $D.(a.i)$ of attribute $a.i$.

2.4 Predicates

A predicate is of the form $((a.1$ in $X.1) \wedge ... \wedge (a.t$ in $X.t))$, where each $a.i$ is an attribute, each $X.i$ is an interval that is contained in the domain $D.(a.i)$ of attribute $a.i$, and $\wedge$ is the logical AND or conjunction operator.

The value of each conjunct $(a.i$ in $X.i)$ in a predicate is *true* iff the value of attribute $a.i$ is an integer in interval $X.i$.

The value of a predicate is *true* iff the value of every conjunct $(a.i$ in $X.i)$ in the predicate is *true*.

A predicate $((a.1$ in $X.1) \wedge ... \wedge (a.t$ in $X.t))$, where each interval $X.i$ is the whole domain of the corresponding attribute $a.i$, is called the ALL predicate.

Let pr and ps denote the following two predicates:
$$pr = ((a.1 \text{ in } X.1) \wedge ... \wedge (a.t \text{ in } X.t))$$
$$ps = ((a.1 \text{ in } Y.1) \wedge ... \wedge (a.t \text{ in } Y.t))$$
Next, we use these two predicates to define two concepts: "two overlapping predicates" and "intersection of two predicates".

Predicates pr and ps are said to be overlapping iff every interval $X.i$ in pr and every corresponding interval $Y.i$ in ps are overlapping.

If predicates pr and ps are overlapping, then the intersection of predicates pr and ps is defined to be the predicate
$$((a.1 \text{ in } Z.1) \wedge ... \wedge (a.t \text{ in } Z.t))$$
where each interval $Z.i$ is the intersection of the two corresponding intervals $X.i$ and $Y.i$.

A request $(v.1, ..., v.t)$ is said to match a predicate
$$((a.1 \text{ in } X.1) \wedge ... \wedge (a.t \text{ in } X.t))$$
iff each integer $v.i$ in the request is an element in the corresponding interval $X.i$ in the predicate.

2.5   Actions

We assume that there are two distinct actions: "accept" and "reject". Henceforth, we write "accept" and "reject" with quotation marks to indicate the "accept" and "reject" actions, respectively. We also write accept and reject without quotation marks to indicate the English words accept and reject, respectively.

2.6   Rules

A rule (in a policy) is defined as a pair, one predicate and one action, written as follows:
$$\langle predicate \rangle \rightarrow \langle action \rangle$$

A rule whose action is "accept" is called an *accept* rule, and a rule whose action is "reject" is called a *reject* rule. An *accept* rule whose predicate is the ALL predicate is called an *accept-ALL* rule, and a *reject* rule whose predicate is the ALL predicate is called the *reject-ALL* rule.

A request is said to *match* a rule iff the request matches the predicate of the rule. (Note that each request matches every ALL rule.)

2.7   Policies

A policy is a nonempty sequence of rules. A policy P is said to *accept* (or *reject*, respectively) a request rq iff P has an accept (or reject, respectively) rule r such that request rq matches rule r and does not match any rule that precedes rule r in policy P.

3   The Policy Implication Problem

Let P and Q be two policies. The pair (P, Q) is called an *accept-implication pair* iff the set of requests accepted by policy P is a subset of the set of requests accepted by policy Q. If a pair (P, Q) is shown to be an accept-implication pair, then policy P is called an accept-implementation of policy Q.

The *policy implication problem* is to develop an algorithm that takes as input any pair of policies (P, Q) and determines whether or not the pair (P, Q) is an accept-implication pair.

Let ALG be any algorithm that can solve the policy implication problem. Also let (P, Q) and (P', Q') be any two policy pairs, where P' is the same policy as P except that each "accept" action in P is replaced by a "reject" action in P' and vice versa, and Q' is the same policy as Q except that each "accept" action in Q is replaced by a "reject" action in Q' and vice versa. Algorithm ALG determines that (P, Q) is an accept-implication pair iff (P', Q') is a "reject-implication pair". (Note that (P', Q') is a reject-implication pair iff every request that is rejected by P' is also rejected by Q'.)

The previous paragraph indicates that any algorithm, that can determine whether any given policy pair is an accept-implication pair, can also determine whether any given policy pair is a reject-implication pair.

Consider any algorithm ALG that can solve the policy implication problem. Algorithm ALG can support the following step-wise refinement method for designing policies:

1. The policy designer starts with a simple policy $P.1$ that accepts more requests than the designer wishes. The designer should be discouraged from jumping directly to a policy that accepts precisely those requests that the designer wishes, because such a policy is likely to be too complicated for the designer to design it correctly.
2. Then the designer designs a second policy $P.2$ that is supposed to implement policy $P.1$ and then uses algorithm ALG to check that indeed the pair $(P.2, P.1)$ is an accept-implication pair. If the pair $(P.2, P.1)$ does not turn out to be an accept-implication pair, then the designer needs to design a different policy $P.2$.
3. Then the designer designs a third policy $P.3$ that is supposed to implement policy $P.2$ and then uses algorithm ALG to check that indeed the pair $(P.3, P.2)$ is an accept-implication pair. (If the pair $(P.3, P.2)$ does not turn out to be an accept-implication pair, then the designer needs to design a different policy $P.3$.)
4. Step 4 is repeated several times where the designer designs the policies $P.4$, ..., $P.k$ until the designer reaches a policy $P.k$ that precisely accepts only those requests that the designer wishes to be accepted.

In this paper, our design of an algorithm to solve the policy implication problem proceeds in three steps:

1. In the first step, we develop an algorithm ALG1 that can solve the policy implication problem for any policy pair (P, Q), where P is any policy that consists of exactly one accept rule.
2. In the second step, we develop an algorithm ALG2 that can use ALG1 to solve the policy implication problem for any policy pair (P, Q), where P is any policy that consists of zero or more discard rules followed by one accept rule.
3. In the third step, we develop an algorithm ALG3 that can use ALG2 to solve the policy implication problem for any policy pair (P, Q), where P is any policy that has at least one accept rule. (Note that the policy implication problem for any policy pair (P, Q) is trivial to solve when policy P has no accept rules.) Our algorithm for solving the policy implication problem is ALG3.

4   Implication of Accept Rules

In this section, we present an algorithm ALG1 that can take as input any policy pair (P, Q), where P is a policy that consists of exactly one accept rule and determine whether (P, Q) is an accept-implication pair. But before we present ALG1, we need to introduce the three concepts: "a property", "a request matching a property", and "a policy satisfying a property".

A *property* (of a policy) is defined as a pair, one predicate and one action, written as follows:

$$\langle predicate \rangle \rightarrow \langle action \rangle$$

A property whose action is "accept" is called an accept property, and a property whose action is "reject" is called a reject property. Note that a rule and a property have the same syntax. Thus, an accept (or reject, respectively) rule can be viewed as an accept (or reject, respectively) property, and vice versa.

A *request rq* is said to *match a property pp* iff *rq* matches the predicate of *pp*.

A *policy P* is said to *satisfy a property pp* iff either *pp* is an accept property and *P* accepts every request that matches *pp* or *pp* is a reject property and *P* rejects every request that matches *pp*.

From these three concepts, the next theorem follows.

Theorem 1. *Let ar denote an accept rule, and (ar) denote a policy that consists only of the accept rule ar. The policy pair ((ar), Q) is an accept-implication pair iff policy Q satisfies the accept property ar.*

Proof: To prove this theorem, we need to consider two cases. In the first case, we assume that $((ar), Q)$ is an accept-implication pair and prove that Q satisfies the accept property ar. Then in the second case, we assume that policy Q satisfies the accept property ar and prove that $((ar), Q)$ is an accept-implication pair.

Case 1: $((ar), Q)$ is assumed to be an accept-implication pair:
From the assumption that $((ar), Q)$ is an accept-implication pair, every request that is accepted by (ar) is accepted by Q. Therefore, every request that matches property ar is accepted by Q. Hence, from the definition of a policy satisfying a property, we conclude that policy Q satisfies property ar.

Case 2: Policy Q is assumed to satisfy the property ar:
From the assumption that policy Q satisfies property ar, Q accepts every request that matches property ar. Therefore, every request that accepted by policy (ar) is also accepted by policy Q. Hence, from the definition of an accept-implication pair, we conclude that $((ar), Q)$ is an accept-implication pair. □

From Theorem 1, to determine whether a policy pair $((ar), Q)$ is an accept-implication pair, one needs to determine whether policy Q satisfies the accept property ar. In the Appendix of this paper, we outline a recent method [2] and [4], called the PSP method, that can take as input a policy Q and an accept property ar and determine whether Q satisfies ar. (It is worth noting that the PSP method can also be used in detecting all redundant rules in a policy [3] and [9].)

Algorithm ALG1, which is presented next, uses the PSP method to determine whether any policy pair $((ar), Q)$ is an accept-implication pair.

Algorithm ALG1
Input: A policy pair $((ar), Q)$ where (ar) is a policy that consists of one accept rule ar
Output: A determination of whether $((ar), Q)$ is an accept-implication pair

Step 1:
Use the PSP method outlined in the Appendix, to determine whether policy Q satisfies the accept property ar

Step 2:
If Q satisfies ar
Then $((ar), Q)$ is an accept-implication pair
Else $((ar), Q)$ is not an accept-implication pair
End Algorithm ALG1

The time complexity of ALG1 is dominated by the time complexity of the PSP method which is of order $\mathcal{O}(n^{t+1})$, where n is the number of rules in policy Q and t is the number of attributes.

5   Implication of Accept Slices

In this section, we present an algorithm ALG2 that can take as input any policy pair (P, Q), where P is a policy that consists of zero or more reject rules followed by one accept rule and determine whether (P, Q) is an accept-implication pair. But before we present ALG2, we need to introduce two concepts: "an accept slice" and "simplification of a policy pair".

An *accept slice* is a policy that consists of zero or more reject rules followed by one accept rule.

Let (P, Q) be a policy pair, where P is an accept slice. The *simplification* of (P, Q) is the policy pair $((ar), Q')$ that satisfies the following two conditions:

1. Policy (ar) consists only of the accept rule ar in P
2. Policy Q' consists of all the reject rules of P, after changing their actions from "reject" to "accept", followed by all the rules in Q

From these concepts, the next theorem follows.

Theorem 2. *Let (P, Q) be a policy pair, where P is an accept slice and let $((ar), Q')$ be the simplification of (P, Q). Then, (P, Q) is an accept-implication pair iff $((ar), Q')$ is an accept-implication pair.*

Proof: Let P be an accept slice that consists of m reject rules $p.1, ..., p.m$ followed by the accept rule ar. Also let Q be a policy that consists of n rules, denoted $q.1, ..., q.n$. Thus, policy Q' consists of m rules $r.1, ..., r.m$ followed by the n rules $q.1, ..., q.n$, where each rule $r.i$ in Q is the same as the reject rule $p.i$ in P except that the action of $r.i$ is "accept" rather than "reject".

To prove this theorem, we need to consider two cases. In the first case, we assume that (P, Q) is an accept-implication pair and prove that $((ar), Q')$ is an accept-implication pair. Then in the second case, we assume that $((ar), Q')$ is an accept-implication pair and prove that (P, Q) is an accept-implication pair.

Case 1: (P, Q) is assumed to be an accept-implication pair:
Let rq be any request that is accepted by the policy (ar). We need to show that rq is accepted by Q'. First, we need to consider two sub-cases 1.1 and 1.2:
Case 1.1: request rq does not match any of the rules $p.1$, ..., $p.m$ in P:
In this case, request rq is accepted by policy P and also by policy Q since (P, Q) is an accept-implication pair. Thus, rq matches some accept rule $q.i$ in Q and does not match any of the preceding rules $q.1$, ..., $q.(i-1)$ in Q. Therefore, rq does not match any of the rules $r.1$, ..., $r.m$, $q.1$, ..., $q.(i-1)$ in Q' and matches the accept rule $q.i$ in Q'. Hence, rq is accepted by Q'.
Case 1.2: request rq matches a rule p.i and does not match any of the preceding rules $p.1$, ..., $p.(i-1)$ in P:
In this case, rq matches the accept rule $r.i$ and does not match any of the preceding accept rules $r.1$, ..., $r.(i-1)$ in Q. Hence, rq is accepted by Q'.

Case 2: $((ar), Q')$ is assumed to be an accept-implication pair:
Let rq be any request that is accepted by policy P. We need to show that rq is also accepted by policy Q. Because rq is accepted by P, rq does not match any of the reject rules $p.1$, ..., $p.m$ and matches the accept rule ar in P. Thus, rq is accepted by the policy (ar) and also by the policy Q' since $((ar), Q')$ is an accept-implication pair. But because rq does not match any of the accept rules $r.1$, ..., $r.m$ in Q', rq matches some accept rule $q.i$ and does not match any of the preceding rules $r.1$, ..., $r.m$, $q.1$, ..., $q.(i-1)$ in Q'. Therefore, rq matches the accept rule $q.i$ and does not match any of the preceding rules $q.1$, ..., $q.(i-1)$ in Q. Hence, rq is accepted by Q.   □

From Theorem 2, to determine whether a policy pair (P, Q), where P is an accept slice, is an accept-implication pair, one needs to determine whether the simplification $((ar), Q')$ of (P, Q) is an accept-implication pair. Because algorithm ALG1 can be used to determine whether $((ar), Q')$ is an accept-implication pair, algorithm ALG2, which is presented next, uses ALG1 to determine whether any policy (P, Q), where P is an accept slice, is an accept-implication pair.

Algorithm ALG2
Input: A policy pair (P, Q) where P is an accept slice
Output: A determination of whether (P, Q) is an accept-implication pair

Step 1:
Construct the simplification $((ar), Q')$ of (P, Q)

Step 2:
Use ALG1 to determine whether the simplification $((ar), Q')$ of (P, Q) is an accept-implication pair

Step 3:
If $((ar), Q')$ is an accept-implication pair
Then (P, Q) is an accept-implication pair
Else (P, Q) is not an accept-implication pair
End Algorithm ALG2

The time complexity of ALG2 is dominated by the time complexity of ALG1 which is of order $\mathcal{O}(n'^{t+1})$, where n' is the number of rules in policy Q'. But (n') is at most $(m + n)$, where m is the number of rules in the accept slice P, and n is the number of rules in policy Q. Therefore, the time complexity of ALG2 is of order $\mathcal{O}((m + n)^{t+1})$, where m is the number of rules in the accept slice P, n is the number of rules in policy Q, and t is the number of attributes.

6   Implication of Accept Policies

A policy that has at least one accept rule is called an accept policy. In this section, we present an algorithm ALG3 that can take as input any policy pair (P, Q), where P is an accept policy and determine whether (P, Q) is an accept-implication pair. (Note that we focus only on policy pairs (P, Q) where P is an accept policy because every policy pair (P, Q), where P is not an accept policy, is in fact an accept-implication pair.) But before we present ALG3, we need to introduce the concept of "primitive accept slices of a policy".

Let P be an accept policy that has k accept rules denoted $ar.1, ..., ar.k$. A *primitive accept slice* of policy P is an accept slice whose accept rule is one of the accept rules $ar.i$ in P and whose reject rules are all the reject rules that precede rule $ar.i$ in P. Note that policy P has k primitive accept slices.

From this concept, the next theorem follows.

Theorem 3. *Let (P, Q) be a policy pair, where P is an accept policy that has k primitive accept slices denoted $P.1, ..., P.k$. Then, (P, Q) is an accept-implication pair iff for every $i \in \{1, ..., k\}$, the pair $(P.i, Q)$ is an accept-implication pair.*

Proof: To prove this theorem, we need to consider two cases. In the first case, we assume that (P, Q) is an accept-implication pair and prove that for every $i \in \{1, ..., k\}$, the pair $(P.i, Q)$ is an accept-implication. Then in the second case, we assume that for every $i \in \{1, ..., k\}$, the pair $(P.i, Q)$ is an accept-implication pair and prove that (P, Q) is an accept-implication pair.

Case 1: (P, Q) is assumed to be an accept-implication pair:
Let rq be any request that is accepted by a primitive accept slice $P.i$ of policy P. We need to show that rq is accepted by Q. Because rq is accepted by $P.i$, rq is

accepted by P and rq is also accepted by Q since (P, Q) is an accept-implication pair.

Case 2: for every $i \in \{1, ..., k\}$, the pair $(P.i, Q)$ is assumed to be an accept-implication pair:

Let rq be any request that is accepted by P. We need to show that rq is accepted by Q. Because rq is accepted by policy P, rq is accepted by at least one primitive accept slice $P.i$ of P and rq is also accepted by Q since $(P.i, Q)$ is an accept-implication pair. □

From Theorem 3, to determine whether a policy pair (P, Q), where P is an accept policy, is an accept-implication pair, one needs to determine whether every primitive accept slice $(P.i, Q)$ of (P, Q) is an accept-implication pair. Because algorithm ALG2 can be used to determine whether each $(P.i, Q)$ is an accept-implication pair, algorithm ALG3, which is presented next, uses ALG2 to determine whether any policy (P, Q), where P is an accept policy, is an accept-implication pair.

Algorithm ALG3
Input: A policy pair (P, Q) where P is an accept policy
Output: A determination of whether (P, Q) is an accept-implication pair

Step 1:
Construct the primitive accept slices $P.1$, ..., $P.k$ of P

Step 2:
Use ALG2 to determine whether each policy pair $(P.i, Q)$, where $P.i$ is a primitive accept slice of P, is an accept-implication pair

Step 3:
If   every policy pair $(P.i, Q)$ is an accept-implication pair
Then (P, Q) is an accept-implication pair
Else (P, Q) is not an accept-implication pair
End Algorithm ALG3

Because the time complexity of ALG2 is of order $\mathcal{O}((m + n)^{t+1})$, where m is the number of rules in policy P, n is the number of rules in policy Q, and t is the number of attributes, and because ALG3 invokes ALG2 at most m times, we conclude that the time complexity of ALG3 is of order $\mathcal{O}((m + n)^{t+2})$. Note that when the number of attributes t is fixed, the time complexity of ALG3 is polynomial.

7   Concluding Remarks

In this paper, we present an algorithm ALG3 that can take any policy pair (P, Q), where P is an accept policy, and determine whether or not (P, Q) is an accept-implication pair. Algorithm ALG3 invokes another algorithm ALG2 that can take any policy pair (P, Q), where P is an accept slice, and determine whether or not (P, Q) is an accept-implication pair. Likewise, Algorithm ALG2 invokes a third algorithm ALG1 that can take any accept property ar and a policy Q, and verify whether or not policy Q satisfies property ar.

Let the time complexity of Algorithm ALG1, denoted C1, to be in the order of some function F over n and t, where n is the number of rules in policy Q and t is the number of attributes of Q. Thus,

$$C1 = \mathcal{O}(F(n, t))$$

The time complexity of Algorithm ALG2, denoted C2, can be computed from the time complexity of Algorithm ALG1 as follows:

$$C2 = \mathcal{O}(F(m + n, t))$$

where m is the number of rules in policy P, n is the number of rules in policy Q, and t is the number of attributes of P or Q. The time complexity of Algorithm ALG3, denoted C3, can be computed from the time complexity of Algorithm ALG2 as follows:

$$C3 = \mathcal{O}((m + n) \times C2)$$

where m is the number of rules in policy P, n is the number of rules in policy Q, and t is the number of attributes of P or Q.

Because Algorithm ALG1 is based on the PSP verification method whose time complexity $F(n, t)$ is of the order $O(n^{t+1})$, the time complexity C1 of ALG1 is

$$C1 = \mathcal{O}(n^{t+1})$$

In this case, the time complexities of ALG2 and ALG3 are as follows:

$$C2 = \mathcal{O}((m + n)^{t+1})$$
$$C3 = \mathcal{O}((m + n)^{t+2})$$

Therefore, the time complexities of all three algorithms are polynomial in those cases where the number of attributes is fixed, as usually the case.

It is also possible to base Algorithm ALG1 on the probabilistic verification method in [1] whose time complexity $F(n, t)$ is of the order $\mathcal{O}(n \times t)$. In this case, the time complexities of the three Algorithms ALG1, ALG2, and ALG3 can be computed as follows:

$$C1 = \mathcal{O}(n \times t)$$
$$C2 = \mathcal{O}((m + n) \times t)$$
$$C3 = \mathcal{O}((m + n)^2 \times t)$$

Note that if we base Algorithm ALG1 on the probabilistic verification method [1], then the three Algorithms ALG1, ALG2, and ALG3 can yield wrong determinations but the probability of this happening is relatively small.

Acknowledgments. Research of M.G. Gouda is supported by NSF Award 1440035. Research of M.J.H. Heule is supported by DARPA Contract N66001-10-2-4087. Research of E.S. Elmallah is supported by NSERC Grant RGPIN 36899.

Appendix: The PSP Method

In this appendix, we briefly discuss a recent method [2] and [4] for verifying whether a policy P satisfies a property pp. For convenience, we refer to this method as the Projection-Slicing-Probing method, or the PSP method for short. Without any loss of generality, we focus our discussion of the PSP method on the case where pp is an accept property.

The PSP method for verifying whether a policy P satisfies an accept property pp consists of three steps: (More explanations about these steps are presented below.)

1. From policy P and the accept property pp, construct a new policy called the projection of policy P over property pp. This new policy is denoted P/pp
2. Divide the projection policy P/pp into a set of special policies $\{RS.1, ..., RS.k\}$ called the reject slices of the projection P/pp.
3. Check whether each reject slice $RS.i$ rejects no request. If every reject slice $RS.i$ is shown to reject no request, then policy P satisfies the accept property pp. Otherwise P does not satisfy pp.

Next we describe these three steps in more detail.

Algorithm A1 (Projection)
Input: A policy P and an accept property pp
Output: A new policy called the projection of policy P over property pp. This new policy is denoted P/pp

Step 1:
Add a reject-ALL rule at the end of policy P

Step 2:
Initially, P/pp is the empty policy

Step 3:
For every rule r in policy P **do**
   If   rule r overlaps property pp
   Then add the intersection of rule r and property pp as a rule at
          the tail of policy P/pp
End Algorithm A1

The next theorem follows from Algorithm A1.

Theorem T1. *A policy P satisfies an accept property pp iff the projection policy P/pp rejects no request.*

Algorithm A2: (Slicing)
Input: A projection policy P/pp of a policy P over an accept property pp

Output: A set of policies $\{RS.1, ..., RS.k\}$, where each policy $RS.i$ is called a reject slice of the projection policy P/pp and k is the number of reject rules in the projection policy P/pp

Step 1:
For each i in the range 1 to k **do**
compute policy $RS.i$ as the sequence of all accept rules that precede the i-th reject rule in policy P/pp followed by the i-th reject rule in policy P/pp
End Algorithm A2
The next theorem follows from Algorithm A2.

Theorem T2. *The projection P/pp of a policy P over an accept property pp rejects no request iff every reject slice of the projection P/pp rejects no request.*

Algorithm A3: (Probing)
Input: A reject slice $RS.i$ of the projection P/pp of policy P over an accept property pp
Output: A determination of whether $RS.i$ rejects no request

Step 1:
For each attribute $a.j$ where j ranges from 1 to t **do**
Compute a set $S.j$ of values of $a.j$ as follows:
$S.j :=$ empty set
For each accept rule ar in $RS.i$ **do**
If   the predicate of ar has the conjunct $(a.j$ in $[u, v])$ **and**
$(v + 1)$ is an element of $D.(a.j)$
Then add element $(v + 1)$ to set $S.j$
End for
If   the predicate of the reject rule rr in $RS.i$ has the conjunct
$(a.j$ in $[u, v])$
Then add element u to set $S.j$

Step 2:
Compute set S of all "probe requests" as the Cartesian product $(S.1 \times ... \times S.t)$

Step 3:
If   no probe request in S is rejected by the reject slice $RS.i$
Then declare that slice $RS.i$ rejects no request
Else   declare that slice $RS.i$ rejects at least one request
End Algorithm A3
The next theorem follows from Theorems T1 and T2 above.

Theorem T3. *A policy P satisfies an accept property pp iff every reject slice of the projection P/pp rejects no request.*

To verify whether a policy P satisfies an accept property pp, one needs to execute Algorithm A1 once, execute Algorithm A2 once, and execute Algorithm A3 an $\mathcal{O}(n)$ times, where n is the number of rules in policy P. Because the time complexity of Algorithms A1 and of Algorithm A2 is $\mathcal{O}(n * t)$, where t is the number of attributes, and because the time complexity of Algorithm A3 is $\mathcal{O}(n^t)$, the time complexity of verifying whether P satisfies pp is $\mathcal{O}(n^{t+1})$.

This large time complexity is to be expected since it has been shown recently that the problem of verifying whether a policy satisfies a property is NP-hard [5]. (Beside resorting to the PSP method, it has been suggested [5] that the large time complexity of policy verification can be faced by using SAT solvers [12] or probabilistic verification techniques [1].)

References

1. Acharya, H.B., Gouda, M.G.: Linear-time verification of firewalls. In: Proceedings of the 17th IEEE International Conference on Network Protocols (ICNP), pp. 133–140. IEEE (2009)
2. Acharya, H.B., Gouda, M.G.: Projection and division: linear-space verification of firewalls. In: Proceedings of the 30th IEEE International Conference on Distributed Computing Systems (ICDCS), pp. 736–743. IEEE (2010)
3. Acharya, H.B., Gouda, M.G.: Firewall verification and redundancy checking are equivalent. In: Proceedings of the 30th IEEE International Conference on Computer Communication (INFOCOM), pp. 2123–2128. IEEE (2011)
4. Elmallah, E.S., Acharya, H.B., Gouda, M.G.: Incremental verification of computing policies. In: Felber, P., Garg, V. (eds.) SSS 2014. LNCS, vol. 8756, pp. 226–236. Springer, Heidelberg (2014)
5. Elmallah, E.S., Gouda, M.G.: Hardness of firewall analysis. In: Noubir, G., Raynal, M. (eds.) NETYS 2014. LNCS, vol. 8593, pp. 153–168. Springer, Heidelberg (2014)
6. Hoffman, D., Yoo, K.: Blowtorch: a framework for firewall test automation. In: Proceedings of the 20th IEEE/ACM International Conference on Automated Software Engineering (ASE), pp. 96–103. ACM (2005)
7. Kamara, S., Fahmy, S., Schultz, E., Kerschbaum, F., Frantzen, M.: Analysis of vulnerabilities in internet firewalls. Computers & Security 22(3), 214–232 (2003)
8. Liu, A.X., Gouda, M.G.: Diverse firewall design. IEEE Transactions on Parallel and Distributed Systems 19(9), 1237–1251 (2008)
9. Liu, A.X., Gouda, M.G.: Complete redundancy removal for packet classifiers in TCAMs. IEEE Transactions on Parallel and Distributed Systems 21(4), 424–437 (2010)
10. Mayer, A., Wool, A., Ziskind, E.: Fang: A firewall analysis engine. In: IEEE Symposium on Security and Privacy, pp. 177–187. IEEE (2000)
11. Wool, A.: A quantitative study of firewall configuration errors. Computer 37(6), 62–67 (2004)
12. Zhang, S., Mahmoud, A., Malik, S., Narain, S.: Verification and synthesis of firewalls using SAT and QBF. In: Proceedings of the 20th IEEE International Conference on Network Protocols (ICNP), pp. 1–6. IEEE (2012)

Verifying Recurrence Properties in Self-stabilization by Checking the Absence of Finite Counterexamples

Oday Jubran$^{(\boxtimes)}$, Eike Möhlmann, and Oliver Theel

Carl von Ossietzky University of Oldenburg, 26111 Oldenburg, Germany
{jubran,eike.moehlmann,theel}@informatik.uni-oldenburg.de

Abstract. A performance-related property of a system can be defined as the ratio of states satisfying some condition in each execution of the system, which we signify as the recurrence of the condition in the execution. In this work, we concern self-stabilization with respect to this property: the convergence to an execution that guarantees a minimum recurrence of a condition. For a system exhibiting infinite executions, it may not be straightforward to verify that the system satisfies the property, while considering the convergence as well. Towards simplifying such a verification, we show that for each system violating the property, there exists a finite execution prefix that is a counterexample with a reasonably short length. Furthermore, we exploit model checking to verify the absence of such counterexamples, to conclude that a system satisfies its property. We apply this approach by using the NUXMV model checker to analyze the service time of a self-stabilizing mutual exclusion algorithm having a finite state space, and running over many topologies.

Keywords: Self-stabilization · Recurrence · Automatic verification · Finite counterexample

1 Introduction

The essence of self-stabilization [1] is the recovery from failures without voluntarily running into such. Self-stabilization is useful when the system's environment is vulnerable to transient faults, e.g., memory allocation problems. Self-stabilization is of a significant impact in distributed systems, since a system's component generally does not have full knowledge about the global configuration of the system, and thus, the components' reaction – with their local knowledge – has to direct the behavior towards preserving the whole system's properties [2].

In the design of self-stabilizing systems, there are two major goals to be achieved: (1) the convergence to a desired behavior, and (2) non-deviating from

This work was partially supported by the German Research Foundation (DFG) as part of the Transregional Collaborative Research Center "Automatic Verification and Analysis of Complex Systems" (SFB/TR 14 AVACS, http://www.avacs.org/).

A. Pelc and A.A. Schwarzmann (Eds.): SSS 2015, LNCS 9212, pp. 124–138, 2015.
DOI: 10.1007/978-3-319-21741-3_9

the desired behavior. Usually, the desired behavior is that all states satisfy some condition, and the convergence time is measured based on the maximum time required to achieve the desired behavior among all executions of the system.

Generally, a system's desired behavior is aimed to satisfy two kinds of properties: (1) safety properties defined by conditions that should hold in each state, and (2) performance-related properties defined by conditions that need to hold periodically to enable running useful actions; they may not hold in each state. The latter properties may reflect the notions of throughput or availability of a system. As an example, consider a TDMA-based wireless sensor network using a limited bandwidth, where message collision may cause message loss. The safety property in such network is collision-free communication, implicated by a correct slot assignment. Furthermore, it may be required that any message should be delivered to a target in bounded time. This property may be impacted by the slot assignment, but may not reflect a condition defined on a single state.

In a recent work [3,4], we considered conditions that do not need to be satisfied in all states, in self-stabilization. We defined the *recurrence of a condition in an execution* as the ratio of states satisfying the condition in the execution. With respect to self-stabilization, the point to be considered is the convergence time to reach an execution suffix that achieves a minimum recurrence. This property is defined over possibly infinite executions. This, in turn, makes it hard to verify whether a system satisfies the property. In this work, our concern is to simplify such verification using formal methods.

Related Work

The competence of self-stabilizing systems is their ability to recover from failures due to transient faults. Basically, the related work concerns variant aspects of such systems' efficiency or performance: shortening the convergence time to a safe behavior, e.g. [5,6], reducing the space requirements, e.g. [7,8], and covering larger underlying topologies and schedulers, e.g. [9]. In contrast to this work, we focus on another aspect of efficiency, namely, the convergence to reach the desired performance, defined by the recurrence of a condition in an execution.

The design and verification of self-stabilizing systems is known to be tough. Some related work considers using formal methods and automatic verification to design self-stabilizing systems. Examples are [10,11]. In [10], the authors present a formal method for algorithmic design of self-stabilizing systems based on variable superposition and backtracking search. In [11], the authors make use of SMT solvers [12] for synthesizing self-stabilizing algorithms. Other approaches consider analyzing notions of performance of self-stabilizing systems. Examples are [13–15]. In [13], the authors use a metric for measuring the expected mean value of the system's convergence time. This value denotes the average case of the convergence time, and is computed by probabilistic model checking. The work [14] considers the occurrence of transient faults during the convergence, and their effect on the convergence time. The approach [15] defines and applies fault tolerance measurements, such as availability, to evaluate self-stabilizing systems, also under the assumption of ongoing transient faults. These approaches and others are basically aimed to evaluate the performance of self-stabilizing systems using formal methods and automatic verification, which is found to be useful.

In our approach, we exploit model checking for proving the absence of counterexamples wrt. the performance property we consider, to conclude that the analyzed system satisfies the property.

Contribution

First, we show that for each system that does not converge to a behavior guaranteeing a minimum recurrence of a condition in c steps, there exists an execution prefix having a length of $c + 1$ states that is a counterexample. Second, we consider the recurrence of a condition also during the convergence time, i.e., starting from the initial state of the execution. We show that if the recurrence is not reached in w steps, then exists a counterexample of length between $w + 1$ and $2w + 1$. Next, for systems having finite state space, model checking can be used to verify the absence of counterexamples, to conclude that a system converges to achieve a minimum recurrence of some condition. As a case study, we use the model checker NUXMV to analyze the service time of a self-stabilizing mutual exclusion algorithm run over many topologies, based on our approach.

Outline. Section 2 presents preliminary notation and formalism. Section 3 presents the formal definition of recurrence properties in self-stabilization. Section 4 presents the counterexample-based approach. Section 5 extends the definitions of Section 3, for considering recurrence also during the convergence. Section 6 presents the case study. Section 7 gives a conclusion and a discussion.

2   Notation and Formalism

In this section, we provide a formalism of the system and the environment we are considering, to be used in the following sections.

We define *system variables* as a vector of variables $[r_0, ..., r_{g-1}]$. A **system state** γ is a vector of values $[v_0, ..., v_{g-1}]$ valuating the system variables. A *condition con* is a boolean expression over the system variables. We say that a state γ *satisfies* a condition *con*, denoted by $\gamma \models con$, iff the condition *con* evaluates to *true* under γ. A *state space* is the set of all states of the system.

An **execution** Ξ is a sequence of states of the state space, which can be *finite* $\gamma_0, ..., \gamma_{k-1}$ or *infinite*. Let $\Xi : \gamma_0, \gamma_1, ...$ be an execution, and let $i, j \in \mathbb{N}_0$.

- A *step of* Ξ is a tuple (γ_i, γ_{i+1}).
- A *subexecution* of Ξ is a finite subsequence $\gamma_i, ..., \gamma_j$ of Ξ, where $j \geq i$.
- An *execution prefix* of Ξ is a finite subexecution $\gamma_0, ..., \gamma_j$.
- An *execution suffix* of Ξ is an execution $\gamma_i, \gamma_{i+1}, ...$

  Let $\Xi : \gamma_0, ..., \gamma_{k-1}$ be a finite execution.
- A *strict subexecution* of Ξ is a finite subsequence $\gamma_i, ..., \gamma_j$ of Ξ, such that $i > 0$ or $j < k - 1$.
- The *length* of Ξ, denoted by $len(\Xi)$, is k; i.e., the number of states in Ξ.

We define a system, while taking self-stabilization into consideration: each state γ in the state space is an initial state. A **system** Ω is a – possibly infinite – set of executions, such that for each subexecution Ξ' of an execution $\Xi \in \Omega$, Ξ' is an execution prefix of an execution $\Xi'' \in \Omega$.

A system Ω is said to be **self-stabilizing** wrt. a property *con* iff for each execution $\gamma_0, \gamma_1, ...$, there exists finally a state γ_j, for $j \geq 0$, such that each state of the execution suffix $\gamma_j, \gamma_{j+1}, ...$ satisfies *con*.

3   Recurrence in Self-stabilization

Considering the definition of self-stabilization wrt. some condition, it is required that each execution finally reaches a state, from which any following state satisfies the condition. In this section, we present an extension of this definition, which is given in [4]. The extension involves the conditions that do not necessarily need to be satisfied by all states after convergence, but are required to be satisfied by a minimum ratio of states.

First, we present the notion of recurrence which denotes the ratio of states satisfying a condition in a finite execution.

DEFINITION 1 (RECURRENCE). Let $\Xi : \gamma_0, ..., \gamma_{k-1}$ be a finite execution, and let *con* be a condition. The *recurrence* of *con* in Ξ, denoted by $Rec_{con}(\Xi)$, is the ratio $\Delta \in [0,1] \subset \mathbb{Q}$ of the states satisfying *con* in Ξ.   ◇

From now on, we use $sat_{con}(\Xi)$ to denote the number of states satisfying *con* in Ξ. This entails that $Rec_{con}(\Xi) = \frac{sat_{con}(\Xi)}{len(\Xi)}$. For example, let $\underline{\gamma}$ denote that a state γ satisfies *con*, and let Ξ be the following finite execution:

$$\Xi : \underline{\gamma_0}, \underline{\gamma_1}, \gamma_2, \gamma_3, \underline{\gamma_4}, \gamma_5, \underline{\gamma_6}, \gamma_7, \gamma_9, \underline{\gamma_9}, \gamma_{10}, \underline{\gamma_{11}},$$

the recurrence of *con* in Ξ can be computed by a simple division operation:

$$Rec_{con}(\Xi) = \frac{sat_{con}(\Xi)}{len(\Xi)} = \frac{6}{12} = 0.5.$$

Our aim is to use the notion of recurrence in self-stabilization. In general, many self-stabilizing systems have infinite executions. The main issue to be concerned with is the worst-case convergence time to a state γ_t, from which any execution $\Xi : \gamma_t, \gamma_{t+1}, ...$ satisfies the following property: each execution prefix of Ξ satisfies a minimum recurrence Δ of some condition *con*. We denote this property by con_Δ. We denote the worst-case convergence time to achieve con_Δ by con_Δ-*convergence time*.

DEFINITION 2 (con_Δ). An execution $\Xi : \gamma_0, \gamma_1, ...$ is said to satisfy con_Δ iff for each $i \geq 0$, the recurrence of *con* in $\gamma_0, ..., \gamma_i$ ($Rec_{con}(\gamma_0, ..., \gamma_i)$) is greater or equal to Δ.   ◇

DEFINITION 3 (con_Δ-CONVERGENCE TIME). Given a system Ω, a condition *con*, and $\Delta \in [0,1] \subset \mathbb{Q}$.

- An execution $\Xi : \gamma_0, \gamma_1, \ldots$ of Ω is said to *have a con_Δ-convergence time of c steps* iff c is the minimum number, such that the execution suffix $\gamma_c, \gamma_{c+1}, \ldots$ of Ξ satisfies con_Δ.
  It is also said that for each $j \geq c$, the execution Ξ *guarantees con_Δ-convergence in j steps*.
- The system Ω is said to have a *con_Δ-convergence time* of c *steps* iff c is the maximum con_Δ-convergence time among all executions of Ω. $\diamond$

For example, the following execution has a $con_{0.5}$-convergence time of 5.

$$\Xi : \gamma_0, \gamma_1, \gamma_2, \gamma_3, \gamma_4, \underline{\gamma_5}, \gamma_6, \underline{\gamma_7}, \gamma_8, \underline{\gamma_9}, \gamma_{10}, \underline{\gamma_{11}}, \gamma_{12}, \underline{\gamma_{13}}, \ldots$$

Note that the con_Δ-convergence notion applies to finite and infinite executions. In addition, for $\Delta = 0$, the property holds always for all systems. Therefore, in the following sections, we assume that $\Delta > 0$.

4   Finite Counterexamples

In general, the property con_Δ is defined over infinite executions, which makes it hard to analyze con_Δ in some systems, especially when the recurrence differs among subexecutions of an execution. In particular, using automatic verification tools to analyze such properties might not be straightforward, due to infinite executions and a large number of initial states.

In this section, we provide an approach for simplifying the procedure of analyzing recurrence. The idea is as follows: we show that for each system that does not satisfy con_Δ-convergence time of c steps, there exists a finite execution (prefix) Ξ that does not satisfy con_Δ-convergence in c steps, and has a length of $c + 1$. We call Ξ a minimal *counterexample wrt. (con, Δ, c)*.

DEFINITION 4. Let con be a condition, $\Delta \in [0, 1] \subset \mathbb{Q}$, and $c \in \mathbb{N}_0$.
- A *counterexample wrt. (con, Δ, c)* is a finite execution Ξ that does not satisfy con_Δ-convergence in c steps.[1]
- A counterexample Ξ wrt. (con, Δ, c) is said to be *minimal* iff there exists no strict subexecution Ξ' of Ξ such that Ξ' is a counterexample. $\diamond$

The interesting point that makes our approach possible, is that each state in a self-stabilizing system is an initial state of some execution, and having a minimal counterexample Ξ' as a subsequence of any execution implies that Ξ' is indeed a separate execution (prefix) in the system. Note that for systems having a finite state space, there exists a finite number of minimal counterexamples.

In the remainder of this section, we prove that for each system that does not satisfy con_Δ-convergence in c steps, there exists a minimal counterexample Ξ', whose length is $c + 1$. The following is a basic Lemma, that regards concatenating two subsequent executions, satisfying particular recurrence properties.

---

[1] We write "counterexample" without "wrt. (con, Δ, c)," if it is clear from the context.

LEMMA 1. Let $\Xi : \gamma_i, ..., \gamma_{j-1}, \gamma_j, ..., \gamma_{k-1}$ be a finite execution, such that $Rec_{con}(\gamma_i, ..., \gamma_{j-1}) \geq \Delta$, and $\forall j \leq s \leq k - 1 \bullet Rec_{con}(\gamma_j, ..., \gamma_s) \geq \Delta$. The following statement holds:

$$\forall j \leq s \leq k - 1 \bullet Rec_{con}(\gamma_i, ..., \gamma_s) \geq \Delta.$$

PROOF: The cases where $len(\gamma_i, ..., \gamma_{j-1}) = 0$ or $len(\gamma_j, ..., \gamma_{k-1}) = 0$ hold trivially. In the following, we assume that $len(\gamma_i, ..., \gamma_{j-1}) \geq 1$ and $len(\gamma_j, ..., \gamma_{k-1}) \geq 1$. By the premises, it follows that

$$Rec_{con}(\gamma_i, ..., \gamma_{j-1}) \geq \Delta. \tag{1}$$

$$\Longleftrightarrow \frac{sat_{con}(\gamma_i, ..., \gamma_{j-1})}{(j-1) - i + 1} \geq \Delta.$$

$$\Longleftrightarrow sat_{con}(\gamma_i, ..., \gamma_{j-1}) \geq \Delta(j - i) \tag{2}$$

Analogous to the derivation of (2):

$$\forall j \leq s \leq k - 1 \bullet sat_{con}(\gamma_j, ..., \gamma_s) \geq \Delta(s - j). \tag{3}$$

By Def. 1 and by (2) and (3), the following derivation applies:

$$\forall j \leq s \leq k - 1 \bullet Rec_{con}(\gamma_i, ..., \gamma_s) = \frac{sat_{con}(\gamma_i, ..., \gamma_s)}{s - i + 1}$$

$$= \frac{sat_{con}(\gamma_i, ..., \gamma_{j-1}) + sat_{con}(\gamma_j, ..., \gamma_s)}{s - i + 1}$$

$$\geq \frac{\Delta(j - i) + \Delta(s - j + 1)}{s - i + 1}$$

$$\geq \Delta. \qquad \square$$

The following Observation and Lemma show that the length of any minimal counterexample wrt. (con, Δ, c) is $c + 1$.

OBSERVATION 1. For each counterexample Ξ wrt. (con, Δ, c), $len(\Xi) \geq c + 1$.

PROOF: It follows by Definitions 3 and 4. $\qquad \square$

LEMMA 2. For each minimal counterexample Ξ wrt. (con, Δ, c): $len(\Xi) = c + 1$.

PROOF: Observation 1 implies that the length of any counterexample is greater or equal to $c + 1$. It remains to show that the length of each minimal counterexample is not greater than $c + 1$.

We prove this by contradiction: assume that there exists a minimal counterexample $\Xi : \gamma_0, ..., \gamma_{k-1}$ wrt. (con, Δ, c), where $k = len(\Xi) > c + 1$. By Definitions 3 and 4, it follows that:

$$\forall i \leq c \bullet \exists j \geq c \bullet Rec_{con}(\gamma_i, ..., \gamma_j) < \Delta. \tag{4}$$

Since Ξ is minimal, by Def. 4, each strict subexecution of Ξ is not a counterexample. Let Ξ' be the strict subexecution $\gamma_1, ..., \gamma_{k-1}$ of Ξ. Since $len(\Xi) > c + 1$, it follows that $len(\Xi') \geq c + 1$. By Def. 3, this implies that:

$$\exists i \leq c + 1 \bullet \forall j \geq c + 1 \bullet Rec_{con}(\gamma_i, ..., \gamma_j) \geq \Delta. \tag{5}$$

By considering (4), the formula holds for any i among $\{1, ..., c\}$. This implies that the formula (5) does not hold for any i among $\{1, ..., c\}$. This implies that i may only be $(c + 1)$ in (5); i.e.:

$$\forall j \geq c + 1 \bullet Rec_{con}(\gamma_{c+1}, ..., \gamma_j) \geq \Delta. \tag{6}$$

By (6) and Def. 1:

$$\gamma_{c+1} \models con \tag{7}$$

By (4), it follows that $\exists j \geq c \bullet Rec_{con}(\gamma_c, ..., \gamma_j) < \Delta$. This, by (6), (7), and Lemma 1, implies that:

$$\gamma_c \not\models con \tag{8}$$

We make a case distinction based on the value of c:

1. $c = 0$. By Def. 4 and (8), γ_c is a counterexample of length $1 = c + 1$. This contradicts the assumption that Ξ, with $len(\Xi) > 1$, is a minimal counterexample.
2. $c > 0$. By assumption, it holds that $len(\gamma_0, ..., \gamma_c) \geq c + 1$. By minimality of Ξ, the strict subexecution $\gamma_0, ..., \gamma_c$ is not a counterexample; i.e. $\exists i \leq c \bullet Rec_{con}(\gamma_i, ..., \gamma_c) \geq \Delta$. However, since $\gamma_c \not\models con$, it follows that $i \neq c$, which implies that:

$$\exists i < c \bullet Rec_{con}(\gamma_i, ..., \gamma_c) \geq \Delta. \tag{9}$$

By Lemma 1, (6), and (9):

$$\exists i < c \bullet \forall j \geq c \bullet Rec_{con}(\gamma_i, ..., \gamma_j) \geq \Delta. \tag{10}$$

There is a contradiction between (4) and (10) $\lightning$. $\qquad\qquad\square$

THEOREM 1. If a system Ω does not satisfy con_Δ-convergence in c steps, then there exists a minimal counterexample wrt. (con, Δ, c) of length $c + 1$, that is a prefix of an execution in Ω.

PROOF: Since Ω does not satisfy con_Δ-convergence in c steps, then by Def. 4, there exists a counterexample Ξ wrt. (con, Δ, c) in Ω. If Ξ is minimal, then the Theorem holds. Otherwise, by Lemma 2, there exists a strict subexecution Ξ' of Ξ, such that $len(\Xi') = c + 1$, and Ξ' is a minimal counterexample. By definition of a system, any subexecution of any execution in Ω is indeed an execution prefix of an execution in Ω. The Theorem holds. $\qquad\square$

5 An Alternative View to con_Δ-convergence

In self-stabilization, it is usually assumed that faults do not happen very frequently. This, in turn, directs the focus to the aspect where the system has to quickly converge to a stable behavior, without voluntarily deviating from it, while not focusing on the delivered quality of service during convergence. However, there are environments where systems are vulnerable to high frequency of faults. Naturally, for such environments, it is important that the system provides a reasonable quality of service, even during system convergence.

Our approach here is to consider such environments in our framework. Towards this end, we use the notion of con_Δ-*warmup time* to denote the time required by a system to accumulatively reach Δ recurrence of a condition con, starting from any initial state. In contrast to the con_Δ-convergence time defined in Section 3, the con_Δ-warmup time considers the recurrence of con starting from the beginning, and not starting from a state that occurs during the con_Δ-convergence time.

DEFINITION 5 (con_Δ-WARMUP TIME). Given a system Ω, a condition con, and $\Delta \in [0,1] \subset \mathbb{Q}$.

- An execution $\Xi : \gamma_0, \gamma_1, ...$ is said to *have a con_Δ-warmup time of w steps* iff w is the minimum number, such that for each $i \geq w$, the execution prefix $\gamma_0, ..., \gamma_i$ of Ξ satisfies con_Δ.
  It is also said that the execution Ξ *guarantees con_Δ-warmup in i steps*.
- The system Ω is said to have a con_Δ-*warmup time* of w *steps* iff w is the maximum con_Δ-warmup time among all executions of Ω.   ◇

To analyze recurrence properties, together with the warmup notion, we follow a similar approach to the one in Section 4: for each system that does not satisfy some con_Δ-warmup time, there exists a minimal counterexample of finite length, even though the system has infinite executions. To avoid confusion, we call any counterexample of the warmup time property a *wu-counterexample*.

DEFINITION 6. Let con be a condition, $\Delta \in [0,1] \subset \mathbb{Q}$, and $w \in \mathbb{N}_0$.

- A *wu-counterexample wrt.* (con, Δ, w) is a finite execution Ξ that does not satisfy con_Δ-warmup in w steps.
- A *wu*-counterexample Ξ wrt. (con, Δ, w) is said to be *minimal* iff there exists no strict subexecution Ξ' of Ξ such that Ξ' is a *wu*-counterexample.   ◇

Considering the warmup time, the length of any minimal *wu*-counterexample lies between $w + 1$ and $2w + 1$. In this case, to find a counterexample via model checking, it is sufficient to check all execution prefixes having any of those lengths.

THEOREM 2. If a system Ω does not satisfy con_Δ-warmup time of w steps, then there exists a minimal *wu*-counterexample $\Xi = \gamma_0, ..., \gamma_{k-1}$ wrt. (con, Δ, w) such that $w+1 \leq k \leq 2w+1$, and Ξ is an execution prefix of an execution in Ω.

PROOF: By Def. 6, and analogous to Observation 1, it follows that any wu-counterexample has a length greater or equal to $w+1$. Thus, it remains to show that the length of each minimal wu-counterexample is not greater than $2w+1$. We prove this by contradiction:

Let $\Xi = \gamma_0, ..., \gamma_{k-1}$ be a minimal wu-counterexample, such that $len(\Xi) = k > 2w+1$. By Definitions 5, 6, and by assumption, it follows that $Rec_{con}(\Xi) < \Delta$, or equivalently

$$sat_{con}(\Xi) < k \cdot \Delta. \tag{11}$$

We split Ξ into two parts: $\Xi = \alpha\beta$ where

$$\Xi = \underbrace{\gamma_0 \cdots \gamma_w}_{\alpha} \underbrace{\gamma_{w+1} \cdots \gamma_{2w} \cdots \gamma_{k-1}}_{\beta}.$$

Since $len(\alpha) = w+1$, by minimality of Ξ, it follows that $Rec_{con}(\alpha) \geq \Delta$, or equivalently:

$$sat_{con}(\alpha) \geq (w+1) \cdot \Delta. \tag{12}$$

Likewise, since $len(\beta) = k - w - 1 > (w+1) - w - 1 = w$, by minimality of the length of Ξ, it follows that: $Rec_{con}(\beta) \geq \Delta$, or equivalently

$$sat_{con}(\beta) \geq (k - w - 1) \cdot \Delta. \tag{13}$$

Considering that $sat_{con}(\alpha) + sat_{con}(\beta) = sat_{con}(\Xi)$, by (12) and (13), we have

$$sat_{con}(\Xi) \geq (w+1) \cdot \Delta + (k - w - 1) \cdot \Delta, \tag{14}$$

which gives

$$sat_{con}(\Xi) \geq k \cdot \Delta. \tag{15}$$

There is a contradiction between (11) and (15) $\lightning$. □

We provide an example showing that $2w+1$ is indeed the least upper bound. The following execution Ξ has length $2w+1$, and is a minimal wu-counterexample wrt. $(con, \Delta = \frac{1}{2}, w = 3)$. Again, $\underline{\gamma}$ indicates that γ satisfies con:

$$\Xi : \gamma_0, \gamma_1, \underline{\gamma_2}, \underline{\gamma_3}, \underline{\gamma_4}, \gamma_5, \gamma_6.$$

6   Model Checking the Absence of Finite Counterexamples

In this section, we show how model checking can be applied to check if a distributed algorithm guarantees the following two properties:

(P1) a con_Δ-convergence time of c steps
(P2) a con_Δ-warmup time of w steps.

Model checking is a verification technique that checks whether a particular system's model satisfies a particular specification. It checks whether each reachable state from an initial state satisfies a condition. Concerning systems' environment of this work, there are two difficulties of applying model checking: (1) having possibly infinite executions, and (2) having possibly infinite state space. In this work, our concern is to simplify the former difficulty (see Sections 4 and 5.) The latter property might be tackled by additional abstraction techniques, which is out of the scope of this work. Therefore, from now on, we consider systems with a finite state space, but not necessarily finite executions.

Since we check a property over executions, and model checking verifies conditions over states, our idea is to add a so-called *observer* process, that (1) runs in parallel to the system, and (2) stores the truth values of *con* for all states in the execution. Next, the model checker verifies if the observer's state satisfies some property, to know whether the recurrence property holds or not.

We used the model checker NUXMV [16]. NUXMV provides a flexible input language for modelling distributed algorithms, defined by guarded commands.

Checking con_Δ-convergence Time of c Steps

To check the property (P1), we add an observer with $c + 1$ registers $b_0, \ldots, b_c$ and a step counter "step," which is initialized with 0 and ranging from 0 to $c + 1$. step is incremented in each step. The observer stores the first $c + 1$ states of an execution Ξ, as follows: In the i-th step, the observer assigns the register b_{i-1} the truth value of *con* in state γ_{i-1}. Thus, in the state γ_{i+1} the value of b_i is assigned correctly and reflects whether $\gamma_i \models con$ is true. Next, the model checker verifies the following formula:

$$\text{step} = c + 1 \rightarrow \exists i \leq c \bullet count(b_i, \ldots, b_c) \geq \Delta \cdot (c - i + 1).$$

If the model checker finds an execution leading to a state that violates the former formula, then this execution corresponds to an execution Ξ of the system which is a counterexample. Hint: since the register b_{i-1} is updated during the i-th step and thus keeps the correct value earliest in state γ_i, the formula has to be checked one step later than expected, i.e., when step $= c + 1$ and not when step $= c$.[2]

Checking con_Δ-warmUp Time of w Steps

To check (P2), we add an observer, with a slight different functionality: the observer has an additional counter "good." Both counters step and good are initialized with 0 and range from 0 to $w + 1$. The counter good is incremented only in each step where *con* holds. This allows us to check whether formula

$$w + 2 \leq \text{step} \wedge \text{step} \leq 2w + 2 \rightarrow \text{good} \geq \Delta * \text{step}$$

holds. Hint: again, we check the formula one step later than expected, i.e., when $w + 2 \leq \text{step} \wedge \text{step} \leq 2w + 2$ instead of $w + 1 \leq \text{step} \wedge \text{step} \leq 2w + 1$.

---

[2] Although it is possible to do check the formula in the state where step $= c$, this would result in a fair readability.

Algorithm 1. Mutual Exclusion Algorithm of Process p [4, Algorithm 2]

Constants

$\epsilon \quad = \lceil D/2 \rceil - 1$
$stab_\chi = \{0, ..., (n + \epsilon - 1)\}$
$tail_\chi^* = \{-D, ..., -1\}$

Predicates

$allCorrect_p \equiv \forall q \in \mathcal{N}_p \bullet r_p = r_q$
$privileged_p \equiv allCorrect_p \wedge r_p = id + \epsilon$
$normal_p \equiv r_p \in stab_\chi \wedge allCorrect_p$
$converge_p \equiv \exists q \in \mathcal{N}_p^* \bullet r_q \in tail_\chi^*$
$reset_p \equiv \forall q \in \mathcal{N}_p^* \bullet r_q \in stab_\chi \wedge \neg allCorrect_p$

Guarded Commands

$NA \quad :: \quad normal_p \quad \longrightarrow \quad r_p := r_p + 1 \mod (n + \epsilon);$
$CA \quad :: \quad converge_p \quad \longrightarrow \quad r_p := \min\{r_s + 1 | s \in \mathcal{N}_p^*\};$
$RA \quad :: \quad reset_p \quad \longrightarrow \quad r_p := -D;$

Benchmarks

As a benchmark, we have chosen a distributed mutual exclusion algorithm – Algorithm 1 – to be analyzed. The algorithm is taken from [4, Algorithm 2]. The algorithm is based on the finite synchronous incrementing system, presented by Boulinier et al. [17], and it follows a similar approach to Dubois et al. [6] in achieving a fast convergence wrt. mutual exclusion. We provide an appropriate clarification of the algorithm, without going into many details, due to the limited space. The full details and correctness proofs can be found in [4].

The general environment is as follows: the system's topology is modelled as a connected graph $G = (P, E)$, with a finite number of processes P and edges E, and uses the shared memory model under synchronous environments [18]. The number of processes is denoted by n, and the diameter of the graph is denoted by D. We assume that $n \geq 2$, which implies that $D \geq 1$. The set of neighbors of a process p is denoted by $\mathcal{N}_p$. We also define $\mathcal{N}_p^* = \mathcal{N}_p \cup \{p\}$.

Each process p has a variable r_p. Let $\epsilon = \lceil D/2 \rceil - 1$. The domain of r_p is the following set of integer values: $\{-D, ..., (n + \epsilon - 1)\}$. This domain is divided into two major subsets: $stab_\chi = \{0, ..., (n + \epsilon - 1)\}$ and $tail_\chi^* = \{-D, ..., -1\}$.

There are three types of actions performed by each process p:

1. *NA* (*Normal Action*): a process p increments its value within $0, ..., (n + \epsilon - 1)$, if $r_p = r_q$ for all $q \in \mathcal{N}_p$.
2. *CA* (*Converge Action*): a process p sets r_p to the minimum-plus-one value of r_q among all $q \in \mathcal{N}_p^*$, if $r_q \in tail_\chi^*$.
3. *RA* (*Reset Action*): a process p sets r_p to $-D$ if there exists a neighbor q, such that $r_q \neq r_p$, and for all neighbors $g \in \mathcal{N}_p^*$, $r_g \in stab_\chi$.

The aim of this design is to achieve a *synchronous unison*: an execution $\Xi : \gamma_0, \gamma_1, ...$ satisfies a synchronous unison – *SU* – iff

1. In each state $\gamma_0, \gamma_1, ...$, for all $p, q \in P$, $r_p = r_q$.
2. Each process $p \in P$ increments r_p in each execution step of Ξ.

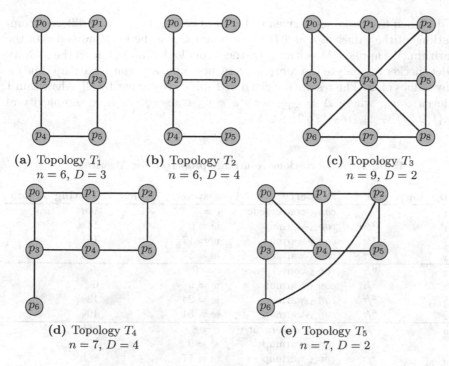

(a) Topology T_1
$n = 6$, $D = 3$

(b) Topology T_2
$n = 6$, $D = 4$

(c) Topology T_3
$n = 9$, $D = 2$

(d) Topology T_4
$n = 7$, $D = 4$

(e) Topology T_5
$n = 7$, $D = 2$

Fig. 1. The topologies, over which Algorithm 1 is tested

Note that with the given parameters, the convergence time complexity wrt. *SU* of this system is $2D$ [17].

This system can be used as a mutual exclusion algorithm [6]. In the specification of mutual exclusion – *ME* –, there exists a condition *privileged*, which is defined over the local state of each process (including the read values of the process's neighbors) – see Algorithm 1. The specification of *ME* is as follows:

1. If $privileged_p$ holds for one process p in a given system state γ, it should not hold for any other process in γ.
2. For each process $p \in P$, $privileged_p$ holds infinitely often.

Algorithm 1 converges wrt. *ME* in $\lceil D/2 \rceil - 1$ steps. This time complexity is optimal, and a complete argument about this time complexity is given in [4].

Model Checking

In the design of Algorithm 1, the main purpose is to achieve a high recurrence of *privileged* for any process, besides the optimal time complexity, based on the basic design of the finite incrementing system [17]. Note that the recurrence of *privileged* refers to the notion of *service time* in mutual exclusion [19]. In the following, we analyze the recurrence of *con*. *con* is defined as follows:

$$con \stackrel{\text{def}}{=} \exists p \in P \bullet privileged_p,$$

We designed five topologies, given in Fig. 1. The topologies have different combinations of the values of n and D, since n and D are the key parameters of the algorithm. We applied Algorithm 1 on these topologies, and we used the NUXMV model checker to analyze the con_Δ-convergence time, and con_Δ-warmup time for many values of Δ. The results are given in Table 1. Note that by [4], Algorithm 1 achieves con_Δ, where $\Delta = \frac{n}{n+\epsilon}$, with a con_Δ-convergence time complexity of $\max\{(\lceil 2.5D \rceil - 1), (n + \lceil D/2 \rceil - 2)\}$.

Table 1. Model checking recurrence properties for Algorithm 1

Topology	Δ	Property	#steps	Holds	Testing Time[3]
T_1	$6/7$	con_Δ-convergence	$c = 7$	✓	10s
T_1	$2/11$	con_Δ-warmup	$w = 9$	✓	14s
T_1	$4/7$	con_Δ-warmup	$w = 17$	✓	15s
T_1	$5/7$	con_Δ-warmup	$w = 37$	✓	29s
T_2	$6/7$	con_Δ-convergence	$c = 9$	✓	4s
T_2	$2/11$	con_Δ-warmup	$w = 9$	✓	6s
T_2	$4/7$	con_Δ-warmup	$w = 24$	✓	13s
T_2	$5/7$	con_Δ-warmup	$w = 51$	✓	19s
T_3	$1/1$	con_Δ-convergence	$c = 8$	✓	86h
T_3	$2/11$	con_Δ-warmup	$w = 9$	✓	73h
T_3	$4/7$	con_Δ-warmup	$w = 17$	✓	86h
T_3	$5/7$	con_Δ-warmup	$w = 37$	✓	88h
T_4	$7/8$	con_Δ-convergence	$c = 8$	X	5m51s
T_4	$7/8$	con_Δ-convergence	$c = 9$	✓	7m15s
T_4	$2/11$	con_Δ-warmup	$w = 8$	X	6m10s
T_4	$2/11$	con_Δ-warmup	$w = 9$	✓	7m55s
T_4	$4/7$	con_Δ-warmup	$w = 23$	X	9m42s
T_4	$4/7$	con_Δ-warmup	$w = 24$	✓	9m27s
T_4	$5/7$	con_Δ-warmup	$w = 43$	X	10m35s
T_4	$5/7$	con_Δ-warmup	$w = 44$	✓	10m44s
T_5	$1/1$	con_Δ-convergence	$c = 3$	X	3m03s
T_5	$1/1$	con_Δ-convergence	$c = 4$	✓	2m42s
T_5	$2/11$	con_Δ-warmup	$w = 2$	X	4m26s
T_5	$2/11$	con_Δ-warmup	$w = 3$	✓	3m24s
T_5	$4/7$	con_Δ-warmup	$w = 7$	X	4m05s
T_5	$4/7$	con_Δ-warmup	$w = 8$	✓	3m29s
T_5	$5/7$	con_Δ-warmup	$w = 11$	X	3m31s
T_5	$5/7$	con_Δ-warmup	$w = 12$	✓	4m

7   Conclusion and Discussion

We presented a formal approach that simplifies verifying recurrence properties in self-stabilizing systems using automatic verification tools. First, we have shown

---

[3] On 64-core AMD Opteron with 2.6GHz, 504GiB of RAM (single-core mode).

that for each system that does not converge to an execution suffix guaranteeing a minimum recurrence in c steps, there exists an execution, whose prefix of length $c + 1$ is a counterexample. Second, we presented the notion of *warmup time*, which denotes the time required by an execution to reach some recurrence of a condition, starting from any state. We have shown that if a system does not satisfy a warmup time wrt. some recurrence in w steps, then the system has an execution prefix that is a counterexample having a length between $w + 1$ and $2w + 1$. Next, given that there exists at least one finite counterexample for each system violating its property, model checking can be used to check the absence of counterexamples, to conclude that a system satisfies its property. As a case study, we analyzed the service time of a self-stabilizing mutual exclusion algorithm. We have modelled the service time as the recurrence of granting privilege to a process. We have used the model checker NUXMV to obtain analysis of the algorithm over many topologies.

For the model checking section we considered systems having finite state space since we were able to apply model checking directly. However, this might not be the case for systems having infinite state space. An infinite state space is the result of having variables with infinite domains. In many cases, such variables have number values. This raises the question whether bounded model checking (BMC) together with abstraction techniques may be used to verify recurrence properties for these systems. To use BMC, it is required that there exists an upper bound on the length of the execution, which is achieved in this work.

Our approach considered analyzing performance properties in self-stabilization. Following this approach, instead of focusing on performance related conditions, one may focus on the consequences of faults during the convergence. In particular, the notion of warmup time can be used to analyze the recurrence of conditions that are followed by non-desired actions during convergence. For example, one may analyze the recurrence of failing to satisfy mutual exclusion; i.e., two or more processes having granted privileges in the same state. This provides more information about the algorithm's behavior during convergence, which might help to improve the quality of service.

References

1. Dolev, S.: Self-Stabilization. The MIT Press (2000)
2. Dijkstra, E.W.: Self-Stabilizing Systems in Spite of Distributed Control. Communications of the ACM **17**(11) (1974)
3. Jubran, O., Theel, O.: Brief announcement: introducing recurrence in self-stabilization. In: [20]
4. Jubran, O., Theel, O.: Introducing Recurrence in Self-Stabilization (Revised Version). Report No. 101 of SFB/TR 14 AVACS, April 2015. http://www.avacs.org/
5. Kravchik, A., Kutten, S.: Time optimal synchronous self stabilizing spanning tree. In: Afek, Y. (ed.) DISC 2013. LNCS, vol. 8205, pp. 91–105. Springer, Heidelberg (2013)
6. Dubois, S., Guerraoui, R.: Introducing Speculation in Self-Stabilization - An Application to Mutual Exclusion. CoRR, abs/1302.2217 (2013)

7. Boulinier, C., Petit, F., Villain, V.: When graph theory helps self-stabilization. In: Proceedings of the 23rd ACM Symposium on Principles of Distributed Computing - PODC. ACM (2004)

8. Datta, A.K., Larmore, L., Vemula, P.: Self-Stabilizing Leader Election in Optimal Space under an Arbitrary Scheduler. Theoretical Computer Science 412(40), 5541–5561 (2011)

9. Dhama, A., Theel, O.: A tranformational approach for designing scheduler-oblivious self-stabilizing algorithms. In: Dolev, S., Cobb, J., Fischer, M., Yung, M. (eds.) SSS 2010. LNCS, vol. 6366, pp. 80–95. Springer, Heidelberg (2010)

10. Klinkhamer, A., Ebnenasir, A.: Synthesizing self-stabilization through superposition and backtracking. In: [20]

11. Faghih, F., Bonakdarpour, B.: SMT-based synthesis of distributed self-stabilizing systems. In: [20]

12. de Moura, L.M., Bjørner, N.: Satisfiability Modulo Theories: Introduction and Applications. Communic. of the ACM 54(9), 69–77 (2011)

13. Fallahi, N., Bonakdarpour, B., Tixeuil, S.: Rigorous performance evaluation of self-stabilization using probabilistic model checking. In: Proceedings of the 32nd Symposium on Reliable Distributed Systems - SRDS. IEEE (2013)

14. Nakaminami, Y., Kakugawa, H., Masuzawa, T.: An advanced performance analysis of self-stabilizing protocols: stabilization time with transient faults during convergence. In: Proceedings of the 20th International Parallel and Distributed Processing Symposium - IPDPS. IEEE (2006)

15. Dhama, A., Theel, O., Warns, T.: Reliability and availability analysis of self-stabilizing systems. In: Datta, A.K., Gradinariu, M. (eds.) SSS 2006. LNCS, vol. 4280, pp. 244–261. Springer, Heidelberg (2006)

16. Cavada, R., et al.: The NUXMV symbolic model checker. In: Biere, A., Bloem, R. (eds.) CAV 2014. LNCS, vol. 8559, pp. 334–342. Springer, Heidelberg (2014)

17. Boulinier, C., Petit, F., Villain, V.: Synchronous vs. Asynchronous Unison. Algorithmica 51(1) (2008)

18. Tel, G.: Introduction to Distributed Algorithms. Cambridge University Press (2000)

19. Johnen, C.: Service time optimal self-stabilizing token circulation protocol on anonymous unidirectional rings. In: Proceedings of the 21st International Symposium on Reliable Distributed Systems - SRDS. IEEE (2002)

20. Proceedings of the 16th International Symposium on Stabilization, Safety, and Security of Distributed Systems - SSS. Springer (2014)

Untangling Partial Agreement: Iterated x-consensus Simulations

Damien Imbs[1(✉)], Sergio Rajsbaum[2], and Adrián Valle[3]

[1] Department of Mathematics, University of Bremen, 28334 Bremen, Germany
imbs@math.uni-bremen.de
[2] Instituto de Matemáticas, UNAM, D.F. 04510 Ciudad de Mexico, Mexico
[3] Oracle, Zapopan, Jalisco, Mexico

Abstract. The basic *read/write shared memory* model where asynchronous and crash prone processes communicate to solve a task is difficult to analyze. A more structured model is the *iterated immediate snapshot* model (IIS), where processes execute communication closed rounds. In each round, they communicate using read/write registers that cannot be reused in later rounds. It is known that a task is solvable in the IIS model if and only if it is solvable in the basic read/write model. Both models are also equivalent when, in addition to read/write registers, processes also have access to stronger communication objects called *01-tasks*.

This paper extends further the task computability equivalence presenting a simulation that includes x-consensus objects, which solve consensus among up to x processes. The simulation implies that an iterated model where processes communicate through a sequence consisting only of x-consensus objects is equivalent to the basic shared memory model augmented with x-consensus objects.

Keywords: Asynchronous systems · Consensus · Distributed computing · Iterated Immediate Snapshot · Read/write shared memory · Task solvability · Wait-freedom

1 Introduction

A central issue in distributed computing is determining which *tasks* are solvable in a given computation model. When solving a task, each process starts the computation with an input value, known only to itself, and after communicating with the other processes, decides an output value. The task specifies the outputs that are compatible with each other, for the given local inputs of the processes. An example is the *k-set agreement* task [14], where at most k different outputs are produced, and all have to be equal to one of the inputs. When $k = 1$, we have the classic *consensus* task [21], where all outputs must be equal to one of the inputs.

S. Rajsbaum—Partially supported by a UNAM-PAPIIT grant.
D. Imbs and A. Valle—Part of this work was done while the authors were at the Instituto de Matemáticas, UNAM.

© Springer International Publishing Switzerland 2015
A. Pelc and A.A. Schwarzmann (Eds.): SSS 2015, LNCS 9212, pp. 139–155, 2015.
DOI: 10.1007/978-3-319-21741-3_10

A basic model is the wait-free *read/write shared memory* model, where n asynchronous processes that may crash, communicate using shared read/write registers. This model is strong enough to implement snapshots [1], where processes can read the whole memory in a single atomic step. However in this model k-set agreement is not solvable [6,37,47], even when $k = n - 1$.

Designing algorithms as well as proving impossibility results in the read/write memory model is difficult. It is easier to analyze algorithms in more structured, *iterated* models of computation [8,10,11,13,18,22,26,28,43–46]. In an iterated model [41], processes proceed in communication closed rounds [20]. In each round, they communicate using shared objects specific to the given round. These objects cannot be reused in later rounds. Iterated models have also been used to facilitate impossibility proofs using topology [30], and for some results the only known proofs are in an iterated model e.g. [11,19,28,34].

Given the usefulness of iterated models both to design algorithms and to prove impossibility results, the main research question in this area is when a model of computation is equivalent to its iterated counterpart (where communication proceeds in rounds, and objects can be used only once, in their corresponding round), with respect to task solvability. Also, this issue is closely related to the question of when a distributed algorithm has a recursive counterpart [7,27,42].

The basic iterated model is the *iterated immediate snapshot* (IIS) model [8], where processes communicate in each round using an *immediate snapshot* object associated to the round. In such an object, a process can invoke a write operation, and receives a snapshot that occurred immediately after the write. The first result in this area was that the IIS model can *simulate* the read/write shared memory model where any number of process can crash [8], and hence both models can solve the same set of tasks.

Later on, the IIS model was extended and a simulation was provided [26], showing that the same tasks can be solved when 01-*objects* are available [23,24]. These objects are stronger than read/write registers, but are not strong enough to solve consensus even among 3 processes; they are strong enough only to solve $(n - 1)$-set agreement.

Contributions. We introduce the *iterated x-consensus* model. In this model, in each round, processes communicate through a single x-consensus object. They do not have access to read/write registers.

- We present a simulation that can execute any wait-free read/write shared memory algorithm that solves a task in the iterated x-consensus model. Thus, x-consensus objects have a "memory effect": they can be used to solve any task that can be solved using read/write registers.
- We present an extension of the previous simulation to shared memory models where processes have, in addition to read/write registers, access to x-consensus objects. This extended simulation proves that the shared memory model where processes have access to x-consensus objects is equivalent to the iterated x-consensus model. This simulation has the following implications.

In the shared memory model, processes can access the x-consensus objects in any order (not necessarily the same for each process). On the other hand, in the iterated x-consensus model, processes access the objects in exactly the same order, just as they access the different rounds in the same order. The simulation shows that there does not exist any algorithm that (in addition to a shared memory) only uses x-consensus objects for which the correctness depends on the fact that processes access the objects in a different order. Object invocations can always be reorganized to happen in the same order for every process (e.g., the simulation shows that in our context, there is no added computational power by a code where one process accesses first O_1 and then O_2 while another process accesses first O_2 and then O_1).

The simulation shows that, when considering *colorless* tasks [9,33,34] (such as set agreement), the wait-free iterated x-consensus model with n processes is equivalent to the wait-free shared memory model with $\lceil n/x \rceil$ processes. This equivalence implies that the problem of determining whether a colorless task can be solved in the iterated x-consensus model consisting of n processes is decidable if and only if $\lceil n/x \rceil \leq 2$. The proof is by reduction to the problem of determining if a given task is wait-free solvable, which is known to be decidable only for 2 processes [25,31,32].

Related Work. The characterisation of the tasks which are solvable in the basic read/write model [37] has an origin going back to [5] and has been extended to various other models using topology [30]. Extensions include randomized characterizations [16,17].

A powerful technique to determine if a task is solvable in a given model is the use of simulations, e.g. [3,8,12,22,26,35,36,44]. One of the results based on a simulation is the equivalence between the shared memory and the message-passing model of computation (under the condition that a majority of processes are correct) [3]. Such simulations allowed to design algorithms in shared memory and export them to message-passing (which is harder to analyze), or to prove impossibilities in the shared memory model, and extend them to the message passing using simulations. Other classes of simulations are between models that have different numbers of processes [9] or tolerate different types of failures [40].

In [26], the read/write model and the iterated snapshot model are strengthened with 01-tasks [23], and it is shown that the equivalence between the two models still holds. In these tasks processes decide either 0 or 1, but they cannot all decide the same value. In executions in which not all processes participate, the valid outputs depend on the specific 01-task. The strongest 01-task can solve $(n, n-1)$-set agreement, but not $(n, n-2)$-set agreement. The x-consensus objects that we consider here are thus more powerful. A study of when simulations exist between certain models and not others has been done in [33], based on topological arguments.

In [44], the possible executions of the IIS model are restricted in such a way that they are equivalent to executions of a read/write system with a failure detector. The resulting model is called the *Iterated Restricted Immediate Snapshot* model. In [45], the IIS model is enriched directly with failure detectors. It is shown that various failure detectors in the read/write model have an equivalent in the IIS model.

In [39], the equivalence between the read/write shared memory model and the shared memory model extended with x-consensus objects is considered. For colorless tasks, the t-resilient model with x-consensus objects is equivalent to the $\lfloor t/x \rfloor$-resilient read/write model.

The objects that allow solving consensus between two processes are computationally equivalent to objects of the *Common2* class [2], which includes Test&Set, Swap, stack, and others. A generalization of 2-consensus objects are x-consensus objects, which can solve consensus among x processes. Also, x-consensus objects can solve k-set agreement among n processes, if and only if $k \geq \lceil n/x \rceil$ e.g. [15,30].

2   Model of Computation

We consider a set Π of n processes $p_1, \ldots, p_n$. Processes are *asynchronous:* there is no assumption on their relative speeds. Processes can crash: they can stop their execution at any time. We briefly recall notions that can be found in textbooks such as [4].

A decision task specifies a one-shot decision problem (the failure model is not part of this definition). Each process can invoke a single operation and can invoke it only once. Formally, a task is defined by a set $\mathcal{I}$ of possible input vectors, a set $\mathcal{O}$ of possible output vectors, and a relation $\Delta : \mathcal{I} \rightarrow 2^{\mathcal{O}}$ that associates each input vector $I \in \mathcal{I}$ to a non-empty set of output vectors $O \in \mathcal{O}$. Informally, an algorithm solves a task if the following holds. Each process p_i starts with an input value $input_i$ and each non-faulty process p_j decides an output value $output_j$. The input vector I is formed by the different inputs such that $I[i] = input_i$. Similarly, the output vector O is formed by the outputs such that $O[i] = output_i$. The output vector O must belong to the set $\Delta(I)$ for the algorithm to satisfy the safety of the task.

2.1   The Shared Memory Communication Model

Processes communicate by shared objects. Informally, an object specifies a set of states, a set of processes that may access it, the set of operations that those processes may apply to the object, and the behavior of the object, described by the effect of each operation on the object's state and the value the operation returns, assuming no other operation is accessing the object at that time. When operations are invoked concurrently *linearizability* [38] says that the object behaves as if each operation had occurred instantaneously, at some point between the time it was invoked and the time it returned its response. The shared memory includes an array of single-writer/multi-reader atomic registers. We may assume [1] that the shared memory is abstracted as a *snapshot* object, denoted $MEM[1..n]$. The entry $MEM[i]$ is associated to process p_i. The snapshot object offers two operations. Process p_i can write the value v to $MEM[i]$ using the operation $MEM.write_i(v)$ (for the sake of conciseness, this will be abbreviated by

$MEM[i] \leftarrow v$). Process p_i can also read the whole content of MEM atomically using the operation $MEM.snapshot_i()$.

```
algo_i(in_i):
(01)   view_i ← in_i;
(02)   while (δ_i(view_i) = ⊥) do
(03)      MEM[i] ← view_i;
(04)      view_i ← MEM.snapshot()
(05)   end while;
(06)   decide(δ_i(view_i)).
```

Fig. 1. Canonical form of a shared memory algorithm

Every distributed algorithm in which processes only communicate using the shared memory described above can be represented in the form presented in Figure 1.

Processes communicate through a single snapshot object MEM. Each process p_i gets an input value in_i, and stores the value in its local variable $view_i$ (line 01). The aim of variable $view_i$ is to store the local state of p_i. The algorithm is *full-information* because a process stores everything it has seen in $view_i$, and repeatedly communicate $view_i$ to the other processes. For computability purposes, we are not interested in saving on communication. Each process p_i repeatedly writes its local state to the shared memory, $view_i$ (line 03, and then takes a snapshot. Each repetition of the loop, p_i applies a decision function δ_i to its local state (line 02). If δ returns a value different from ⊥, the process decides this value (line 06).

In the following, we will only consider algorithms in their canonical form. Because each process writes its whole local state (the variable $view_i$) when it writes (line 03), any other value it could have written can be deduced from this information. If an algorithm writes twice without taking a snapshot, or takes two snapshots without writing, the missing operations can be inserted.

2.2   Model with x-consensus

In addition to a shared memory, processes may also have access to x-*consensus* objects. Recall that we assume that an object specifies which processes may access it. An x-consensus object is similar to the well-known consensus object e.g. [4,12], except that it can it be accessed only by a statically predefined subset of x processes, $1 \leq x \leq n$. Thus, it offers a single operation propose to the subset of processes that can access it, and it satisfies the usual consensus requirements.

- **Agreement.** No two distinct values are returned by different processes.
- **Validity.** A decided value is a proposed value.
- **Wait-freedom.** Any invocation by a correct process terminates.

An x-consensus object cannot be implemented using a read/write shared memory in a wait-free manner [29], except in the trivial case, $x = 1$, where only one process can invoke the object. When $x = n$ we have the usual consensus object.

Shared Memory Extended with x-consensus Objects. In the shared memory model extended with x-consensus objects, an infinite supply of these object is available to the processes. Processes can invoke any object at any time. The canonical form presented in Figure 2 is an extension of the one in Figure 1. Here, a process may invoke an x-consensus object after each time it writes to the shared memory (and before it takes the snapshot of the corresponding iteration).

```
algo_i(in_i):
(01)   view_i ← in_i; last_call ← ⊤;
(02)   while (δ_i(view_i) = ⊥) do
(03)       MEM[i] ← ⟨view_i, last_call⟩;
(04)       if (φ_i(view_i) ≠ ⊥)
(05)           then last_call ← φ_i(view_i).propose(view_i)
(06)           else last_call ← ⊤ end if;
(07)       view_i ← MEM.snapshot()
(08)   end while;
(09)   decide(δ_i(view_i)).
```

Fig. 2. Canonical form of a shared memory algorithm accessing x-consensus objects

The algorithm presented in Figure 1 is generic; the only task-specific element being the decision function δ. Here, an algorithm must also specify the x-consensus object to be invoked in each iteration of the loop. The object to be invoked by p_i is specified using a function ϕ_i. Given the local state of the process, ϕ_i returns either the identity of the object to be invoked, or $\perp$ if no x-consensus object will be invoked in the iteration (line 04). The object $\phi_i(view_i)$ is invoked (in line 05) with the operation $\phi_i(view_i).\mathsf{propose}(view_i)$, and the value returned by the object is stored in the local variable $last\_call$. The returned value will be communicated to the other process in the next iteration. The value returned by the object is stored in the local variable $last\_call$. If an object has been invoked, it contains the result of this invocation (line 05). If no object has been invoked, it contains the special value $\top$ (line 06).

2.3 The *Iterated x-consensus* Model

In the Iterated x-consensus model, processes proceed by rounds. An x-consensus object is associated to each round r. Processes communicate in each round only through the corresponding x-consensus object. Processes must access the x-consensus objects in the order imposed by the rounds: if a process does not access the x-consensus object of a given round, it cannot access it in later rounds.

The set of x processes that are allowed to access the object that corresponds to a round r is defined by a function μ. The sets returned by $\mu(r)$ evolve in a round-robin fashion: each subset of x processes is returned every $\binom{n}{x}$ rounds. Any other function that allows all subsets of x processes to run infinitely often would work.

3   The Base Simulation

Consider an algorithm solving some task in the shared memory model, given in the form of Figure 1. We show how to *simulate* the algorithm in the iterated x-consensus model with $x > 1$. Informally, in the simulation algorithm there are variables that represent the SWMR registers of the original algorithm, one variable per simulator. Each run of the simulation will correspond to a valid execution of the simulated algorithm, represented in these variables, until the decision function δ_i can be applied by each (simulator) process p_i. The simulation implies that if a task is solvable in the wait-free read/write shared memory model, then it is solvable in the x-consensus model. Thus, although x-consensus objects have no persistent value beyond the round in which they are accessed, they can be used to simulate a single array of shared registers, in order to solve a task.

Mechanism of the Simulation Algorithm. Each process stores in its local memory an array of values that represents its view of the simulated Single-Writer/Multi-Reader (SWMR) registers (one register per process). Initially, its view contains its input value for its own register and a special value $\bot$ for the registers of other processes.

In a given round, the x processes that can access an x-consensus object communicate their views using the object. The communication is one-way; only the winner (the process whose value is chosen by the x-consensus object) can communicate its view to the others. When a process observes a stable view of the memory with respect to all the other processes (in x-consensus invocations that include all other processes, it has either won or the winner had the same input), it simulates a snapshot and a write: in its local view, it updates its own register with the content of its previous view.

3.1   The Simulation Algorithm

The simulation algorithm is presented in Figure 3. It produces an execution of the given shared memory algorithm in the iterated x-consensus model.

Local Variables. The shared memory consists only of the x-consensus objects that processes access in each round. The local variables of a process p_i are the following.

- The round number r. This indicates to p_i the current round number. As required by the iterated x-consensus model, r is increased by 1 in each round (line 03).

```
Procedure BaseSimulation_i(input_i):
(01)  for all j ∈ [1..n], j ≠ i do c[j].val ← ⊥; c[j].clock ← 0 end for;
      c[i].val ← input_i; c[i].clock ← 1; ready_i ← ∅; view_i ← input_i; r ← 0;
(02)  loop forever
(03)    r ← r + 1;
(04)    if (i ∈ μ(r)) then
(05)      xcons_mem_i ← x_cons_r.propose(c);
(06)      if (xcons_mem_i ≠ c) then ready_i ← ∅; update_c(xcons_mem_i)
(07)                          else ready_i ← ready_i ∪ μ(r) end if;
(08)      if (ready_i = Π) then
(09)        view_i ← c.val;
(10)        if (δ_i(view_i) ≠ ⊥) then return(δ_i(view_i))
(11)                          else c[i].val ← view_i; c[i].clock ← c[i].clock + 1;
(12)                               ready_i ← ∅ end if
(13)  end if end if end loop.
```

Fig. 3. The base simulation algorithm (code for process p_i)

- The array $c[1..n]$. This array contains the values of the most recent simulated writes that process p_i has observed by other processes. Each entry contains two fields: *clock* and *val*. The field $c[j].val$ contains the value of the $c[j].clock^{th}$ simulated write by process p_j. Note that at line 09, $view_i$ gets $c.val = [c[1].val, \ldots, c[n].val]$.
- The array $xcons\_mem_i[1..n]$. This array contains the result of the last x-consensus invocation. Because processes propose their array c in each round in which they participate, each entry $xcons\_mem_i[j]$ contains the state of the simulation of the register of p_j as observed (directly or indirectly) by the winner of the last x-consensus invocation in which p_i participated.
- The set $ready_i$. This set contains the identities of all the processes that have participated in an x-consensus invocation with p_i since the last time p_i received a view different from its own in such an invocation.
- The variable $view_i$. This variable is used to simulate the local state of process p_i in the shared memory algorithm. It corresponds to the variable $view_i$ used in the full-information algorithm presented in Fig. 1. It is initialized with the input of p_i.

For the sake of simplifying the presentation of the algorithm, the code includes the local operation update_c (line 06). It updates the local array c using the most recent values obtained during the x-consensus invocation. The code is the following:

update_c($xcons\_mem_i$):
  for all $x \in [1..n]$ do
    if ($xcons\_mem_i[x].clock > c[x].clock$) then $c[x] ← xcons\_mem_i[x]$ end if
  end for.

Code Description. Process p_i initializes the array c with $\{⊥, 0\}$ for all clock entries except its own, indicating that it has not yet observed any write by any other process. It initializes its own entry $c[i]$ with $\{input_i, 1\}$, indicating its own clock value is 1, and its first write announces its own input. It then sets $ready_i$ to $\emptyset$ and enters the loop.

Process p_i increases its round number (line 03) until it can invoke the corresponding x-consensus object (test at line 04 using the function μ). It then invokes the object of the corresponding round, using its array c as its input line 05). This is the only way in which it communicates with other processes. There are two cases.

1. The result of the invocation is not equal to the value of its array c (line 06) because another process with a different input won it. In this case, p_i resets its set $ready_i$ to prevent simulating an inconsistent snapshot. It then updates c with the new values it learned from the invocation.
2. The result of the invocation is equal to the array c (line 07) because p_i won the x-consensus or because another process with the same input c won it. Process p_i then adds the set $\mu(r)$ of processes that are allowed to participate in this round to its set $ready_i$: all the processes p_j in $\mu(r)$ that do not propose the same array c will then have to reset their sets $ready_j$ (line 06 of p_j's code).

If the set $ready_i$ contains the identities of all the processes (test at line 08), p_i is ready to simulate a consistent snapshot using the values contained in c (line 09). If p_i can obtain a decision value for the simulated algorithm using the simulated snapshot (test at line 10 using the function δ), it returns this value and stops its execution. Otherwise, it simulates a write (line 11): it updates its own entry of c and resets its set $ready_i$.

3.2   Proof of the Simulation

Lemma 1. *All the processes that satisfy the condition $ready_i = \Pi$ at line 08 during round r do so with the same array c.*

Proof. Process p_i may execute line 08 during round r only if its identifier belongs to $\mu(r)$ (line 04) and thus only if it invoked the x-consensus operation at line 05. Because of the agreement property of the x-consensus objects, every process that invokes the x-consensus operation at round r receives the same array $xcons\_mem$.

If the array $xcons\_mem_i$ that p_i receives from this invocation is different from its array c (test at line 06), it resets its set $ready_i$ and does not satisfy the condition at line 08. All the processes that satisfy the condition at line 08 during round r thus do so with the same array c.

Define a partial order on the arrays c as follows. If $\forall x \in [1..n] : c[x].clock \leq c'[x].clock$, then $c \leq c'$. If $c \leq c' \wedge c' \not\leq c$, then $c < c'$.

Lemma 2. *If p_i satisfies the condition at line 08 during round r with the array c and p_j satisfies it during round r' with the array c', with $r < r'$, then $c \leq c'$.*

Proof. Let r'' be the last round before r at which p_i adds p_j to its set $ready_i$ (line 07). Because p_i needs to have all the processes in its set $ready_i$ to satisfy the condition at line 08, r'' is well-defined. Because p_i must reset its set $ready_i$ every time that it receives an array $xcons\_mem_i$ different from its array c (test at line 06), the array c of p_i is the same during round r'' and round r, and is equal to the array $xcons\_mem_i$ that p_i received during its x-consensus invocation at round r''.

During round r'', p_i can only add processes that belong to $\mu(r'')$ (line 07). Process p_j thus belongs to $\mu(r'')$ and receives the same value as p_i during the x-consensus invocation during round r''. Process p_j thus either updates its array c' during round r'' with values at least as recent at the values in c (line 06), or has an array c' equal to c (line 07). We can then conclude that $c \leq c'$.

Lemma 3. *If there are correct undecided processes at round r, at least one of them satisfies the condition $ready_i = \Pi$ at line 08 at round $r' \geq r$.*

Proof. Let P be the set of correct processes that have not decided at round r. By way of contradiction, suppose that there is an execution in which the processes in P never satisfy the condition at line 08 after round r.

There are two cases when a process p_i fills its set $ready_i$, and hence must satisfy the condition at line 08. If either (1) $p_i \in P$ does not participate in a round (because it does not belong to the set of x processes that can participate in this round), or (2) p_i does not satisfy the condition at line 06 (because $xcons\_mem_i = c$) during $\binom{n}{x}$ consecutive rounds, p_i fills its set $ready_i$ and it must satisfy the condition at line 08, a contradiction. Process p_i thus satisfies the condition at line 06 at least once every $\binom{n}{x}$ rounds. This can happen because (1) p_i observes values more recent than its own in $xcons\_mem_i$ or (2) it observes older values (less than in the vector clock).

Every time process $p_i \in P$ satisfies the condition at line 06 because it observes values more recent than its own, it updates its vector c with at least one entry of $xcons\_mem$ strictly more recent than its own (function update_c, line 06). Because the processes in P never satisfy the condition at line 08 after round r, they can never update their entry of c at line 11. Let c_{max} be the vector constituted by the highest entries (when considering the clock value) of the vectors c of the processes of P at round r. Process p_i cannot update the entries of its vector c to entries more recent than the entries of c_{max}. Every process in P thus eventually satisfies the condition at line 06 only because it observes older values.

Let r' be the first round after which processes in P only observe older values. Let p_i and p_j be two processes such that, at a round $r'' > r'$, p_i satisfies the condition at line 06 because it observes an older value from p_j (p_j wins the consensus at line 06 during round r'). Because processes never observe values more recent than their own after r', p_i never wins an x-consensus in which p_j participates after r'. By repeating the same reasoning, we obtain that either (1) no process in P ever wins an x-consensus or (2) a process in P never observes older values. Both cases lead to contradictions, which concludes the proof of the lemma.

Lemma 4. *The simulated execution is a correct execution of the shared memory model.*

Proof. Process p_i simulates a snapshot by writing the content of its array c into its variable $view_i$ (line 09) and a write by updating its entry of its array c (line 11). It does so every time it satisfies the condition at line 08.

By Lemmas 1 and 2, the simulated snapshots (the contents of c written into the variable $view$) can be totally ordered. Moreover, process p_i simulates a write (by updating $c[i]$) every time it simulates a snapshot. The simulated execution thus corresponds to a correct execution of the shared memory model.

Lemma 5. *If the simulated algorithm is a wait-free algorithm, then every correct process decides.*

Proof. By Lemma 3, after any given round r, if there are undecided processes, at least one of them satisfies the condition at line 08 and thus completes its simulation of a snapshot and a write. If the simulated algorithm is wait-free, at least one correct process will then make enough progress to decide. Because a process that decides stops participating (it returns its decision value at line 10), every correct process eventually decides.

Theorem 1. *The algorithm presented in Figure 3 is a correct simulation of a wait-free shared memory algorithm.*

Proof. The proof follows from Lemmas 4 (safety), and 5 (progress).

4   The Extended Simulation

The simulation presented in this section takes as input a wait-free algorithm designed for the shared memory model extended with x-consensus objects, and simulates it in the iterated x-consensus model. It shows that, with respect to wait-free task solvability, the iterated x-consensus model is equivalent to the shared memory model augmented with x-consensus objects, because simulating an algorithm for the iterated x-consensus model in the shared memory model extended with x-consensus objects is trivial.

Extending the Previous Simulation. The simulation algorithm is presented in Figure 4. It is based on the simulation presented in the previous section. The algorithm to be simulated is designed for the shared memory model extended with x-consensus objects, as in Figure 2. Thus, it is defined by a decision function δ, and by a function ϕ_i that specifies the x-consensus object to be invoked in each iteration of the loop.

```
Procedure ExtendedSimulationᵢ(inputᵢ):
```

Procedure ExtendedSimulation$_i$($input_i$):
(01) **for all** $j \in [1..n], j \neq i$ **do** $c[j].val \leftarrow \bot$; $c[j].clock \leftarrow 0$ **end for**;
$\quad\quad$ $c[i].val \leftarrow input_i$; $c[i].clock \leftarrow 1$;
$\quad\quad$ $ready_i \leftarrow \emptyset$; $solved \leftarrow \emptyset$; $to\_solve \leftarrow \emptyset$; $view_i \leftarrow input_i$; $r \leftarrow 0$;
(02) **loop forever**
(03) $\quad$ $r \leftarrow r + 1$;
(04) $\quad$ **if** $(i \in \mu(r))$ **then**
(05) $\quad\quad$ **if** $(\exists \langle xcons\_id, xcons\_in \rangle \in to\_solve_i : \mathsf{procs}(xcons\_id) = \mu(r))$ **then**
(06) $\quad\quad\quad$ $(xcons\_mem_i, xcons\_inv_i) \leftarrow \mathsf{x\_cons}_r.\mathsf{propose}(c, \langle xcons\_id, xcons\_in \rangle)$;
(07) $\quad\quad$ **else if** $(\exists \langle xcons\_id, xcons\_in \rangle \in to\_solve_i)$ **then**
(08) $\quad\quad\quad$ $(xcons\_mem_i, xcons\_inv_i) \leftarrow \mathsf{x\_cons}_r.\mathsf{propose}(c, \langle xcons\_id, xcons\_in \rangle)$;
(09) $\quad\quad$ **else**
(10) $\quad\quad\quad$ $(xcons\_mem_i, xcons\_inv_i) \leftarrow \mathsf{x\_cons}_r.\mathsf{propose}(c, \bot)$;
(11) $\quad\quad$ **end if**;
(12) $\quad\quad$ **if** $(xcons\_inv_i \neq \bot)$ **then**
(13) $\quad\quad\quad$ **if** $(\mathsf{procs}(xcons\_inv_i.id) = \mu(r))$ **then**
(14) $\quad\quad\quad\quad$ **for all** $\langle xcons\_inv_i.id, x \rangle \in to\_solve_i$ **do**
(15) $\quad\quad\quad\quad\quad$ $to\_solve_i \leftarrow to\_solve_i \setminus \{\langle xcons\_inv_i.id, x \rangle\}$ **end for**;
(16) $\quad\quad\quad\quad$ $solved_i \leftarrow solved_i \cup \{xcons\_inv_i\}$
(17) $\quad\quad\quad$ **else if** $((i \in \mathsf{procs}(xcons\_inv_i.id)) \wedge (\nexists \langle xcons\_inv_i.id, - \rangle \in to\_solve_i))$
(18) $\quad\quad\quad\quad\quad$ **then** $to\_solve_i \leftarrow to\_solve_i \cup \{xcons\_inv_i\}$
(19) $\quad\quad\quad$ **end if**
(20) $\quad\quad$ **end if**;
(21) $\quad\quad$ **if** $(xcons\_mem_i \neq c)$ **then** $ready_i \leftarrow \emptyset$; $\mathsf{update\_c}(xcons\_mem_i)$
(22) $\quad\quad\quad\quad\quad\quad\quad\quad$ **else** $ready_i \leftarrow ready \cup \mu(r)$ **end if**;
(23) $\quad\quad$ **if** $((ready_i = \Pi) \wedge ((\phi_i(view_i) = \bot) \vee (\exists \langle \phi_i(view_i), xcons\_res \rangle \in solved_i)))$
(24) $\quad\quad\quad$ **then** $last\_view_i \leftarrow view_i$; $view_i \leftarrow c.val$;
(25) $\quad\quad\quad\quad$ **if** $(\delta(view_i) \neq \bot)$ **then** $\mathsf{return}(\delta(view_i))$
(26) $\quad\quad\quad\quad\quad\quad\quad\quad$ **else if** $(\phi_i(last\_view_i) \neq \bot)$
(27) $\quad\quad\quad\quad\quad\quad\quad\quad\quad$ **then** $c[i].val \leftarrow \langle view_i, xcons\_res \rangle$
(28) $\quad\quad\quad\quad\quad\quad\quad\quad\quad$ **else** $c[i].val \leftarrow \langle view_i, \top \rangle$ **end if**;
(29) $\quad\quad\quad\quad\quad\quad\quad\quad$ $c[i].clock \leftarrow c[i].clock + 1$; $ready_i \leftarrow \emptyset$;
(30) $\quad\quad\quad\quad\quad\quad\quad\quad$ **if** $(\phi_i(view_i) \neq \bot)$ **then**
(31) $\quad\quad\quad\quad\quad\quad\quad\quad\quad$ $to\_solve_i \leftarrow to\_solve_i \cup \{\langle \phi_i(view_i), view_i \rangle\}$
(32) **end if end if end if end if end loop**.

Fig. 4. The simulation algorithm extended to x-consensus objects (code for process p_i)

Additional Local Variables. In addition to the local variables used in the base simulation, the algorithm uses the following variables:

- A set to_solve_i. This set contains pairs consisting of the identifier of an x-consensus object and an input for this object. These pairs represent the x-consensus invocations that have not been simulated yet. The pairs contained in to_solve_i can represent invocations by p_i or invocations by other processes that p_i has learned in an earlier round.
- A set $solved_i$. This set contains pairs consisting of the identifier of an x-consensus object and an output for this object. These pairs represent the x-consensus invocations that have already been simulated.
- A variable $xcons\_inv_i$. This variable contains a pair representing the simulation of an x-consensus invocation. If the set of processes that can invoke

the corresponding object corresponds to the set of processes that are allowed to participate in this round, then the simulation of the invocation succeeds. Otherwise, this variable is used as a helping mechanism: when p_i receives a pair that does not correspond to the current round, it can propose it during a later x-consensus invocation.

Additionally, the simulation uses a function $\mathsf{procs}(X)$ to determine the set of processes that can access a simulated x-consensus object X.

Modifications to the Behavior of the Algorithm. Process p_i checks if it is aware of an x-consensus simulation that corresponds to the set of processes that can participate in the current round by checking its set to_solve_i (test at line 05). If it does, it proposes it with its current simulation of the memory (line 06). Otherwise, it checks if it is aware of another pending x-consensus simulation (line 07). If it does, it proposes it (line 08). This is used as a helping mechanism to avoid processes blocking each other when they need to simulate x-consensus objects that correspond to different sets of processes. If p_i is not aware of any pending x-consensus simulation, it proposes the special value $\bot$ along with its current simulation of the memory (line 10).

Process p_i then checks the part of the result of the x-consensus invocation that corresponds to the simulation of x-consensus objects. If it receives a pair that corresponds to the set of processes that can participate in the current round (test at line 13), it considers the invocation as simulated by placing the pair in its set $solved_i$ and by removing any pair that corresponds to the same object from its set to_solve_i. Otherwise, if the pair corresponds to an object it can access, it places it in its set to_solve_i (line 18).

An additional test is performed before the simulation of a snapshot is allowed. Process p_i checks if it has a pending x-consensus invocation, and if it has already been simulated (line 23). When simulating a write, p_i writes the result of its simulated x-consensus invocation if it has one (line 27) or $\top$ if it doesn't (line 28). Note that at line 29, $xcons\_res$ is only defined when $\phi_i(view_i) \neq \bot$, which is fine because of the previous **if** condition. Finally, if it has to simulate an x-consensus invocation before its next simulation of a snapshot, p_i adds the corresponding pair to its set to_solve_i (line 31).

Due to page limitations, the proof of the extended simulation is omitted.

5 Implications of the Simulation

Simulation of a Memory. The simulation from Section 3 shows that x-consensus objects can be used without an additional memory to solve any task that can be solved in a wait-free manner in a shared memory system.

Order of the x-consensus Invocations. One could think that the basis of some algorithms is that different processes must invoke x-consensus objects in different orders. The simulation from Section 4 shows that this is actually never true.

The invocations of x-consensus objects can always be reordered so that all processes invoke the objects in the same order (i.e. in the resulting algorithm, there is no pair of objects A and B, and processes p_i and p_j, such that p_i first invokes A then B, while p_j invokes B before A).

Equivalence with Pure Read/Write Models for Colorless Tasks. When considering colorless tasks, a shared memory model consisting of n processes, of which at most t can crash, and which can access x-consensus objects, is equivalent to a model of $\lfloor t/x \rfloor + 1$ processes, of which at most $\lfloor t/x \rfloor$ can crash, and which can only access shared registers (the result is from [39], and the equivalence is partly based on the BG simulation [9]).

By combining the previous equivalence with the simulation from Section 4, we obtain that, when considering colorless tasks, the wait-free iterated x-consensus model consisting of n processes is equivalent to a wait-free shared memory model of $\lceil n/x \rceil$ processes. The previous equivalences are presented in Figure 5.

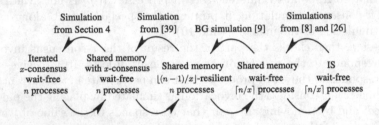

Fig. 5. Model equivalence for colorless tasks

Decidability. Consider the following problem, which is undecidable [25,31,32]: is a task solvable in a wait-free shared memory system of $n \geq 3$ processes (and thus with $t \geq 2$ crashes)? The same problem is decidable if there are only 2 processes (see [30] for decidability results in this and other models). The simulation, combined with the previous equivalence, gives the following result: the problem of knowing if a colorless task is solvable in a wait-free iterated x-consensus model consisting of n processes is undecidable if and only if $\lceil n/x \rceil \geq 3$. For instance, when $x = 2$, it is undecidable for 5 processes and decidable for 4 processes.

References

1. Afek, Y., Attiya, H., Dolev, D., Gafni, E., Merritt, M., Shavit, N.: Atomic snapshots of shared memory. J. ACM **40**(4), 873–890 (1993)
2. Afek, Y., Weisberger, E., Weisman, H.: A completeness theorem for a class of synchronization objects. In: Proceedings of the 12th ACM Symposium on Principles of Distributed Computing, PODC 1993, pp. 159–170. ACM (1993)
3. Attiya, H., Bar-Noy, A., Dolev, D.: Sharing memory robustly in message-passing systems. J. ACM **42**(1), 124–142 (1995)

4. Attiya, H., Welch, J.: Distributed Computing: Fundamentals, Simulations, and Advanced Topics. Synthesis Lectures on Distributed Computing Theory. Wiley (2004)
5. Biran, O., Moran, S., Zaks, S.: A combinatorial characterization of the distributed 1-solvable tasks. J. Algorithms **11**(3), 420–440 (1990)
6. Borowsky, E., Gafni, E.: Generalized FLP impossibility result for t-resilient asynchronous computations. In: Proceedings of the 25th ACM Symposium on Theory of Computing, STOC 1993, pp. 91–100. ACM (1993)
7. Borowsky, E., Gafni, E.: Immediate atomic snapshots and fast renaming. In: Proc. of the 12th ACM Symp. on Principles of Dist. Computing, PODC 1993, pp. 41–51. ACM (1993)
8. Borowsky, E., Gafni, E.: A simple algorithmically reasoned characterization of wait-free computation (extended abstract). In: Proceedings of the 16th ACM Symposium on Principles of Distributed Computing, PODC 1997, pp. 189–198. ACM (1997)
9. Borowsky, E., Gafni, E., Lynch, N., Rajsbaum, S.: The BG distributed simulation algorithm. Distributed Computing **14**(3), 127–146 (2001)
10. Bouzid, Z., Gafni, E., Kuznetsov, P.: Strong equivalence relations for iterated models. In: Aguilera, M.K., Querzoni, L., Shapiro, M. (eds.) OPODIS 2014. LNCS, vol. 8878, pp. 139–154. Springer, Heidelberg (2014)
11. Castañeda, A., Imbs, D., Rajsbaum, S., Raynal, M.: Renaming is weaker than set agreement but for perfect renaming: a map of sub-consensus tasks. In: Fernández-Baca, D. (ed.) LATIN 2012. LNCS, vol. 7256, pp. 145–156. Springer, Heidelberg (2012)
12. Chandra, T., Hadzilacos, V., Jayanti, P., Toueg, S.: Generalized irreducibility of consensus and the equivalence of t-resilient and wait-free implementations of consensus. SIAM Journal on Computing **34**(2), 333–357 (2005)
13. Charron-Bost, B., Schiper, A.: The heard-of model: computing in distributed systems with benign faults. Distributed Computing **22**(1), 49–71 (2009)
14. Chaudhuri, S.: More choices allow more faults: Set consensus problems in totally asynchronous systems. Inf. Comput. **105**(1), 132–158 (1993)
15. Chaudhuri, S., Reiners, P.: Understanding the set consensus partial order using the borowsky-gafni simulation. In: Babaoğlu, Ö., Marzullo, K. (eds.) WDAG 1996. LNCS, vol. 1151, pp. 362–379. Springer, Heidelberg (1996)
16. Chor, B., Moscovici, L.: Solvability in asynchronous environments. In: Proc. of the 30th Annual Symposium on Foundations of Computer Science, FOCS 1989, pp. 422–427 (1989)
17. Chor, B., Nelson, L.-B.: Solvability in asynchronous environments II: Finite interactive tasks. SIAM J. Comput. **29**(2), 351–377 (1999)
18. Chou, C.T., Gafni, E.: Understanding and verifying distributed algorithms using stratified decomposition. In: Proceedings of the 7th ACM Symposium on Principles of Distributed Computing, PODC 1988, pp. 44–65. ACM (1988)
19. Conde, R., Rajsbaum, S.: The complexity gap between consensus and safe-consensus. In: Halldórsson, M.M. (ed.) SIROCCO 2014. LNCS, vol. 8576, pp. 68–82. Springer, Heidelberg (2014)
20. Elrad, T., Francez, N.: Decomposition of distributed programs into communication-closed layers. Sci. Comput. Program. **2**(3), 155–173 (1982)
21. Fischer, M.J., Lynch, N.A., Paterson, M.: Impossibility of distributed consensus with one faulty process. J. ACM **32**(2), 374–382 (1985)

22. Gafni, E.: Round-by-round fault detectors (extended abstract): unifying synchrony and asynchrony. In: Proceedings of the 17th ACM Symposium on Principles of Distributed Computing, PODC 1998, pp. 143–152. ACM (1998)

23. Gafni, E.: The 0–1-exclusion families of tasks. In: Baker, T.P., Bui, A., Tixeuil, S. (eds.) OPODIS 2008. LNCS, vol. 5401, pp. 246–258. Springer, Heidelberg (2008)

24. Gafni, E., Herlihy, M.: Sporadic solutions to zero-one exclusion tasks. In: Esparza, J., Fraigniaud, P., Husfeldt, T., Koutsoupias, E. (eds.) ICALP 2014. LNCS, vol. 8572, pp. 1–10. Springer, Heidelberg (2014)

25. Gafni, E., Koutsoupias, E.: Three-processor tasks are undecidable. SIAM J. Comput. 28(3), 970–983 (1999)

26. Gafni, E., Rajsbaum, S.: Distributed programming with tasks. In: Lu, C., Masuzawa, T., Mosbah, M. (eds.) OPODIS 2010. LNCS, vol. 6490, pp. 205–218. Springer, Heidelberg (2010)

27. Gafni, E., Rajsbaum, S.: Recursion in distributed computing. In: Dolev, S., Cobb, J., Fischer, M., Yung, M. (eds.) SSS 2010. LNCS, vol. 6366, pp. 362–376. Springer, Heidelberg (2010)

28. Gafni, E., Rajsbaum, S., Herlihy, M.P.: Subconsensus tasks: renaming is weaker than set agreement. In: Dolev, S. (ed.) DISC 2006. LNCS, vol. 4167, pp. 329–338. Springer, Heidelberg (2006)

29. Herlihy, M.: Wait-free synchronization. ACM Trans. Program. Lang. Syst. 13(1), 124–149 (1991)

30. Herlihy, M., Kozlov, D., Rajsbaum, S.: Distributed Computing Through Combinatorial Topology. Morgan Kaufmann, Elsevier (2013)

31. Herlihy, M., Rajsbaum, S.: The decidability of distributed decision tasks (extended abstract). In: Proceedings of the 29th ACM Symposium on Theory of Computing, STOC 1997, pp. 589–598. ACM (1997)

32. Herlihy, M., Rajsbaum, S.: A classification of wait-free loop agreement tasks. Theoretical Computer Science 291(1), 55–77 (2003)

33. Herlihy, M., Rajsbaum, S.: Simulations and reductions for colorless tasks. In: Proc. of the 31st ACM Symp. on Principles of Dist. Computing, PODC 2012, pp. 253–260. ACM (2012)

34. Herlihy, M., Rajsbaum, S.: The topology of distributed adversaries. Distributed Computing 26(3), 173–192 (2013)

35. Herlihy, M., Rajsbaum, S., Raynal, M.: Power and limits of distributed computing shared memory models. Theoretical Computer Science 509, 3–24 (2013)

36. Herlihy, M., Rajsbaum, S., Tuttle, M.R.: Unifying synchronous and asynchronous message-passing models. In: Proceedings of the 17th ACM Symposium on Principles of Distributed Computing, PODC 1998, pp. 133–142. ACM (1998)

37. Herlihy, M., Shavit, N.: The topological structure of asynchronous computability. J. ACM 46(6), 858–923 (1999)

38. Herlihy, M., Wing, J.M.: Linearizability: A correctness condition for concurrent objects. ACM Trans. Program. Lang. Syst. 12(3), 463–492 (1990)

39. Imbs, D., Raynal, M.: The multiplicative power of consensus numbers. In: Proc. of the 29th ACM Symp. on Principles of Dist. Computing, PODC 2010, pp. 26–35. ACM (2010)

40. Neiger, G., Toueg, S.: Automatically increasing the fault-tolerance of distributed algorithms. J. Algorithms 11(3), 374–419 (1990)

41. Rajsbaum, S.: Iterated shared memory models. In: López-Ortiz, A. (ed.) LATIN 2010. LNCS, vol. 6034, pp. 407–416. Springer, Heidelberg (2010)

42. Rajsbaum, S., Raynal, M.: An introductory tutorial to concurrency-related distributed recursion. Bulletin of the EATCS, p. 111 (2013)

43. Rajsbaum, S., Raynal, M., Travers, C.: An impossibility about failure detectors in the iterated immediate snapshot model. Inf. Process. Lett. **108**(3), 160–164 (2008)
44. Rajsbaum, S., Raynal, M., Travers, C.: The iterated restricted immediate snapshot model. In: Hu, X., Wang, J. (eds.) COCOON 2008. LNCS, vol. 5092, pp. 487–497. Springer, Heidelberg (2008)
45. Raynal, M., Stainer, J.: Increasing the power of the iterated immediate snapshot model with failure detectors. In: Even, G., Halldórsson, M.M. (eds.) SIROCCO 2012. LNCS, vol. 7355, pp. 231–242. Springer, Heidelberg (2012)
46. Raynal, M., Stainer, J.: Synchrony weakened by message adversaries vs asynchrony restricted by failure detectors. In: Proceedings of the 2013 ACM Symposium on Principles of Distributed Computing, PODC 2013, pp. 166–175. ACM (2013)
47. Saks, M.E., Zaharoglou, F.: Wait-free k-set agreement is impossible: The topology of public knowledge. SIAM J. Comput. **29**(5), 1449–1483 (2000)

Automated Analysis of Impact of Scheduling on Performance of Self-stabilizing Protocols

Saba Aflaki[1], Borzoo Bonakdarpour[2(✉)], and Sébastien Tixeuil[3]

[1] University of Waterloo, Waterloo, Canada
saflaki@uwaterloo.ca
[2] McMaster University, Hamilton, Canada
borzoo@mcmaster.ca
[3] Université Pierre and Marie Curie, Paris, France
sebastien.tixeuil@lip6.fr

Abstract. In a concurrent computing system, a *scheduler* determines at each time which computing task should execute next. Thus, a scheduler has tremendous impact on the performance of the tasks that it orchestrates. Analyzing the impact of scheduling in a *distributed* setting is a challenging task, as it is concerned with subtle dimensions such as geographical distance of processes and the achievable level of parallelism. In this paper, we propose an automated method based on probabilistic verification for analyzing fault recovery time in distributed *self-stabilizing* protocols. We exhibit the usefulness of our approach through a large set of experiments that demonstrate the impact of different types of scheduling policies on recovery time of different classes of stabilizing protocols, and the practical efficiency of classical self-stabilizing scheduler transformers.

1 Introduction

Self-stabilization [5] is a versatile technique for forward recovery to a good behavior when transient faults occur in a distributed system or the system is initialized arbitrarily. Moreover, once the good behavior is recovered, the system preserves this behavior in the absence of faults. In [7,8], we demonstrated that *expected recovery time* is a more descriptive metric than the traditional asymptotic complexity measures (e.g., the big O notation for the number of recovery steps or rounds) to characterize the performance of stabilizing programs. Average recovery time can be measured by giving weights to states and transitions of a stabilizing program and computing the expected value of the number of steps that it takes the program to reach a legitimate state. These weights can be assigned by a uniform distribution (in the simplest case), or by more sophisticated probability distributions. This technique has been shown to be effective in measuring the performance of weak-stabilizing programs, where not all computations converge [7], and cases where faults hit certain variables or locations more often, as well as in synthesizing stabilizing protocols [1].

A vital factor in designing self-stabilizing protocols is the scheduling assumptions. For instance, certain protocols are stabilizing under a (1) fair scheduler [4],

© Springer International Publishing Switzerland 2015
A. Pelc and A.A. Schwarzmann (Eds.): SSS 2015, LNCS 9212, pp. 156–170, 2015.
DOI: 10.1007/978-3-319-21741-3_11

(2) probabilistic scheduler [12,16], or (3) scheduler that disallows fully parallel execution of processes [10]. In addition to the issue of correctness, different scheduling policies may have a totally different impact on the *performance* of a self-stabilizing protocol [3]. To the best of our knowledge, there is no work on rigorous analysis of how a scheduling policy alters the performance of self-stabilization.

With this motivation, in this paper, we extend our work in [7,8] to incorporate different scheduling policies in evaluating the performance of self-stabilizing algorithms. In particular, we consider the following scheduling criteria:

- *Distribution* imposes spatial constraints on the selection of processes whose transitions will be executed.
- *Boundedness* of a scheduler ensures that a process is not scheduled for execution more than certain number of times between any two schedulings of any other process.
- *Fairness* of a scheduler guarantees that every process is given a fair share of execution.

Our contributions in this paper are the following: We

- rigorously formalize the aforementioned scheduling criteria;
- propose an automated compositional method for (1) augmenting a self-stabilizing protocol with different types of scheduling policies, and (2) evaluating the performance (*i.e.*, expected recovery time) of the augmented protocol using probabilistic verification techniques, and
- conduct a large set of experiments to demonstrate the application of our approach in analyzing the performance of self-stabilizing protocols under different scheduling policies.

In particular, we studied the effect of distribution, boundedness and fairness of a scheduler on the possibility of convergence as well as the expected recovery time of three self-stabilizing algorithms [10], and a few variants. We show that the first algorithm needs refinement to be able to stabilize under weaker scheduling constraints. One approach is to compose the algorithm with a stabilizing local mutual exclusion algorithm. In this regard, we compose the algorithm with a snap-stabilizing dining philosophers algorithm [13] and demonstrate that ensuring safety comes at a cost of higher expected recovery time. Another approach suggested in [10,11] is to randomize the actions of processes for which we explore three different strategies for choosing the randomization parameter (two static and one dynamic). Furthermore, we consider the solution of [10] for an identified network. This algorithm is deterministic.

We measure the expected recovery time of all these six strategies under different scheduling constraints. Our experiments show that, in general, the deterministic algorithms outperform the randomized ones. Moreover, an adaptive randomized algorithm which dynamically chooses the randomization parameter has a promising performance. It also has the benefit of no pre-tuning requirements.

Organization. Section 2 presents our computation model for distributed programs, the concept of self-stabilization and recovery time. We present the formal semantics of different types of schedulers in Section 2.3. Our approach for augmenting a distributed program with a scheduling scheme is presented in Section 3. Experimental results and analysis are discussed in Section 4. Finally, we make concluding remarks and discuss future work in Section 5.

2   Preliminaries

2.1   Distributed Programs

A distributed system consists of a finite set of processes Π operating on a finite set of variables V. Each variable $v \in V$ has a finite domain D_v. A valuation of all variables determines a state of the system. We denote the value of a variable v in state s by $v(s)$. The *state space* of a distributed system is the set of all possible states spanned by V denoted by S_V.

Each process $\pi \in \Pi$ can read (respectively, write) a subset of V called its read (respectively, write)-set. We denote the read and write sets of a process by R_π and W_π respectively. In our model, processes communicate through *shared memory*, i.e. several processes can read the same variable. However, only one process can write to a variable. We say that two processes π and π' are *neighbors* if $R_\pi \cap R_{\pi'} \neq \emptyset$. Thus, the communication network of a distributed system can be modelled by a graph $G = (\Pi, E)$, where a vertex represents a process, and there is an edge between any two processes that are neighbors. We denote the shortest path between two vertices (processes) π and π' in G by $dist(\pi, \pi')$ and the diameter of the graph by $diam(G)$.

Definition 1. *A distributed program is a tuple $dp = (\Pi, V, T)$, where*

- *Π is a finite set of processes,*
- *V is a finite set of variables,*
- *$T \subseteq S_V \times S_V$ is the transition relation.*   □

In order to analyze the performance of distributed programs, we view them as a *discrete-time Markov chain* (DTMC).

Definition 2. *A DTMC is a tuple $M = (S, S_0, \iota_{init}, \mathbf{P_M}, L, AP)$ where,*

- *S is a finite set of states,*
- *S_0 is the set of initial states,*
- *$\iota_{init} : S \to [0,1]$ is the initial distribution such that $\sum_{s \in S} \iota_{init}(s) = 1$,*
- *$\mathbf{P_M} : S \times S \to [0,1]$ is the transition probability matrix (TPM) such that*

$$\forall s \in S : \sum_{s' \in S} \mathbf{P_M}(s, s') = 1$$

- *$L : S \to 2^{AP}$ is the labelling function that identifies which atomic propositions from a finite set AP hold in each state.*   □

Given Def. 1 and Def. 2, it is straightforward to model the transition system of a distributed program with a DTMC. The state space of the distributed program forms the set of states DTMC (i.e., $S = S_V$). S_0 and ι_{init} can be determined based on the program. If the distributed program is probabilistic, then the value of the elements of $\mathbf{P_M}$ are known. Otherwise, without loss of generality, we can consider uniform distribution over transitions. In that case:

$$\mathbf{P_M}(s, s') = \frac{1}{|\{(s, s'') \in T(dp)\}|}$$

L assigns atomic propositions to states which facilitates computation and verification of certain quantitative and qualitative properties. Later, in Section 2.2, we will see how a single atomic proposition ls can define an important class of distributed programs namely, self-stabilizing programs. Throughout this paper, We use dp and M interchangeably to refer to a distributed program.

Definition 3. *A computation σ of a distributed program $dp = (\Pi, V, T)$ (respectively, DTMC $M = (S, S_0, \iota_{init}, \mathbf{P_M}, L, AP))$, over state space S, is a maximal sequence of states: $\sigma = s_0 s_1 s_2 \cdots$, where*

- *$s_0 \in S_0$,*
- *$\forall i \geq 0, (s, s') \in T(dp)$ (respectively, $\mathbf{P_M}(s_i, s_{i+1}) > 0$).*   □

Notation 1. *σ_s indicates a computation that starts in state s. We denote the set of all possible distributed programs by DP, the set of all computations of a distributed program by $\Sigma(dp)$ and the set of finite computations by $\Sigma_{fin}(dp)$.*

2.2   Self-stabilization and Convergence Time

Definition 4 (self-stabilization). *A distributed program $M = (S, S_0 = S, \mathbf{P_M}, L, \{ls\})$ is self stabilizing iff the following conditions hold:*

- *Strong convergence: $\forall s \in S$, all computations σ_s eventually reach a state in $LS = \{s \mid ls \in L(s)\}$,*
- *Closure: $\forall s \in LS : (\mathbf{P_M}(s, s') > 0) \Rightarrow (s' \in LS)$.*   □

In **weak-stabilization** [9], for every state $s \in S$ there *exists* a computation σ_s that eventually reaches a state in LS. In **probabilistic-stabilization** [12], for all $s \in S$, a computation σ_s reaches a state in LS with probability one. Closure is the same in all types of stabilization. In the sequel, we use the term *stabilizing* algorithm to refer to either of the three types of stabilization mentioned above.

Definition 5. *For a stabilizing program M, the convergence or recovery time of a computation σ with an initial fragment $s_0 s_1 \cdots s_n$ such that $s_0 s_1 \cdots s_{n-1} \notin LS$ and $s_n \in LS$ equals n.*

2.3 Scheduler Types

Schedulers determine the degree of parallelism in a distributed program. They are specifically important in stabilizing programs as they affect both the possibility of convergence and convergence time. A detailed survey of schedulers in self-stabilization can be found in [6]. We review the four classification factors of schedulers *k-centrality*, *fairness*, *boundedness* and *enabledness* studied in [6].

A **k-central** scheduler allows processes in distance at least k to execute simultaneously. In particular, 0-central and $diam(G)$-central schedulers are called *distributed* and *central* respectively. In the former, any subset of the enabled processes can be scheduled at any time. In the latter, a single process can execute at a time.

A **weakly fair** scheduler ensures that a continuously enabled process is eventually scheduled. A **strongly fair** scheduler ensures that a process that is enabled infinitely often is eventually scheduled.

A scheduler is **k-bounded** if it does not schedule a process more than k times between any two schedulings of any other process.

3 Augmenting a Distributed Program with a Scheduler

To concisely specify the behavior of a process π, we utilize a finite set of *guarded commands* $(\mathcal{G}_\pi)$. A guarded command has the following syntax:

$$\langle label \rangle \ : \ \langle guard \rangle \ \rightarrow \ \langle statement \rangle;$$

The *guard* is a Boolean expression over the read-set of the process. The statement is executed whenever the guard is satisfied. Execution of guarded commands updates variables and causes transitioning from one state to another. In *probabilistic programs* commands are executed with a probability. Hence, transitions among states in the system are executed according to a probability distribution.

$$\langle label \rangle \ : \ \langle guard \rangle \ \rightarrow \ p_1 : \langle statement_1 \rangle + \cdots + p_n : \langle statement_n \rangle;$$

where

$$\sum_{i=1}^{n} p_i = 1$$

A guarded command is *enabled* if its guard evaluates to true. A process is enabled if at least one of its guarded commands is enabled. The set of guarded commands of a distributed program is formed by the union of the guarded commands of its constituent processes. In a parallel (i.e., simultaneous) execution, all enabled processes execute their enabled commands. In contrast, in a serial (i.e., interleaving) execution, only one enabled process runs its enabled commands. We use labels to synchronize (parallelized) guarded commands of different processes. More specifically, if all guarded commands (possibly belonging to different processes) that have identical labels are enabled, they will all be executed. If at least one of them is not enabled, none of them will be executed. The synchronization of guarded commands with guards $g_1, \cdots, g_n$ is equivalent to having one guarded command with guard $g_1 \wedge \cdots \wedge g_n$ and the union of all statements. We omit the label from a guarded command whenever it is not used.

3.1   Encoding Schedulers in a Distributed Program

In this section, we describe how we modify a distributed program dp to obtain a program that behaves as if dp was executed under a certain type of scheduler, when only serial executions are available.

k-Central Scheduler. Given a distributed system composed of processes Π. Let each process π in Π consist of a set of guarded commands $\mathcal{G}_\pi$. We augment Π with a k-central scheduler as follows. For every process $\pi \in \Pi$, let

$$KValid_\pi = \{\pi' \mid dist(\pi, \pi') > k\}$$

be the set of processes that are at least $k + 1$ hops away from π. To encode a k-central scheduler, we synchronize every guarded command of a process π with the guarded commands of every subset of $KValid_\pi$. Thus, each process of the new program consists of the following guarded commands:

$for\ all\ \langle g_{\pi,i} \rangle \rightarrow \langle s_{\pi,i} \rangle \in \mathcal{G}_\pi : for\ all\ kval_\pi \subseteq KValid_\pi : for\ all\ \pi' \in kval :$
$for\ all\ \langle g_{\pi',j} \rangle \rightarrow \langle s_{\pi',j} \rangle \in \mathcal{G}_{\pi'} :$

$\langle g_{\pi,i} \wedge (\bigwedge g_{\pi',j}) \rangle \rightarrow \langle s_{\pi,i} \rangle;$

Note that $kval_\pi = \emptyset$ yields the original guarded command of the process. It is necessary to include this case to model a central scheduler.

k-Bounded and k-Enabled Schedulers. To simulate the behavior of a k-bounded (similarly, k-enabled) scheduler, we add a counter (variable) per every ordered pair of processes in the system. A command of a process is allowed to execute only if it has been executed less than k times between any two executions of every other process. Once a process π executes a command, the variables which count the number of executions of other processes between any two executions of π are reset to zero. In a distributed system with n processes $\Pi = \{\pi_1, \cdots, \pi_n\}$, we add variables $\{count_{\pi_i, \pi_j} \mid 1 \leq i, j \leq n\}$. Thus, we replace each guarded command $\langle g_{\pi_i} \rangle \rightarrow \langle s_{\pi_i} \rangle$ in $\mathcal{G}_{\pi_i}$ with the following:

$$\langle g_{\pi_i} \wedge (\bigwedge_{\substack{1 \leq j \leq n \\ i \neq j}} count_{\pi_i, \pi_j} < k) \rangle \rightarrow \langle s_{\pi_i} \rangle; \{\langle count_{\pi_j, \pi_i} := 0 \rangle; \}_{\substack{1 \leq j \leq n \\ i \neq j}}$$

Fairness. Schedulers that generate the worst and best cases are unfair. They can be achieved by modelling the program with a Markov decision process (MDP) instead of a DTMC (for more information see [15]). A probabilistic scheduler which uniformly chooses transitions produces average case expected recovery time, which is both fair and unfair.

Algorithm 1. Deterministic Self-stabilizing Vertex Coloring Program

1: **Shared Variable:** $c_\pi : int \in [0, B]$
2: **Guarded Command:** $action_\pi : \neg(c_\pi = max(\{0, \cdots, B\} \setminus \bigcup_{\pi' \in N(\pi)} c_{\pi'})) \rightarrow$
   $c_\pi := max(\{0, \cdots, B\} \setminus \bigcup_{\pi' \in N(\pi)} c_{\pi'})$

---

4 Experiments and Analysis

We use probabilistic model-checking (in particular, the tool PRISM [14]) to investigate the significance of the choice of a scheduler on the expected recovery time of a stabilizing distributed algorithm. We chose the *vertex coloring in arbitrary graphs* problem as our case study. It is a classic problem in graph theory that has many applications in scheduling, pattern matching, etc. Furthermore, we study several stabilizing programs that solve this problem. One nonprobabilistic algorithm that requires a network, where each process must have a unique id. A probabilistic algorithm where a static probability is assigned to each process, and one with adaptive probability. We compare the expected recovery time of these strategies under all types of schedulers. In our experiments, the choice of graph structure/size and some other parameters was influenced and limited by the computational power of the machine used to do the experiments.

4.1 Self-stabilizing Vertex Coloring in Arbitrary Graphs

Definition 6 (Vertex Coloring). *In a graph $G = (V, E)$, the* vertex coloring *problem asks for a mapping from V to a set C of colors, such that no two adjacent vertices (connected directly by an edge) share the same color.*   □

We say two vertices are in *conflict* iff they are neighbors and they have the same color. The first deterministic self-stabilizing vertex coloring program of [10] is designed for an anonymous network with an arbitrary underlying communication graph structure $G = (\Pi, E)$ and a non-distributed scheduler. We call this program *deterministic*. Each process has a variable c_π representing its color with domain $c_\pi \in [0, B]$, where B is the maximum degree (number of neighbors) of a vertex (process) in G. In every state, if a process's color is not equal to the maximum available color (the maximum number not taken by any of its neighbors) max_π, it changes its color to max_π. Otherwise, it does not do anything. In this algorithm, a legitimate state is one that the color of each process is equal to max_π. We denote the neighbors of a process by $N(\pi)$ (see Algorithm 1).

The Effect of Schedulers on Expected Recovery Time. We investigate the effect of four attributes of schedulers: centrality, boundedness, enabledness, and fairness, on the expected recovery time of Algorithm 1.

k-Centrality: We calculate the average case expected recovery time for a linear graph, where the size varies from $5 - 7$ and k varies from $0 - Diam(G)$. In a

Table 1. Effect of centrality, boundedness and enabledness

(a) Effect of centrality on expected recovery time (average case)

Size\k	0	1	2	3	4	5	6
5	5.6	9.1	13.1	14.4	15.7	-	-
6	7.1	10.7	14.6	18.6	19.6	20.9	-
7	7.6	11.6	16.1	21.2	24.5	24.6	25.8

(b) Effect of boundedness/enabledness on expected recovery time

	Complete			Star			Linear		
	R_{min}	R_{max}	R_{exp}	R_{min}	R_{max}	R_{exp}	R_{min}	R_{max}	R_{exp}
1	3.24	4.64	3.88	10.25	13.33	11.78	6.84	10.30	8.48
2	2.68	7.14	4.10	6.74	24.20	12.52	4.48	19.40	9.03
3	2.57	9.63	4.28	5.74	35.04	13.39	3.87	28.61	9.60

Table 2

(a) $R_{max} - R_{min}$

	Complete	Star	Linear
1	1.40	3.08	3.46
2	4.46	17.46	14.92
3	7.06	29.30	24.74

(b) Cost of ensuring safety in executions

	Fair		Unfair	
Deg	deterministic 1-central	composed distributed	deterministic 1-central	composed distributed
2	1.72	2.54	2.44	2.91
3	2.29	3.73	3.52	4.75
4	2.72	4.69	4.61	6.56
5	3.05	5.49	5.69	8.34
6	3.33	6.16	6.77	10.08
7	3.56	6.72	7.82	11.77
8	3.76	7.21	8.87	13.43

linear graph, $Diam(G) = size - 1$. As expected, Table 1(a) validates that, in average, parallelism helps improve the recovery time. However, there can be cases in which it shows detrimental effect. The impact of centrality also depends on the fairness of the scheduler. In the worst case this program does not stabilize under a distributed $(0 - central)$ scheduler.

Boundedness/Enabledness: We study the effect of boundedness/enabledness on graphs of size 4 with complete, star, and linear structures for $k = 1, 2, 3$. For each graph structure and each value of k, Table 1(b) contains three numbers: R_{min} (best case expected recovery time), R_{avg} (average case expected recovery time), and R_{max} (worst case expected recovery time). Table 2(a) demonstrates that as k increases so does the gap between the best case and the worst case. This is the result of allowing more computations as we increase k. That is, all executions corresponding to a k-bounded (respectively, k-enabled) scheduler are also included in the executions of a $(k-1)$-bounded (respectively, $(k-1)$-enabled) scheduler.

Fairness: Fairness alongside centrality can determine possibility of convergence. An unfair distributed scheduler can prevent Algorithm 1 from converging. Consider, for example, a state in which two neighbors have identical colors

$(\langle 1, 1 \rangle)$ and the same maximum available color (2). A computation that infinitely alternates between states $\langle 1, 1 \rangle$ and $\langle 2, 2 \rangle$ never converges to a correct state. Such a computation can be produced by a distributed unfair scheduler. In the rest of our experiments, by unfair scheduler we mean a scheduler that results in worst case expected recovery time, unless otherwise specified.

4.2   Composition with Dining Philosophers and the Cost of Ensuring Safety

Recall that Algorithm 1 needs to be refined to work under distributed unfair schedulers. We compose Algorithm 1 with an optimal *snap-stabilizing* (i.e., zero recovery time) dining philosophers distributed program for trees of [13] and refer to it as the *composed strategy*. The solution to the dining philosophers problem provides local mutual exclusion. Since this algorithm is designed specifically for tree structures, in the rest of this section, we use balanced trees in our experiments to ensure fair comparison. Figs. 1 and 2 depict the expected recovery time of the composed algorithm under fair (central, 1-central, distributed) and unfair (central, 1-central, distributed) schedulers, respectively.

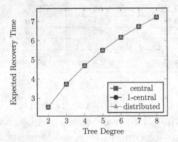

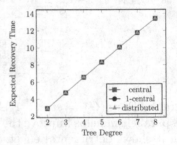

Fig. 1. Composed program with a fair scheduler

Fig. 2. Composed program with an unfair scheduler

Observe that composing a distributed program with dining philosophers and running the composition under a distributed scheduler is in principle equivalent to running the original distributed program under a 1-central scheduler. However, the 1-central scheduler that is produced by the dining philosopher algorithm may only be able to produce a subset of the possible schedules. Table 2(b) shows the expected recovery time of the deterministic algorithm under 1-central scheduler and the composed algorithm under distributed scheduler (both fair and unfair) for trees with height one and degrees 2 − 8. The difference is explained by the fact that the dining philosophers layer itself forces processes that are normally not activatable (that is, they already have a non-conflicting color) to act; that is, the enforcement of fairness between nodes induces unnecessary computation steps.

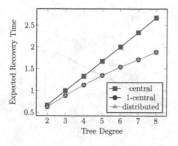

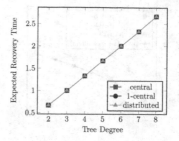

Fig. 3. ID-based deterministic program with a fair scheduler

Fig. 4. ID-based deterministic program with an unfair scheduler

4.3 ID-Based Prioritization

This strategy corresponds to the second deterministic self-stabilizing algorithm of [10], and requires an identified network where each process has a unique id. When several processes are in conflict with the same color, only the process with the highest id will execute its command. As a result, no two similarly colored enabled neighbors will ever execute their commands simultaneously. In some rare cases, this algorithm may not produce 1-central schedules: consider a line of 4 processes c, a, b, d (where identifiers are ordered alphabetically), such that c and a have the same color α, and b and d have the same color β (with $\alpha \neq \beta$). Then, a distributed scheduler may schedule both a and b in a particular step from this situation, resulting in neighboring nodes executing their actions simultaneously. In trees of height 1, this situation cannot occur, and all produced schedules are 1-central. This explains in our results (see Figs. 3 and 4) why running this program under 1-central and distributed schedulers produces the same expected recovery time.

4.4 Probabilisitic-Stabilizing Vertex Coloring Programs

The random conflict manager [11] is a lightweight composition scheme for self-stabilizing programs that amounts to executing the original algorithm with some probability p (rather than always executing it). The probabilistic conflict manager does *not* ensure that two neighboring nodes are *never* scheduled simultaneously, but anytime the (possibly unfair) scheduler activates two neighboring nodes u and v, there is a $1 - p^2$ probability that u and v do *not* execute simultaneously. Composing the random conflict manager with the deterministic coloring protocol yields a probabilistic coloring algorithm. Fine tuning the parameter p is challenging: a higher p reduces the possibility that a conflict persists when two neighboring conflicting nodes are activated simultaneously (reducing the stabilization time), but also reduces the possibility to make progress by executing the algorithm (increasing the stabilization time). Thus, we consider three strategies for choosing p: (1) p is a constant, for all nodes, throughout the entire execution; (2) p depends on local topology (*i.e.* the current node degree); (3) p is

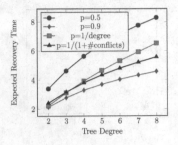

Fig. 5. Probabilistic programs with a fair distributed scheduler

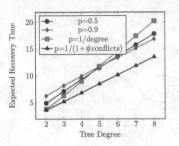

Fig. 6. Probabilistic programs with an unfair distributed scheduler

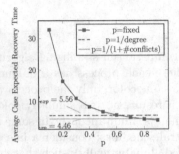

Fig. 7. Evaluating the effect of the randomization parameter on expected recovery time (on a tree of height=2, degree=2) with a fair distributed scheduler

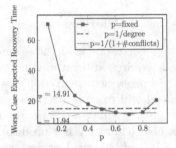

Fig. 8. Evaluating the effect of the randomization parameter on expected recovery time (on a tree of height=2, degree=2) with an unfair distributed scheduler

dynamically computed (*i.e.* depending on the current number of conflicts at the current node).

Constant Randomization Parameter. In this strategy, p is a fixed constant for all processes during the program execution. In the original third probabilistic algorithm [10], this probability is equal to 0.5. Figs. 5 and 6 show that with fixed probability of execution, the stabilization time increases as the number of potential initial conflicts rises. Figs 7 and 8 demonstrate that for a fixed topology, fine tuning the probability used can result in significantly lower stabilization time. We observe that the stabilization time is not necessarily monotonous with respect to the probability used, as the unfair case demonstrates that increasing the probability of execution too much may have detrimental effects (more conflicts can be preserved in the worst case).

Vertex Degree. This strategy depends on the local structure of the network to let a process execute its commands. It is based on the intuitive reasoning that nodes with fewer neighbors have a lower chance of being in conflict with

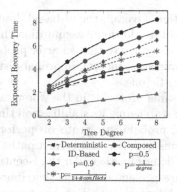

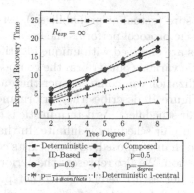

Fig. 9. Fair distributed scheduler

Fig. 10. Unfair distributed scheduler

one of them. The protocol gives higher priority to processes with less number of neighbors. Although processes can have distinct values of p, their values are statically chosen and fixed during the execution. Fig. 5 shows that this strategy works remarkably better than a fair coin under a fair scheduler. However, it gradually falls behind a fair coin in the worst case under an unfair scheduler. This is explained by the existence of a central node with an increasing number of neighbors. If executed, this central node can resolve many conflicts at the same time (expediting stabilization) in the initial case where it has many conflicts. However, the vertex degree approach pushes towards that these many conflicts are resolved by satellite nodes with a higher probability, causing stabilization to require additional steps, in the worst case.

Number of Conflicts. This strategy refines the vertex degree approach to dynamically take into account the number of potential conflicts. It prioritizes processes with more conflicts over processes with fewer conflicts. Figures 5- 8 indicate that except for a few biased coins, this adaptive method defeats the other two strategies. It also has the clear advantage of no pre-tuning of the system.

4.5   Comparing Strategies and Schedulers

This section is devoted to analyzing the results of our technique to select a protocol variant for a particular environment (topology and scheduler). Figure 9 presents a comparison of protocol variants (deterministic, composed, id-based, and the three probabilistic ones) when the scheduler is fair, varying the number of nodes in the network. One interesting lesson learned is that the original protocol (deterministic), which is not self-stabilizing for the distributed scheduler (only weakly stabilizing) performs in practise better than actually self-stabilizing protocols (composed, and the three probabilistic variants), so there is a price to pay to ensure (actual or probabilistic) self-stabilization. Overall, the id-based deterministic protocol performs the best (but requires the additional assumption that nodes are endowed with unique identifiers). We also observe that smarter probabilistic variants outperform the composed deterministic protocol, so probabilistic stabilization can come cheaper than a deterministic one.

Figure 10 describes the performance of the same protocols in the worst case (unfair scheduler). As deterministic is only weak-stabilizing, its stabilization time with unfair scheduler is infinite. In that case, all probabilistic protocols perform worse than composed, as there exists computations with longer incorrect paths of execution. We also represent the performance of deterministic under the 1-central scheduler as a reference (all other protocols are presented for the distributed scheduler) for best case situation where only 1-central execution are present. It turns out that both probabilistic variants and composed introduce overhead. The overhead of composed has been discussed in Section 4.2, while the overhead of probabilistic variants is that more executions (including executions that are not 1-central) remain possible (with respect to 1-central ones). Again, id-based outperforms all others, including those of deterministic under 1-central scheduler.

The most complex topology is presented in Fig. 11, and the relative order of strategies is preserved also for this setting. If the scheduling is fair and identifiers are not available, leaving the algorithm unchanged is the best option. Otherwise, the choice can be to use the refined probabilistic option (that is depending on the current number of conflicts) when there are no identifiers, and the id-based deterministic protocol whenever they are available.

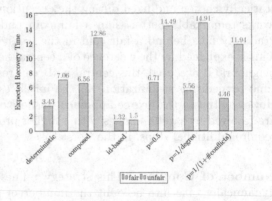

Fig. 11. Expected recovery time of the six algorithms under fair and unfair schedulers for a tree of height 2 and degree 2. Deterministic is presented for the 1-central scheduler. All others are presented for the distributed scheduler.

5   Conclusion

In this paper, we studied the role of schedulers in the correctness and performance of stabilizing programs. We adopted a rigorous method based on probabilistic model checking proven to be more descriptive by previous work [7,8]. We investigated the impact of different scheduling criteria, namely distribution, boundedness, and fairness on the performance of the self-stabilizing vertex coloring protocols of arbitrary graphs algorithm of [10]. We explored two methods to transform the first deterministic algorithm to a scheduler-oblivious self-stabilizing program that works under distributed unfair schedulers as well. First, we composed the algorithm with a stabilizing dining philosophers algorithm at the cost of slower recovery due to the overhead induced by the additional layer (even though this layer has zero stabilization time). Second, we used a probabilistic conflict manager to ensure convergence with probability one. We studied three strategies for picking the randomization parameter p: (i) a constant value, (ii) a static value inversely proportional to the degree of the vertex (process), and (iii) a dynamic value inversely proportional to the number of conflicts. Our experiments establish the superiority of the final strategy, especially in the light of no tuning requirements. We also evaluated the id-based deterministic algorithm of [10] for a non-anonymous network.

In general, our results demonstrate that the deterministic algorithms outperform the probabilistic ones. The id-based algorithm is the best among all deterministic ones as well as defeating all probabilistic algorithms. The price to pay is that unique identifiers must preexist in the network. To run an id-based self-stabilizing algorithm on an anonymous network, the algorithm should be composed with a self-stabilizing unique naming algorithm. This approach, however, is likely to downgrade the performance significantly. Furthermore, precisely evaluating this performance hit requires to formally include more advanced composition techniques [2] in our framework, an interesting open challenge.

For future work, we are planning to study the impact of scheduling policy along with other factors that can affect the performance of a self-stabilizing protocol, such as the likelihood and locality of occurrence of faults.

Acknowledgments. This work was partially sponsored by Canada NSERC Discovery Grant 418396-2012 and NSERC Strategic Grant 430575-2012.

References

1. Aflaki, S., Faghih, F., Bonakdarpour, B.: Synthesizing self-stabilizing protocols under average recovery time constraints. In: Proceedings of the 35th International Conference on Distributed Computing Systems (ICDCS) (to appear, 2015)
2. Arora, A., Gouda, M.G., Herman, T.: Composite routing protocols. In: Proceedings of the Second IEEE Symposium on Parallel and Distributed Processing (SPDP), pp. 70–78 (1990)
3. Beauquier, J., Johnen, C.: Analyze of probabilistic algorithms under indeterministic scheduler. In: IEEE International Symposium on Parallel and Distributed Processing with Applications (ISPA), pp. 553–558 (2008)
4. Devismes, S., Tixeuil, S., Yamashita, M.: Weak vs. self vs. probabilistic stabilization. In: Proceedings of the 28th International Conference on Distributed Computing Systems (ICDCS), pp. 681–688 (2008)
5. Dijkstra, E.W.: Self-stabilizing systems in spite of distributed control. Communications of the ACM **17**(11), 643–644 (1974)
6. Dubois, S., Tixeuil, S.: A taxonomy of daemons in self-stabilization. CoRR, abs/1110.0334 (2011)
7. Fallahi, N., Bonakdarpour, B.: How good is weak-stabilization? In: Higashino, T., Katayama, Y., Masuzawa, T., Potop-Butucaru, M., Yamashita, M. (eds.) SSS 2013. LNCS, vol. 8255, pp. 148–162. Springer, Heidelberg (2013)

8. Fallahi, N., Bonakdarpour, B., Tixeuil, S.: Rigorous performance evaluation of self-stabilization using probabilistic model checking. In: Proceedings of the 32nd IEEE International Conference on Reliable Distributed Systems (SRDS), pp. 153–162 (2013)
9. Gouda, M.G.: The theory of weak stabilization. In: Datta, A.K., Herman, T. (eds.) WSS 2001. LNCS, vol. 2194, pp. 114–123. Springer, Heidelberg (2001)
10. Gradinariu, M., Tixeuil, S.: Self-stabilizing vertex coloring of arbitrary graphs. In: Proceedings of 4th International Conference on Principles of Distributed Systems (OPODIS), pp. 55–70 (2000)
11. Gradinariu, M., Tixeuil, S.: Conflict managers for self-stabilization without fairness assumption. In: Proceedings of the 27th International Conference on Distributed Computing Systems (ICDCS), pp. 46–46 (2007)
12. Herman, T.: Probabilistic self-stabilization. Information Processing Letters **35**(2), 63–67 (1990)
13. Johnen, C., Alima, L.O., Datta, A.K., Tixeuil, S.: Optimal snap-stabilizing neighborhood synchronizer in tree networks. Parallel Processing Letters **12**(3–4), 327–340 (2002)
14. Kwiatkowska, M., Norman, G., Parker, D.: PRISM 4.0: verification of probabilistic real-time systems. In: Gopalakrishnan, G., Qadeer, S. (eds.) CAV 2011. LNCS, vol. 6806, pp. 585–591. Springer, Heidelberg (2011)
15. Simaitis, A.: Automatic Verification of Competitive Stochastic Systems. PhD thesis, Department of Computer Science, University of Oxford (2014)
16. Yamauchi, Y., Tixeuil, S., Kijima, S., Yamashita, M.: Brief announcement: probabilistic stabilization under probabilistic schedulers. In: Aguilera, M.K. (ed.) DISC 2012. LNCS, vol. 7611, pp. 413–414. Springer, Heidelberg (2012)

Efficient and Decentralized Polling Protocol for General Social Networks

Bao-Thien Hoang[1]([⊠]) and Abdessamad Imine[2]

[1] LCOMS EA7306, Université de Lorraine, Metz, France
bao-thien.hoang@univ-lorraine.fr
[2] Université de Lorraine and LORIA/INRIA, Nancy, France
abdessamad.imine@loria.fr

Abstract. We address the polling problem in social networks where users want to preserve the confidentiality of their votes, obtain the correct final result, and hide, if any, their misbehaviors. Guerraoui *et al.* [15,16] recently proposed polling protocols that neither rely on any central authority nor cryptography system. However, these protocols can be deployed safely and efficiently provided that the social graph structure should be transformed into a ring structure-based overlay and the number of participating users is a perfect square. Consequently, designing *secure* and *efficient* polling protocols regardless these constraints remains a challenging issue.

In this paper, we present EPol, a simple decentralized polling protocol that is deployed on more general social graphs. More explicitly, we define a family of social graphs that satisfy what we call the m-broadcasting property (where m is not greater than the minimum node degree) and show their structures enable low communication cost and constitute necessary and sufficient condition to ensure vote privacy and limit the impact of dishonest users on the accuracy of the polling output. In a social network of N users with diameter Δ_G and $D \leq (m-1)\Delta_G/2$ dishonest users (and similarly to the work [15,16] where they considered $D < \sqrt{N}$), a *privacy parameter* k enables us to obtain the following results: (i) the maximum probability of vote disclosure with certainty is $(D/N)^{k+1}$ and without certainty is $\left(\frac{D}{N}/(1 - 2\frac{D}{N})\right)\left[1 - \sum_{i=0}^{k} \gamma_i(2\frac{D}{N})^{2i+1}\right]$, where γ_i is the proportion of nodes voting for $2i + 1$ shares and $0 \leq i \leq k$; (ii) up to $2D$ votes can be revealed with certainty; (iii) the maximum impact on the final result is $(6k+4)D$, and the average impact is $\left[\left(\sum_{i=0}^{k} \gamma_i(2i+1)\right)\left(1 + 2\sum_{i=0}^{k} \gamma_i\frac{i+\alpha}{2i+1}\right) + 1\right]D$, where α is the proportion of users correctly voting; (iv) unlike [15,16], EPol is effective to compute more precisely the final result; and (v) the communication and spatial complexities of EPol are close to be linear.

Keywords: Social networks · Polling protocol · Secret sharing · Privacy

1 Introduction

Polling is one of the current practical and useful topics in online social networks (OSNs). In general, that is the problem of providing to all participants the

Funded by ANR Streams project.

© Springer International Publishing Switzerland 2015
A. Pelc and A.A. Schwarzmann (Eds.): SSS 2015, LNCS 9212, pp. 171–186, 2015.
DOI: 10.1007/978-3-319-21741-3_12

outcome of a poll conducted among themselves, thus giving the most favorite choice among some options. Each participant can express his/her preference by submitting a vote, then all votes are aggregated and the majority option will be chosen as the final result. Just to demonstrate one typical example, a university has just launched a new administrative procedure and may ask students whether or not this method is helpful, and each user will choose one option between "Yes" and "No". For the sake of simplicity, we here consider such a polling problem with only two options "+1" and "−1" for the concerning question.

The goal of studying this problem is to devise a polling protocol that can perform a secure and accurate process to sum up the initial votes with the presence of dishonest users, who try to bias the outcome and disclose the votes of honest ones. Despite the simplicity characteristics of this problem, it takes an important part in incorporating user's opinion online. Thus, currently, several studies and solutions for this problem using two settings, centralized and distributed networks, are proposed. In the centralized OSN, for instance Facebook Poll[1] and Doodle[2], such a computation process may be easily achieved through a central server which is used to collect the users' votes before summing up them to obtain the output. Nevertheless, this solution suffers from server failures and particularly privacy problems: user might generally not want his/her vote to be known by a central entity, and it is not guaranteed the server will neither bias nor disclose the votes.

Problem Statement. We deal with the polling problem in the decentralized OSN where information is not concentrated in a central point, and hence, user privacy is improved. In addition, we do not want to rely on cryptography for ensuring privacy or accuracy because cryptography uses complicated computation that impacts to the scalability and practicality of the protocols. Moreover, some traditional distributed computing problems can be solved without cryptography as motivated in [22,27].

Guerraoui et al. [15,16] proposed DPol, a simple decentralized polling protocol based on the secret sharing scheme (without using cryptography). DPol ensures the privacy of votes and limits the impact of dishonest users on accuracy. However, DPol has some disadvantages. First, DPol relies on a structured overlay (a cluster-ring-based structure) inspired from [12]. Although it is efficient in terms of the communication cost, it is on top and independent of the social graph. It does not take into account the social links among users in the sense that it builds a uniform distribution of users into groups. It means that we have to target a special case of graphs using the notion of group with potentially different links. Yet, the original social links may increase the confidence/trust of user interactions, as these links are chosen and agreed by users themselves. Second, to get a minimum communication cost (i.e., $\mathcal{O}(\sqrt{N})$), the number of users should be a perfect square in such a way that a graph with N users is divided into $\sqrt{N}$ groups of size $\sqrt{N}$. Third, transforming a graph into an overlay might not be useful since some security properties like accuracy may be affected, and

[1] http://apps.facebook.com/opinionpolls/
[2] http://www.doodle.com/

accordingly, this transformation may incur some additional communication costs. For instance, if the social graph is a clique, then each user can obtain easily the data sent by other ones because they are fully connected. However, when using a ring overlay on the top of this social graph, a user's data may be corrupted by intermediate users. To preserve accuracy, users should do verification procedures which may also increase the communication cost. In addition, as stated in DPol, an honest user may decide on the arbitrary data sent by dishonest ones, and thus, the impact of dishonest users on accuracy may be high.

Later, several protocols and extensions inspired from the idea of DPol have been proposed such as MPOL [11], PDP [3] and DiPA [2]. However these protocols rely on the same ring-based overlay structure, give the high impact of dishonest participants on the final result, and, generally, have minor contribution compared to DPol. Unlike these work, authors of [18] introduced a distributed polling protocol and a family of more general social graphs which ensures the correctness of the protocol and vote privacy of nodes. Nonetheless, the communication model is *synchronous* and the communication cost is super-linear in N, and is $\mathcal{O}(N^2)$ in the worst case, with the presence of dishonest nodes.

Accordingly, devising efficient and decentralized polling protocols without cryptography and constraints (such as the use of overlay structure and perfect square number of users) imposed in [15,16] remains a challenging problem.

Contributions. In this paper, we propose the design of a simple decentralized polling protocol that neither requires a central authority nor cryptography system. Unlike [15,16], our protocol is deployed on more social networks in such a way that each individual can perform the voting process privately and securely without resorting to the group division. Despite the use of richer social graph structures (which also include a ring-based structure given in [15,16]), a node can receive/send so many duplicated messages from/to other nodes. This can lead to flooding the local storage and getting the high communication cost. Inspired from [29], we introduce a method for efficiently broadcasting messages by using the concept called *m-broadcasting property*. A graph satisfies the m-broadcasting property for a parameter $m \in \mathbb{N}$ such that $1 \leq m \leq d_{min}$, where d_{min} is the minimum node degree, if for each source node, there exists a topological ordering of the nodes such that every node connects directly either to the source or to some m nodes preceding it in the ordering w.r.t. the source. (A node knows only its direct neighbors' ordering.) Consequently, instead of accepting all messages originating from the source, a node stores only m ones passed by *ordered paths*. The construction of this kind of graphs is not presented here due to limited space. (See [19] for more details about this construction and some graph examples.)

To describe carefully the distributed implementation of a polling problem, we consider the following fundamental criteria: accuracy, privacy, resilience to dishonest nodes, and asymptotic complexity. Using the same notion of privacy parameter k given in [15,16], we get the following results in a system of size N with D dishonest users: (i) the probability of vote disclosure with certainty is at most $(D/N)^{k+1}$; (ii) up to $2D$ votes can be revealed with certainty (if all honest nodes do not not vote for the same value); (iii) in practice, dishonest

Table 1. Comparison of distributed polling protocols where "Max. Impact": the maximum difference between the output and the expected result, "Privacy": the probability of vote disclosure, "Nb. of Dishonest Nodes": the number of dishonest nodes the system can tolerate, "Spatial complexity": the total space a node must hold, "Message complexity": the number of messages sent by a node, k: privacy parameter $(0 \leq k \leq \min\{d_{min}, \lfloor (\sqrt{N} - 1)/2 \rfloor\})$, r: number of groups $(r \leq \sqrt{N})$, $|g_i|$: group size $(|g_i| \leq \sqrt{N})$, d_0: maximum node degree, Δ_G: network diameter. Entries marked with an asterisk (*) show the results for binary polling.

Algorithm	Graph	Max. Impact	Privacy	Nb. of Dishonest Nodes	Complexity Spatial	Message	Crash
DPol [15]	Overlay	$(6k+2)D$	$(D/N)^{k+1}$	$D < \sqrt{N}$	$\mathcal{O}(rk + |g_i|)$	$\mathcal{O}(rk + |g_i|)$	Yes
DPol* [16]	Overlay	$(6k+4)D$	$(D/N)^{k+1}$	$D < \sqrt{N}$	$\mathcal{O}(rk + |g_i|)$	$\mathcal{O}(rk + |g_i|)$	Yes
Pol [18]	General	$(6k+4)D$	$(D/N)^{k+1}$	$D \leq N/10$	$\mathcal{O}(N^2)$	$\mathcal{O}(k + N^2)$	No
MPOL* [11]	Overlay	$(6k+2)D$	$(D/N)^{k+1}$	$D < \sqrt{N}$	$\mathcal{O}(rk^2|g_i|)$	$\mathcal{O}(rk + |g_i|)$	No
PDP [3]	Overlay	$2(k+\sqrt{N})D$	$(D/N)^{k+1}$	$D < \sqrt{N}$	$\mathcal{O}(rk + |g_i|)$	$\mathcal{O}(rk + |g_i|)$	No
DiPA [2]	Overlay	$2(k+\sqrt{N})D$	$(D/N)^{k+1}$	$D < \sqrt{N}$	$\mathcal{O}(rk + |g_i|)$	$\mathcal{O}(rk + |g_i|)$	No
This work	General	$(6k+4)D$	$(D/N)^{k+1}$	$D \leq (m-1)\Delta_G/2$	$\mathcal{O}(mN)$	$\mathcal{O}(N(d_0 - m))$	Yes

nodes may also try to reveal a node's vote even if they hold only partial information of the vote (e.g., some shares of that vote). We consider the cases where dishonest nodes agree on some rules for disclosing a node's vote without certainty (section 4.2), then the maximum probability of greedy (i.e., analyzing *some* shares of the vote) and non-greedy (i.e., analyzing *all* shares of the vote) vote detection are respectively $\sum_{i=\rho}^{k} \gamma_i \frac{N+1}{N-D+\rho+2} (\frac{D}{N-D+\rho+1})^{\rho+1}$ and $\left(\frac{D}{N}/(1 - 2\frac{D}{N})\right)\left[1 - \sum_{i=0}^{k} \gamma_i (2\frac{D}{N})^{2i+1}\right]$, where γ_i is the proportion of nodes voting with $2i + 1$ shares and $0 \leq \rho \leq i \leq k$; (iv) the maximum impact of a dishonest coalition on the final result is $(6k + 4)D$, and the average impact is $\left[\left[\sum_{i=0}^{k} \gamma_i (2i+1)\right]\left[1 + 2\sum_{i=0}^{k} \gamma_i \frac{i+\alpha}{2i+1}\right] + 1\right]D$, where α is the proportion of users correctly voting; (v) the maximum number of dishonest nodes that the system can tolerate is $(m - 1)\Delta_G/2$, where Δ_G is the network diameter; and (vi) the communication and spatial complexities of our protocol are close to be linear.

We are aware that due to the presence of dishonest nodes, an honest node may receive distinct values of a source. As opposed to DPol [15,16], we ensure each node can decide the most represented value to obtain *correct* data of other ones. In addition, we analyze the effect of message loss and node crash on accuracy and termination of the protocol.

We illustrate the comparison of contributions in Table 1. This table shows that our protocol *tolerates more* dishonest nodes than other ones. For instance, if the graph is a ring overlay, compared to DPol [15,16], our protocol has the same message complexity, but tolerates more dishonest nodes and computes more accurately the poll outcome. It is also noted that DPol investigates the effect of crash only, rather the combination with message loss.

Outline. This paper is organized as follows. Section 2 describes our polling model, and introduces a family of social graphs. Section 3 presents our polling protocol and Section 4 analyzes its correctness with and without the presence of dishonest nodes. Section 5 discusses the impact of crash and message loss on accuracy and termination of the protocol. We give an overview of related work in Section 6, followed by a discussion of results in Section 7. Proofs for the correctness of our solution and examples of graph structures are given in [19].

2   Social Network Model

This section describes user behaviors and social graph models. It should be noted that we consider the same assumptions given in [15,16].

2.1   User Behaviors

The polling problem consists of a system modeled as the form of an undirected social graph $G = (V, E)$ with $N = |V|$ uniquely identified nodes representing users and a set E of social links. Each participant n expresses its opinion by giving a vote $v_n \in \{-1, 1\}$. After collecting the votes of all nodes, the expected outcome is $\sum_n v_n$. In this work, we consider the following assumptions:

We consider an *asynchronous* model where each node can communicate (send/receive messages) with its neighbors (e.g., direct friends). Some messages may arrive to the destination with some delay. All nodes have to send/receive/forward messages if they are requested.

Each node is either *honest* or *dishonest*. Honest nodes completely comply with the protocol and take care about their privacy while dishonest ones might not. All dishonest nodes can form a coalition to get the full network knowledge and try to do everything to achieve these goals without being detected: (i) bias the result of the election by promoting their votes or changing the values they received from other honest nodes; (ii) infer the opinions of other nodes. However, they also want to protect their reputation from being affected.

In order to unify the opinions and do not give compensating effects, all dishonest nodes make the single coalition $\mathcal{D}$ of size D. However, they are selfish in the sense that each dishonest node prefers to take care about its own reputation to covering up each other [15,16]. As such the dishonest nodes are rather restricted but more reflective of the real human behavior than Byzantine nodes [21]. Byzantine nodes may do anything they wish. When messages reach to Byzantine nodes, they can drop or do not forward these messages to their neighbors even if requested.

To tolerate the existence of dishonest nodes with a limited vote corruption, we assume each node has at least one honest friend but it does not know which friend is honest or not. To dissuade the user misbehaviors, an activity affected to the profile of the concerned node is given. More precisely, if node u is detected as dishonest one by v then u's profile is tagged with the statement "v accused u of being a dishonest user" and v's profile has the statement "u is a bad guy". Notice that in social networks, no one would like to be tagged as dishonest. Furthermore, we do not take into account the Sybil attacks and spam since those kinds of misbehaviors can be detected by some tools or several systems such as SybilGuard[33], SybilLimit [32], and [24,31] (for mitigating spam). Moreover, as in [15,16], we assume that dishonest nodes cannot wrongfully blame other ones.

2.2 Social Graph Model

In this section, we define the terms and notations of the social graph used throughout this work, and describe the graphs with low communication cost.

Notations. A node n maintains a set of direct neighbors $\Gamma(n)$ of size d_n, and two subsets of $\Gamma(n)$: a set $\mathcal{S}_n$ of *consumers* containing nodes that n sends messages to, and $\mathcal{R}_n$ of *producers* relating to nodes for which n acts as a consumer. They might not be disjoint, i.e., $\mathcal{S}_n \cap \mathcal{R}_n \neq \varnothing$, as depicted in Fig. 1 (where node z is both a producer and a consumer). We denote Δ_G as the diameter of the network G. The distributed algorithms for computing exact diameter take time $\mathcal{O}(N)$ [20,25].

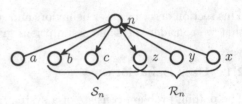

Fig. 1. Producers and consumers of n

Graphs with Low Communication Cost. We define a social graph that satisfies what we call the *m-broadcasting property* (described in the introduction). For a certain source node s, let $\beta_n(s)$ be a number of neighbors of n preceding it in the ordering w.r.t. s.[3] (We sometimes omit the mentioned source where no confusion arises.)

2.3 Secret Sharing Based Graphs

In this part, we present the family of graphs without and with the presence of dishonest nodes. We use a predefined parameter $k \in \mathbb{N}$ and $k \leq \min\{d_{min}, \lfloor (\sqrt{N} - 1)/2 \rfloor\}$ (like [15,16]) and a parameter $m \in \mathbb{N}$ to present the features of our social graphs. Let $G = (V, E)$ be a social graph with the following properties:

Property 1 (P_{g_1}). $d_n \geq 2k+1$, $|\mathcal{S}_n| = 2i+1$ and $|\mathcal{R}_n| \leq 2k+1$ where $0 \leq i \leq k$, for every $n \in V$.

Property 2 (P_{g_2}). G satisfies the *m*-broadcasting property.

Property 3 (P_{g_3}). For a source node, each other node has less than $m/2$ dishonest neighbors preceding it in the ordering (w.r.t. source node).

According to Property P_{g_1}, the set of consumers and the set of producers of a node have the size of *at most* $2k+1$ and might *not be disjoint*. This condition distinguishes our graph family from other structures in [11,15,16] and is more flexible than a graph family in [18] since they all consider the restricted condition where each node has *exactly* $2k+1$ consumers. In addition, it also differs from [2,3] which do not impose any condition to the upper bound on the number of

---

[3] The list of neighbors is determined by a preprocessing step (not detailed here due to space limitation) before the polling process.

producers (that one node should have), thus, a dishonest node can send arbitrary summing data to others and the accuracy of the global outcome is easily affected. Property P_{g_2} enables us to reduce the communication cost in the system. It is also noted that this condition implicitly implies the condition that G is an honest graph mentioned in [18], i.e., for every honest nodes u, v, there exists a path between u and v containing only intermediate honest nodes. Property P_{g_3} ensures each honest node always obtains one correct version of data from other honest ones. Property P_{g_3} also enables us to limit the size of dishonest users, that is $D \leq \frac{m-1}{2}\Delta_G$ (presented in Theorem 8).

From these properties, we characterize two families of graphs:

  (i) $\mathcal{G}_1 = \{G \mid \mathcal{D}(G) = \varnothing$ and G satisfies $P_{g_1}, P_{g_2}\}$.
  (ii) $\mathcal{G}_2 = \{G \mid \mathcal{D}(G) \neq \varnothing$ and G satisfies P_{g_1}, P_{g_2} and $P_{g_3}\}$.

Graphs in $\mathcal{G}_1$ contain only honest nodes and satisfy property P_{g_1} and P_{g_2}. Graphs in $\mathcal{G}_2$ contain honest and dishonest nodes and satisfy properties P_{g_1}, P_{g_2} and P_{g_3}.

3   Polling Protocol

We present here our polling protocol, EPol, for the network without crash and message loss. EPol is composed of the following phases:

Sharing. In this phase, node n contributes its opinion by sending a set of shares expressing its vote $v_n \in \{-1, 1\}$ to its consumers. We inspired the sharing scheme proposed in [9]. Namely, first n chooses *randomly* a value i such that $i \in \{0, 1, ..., k\}$ and i is not known by other nodes. Then it generates $2i + 1$ shares $\mathcal{P}_n = \{p_1, p_2, ..., p_{2i+1}\}$, where $p_j \in \{-1, 1\}$ and $1 \leq j \leq 2i+1$, including: $i + 1$ shares of value v_n, and i shares of opposite v_n's value. The intuition of this creation is to regenerate the vote v_n when the shares are summed. Later it randomly generates a permutation μ_n of $\mathcal{P}_n$, and sends shares to $2i + 1$ consumers. Lines 4–8 in Algorithm 1 describe this activity. Node also receives $|\mathcal{R}_n|$ shares from its producers. Note that $\mathcal{S}_n$ and $\mathcal{R}_n$ might not be disjoint.[4]

After each node collects shares from its producers, and sums into *collected data* c_n (lines 9–14 in Algorithm 1), this phase is over. It is also noted that because the votes and their generating shares belong to the set $\{-1, +1\}$, nodes cannot distinguish between a vote and a share. Hence, if a node opts a value $i = 0$ and generates only $2i + 1 = 1$ share, the dishonest consumer receiving a message from that node could not distinguish if such share was generated as a single one or it is one among many generated shares of that node.

Fig. 2 illustrates an example of the protocol for $i = k = 1$. Fig. 2a presents the network and the ordering of nodes w.r.t. source A in the parentheses. Figure 2b depicts the sharing phase at node A. Node A would like to vote $+1$, thus, it generates a set of $2i + 1 = 3$ shares $\{+1, -1, +1\}$. Node A collects the shares from its producers and computes the collected data $c_A = 3$.

---

[4] This distinguishes our protocol from approaches in [2,3,11,15,16]. The set of consumers and producers in these approaches are separated for each of size $2k + 1$.

Algorithm 1. POLLING ALGORITHM AT NODE $n \in \{0, 1, ..., N-1\}$

Input:
  v_n: A vote of node n, value in $\{-1, 1\}$
  k : privacy parameter
  m : positive integer where $1 \leq m \leq d_{min}$
   i: integer value in $[0, k]$
  $\mathcal{S}_n$: set of consumers to send shares
  $\mathcal{R}_n$: set of producers to receive shares

Variables:
  c_n: collected data, $c_n = 0$
  $\mathcal{C}_n$: set of possible collected data
     $\mathcal{C}_n[\{0, 1, ..., N-1\} \rightarrow \varnothing]$
  h_n: set of final deciding collected data
     $h_n[\{0, 1, ..., N-1\} \rightarrow \perp]$

Output: result

Polling Algorithm

1 Sharing($v_n, \mathcal{S}_n, i$)
2 Broadcasting(c_n)
3 Aggregating()

Procedure Sharing($v_n, \mathcal{S}_n, i$)

4 $\mathcal{P}_n \leftarrow \{v_n\}$
5 **for** $j \leftarrow 1$ **to** i **do** $\mathcal{P}_n \leftarrow \mathcal{P}_n \cup \{v_n\} \cup \{-v_n\}$
6 $\mu_n \leftarrow_{rand} \mathcal{P}_n$
7 **for** $j \leftarrow 0$ **to** $2i$ **do**
8 $\lfloor$ send (SHARE, $\mu_n[j]$) to $\mathcal{S}_n[j]$

9 $count \leftarrow 0$
10 **while** ($count < |\mathcal{R}_n|$) **do**
11 | **upon event** (receive (SHARE, p) from
    | neighbor r in the first time) **do**
12 | | **if** ($r \in \mathcal{R}_n$ and $p \in \{-1, 1\}$) **then**
13 | | | $c_n \leftarrow c_n + p$
14 | | | $count \leftarrow count + 1$

Procedure Broadcasting(c_n)

15 **foreach** ($r \in \Gamma(n)$) **do**
16 $\lfloor$ send (DATA, n, c_n) to r

17 $count \leftarrow 0$
18 **while** ($count < N-1$) **do**
19 | **upon event** (receive message (DATA, s,
    | c_s) from direct neighbor r preceding n in
    | the ordering w.r.t. source s) **do**
20 | | **if** ($r = s$) **then**
21 | | | $h_n[s] \leftarrow c_s$
22 | | | $count \leftarrow count + 1$
23 | | | Forward (DATA, s, c_s) to other
    | | | friends succeeding n in the
    | | | ordering w.r.t. source s
24 | | **else if** ($s \notin \Gamma(n)$) **then**
25 | | | $\mathcal{C}_n[s] \leftarrow \mathcal{C}_n[s] \cup \{c_s\}$
26 | | | **if** ($|\mathcal{C}_n[s]| = m$) **then**
27 | | | | $h_n[s] \leftarrow$ Decide($\mathcal{C}_n[s]$)
28 | | | | $count \leftarrow count + 1$
29 | | | | send (DATA, s, $h_n[s]$) to
    | | | | other $d_n - \beta_n(s)$ friends
    | | | | succeeding n in the ordering
    | | | | w.r.t. source s

Function Decide($\mathcal{Z}$)

30 **return** the most represented value in $\mathcal{Z}$

Procedure Aggregating()

31 result $\leftarrow 0$
32 **for** $s \leftarrow 0$ **to** $N-1$ **do**
33 | **if** ($s \neq n$) **then**
34 | | result $\leftarrow$ result $+ h_n[s]$
35 | **else** result $\leftarrow$ result $+ c_n$

Broadcasting. In this phase, each node needs to broadcast its collected data in such a way that each recipient node eventually obtains that correct data. In the naive approach, upon receiving a message from the neighbor, a node stores the data then forwards it on every other edge. Despite the use of richer social graph structures, and with the presence of dishonest nodes which can corrupt data, one node can receive/send so many duplicated messages (which may be passed by many paths) from/to other nodes. This leads to flooding the local storage. As motivated in the introduction, we propose a method for efficiently broadcasting messages by using the concept m-broadcasting property. For a graph satisfying the m-broadcasting property, each node n sends its collected data to all neighbors (lines 15–16). Then, upon receipt of the message containing the collected data of source s from neighbor r preceding it in the ordering (w.r.t. source s), node n does one of the following activities:

 - $r = s$: It decides on the data of source s by storing the value c_s in $h_n[s]$. When the value $h_n[s]$ is assigned, it is further forwarded to all $d_n - \beta_n(s)$ nodes

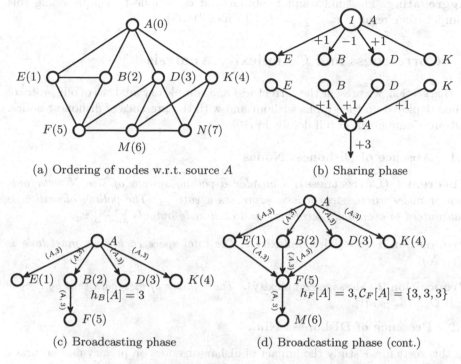

(a) Ordering of nodes w.r.t. source A

(b) Sharing phase

(c) Broadcasting phase

(d) Broadcasting phase (cont.)

Fig. 2. Polling algorithm for $i = k = 1$ and $m = 3$

succeeding it in the ordering (lines 20–23). In Fig. 2c, node A broadcasts its data, then B receives, stores that data in $h_B[A]$, and forwards it to F.

- $r \neq s$: To avoid the case that value $h_n[s]$ might be calculated (and broadcast) twice for the direct neighbor s, node n only considers the case $r \neq s \wedge s \notin \Gamma(n)$. If this condition is satisfied, it adds the value c_s to the multiset $\mathcal{C}_n[s]$ of possible collected data for s (line 25). When node n has received the expected number m of possible collected data for a given source s, it decides on the collected data by choosing the most represented value in $\mathcal{C}_n[s]$ and puts it in $h_n[s]$. (Since the decision is based on the most represented value, instead of waiting for receiving all m forwarded data, node n can decide the source's data upon receipt of more than $m/2$ identical data.) Node n then forwards the data to all $d_n - \beta_n(s)$ nodes succeeding it (lines 26–29).

In Fig. 2d, node F has four friends, but receives only $m = 3$ messages from preceding neighbors E, B, D. As all values in $\mathcal{C}_F[A]$ are 3, node F decides that value as the collected data of A and stores it in $h_F[A]$. It then forwards that data to its succeeding node M.

When a node decides the collected data of s and has no succeeding friend, the value $h_n[s]$ is no longer forwarded. This phase is complete if a node decides on the collected data of all other ones in the network.

Aggregating. The final result is obtained at each node by simply doing this computation: $\text{result} = c_n + \sum_{j \neq n} h_n[j]$ (lines 31–35).

4   Correctness and Complexity Analysis

In this section, we present the correctness and complexity analysis of our protocol when deployed on the graphs without and with the presence of dishonest nodes. All proofs are given in full details in [19].

4.1   Absence of Dishonest Nodes

Theorem 1 (Correctness). *Consider a polling system of size N with only honest nodes where each node n expresses a vote v_n. The polling algorithm is guaranteed to eventually terminate and each node outputs $\sum_{n=0}^{N-1} v_n$.*

Proposition 1 (Spatial complexity). *The total space each node must hold is $\mathcal{O}(mN)$.*

Proposition 2 (Message complexity). *The number of messages sent by a node n is $\mathcal{O}(N(d_n - m))$.*

4.2   Presence of Dishonest Nodes

In this section, we study the impact of dishonest nodes on privacy and accuracy when EPol is deployed on the graphs of $\mathcal{G}_2$ in the worst and average cases.

Privacy Analysis

Let γ_i be the proportion of nodes voting with $2i + 1$ shares in the sharing phase, where $0 \leq i \leq k$ and $\sum_{i=0}^{k} \gamma_i = 1$. A node's vote could be revealed with: (i) *certainty* if dishonest nodes are sure about this disclosure, or (ii) *uncertainty* otherwise. Assuming $D \leq (m - 1)\Delta_G/2$ (presented later in Theorem 8), we consider these cases of vote disclosure as follows.

Vote Disclosure with Certainty. We discuss the probability that the vote of a given node may be disclosed with certainty in the following theorem.

Theorem 2 (Certain Privacy). *Assume a coalition of D dishonest nodes knows the number of shares sent by a node. The probability P_{ce} this coalition reveals correctly with certainty the vote of an honest node voting with $2i + 1$ shares $(0 \leq i \leq k)$ is at most $\gamma_i \left(\frac{D}{N}\right)^{i+1}$.*

Corollary 1. *If all nodes send $2k + 1$ shares in the sharing phase, then the probability that a coalition of D dishonest nodes reveals correctly with certainty an honest node's vote is at most $\left(\frac{D}{N}\right)^{k+1}$.*

We see that P_{ce} increases with the increase of γ_i and the decrease of i. Thus, we get the maximum privacy when all nodes generate $2k + 1$ shares, and the minimum privacy when all nodes generate only one share.

If the poll outcome is N (resp. $-N$), it infers all nodes vote for "+1" (resp. "−1") and they all are disclosed. Moreover, w.l.o.g., assume dishonest nodes always vote for "−1", thus, if the result is $N - 2D$ (resp. $-N$) then it implies all honest nodes vote for "+1" (resp. "−1"). Without considering these cases, i.e., all honest nodes do not vote for the same option, Theorem 3 shows us the maximum number of votes that a dishonest coalition could discover.

Theorem 3. *If all honest nodes do not vote for the same option, a coalition of D dishonest nodes can reveal at most $2D$ votes of honest nodes.*

Vote Disclosure with Uncertainty. This part examines the case that dishonest nodes collude to reveal an honest node's vote without sureness. The coalition decides a node's vote based on the received shares in the sense they can decide the vote after getting some shares or after getting all shares from that node. Thus, they choose one of the following *strategies*: (a) Upon receipt of $\rho + 1$ identical shares (for some $0 \leq \rho \leq k$) from a given node, they will be considered as its vote; (b) After receiving all shares from a given node, the most represented value of the received shares will be considered as its vote. The former strategy is used by "greedy" dishonest users who want to reveal rapidly an honest user's vote (even if they have just received one share). The latter one is used by "non-greedy" dishonest users who are patient and wait for receiving all shares of the honest user before trying to disclose his/her vote. We present the probabilities that a coalition of dishonest nodes discloses an honest node's vote for these situations in Theorems 4 and 5. Recall that each node does not know the number of shares generated by other ones.

Theorem 4 (Greedy vote disclosure). *Assume a coalition of D dishonest nodes agrees on the following rule "upon receipt of $\rho + 1$ identical shares $(0 \leq \rho \leq k)$ from a given node, they will be considered as the node's vote". The probability this coalition reveals correctly a node's vote is $P_{gr}(\rho) = \sum_{i=\rho}^{k} \gamma_i \cdot \binom{D}{\rho+1} \sum_{j=0}^{\rho} \binom{D-\rho-1}{j} / \binom{N}{j+\rho+1}$ and is bounded by $\sum_{i=\rho}^{k} \gamma_i \frac{N+1}{N-D+\rho+2} (\frac{D}{N-D+\rho+1})^{\rho+1}$.*

In Theorem 4, the vote v of an honest node is discovered if that node has sent $2i + 1 \geq 2\rho + 1$ shares in which $\rho + 1$ identical ones representing v and up to ρ shares of value $-v$ were received by the dishonest consumers. Moreover, by Theorem 4, value P_{gr} increases when γ_i decreases (and i increases) and D increases.

Theorem 5 (Non-greedy vote disclosure). *Assume a coalition of D dishonest nodes agrees on the following rule "the most represented value of the received shares from a given node will be considered as the node's vote". The probability this coalition reveals correctly a node's vote is $P_{un} = \sum_{i=0}^{k} \gamma_i \cdot \sum_{j=1}^{i+1} \sum_{t=0}^{j-1} \binom{D}{j} \binom{D-j}{t} / \binom{N}{j+t}$ and is bounded by $(\frac{D}{N} / (1 - 2\frac{D}{N})) [1 - \sum_{i=0}^{k} \gamma_i (2\frac{D}{N})^{2i+1}]$.*

By Theorem 5, the quantity P_{un} increases when both values γ_i and D increase (and i also increases).

Combining Vote Disclosure with and Without Certainty. The objective of this part is to present the situation where dishonest nodes may try to reveal an honest node's vote either in certainty or uncertainty. Assume they respect the rules of vote disclosure with and without certainty. From the viewpoint of dishonest nodes, they always want their vote detection to be as certain as possible, i.e., they prefer a node's vote being revealed with certainty to other cases. Hence their strategy is as follows: they first try to disclose a vote of node with sureness. If they do not succeed, for instance, because of lacking of messages, they will consider the way to detect that vote without certainty. It implies the probability a vote is disclosed in this case is $P_{com} = \max\{P_{ce}, P_{gr}, P_{un}\}$.

Accuracy Analysis

In this section, we evaluate the maximum and average impact on accuracy caused by the dishonest coalition when we deploy EPol on the graphs of $\mathcal{G}_2$. From the attacking model introduced in Section 2.1, a dishonest node may affect the poll outcome with the following *misbehaviors*:

(i) Since a node can only generate and send shares to its consumers it is assigned (otherwise the shares are dropped) and there are at most $2k + 1$ consumers to be assigned, it must send at most $2k + 1$ shares in which at most $k + 1$ ones are identical. Hence a dishonest node may misbehave by sending more than $k + 1$ (but not greater than $2k + 1$) identical shares.

(ii) It inverts each receiving "+1"-share into a "−1"-share

(iii) It modifies the collected data of other honest node or sends a forged message in the broadcasting phase.

Verification procedures: in the first attack, the worst case is when a dishonest node sends all $2k + 1$ shares of value "−1". In the attack (ii), a node receives at most $2k + 1$ shares (since at most $2k + 1$ producers are assigned) and thus, the computing collected data must be inside the range $[-(2k + 1), 2k + 1]$. The misbehaviors (i) and (ii) cannot be detected without inspecting the content of the shares themselves, but the misbehavior (iii) is detected with certainty if the dishonest nodes transmit or corrupt the collected data outside the range $[-(2k + 1), 2k + 1]$. Noted that we do not consider the Sybil attacks, hence, in case (iii) a dishonest node cannot create a forged message containing identity of other node. Moreover, this activity does not affect the final result since a node receives directly a message from source s (if it is a neighbor of s) or gets a majority of receiving messages ($\lceil (m + 1)/2 \rceil$) containing the correct data of s. We show the impact of these misbehaviors on accuracy in Theorems 6 and 7.

Theorem 6 (Maximum impact). *Each dishonest node may affect the final result up to* $6k + 4$.

Note that, since $0 \leq k \leq \min\{d_{min}, \lfloor (\sqrt{N} - 1)/2 \rfloor\}$ and, theoretically, the maximum impact is $2N$, the relative error is $(6k + 4)/(2N) = \mathcal{O}(1/\sqrt{N})$.

Theorem 7 (Average impact). *Let α be the proportion of nodes voting for "+1". The average impact of a dishonest node on accuracy is* $I_{avg} = \left[\sum_{i=0}^{k} \gamma_i(2i + 1)\right]\left[1 + 2\sum_{i=0}^{k} \gamma_i \frac{i+\alpha}{2i+1}\right] + 1.$

The quantity I_{avg} is minimized when all nodes generate the same number of shares, e.g., $2i + 1$, and thus $I_{avg} = 2(2i + \alpha + 1)$. In the worst case, a dishonest node sends $2k + 1$ shares, the minimized average impact is $I_{avg} = 2(2k + \alpha + 1)$.

From Theorems 6 and 7 we demonstrate the range of the biased result in Corollary 2.

Corollary 2. *The expected biased result is in the range* $[(2\alpha - 1)N - (6k + 4)D;$ $(2\alpha - 1)N]$. *More particularly, if all nodes send $2k + 1$ shares, then the expected biased result is* $(2\alpha - 1)N - (4k + 2\alpha + 2)D$.

By Theorems 2–7 and Corollaries 1 and 2, for a fixed parameter k, the number of users voting with a high number of shares (e.g., $2k + 1$ shares) affects the privacy and accuracy. More concretely, if we care about vote privacy, we should augment the number of nodes generating $2k + 1$ shares since the probability to disclose a node's vote with certainty (P_{ce}) and with greedy uncertainty (P_{gr}) will decrease. But this rises up the probability P_{un} of non-greedy vote disclosure and the impact on the final outcome. In contrast, if we take care of the accuracy of the final result, we should decrease the number of nodes voting with $2k + 1$ shares since that reduces the impact on the final outcome. It also decreases P_{un}. However this increases the values P_{ce} and P_{gr}.

Security Analysis

In this part, first we justify the maximum number of dishonest nodes that EPol can tolerate in Theorem 8. We then prove that the probability for a node decides wrongly the data of a certain source converges fast in N in Corollary 3. Recall that Δ_G is a network diameter.

Theorem 8 (Tolerance to dishonest nodes). *The maximum number of dishonest nodes that EPol can tolerate is* $\frac{m-1}{2}\Delta_G$.

Corollary 3. *If $D \leq \frac{m-1}{2}\Delta_G$ then a node decides wrongly the collected data of some other node with the probability converging to 0 exponentially fast in N (and Δ_G).*

5 Crash and Message Loss Analysis

This part analyzes the effect of node crashes and message losses on accuracy and termination of the protocol. We assume the system contains no dishonest nodes. Proofs are presented in [19].

Impact on Termination. Suppose nodes crash with probability r (and never recover from a crash), a message is lost (throughout transmitting) with probability l, a node *fails to send shares* to its consumers with probability $q = r + (1 - r)l$. A node n *fails to decide* a collected data of source s since:

1. $n = s$: s fails to compute its collected data c_s.
2. $n \in \Gamma(s)$: n does not receive a broadcast message from s.

3. $n \notin \Gamma(s)$: more than $\beta_n(s) - m$ (preceding) neighbors *fail to forward* the collected data as they either: (i) crashed, or (ii) have themselves not decided on the collected data, or (iii) have forwarded messages but they are lost.

We define by e_{n_i} and z_{n_i} respectively the probability for a node n at distance i from source s to fail to forward and fail to decide a collected data of s. We have $e_{n_i} = r + (1-r)[z_{n_i} + (1 - z_{n_i})l]$, where $z_{n_0} = z_s = \sum_{j=0}^{|\mathcal{R}_s|-1} \binom{|\mathcal{R}_s|}{j}(1-q)^j q^{|\mathcal{R}_s|-j}$, $z_{n_1} = e_{n_0}$, and $z_{n_i} = \sum_{j=0}^{m-1} \left[\binom{\beta_n(s)}{j} \prod_{t=1}^{j}(1 - e_{n_{t_{l_t}}}) \prod_{p=j+1}^{\beta_n(s)} e_{n_{p_{l_p}}} \right]$ where $i \geq 2$, $\{n_1, n_2, \ldots, n_{\beta_n(s)}\}$ and $\{l_1, l_2, \ldots, l_{\beta_n(s)}\}$ are respectively the sets of preceding friends of n (w.r.t. s) and their corresponding distances to s. Notice that l_j could be greater than i for $j = 1, 2, \ldots \beta_n(s)$. A node does not decide on the outcome if it has not decided on at least one collected data of some source, that is $z_{n_{\Delta_G}}$.

Impact on Accuracy. We show the impact on accuracy in Theorem 9

Theorem 9. *The maximum impact on accuracy of a node crash is $3k + 2$.*

6   Related Work

Several recent work related to secret sharing and distributed polling have been proposed. We introduce some work not based on any overlay structure and heavy computation. Secret sharing schemes [1,30] may be used for polling with respect to addition. However, as they do not give the protection for the initial shares, the outcome is likely impacted with the presence of dishonest nodes. Verifiable Secret Sharing Scheme (VSS) and Multi-party Computation protocol (MPC) in [4,26] privately compute the node's shares and give output with small error if a majority of nodes is honest. Nonetheless, without the condition of the initial input, a dishonest node can share arbitrary data, and bias the output. These protocols also use cryptography. This drawback is also applied for other studies based on MPC such as [5–8] even the time and communication complexity are improved. Authors of [23] proposed AMPC which provides users anonymity without using cryptography, but this work used the notion of group. Based on AMPC and enhanced check vectors, E-voting protocol [22] is the information-theoretically secure protocol. But it defines different roles for users and thus, is different from our direction. The distributed ranking schemes are also related to our concern. However, they try to design accurate grading mechanism rather than providing efficient polling schemes [17,28] and not address to privacy [10]. In [29], the m-propagating condition enables the use of minimal shares for the secret. But, in our work, it is used to create a majority for deciding the correct value during the broadcasting phase of our protocol. The protocol in [13] and *AG-S3* [14] can be used for polling in a scalable and secure way, but they either use (i) a ring-based overlay, or (ii) cryptography.

7   Conclusion

This paper presented EPol, a distributed polling protocol for a general family of social graphs, while preserving vote privacy and limit the impact on accuracy of the polling outcome. Unlike other work, our protocol is deployed in a more general family of graphs, and we obtained some similar and better results. In addition, we introduced some uncertain vote disclosure rules for dishonest nodes, and presented the probabilities of vote detection in these cases. We also analyzed the effect of message losses and nodes crashes on accuracy and termination. Despite the use of richer social graph structures, the communication and spatial complexities of EPol are close to be linear. In future work, we plan to implement our protocol in decentralized social networks like Diaspora and Tent.

References

1. Benaloh, J.C.: Secret sharing homomorphisms: keeping shares of a secret sharing. In: Odlyzko, A.M. (ed.) CRYPTO 1986. LNCS, vol. 263, pp. 251–260. Springer, Heidelberg (1987)
2. Benkaouz, Y., Erradi, M.: A distributed protocol for privacy preserving aggregation with non-permanent participants. Computing (2014)
3. Benkaouz, Y., Guerraoui, R., Erradi, M., Huc, F.: A distributed polling with probabilistic privacy. In: SRDS, pp. 41–50 (2013)
4. Chor, B., Goldwasser, S., Micali, S., Awerbuch, B.: Verifiable secret sharing and achieving simultaneity in the presence of faults. In: FOCS, pp. 383–395 (1985)
5. Cramer, R., Franklin, M.K., Schoenmakers, B., Yung, M.: Multi-authority secret-ballot elections with linear work. In: Maurer, U.M. (ed.) EUROCRYPT 1996. LNCS, vol. 1070, pp. 72–83. Springer, Heidelberg (1996)
6. Cramer, R., Gennaro, R., Schoenmakers, B.: A secure and optimally efficient multi-authority election scheme. European Trans. on Telecom. 8(5), 481–490 (1997)
7. Damgård, I., Ishai, Y., Krøigaard, M., Nielsen, J.B., Smith, A.: Scalable multi-party computation with nearly optimal work and resilience. In: Wagner, D. (ed.) CRYPTO 2008. LNCS, vol. 5157, pp. 241–261. Springer, Heidelberg (2008)
8. Damgård, I.B., Nielsen, J.B.: Scalable and unconditionally secure multiparty computation. In: Menezes, A. (ed.) CRYPTO 2007. LNCS, vol. 4622, pp. 572–590. Springer, Heidelberg (2007)
9. Delporte-Gallet, C., Fauconnier, H., Guerraoui, R., Ruppert, E.: Secretive birds: privacy in population protocols. In: Tovar, E., Tsigas, P., Fouchal, H. (eds.) OPODIS 2007. LNCS, vol. 4878, pp. 329–342. Springer, Heidelberg (2007)
10. Dutta, D., Goel, A., Govindan, R., Zhang, H.: The design of a distributed rating scheme for peer-to-peer systems. In: P2P Econ (2003)
11. Englert, B., Gheissari, R.: Multivalued and deterministic peer-to-peer polling in social networks with reputation conscious participants. In: TrustCom (2013)
12. Galil, Z., Yung, M.: Partitioned encryption and achieving simultaneity by partitioning. Inf. Process. Lett., 26(2) (1987)
13. Gambs, S., Guerraoui, R., Harkous, H., Huc, F., Kermarrec, A.-M.: Scalable and secure polling in dynamic distributed networks. In: SRDS, pp. 181–190 (2012)
14. Giurgiu, A., Guerraoui, R., Huguenin, K., Kermarrec, A.-M.: Computing in social networks. Infor. and Comp. 234, 3–16 (2014)
15. Guerraoui, R., Huguenin, K., Kermarrec, A.-M., Monod, M.: Decentralized polling with respectable participants. In: Abdelzaher, T., Raynal, M., Santoro, N. (eds.) OPODIS 2009. LNCS, vol. 5923, pp. 144–158. Springer, Heidelberg (2009)
16. Guerraoui, R., Huguenin, K., Kermarrec, A.-M., Monod, M., Vigfusson, Y.: Decentralized polling with respectable participants. JPDC 72(1), 13–26 (2012)

17. Gupta, M., Judge, P., Ammar, M.: A reputation system for peer-to-peer networks. In: NOSSDAV. ACM, New York (2003)
18. Hoang, B.-T., Imine, A.: On the polling problem for social networks. In: Baldoni, R., Flocchini, P., Binoy, R. (eds.) OPODIS 2012. LNCS, vol. 7702, pp. 46–60. Springer, Heidelberg (2012)
19. Hoang, B.-T., Imine, A.: Efficient polling protocol for decentralized social networks (2014). CoRR, abs/1412.7653
20. Holzer, S., Wattenhofer, R.: Optimal distributed all pairs shortest paths and applications. In: PODC, pp. 355–364 (2012)
21. Lamport, L., Shostak, R.E., Pease, M.C.: The byzantine generals problem. ACM Trans. Program. Lang. Syst., **4**(3) (1982)
22. Malkhi, D., Margo, O., Pavlov, E.: E-voting without 'cryptography'. In: Blaze, M. (ed.) FC 2002. LNCS, vol. 2357, pp. 1–15. Springer, Heidelberg (2003)
23. Malkhi, D., Pavlov, E.: Anonymity without 'cryptography'. In: Syverson, P.F. (ed.) FC 2001. LNCS, vol. 2339, pp. 117–135. Springer, Heidelberg (2002)
24. Mislove, A., Post, A., Druschel, P., Gummadi, P.K.: Ostra: Leveraging trust to thwart unwanted communication. In: NSDI (2008)
25. Peleg, D., Roditty, L., Tal, E.: Distributed algorithms for network diameter and girth. In: Czumaj, A., Mehlhorn, K., Pitts, A., Wattenhofer, R. (eds.) ICALP 2012, Part II. LNCS, vol. 7392, pp. 660–672. Springer, Heidelberg (2012)
26. Rabin, T., Ben-Or, M.: Verifiable secret sharing and multiparty protocols with honest majority (extended abstract). In: STOC (1989)
27. Rivest, R.L.: Chaffing and winnowing: confidentiality without encryption. RSA Laboratories CryptoBytes **4** (1998)
28. Rodriguez-Perez, M., Esparza, O., Muñoz, J.L.: Analysis of peer-to-peer distributed reputation schemes. In: CollaborateCom (2005)
29. Shah, N.B., Rashmi, K.V., Ramchandran, K.: Secure network coding for distributed secret sharing with low communication cost. In: ISIT (2013)
30. Shamir, A.: How to share a secret. Commun. ACM **22**(11), 612–613 (1979)
31. Sirivianos, M., Kim, K., Yang, X.: Socialfilter: introducing social trust to collaborative spam mitigation. In: INFOCOM (2011)
32. Yu, H., Gibbons, P.B., Kaminsky, M., Xiao, F.: Sybillimit: A near-optimal social network defense against sybil attacks. Trans. Netw. **18**(3), 885–898 (2010)
33. Yu, H., Kaminsky, M., Gibbons, P.B., Flaxman, A.D.: Sybilguard: defending against sybil attacks via social networks. Trans. Netw. **16**(3), 576–589 (2008)

Constructing Self-stabilizing Oscillators in Population Protocols

Colin Cooper[1], Anissa Lamani[2]([⊠]), Giovanni Viglietta[3],
Masafumi Yamashita[2], and Yukiko Yamauchi[2]

[1] Department of Informatics, Kings College, London, UK
[2] Department of Informatics, Graduate School of ISEE, Kyushu University,
Fukuoka, Japan
anissa.lamani@gmail.com
[3] School of Electrical Engineering and Computer Science,
University of Ottawa, Ottawa, Canada

Abstract. Population protocols (PPs) are a model of passive distributed systems in which a collection of finite-state mobile agents interact with each other to accomplish a common task. Unlike other works, which investigate their computation power, this paper throws light on an aspect of PPs as a model of chemical reactions. Motivated by the well-known *BZ reaction* that provides an autonomous chemical oscillator, we address the problem of autonomously generating an oscillatory execution from any initial configuration (i.e., in a self-stabilizing manner). For deterministic PPs, we show that the self-stabilizing leader election (SS-LE) and the self-stabilizing oscillator problem (SS-OSC) are equivalent, in the sense that an SS-OSC protocol is constructible from a given SS-LE protocol and vice versa, which unfortunately implies that (1) resorting to a leader is inevitable (although we seek a decentralized solution) and (2) n states are necessary to create an oscillation of amplitude n, where n is the number of agents (although we seek a memory-efficient solution). Aiming at reducing the space complexity, we present and analyze some randomized oscillatory PPs.

Keywords: Population protocol · Self-stabilization · Oscillatory behavior · Leader election · Distributed algorithm

1 Introduction

The motivation of our study is to understand how autonomy emerges in biological systems, and to apply such understanding in giving artificial distributed systems autonomous properties. Specifically, we focus on self-oscillations, which play fundamental roles in autonomous biological reactions, and investigate them as a phenomenon in distributed computing. Self-oscillations are often understood as a chemical oscillator provided by certain reactions, such as the Belousov–Zhabotinsky reaction. We use the population protocol model for our investigation, since it was introduced in part to model chemical reactions.

© Springer International Publishing Switzerland 2015
A. Pelc and A.A. Schwarzmann (Eds.): SSS 2015, LNCS 9212, pp. 187–200, 2015.
DOI: 10.1007/978-3-319-21741-3_13

The *population protocol* (PP) model introduced by Angluin et al. [2] is a model of passive distributed systems. It is used as a theoretical model of a collection of finite-state mobile agents that interact with each other in order to solve a given problem in a cooperative fashion. Computations are done through pairwise interactions, i.e., when two agents interact, they exchange their information and update their states accordingly. The interaction pattern, however, is unpredictable, and the agents have no control over which agent they interact with. We thus assume the presence of an abstract mechanism called *scheduler* that chooses at any time instant the pair of agents that interact with each other. PPs can represent not only artificial distributed systems such as sensor networks and mobile agent systems, but also natural distributed systems such as chemical reactions and biological systems.

In the past few years, many problems have been investigated on PPs, including the problems of computing a function, electing a leader, counting, coloring, synchronizing and naming [1–4,7,8]. Most of the problems consider the computational power of the population and hence are *static*; the agents are requested to eventually reach a configuration that represents the answer to the given computation problem.

The notion of termination is typically intended in the Noetherian sense (in the context of abstract rewriting systems); however the agents are not requested to eventually terminate, but the execution is requested to repeat the same configuration forever.

Unlike most of the past works in PPs, we throw light on an aspect of PPs as a model of chemical reactions. Specifically, we investigate the problem of designing a PP that stabilizes to an oscillatory execution, no matter from which initial configuration it starts; that is, we explore a *self-stabilizing* PP that generates an oscillatory execution. The problem emerges in the project of designing molecular robots [9], and is directly motivated by the Belousov–Zhabotinsky reaction, which is an example of non-equilibrium thermodynamics providing a non-linear chemical oscillator. We show that under a deterministic scheduler governed by an adversary, the self-stabilizing leader election problem and the self-stabilizing oscillator problem are equivalent, and hence costly in term of space complexity. Aiming at space reduction, we then propose and analyze some approximate solutions assuming a randomized scheduler.

In biological systems, the oscillatory behavior is used as a natural clock to transmit signals and hence transfer information. In artificial distributed systems, PPs that exhibit an oscillatory behavior could be used to distributely and autonomously implement a clock.

Apart from the difference of motivation, a few works on *dynamic* problems are related to our work. Angluin et al. [4] provided a self-stabilizing token circulation protocol in a ring with a pre-selected leader. Beauquier and Burman investigated the self-stabilizing mutual exclusion, group mutual exclusion problems [6] and also the self-stabilizing synchronization problem [5]. In the latter work, they have shown that the synchronization problem in the PP model under a deterministic scheduler is impossible to solve, and hence they proposed a solution assuming the presence of an unlimited-resource agent called *Base Station*. Our problem also belongs to the class of dynamic problems.

After introducing some concepts and notions in Section 2, we consider a *deterministic scheduler* governed by an adversary in Section 3. Under this scheduler, we focus on the self-stabilizing oscillator (SS-OSC) problem. We show that the self-stabilizing leader election (SS-LE) problem and the SS-OSC problem are equivalent; that is, an SS-OSC protocol is constructible from a given SS-LE protocol, and vice versa. In Section 4, we consider a *probabilistic scheduler*, i.e., the interacting agents are chosen uniformly at random. Under the probabilistic scheduler, we present and analyze some oscillatory PPs, mainly aiming to reduce space complexity. Section 5 is devoted to the conclusions.

In this paper, we use results from [7] that concern the SS-LE problem. In [7], it has been shown that the SS-LE is impossible to solve with less than n states where n is the size of the population. Also, a PP that solves the SS-LE was proposed. The protocol ensures that eventually each agent has unique state.

2   Preliminaries

In this paper, we consider a population of n anonymous finite-state agents that update their state by interacting with other agents. We consider only pairwise interactions, i.e., each interaction involves exactly two agents. When two agents interact, they update their state according to a common protocol. We denote by $A = \{0, 1, \ldots, n-1\}$, the set of agents in the population, that is, $|A| = n$. Indices are used for notation purposes only; in fact, the agents are anonymous, i.e., they have no identity and cannot be distinguished from each other. Any pair of agents a_1 and a_2 $(a_1 \neq a_2)$ in the population are susceptible to interact and the interactions are undirected.

A *protocol* $P = (Q, \delta)$ is a pair of a finite set of states Q and a transition function $\delta : Q \times Q \to Q \times Q$. When two agents interact with each other, δ determines the next state of both agents. Let p and q be the states of agents a_1 and a_2, respectively. $\delta(p, q) = (p', q')$ indicates that the states of agents a_1 and a_2, after interacting with each other, are p' and q', respectively. We assume that if $\delta(p, q) = (p', q')$ then $\delta(q, p) = (q', p')$.

A *configuration* C is a mapping $A \to Q$ that specifies the state of all the agents in the population. By $C(i)$, we refer to the state of agent i in configuration C. By $\mathcal{C}$ we refer to the set of all possible configurations of the system. Given a configuration $C \in \mathcal{C}$ and an interaction between the two agents a_1 and a_2, $r = (a_1, a_2)$, we say that C' is obtained from C via the interaction r, denoted by $C \xrightarrow{r} C'$, if $(C'(a_1), C'(a_2)) = \delta(C(a_1), C(a_2))$.

Let C_t be the configuration at time t and let r_t be the interaction on C_t at time t. An *execution* E of a protocol P is a sequence of configurations and transitions $(C_0, r_0, C_1, r_1, \cdots)$ such that $\forall\, i \geq 0$, r_i is a transition of δ and $C_i \xrightarrow{r_i} C_{i+1}$. When a configuration C' is reachable from C after a finite number of transitions we note $C \xrightarrow{*} C'$.

A *scheduler* chooses a pair of agents to interact at each time $t \geq 0$. In this paper, we consider two types of schedulers: (i) A deterministic but globally fair scheduler that guarantees that if there is a configuration that is reachable infinitely often, then the configuration is eventually reached. (*ii*) A uniform random scheduler, i.e., the pair of agents that are chosen for the interaction are selected at random, independently and uniformly from the set of all the agents in the system.

In the sequel, we define some important notions that will be used in the paper.

Definition 1. *(Oscillation)* Let $f: [a,b] \subset \mathbb{N} \to \mathbb{R}$ be a function. We say that f is an oscillation if there exists $c \in \mathbb{N}$ such that:

1. $a < c < b$,
2. $f(a) < f(c) > f(b)$,
3. f is weakly increasing in $[a,c]$ and weakly decreasing in $[c,b]$.

The value $f(c) - (f(a) + f(b))/2$ is called the amplitude of the oscillation and is denoted by ι_a, whereas $b - a$ is called the period of the oscillation and is denoted by ι_p. The increasing phase (respectively, decreasing phase) of the oscillation is the interval in which f is weakly increasing (respectively, weakly decreasing).

Definition 2. *(Oscillatory behavior)* Given an execution E of a population protocol $\mathcal{P}$ on n agents and a set of states S, let $f_S : \mathbb{N} \to [0,n] \subset \mathbb{N}$ be the function mapping a time instant t into the number of agents whose state is in S at time t. Let $\{t_0, t_1, \dots\}$ be a strictly increasing sequence of time instants. We say that E exhibits an oscillatory behavior for the set of states S, if for every $i \geq 0$, the restriction of f_S to $[t_i, t_{i+1}]$ is an oscillation.

Note that, according to the previous definitions, any execution exhibits oscillatory behavior, unless the number of agents whose state is in S eventually stabilizes. However, we are also interested in evaluating the "quality" of the oscillations, in terms of their amplitude and period.

3   Deterministic Scheduler

We investigate in this section the problem of generating oscillatory executions under a global fair deterministic scheduler and starting from an arbitrary configuration. We show that the SS-LE problem and SS-OSC problem are equivalent. By using the results in [7], we can deduce then, that the SS-OSC problem is impossible to solve if $|Q| < n$ or if n is arbitrary.

Let us first define the deterministic self-stabilizing oscillator.

Definition 3. *(Deterministic oscillator)* A population of agents executing a deterministic protocol $\mathcal{P}$, under a globally fair scheduler, is a (C, S, ι_a, ι_p)-oscillator if any execution $E = (C, r, C', r', \dots)$ of $\mathcal{P}$ exhibits an oscillatory behavior for the set of states S, with amplitude ι_a and period ι_p.

Definition 4. *(Deterministic self-stabilizing oscillator)* *A population of agents executing a deterministic protocol* $\mathcal{P}$*, under a globally fair scheduler, is a self-stabilizing oscillator for the set of states* S *if, starting from an arbitrary configuration* $C_0 \in \mathcal{C}$*, every execution* $E = (C_0, r_0, C_1, r_1, \dots)$ *of Protocol* $\mathcal{P}$*, reaches a configuration* $C \in \mathcal{C}$ *such that* (C, S, ι_a, ι_p) *is a deterministic oscillator.*

Observe that since the deterministic globally fair scheduler can delay any particular transition of the system for an arbitrary amount of time, it is not possible to bound the period using the classical definition of an interaction. Hence, we use the notion of active interactions that was introduced in [7]. Basically, an interaction r is said to be active in a given configuration $C \in \mathcal{C}$, if it updates the state of at least one of the two agents that have participated in r. More precisely, an interaction $r = (a, b)$, is said to be active in $C \in \mathcal{C}$, if $C \xrightarrow{r} C'$ and either $C(a) \neq C'(a)$ or $C(b) \neq C'(b)$.

When ι_p is omitted, it means that the period of the oscillator is not specified, or that the oscillator is not periodic (i.e., not all oscillations have the same period). We consider in the following (C, S, n, ι_p)-oscillators.

Starting from an arbitrary initial configuration $C_0 \in \mathcal{C}$, we show the following two results:

1. If the SS-LE problem is solvable using M_{LE} states, then it is possible to solve the SS-OCS problem using $M_{LE} + O(n)$ states.
2. If the SS-OSC problem is solvable using M_{OSC} states, then it is possible to solve the SS-LE problem using $M_{OSC} + O(1)$ states.

(1) SS-LE $\Rightarrow$ SS-OSC. We show that a deterministic population protocol $\mathcal{P}_{OSC}$ exists using $M_{LE} + 2^n$ states per agent (M_{LE} being the number of states necessary to solve the self-stabilizing leader election problem). A solution with $M_{LE} + O(n)$ states is also presented later in Discussion (1). The idea of the solution is as follows: we combine our SS-OSC protocol $\mathcal{P}_{OSC}$ with the SS-LE protocol $\mathcal{P}_{LE}$ proposed in [7] and that uses n distinct states per agent. When an interaction occurs between two agents, the two agents execute the enabled actions of both $\mathcal{P}_{OSC}$ and $\mathcal{P}_{LE}$. Protocol $\mathcal{P}_{LE}$ ensures that eventually one leader is elected and all the agents have a unique state [7]. Our solution takes advantage of this "identification" to create an oscillatory behavior. Indeed, using the identification created by Protocol $\mathcal{P}_{LE}$, the leader can somehow remember the agents it has already interacted with.

The state of each agent a_i consists of a triplet of variables $(id_{a_i}, p_{a_i}, T_{a_i})$. Variable id_{a_i} is used by Protocol $\mathcal{P}_{LE}$ ($id_{a_i} \in \{0, 1, 2, \dots, n-1\}$), where 0 is the leader's state. According to [7], eventually each agent has a unique value for id_{a_i}. Variable $p_{a_i} \in \{0, 1\}$, indicates the phase of the oscillation Agent a_i is part of (increasing or decreasing phase). Variable T_{a_i} is an array of n entries such that $\forall j \in \{1, \dots, n-1\}$, $T_{a_i}[j] \subset [0, 1]$. The array is used only by the leader to keep track of the agents the leader has already interacted with, hence, in the sequel, the state of a non-leader agent a_j is only represented by the pair (id_{a_j}, p_{a_j}). Let a_i and a_j be the two interacting agents at time t. Without loss of generality, assume that $id_{a_i} < id_{a_j}$. Protocol 1 describes how agents a_i and a_j update their state.

Protocol 1. Self-stabilizing deterministic oscillator with central control ($\mathcal{P}_{OSC}$)

```
 1: if (id_{a_i} = 0) then
 2:     if (∀ k ∈ [1, n − 1], T_{a_i}[k] = 1) then
 3:         ∀ k ∈ [1, n − 1], T_{a_i}[k] := 0
 4:         if (p_{a_i} = 0) then  p_{a_i} := 1
 5:         else  p_{a_i} := 0
 6:         end if
 7:     else
 8:         if (p_{a_i} = p_{a_j}) then
 9:             if (T_{a_i}[id_{a_j}] = 0) then  T_{a_i}[id_{a_j}] := 1
10:             end if
11:         else
12:             p_{a_j} := p_{a_i}
13:             if (T_{a_i}[id_{a_j}] = 0) then  T_{a_i}[id_{a_j}] := 1
14:             end if
15:         end if
16:     end if
17: end if
```

By executing Protocol $\mathcal{P}_{LE}$, eventually a unique leader is elected and each agent $a_i \in A$ has a unique value for its variable id_{a_i} (refer to [7]). Hence, id_{a_i} can be used to identify Agent a_i. Let us consider the population after the stabilization of Protocol $\mathcal{P}_{LE}$, i.e., $\exists! \, a_i \in A$ such that $id_{a_i} = 0$ and $\forall \, a_j, a_{j'} \in A, a_j \neq a_{j'} \Rightarrow id_{a_j} \neq id_{a_{j'}}$. Let us refer to the elected leader by a_i. Recall that the array T is only used by a_i. Each entry $k \in \{1, \ldots, n-1\}$ of Array T_{a_i} corresponds to the entry of Agent a_j such that $id_{a_j} = k$. Every time a_i interacts with another agent, say a_j, Agent a_j updates its variable p_{a_j} to be in the same phase as the leader (refer to Line 12 in Protocol 1) and the leader updates the entry of a_j to 1 to indicate that it has already interacted with a_j (Lines 9 and 13). When all the entries of T_{a_i} are set to 1, the leader toggles its phase and re-initializes its array (Lines 3-5). Since the initial configuration is arbitrary, some of the entries in the leader's array might be equal to 1 even if the leader did not interact with the corresponding agents. However, since the leader's array is eventually re-initialized, we are sure that after the first re-initialization of T, if an entry of T is equal to 1, then the leader has indeed interacted with the corresponding agent and thus, all agents update their phase to be in the same phase as the leader. Let S be the set of state such that $p = 1$ (Phase 1). Hence, starting from any arbitrary configuration $C_0 \in \mathcal{C}$, every execution $E = (C_0, r_0, C_1, r_1, \ldots)$ of $\mathcal{P}_{LE} \circ \mathcal{P}_{OSC}$ reaches a configuration $C \in \mathcal{C}$ such that (C, S, n, ι_p) is a deterministic oscillator with $\iota_p = O(n)$ active interactions.

Discussion (1). The number of states per agent can be reduced to $M_{LE} + O(n)$ by using the same idea as in Protocol 1, but instead of using an array, the leader uses a counter that we denote by N_{ext} ($N_{ext} \in \{1, \ldots, n-1\}$). The counter is used to indicate the next agent the leader needs to interact with in order to update its state, i.e., the agents update their state in a given order so that the leader is sure to have interacted with everyone. While interacting with the leader, the agents update their phase to be in the same phase as the leader.

Protocol 2. Self-stabilizing deterministic oscillator with central control (second approach)

$(C(\text{Leader}), C(\neg~\text{Leader})) \rightarrow \delta(C(\text{Leader}), C(\neg~\text{Leader}))$	
1. $(0,0,i),(i,0) \rightarrow (0,0,i+1),(i,1)$	if $i < n-1$
2. $(0,0,i),(i,1) \rightarrow (0,0,i+1),(i,1)$	if $i < n-1$
3. $(0,0,n-1),? \rightarrow (0,1,1),~?$	
4. $(0,1,i),(i,0) \rightarrow (0,1,i+1),~(i,0)$	if $i < n-1$
5. $(0,1,i),(i,1) \rightarrow (0,1,i+1),(i,0)$	if $i < n-1$
6. $(0,1,n-1),? \rightarrow (0,0,1),?$	

The formal description of the solution is given in Protocol 2. Character '?' indicates any state of a non leader agent. If '?' is used then, the corresponding non-leader agent does not update its state in the interaction. The state of a leader agent a_i consists of a triplet of variables $(id_{a_i}, p_{a_i}, N_{ext})$ where id_{a_i} and p_{a_i} have the same role as in Protocol 1. The state of a non leader agent a_j is only represented by the couple (id_{a_j}, p_{a_j}). Protocol 1 was introduced to get rid of the state update order induced while using the counter in Protocol 2. We state the following result:

Theorem 1. *Under the global fair scheduler, if there exists a population protocol that solves the SS-LE problem using M_{LE} states then, there exists a population protocol that solves the SS-OSC problem using $M_{LE} + O(n)$ states.*

Discussion (2). From Discussion (1) we know that the number of states per agent can be reduced to $M_{LE}+O(n)$ to create oscillations with amplitude $\iota_a = n$. In fact, the result can be generalized to $M_{LE}+O(\iota_a)$ states where ι_a is the desired amplitude of the oscillator. By using the same strategy as in Discussion (1), it is sufficient to set maximum value of N_{ext} to $\iota_a - 1$. In addition, when the leader interacts with a non leader agent a_j such that $id_{a_j} > N_{ext}$, Agent a_j updates its phase p_{a_j} to 0. Since the scheduler is globally fair, $\forall~a_j \in A$ such that $id_{a_j} > N_{ext}$, a_j eventually interacts with the leader and hence $p_{a_j} = 0$. Thus, only $(\iota_a - 1)$ agents toggle their phase with the leader.

(2) SS-OSC $\Rightarrow$ SS-LE. We show that if the deterministic SS-OSC problem is solvable using M_{OSC} states, then it is also possible to solve the deterministic SS-LE problem using $M_{OSC}+O(1)$ states. To show this result, we build our self-stabilizing SS-LE protocol $\mathcal{P}'_{LE}$ on the top of the SS-OSC protocol $\mathcal{P}'_{OSC}$. By executing Protocol $\mathcal{P}'_{OSC}$, the system eventually exhibits an oscillatory behavior with respect to a given set of state S. Let us consider the population after the stabilization of $\mathcal{P}'_{OSC}$. We first show some important properties of a population that exhibits an oscillatory behavior. We assume that $\iota_a = n$. Given a configuration $C \in \mathcal{C}$, let $N_{C(S)}$ be the set of agents such that $\forall~a_i \in A$, $a_i \in N_{C(S)}$ if $C(a_i) \in S$. The number of agents part of $N_{C(S)}$ is denoted by $|N_{C(S)}|$. By C^+, we denote the set of configurations that can appear during the increasing phase of any oscillation before reaching the amplitude, that is, $\forall~C \in C^+$, $|N_{C(S)}| < n$. By C^*, we refer to the set of configurations such that $\forall~C \in C^*$, $|N_{C(S)}| = n$ (configurations in which all the agents have their states part of S, i.e., the amplitude is reached). The first step is to show that there is a non-empty subset of states that can only appear when the amplitude of the oscillation is reached. More precisely, in any configuration $C \in C^+$, the transition $\delta(C(a_i), C(a_j)) = (C'(a_i), C'(a_j))$ such that $|N_{C(S)}| > |N_{C'(S)}|$ is never enabled when the system is stabilized. Let Q' be the set of states that enable such a transition then, $\forall\, C \in C^+$, $\forall\, a_i \in A$, $C'(a_i) \notin Q'$ and $\forall\, C' \in C^*$, $\exists\, a_i \in A$, $C'(a_i) \in Q'$ (States in Q' indicates that the next phase of the oscillation can be initiated). Next, we define a subset of special configurations that we denote by $C_{sp} \subset C^+$. A configuration $C \in C_{sp}$ satisfies the two following conditions: (1) $\exists!\, a_j \in A$ such that $C(a_j) \notin S$ and (2) $\forall\, a_i \in A$, $C(a_i) \notin Q'$. Observe that Condition (1) implies that $\forall\, a_i \in A \setminus \{a_j\}$, $C(a_i) \in S$. We show that a configuration $C \in C_{sp}$ is eventually reached and $\exists$ $a_i, a_j \in A$ such that $\delta(C_{sp}(a_i), C_{sp}(a_j)) = (C'(a_i), C'(a_j))$ with $C(a_j) \notin S$ and $C'(a_j) \in S$ and either $(C'(a_i) \in Q')$ or $(C'(a_j) \in Q')$. That is, the amplitude is reached and at least one of the two interacting agents has a state part of Q'. We refer to such an interaction by r_{sp}. Finally, we prove that from a configuration $C \in C^*$, if $\exists\, a_i \in A$ such that $C(a_i) \notin Q'$ and $\exists a_j \in A$ such that $\delta(C(a_i), C(a_j)) = (C'(a_i), C'(a_j))$ with $C'(a_i) \in Q'$ then $C(a_j) \in Q'$, that is, when the amplitude is reached, a given agent can change its state to a state in Q' only if it interacts with an agent already in a state part of Q'.

Protocol. In order to elect a leader starting from an arbitrary configuration $C_0 \in C$ using the SS-OSC population protocol $\mathcal{P}'_{OSC}$, we add to the state of each agent one bit of memory to indicate whether the agent is a leader or not ($l \in \{0, 1\}$). When r_{sp} is executed, if C' is the resulting configuration, then $\exists\, a_i \in A$ such that $C'(a_i) \in Q'$ (recall that $r_{sp}{:}\delta(C_{sp}(a_i), C_{sp}(a_j)) = (C'(a_i), C'(a_j))$ such that (i) $C(a_j) \notin S$. (ii) $C'(a_j) \in S$. (iii) $((C'(a_i) \in Q') \vee (C'(a_j)) \in Q'))$. Assume that after the execution of r_{sp}, $\exists!\, a_i \in A$ such that $C'(a_i) \in Q'$ (let us refer to this agent by a_{sp}). The idea of the protocol is as follows: when r_{sp} is executed, Agent a_{sp} becomes a leader. In addition, when a given agent a_i interacts with a leader then, a_i does not update its state (keep the same state). Observe that since we assume an arbitrary initial configuration, such a transition can be executed even if the population is not yet stabilized with respect to $\mathcal{P}'_{OSC}$. To be sure to create only one leader, if in a given configuration $C \in C$, a_i is a leader then a_i becomes a non-leader in the next interaction if $C(a_i) \notin Q'$ or $C(a_i) \notin S$. In the same manner, a_i becomes a non leader if it interacts either with another leader or with an agent a_j such that $C(a_j) \notin S$. Observe that if $\exists\, a_i \in A$ such that a_i is a leader, then a_i can only be enabled to become a non-leader, We show that:

Theorem 2. *Under the global fair scheduler, if there exists a population protocol $\mathcal{P}'_{OSC}$ that solves the SS-OSC problem with amplitude n using M_{OSC} states, then the SS-LE problem is also possible to solve using $M_{OSC} + O(1)$ states.*

Remark. Theorem 2 can be generalized to any amplitude $\iota_a \leq n$. Indeed, the main idea of the solution is to make any leader becomes a non leader infinitely often during the stabilization time to ensure the convergence of Protocol $\mathcal{P}'_{OSC}$. Once the population converges to an oscillatory behavior, the properties of the oscillatory behavior ensure that only one leader is created. The leader then prevents the second phase of the oscillation to be initiated thus, no more leaders are created.

Recall that it has been proved in [7] that the SS-LE problem is not solvable when the number of states is less than the size of the population n and hence impossible to solve in the case where n is arbitrary. Using Theorems 1 and 2, we can deduce the following corollary:

Corollary 1. *There exists no deterministic self-stabilizing oscillator if the number of states by agent is less than n, or if the size of the population is arbitrary.*

4 Stochastic Scheduler

Aiming at the reduction of the space complexity, we investigate in this section the SS-OSC problem under a uniform random scheduler, i.e., the pair of agents that are selected for the interaction are chosen at random, independently and uniformly from the set of all the agents of the population. Let us first define the notion of the self-stabilizing *stochastic oscillator*.

Definition 5. *(Self-stabilizing stochastic oscillator) A (sufficient large) population of agents executing a deterministic protocol $\mathcal{P}$, under a uniform random scheduler, is a (C, S, ι_a, ι_p)-oscillator, if starting from any arbitrary configuration $C_0 \in \mathcal{C}$, any execution $E = (C_0, r_0, C_1, r_1, \dots)$ of $\mathcal{P}$, reaches a configuration $C \in \mathcal{C}$ such that (C, S, ι_a, ι_p) exhibits an oscillatory behavior for the set of states S with an expected average amplitude ι_a and an expected average period ι_p.*

We present in this section, three deterministic protocols. Each of them assumes an arbitrary initial configuration and also the presence of a leader, that is, the agents need first to elect a leader in order to achieve the oscillatory behavior. Recall that, without a leader detector oracle, the SS-LE problem is impossible to solve with less than n states. That is, $\Omega(n)$ states are necessary to achieve the election [7]. We aim in the following at the reduction of the extra-cost used to create the oscillatory behavior.

In the sequel, the state of the leader is represented by the couple (L_p, c) where L_p indicates that the agent is a leader in Phase p ($p \in \{0, 1\}$) and $c \in \{0, \dots k\}$ represents the current value of the leader's counter where $k \in \mathbb{N}$, is the maximum value that the counter can reach. The state of a non-leader agent consists of only one variable p such that $p \in \{0, 1\}$. Variable p indicates which phase of the oscillation the agent is part of. An agent is said to be *a follower* (respectively *a non-follower*) if it is not a leader and if the value of its variable p is the same as (respectively different from) the leader's.

First Approach. The idea of the solution is as follows: at each time the leader interacts with a follower agent, the leader increments its counter. If it interacts with a non-follower agent, the leader re-initializes its counter and the non-follower agent part of the interaction updates its phase to become a follower. When the leader's counter reaches its maximum value, it toggles its phase and re-initializes

Protocol 3. Self-stabilizing stochastic oscillator with central control

(C(Leader), C(¬ Leader)) → δ(C(Leader), C(¬ Leader))	
1. $(L_0,i), 0 \to (L_0,i+1), 0$	$i < k$
2. $(L_0,i), 1 \to (L_0,0), 0$	$i < k$
3. $(L_0,k), 0 \to (L_1,0), 0$	
4. $(L_1,i), 0 \to (L_1,0), 1$	$i < k$
5. $(L_1,i), 1 \to (L_1,i+1), 1$	$i < k$
6. $(L_1,k), 1 \to (L_0,0), 1$	

its counter. The formal description of the protocol is given in Protocol 3. We show in the following that for any counter size $k \gg \log n$, the remaining non-follower agents at the end of a phase is $O((n/k) \log n)$ with high probability (provided that n is sufficiently large).

Suppose without loss of generality that the leader's phase is 0 (L_0), and there are initially $B_0 \leq n$ non-follower agents. Let $X(k) = X(k, B_0)$ be the number of non-follower agents at the end of the phase (when the leader toggles its phase from 0 to 1). Let $P(J)$ be the probability the switch of phase by the leader occurs when J non-follower agents remain. Then:

$$P(J) = \prod_{j=B_0}^{J+1}(1 - (1 - j/n)^k)(1 - J/n)^k$$

Note that only interactions with the leader matter in this calculation. Let E be the expected value of $X(k)$ then: $E = \sum_{J=0}^{B_0} JP(J)$.

Let $\omega = \omega(n)$ be some slowly growing function of n and assume $B_0 = n$ (worst case), and $J \geq \omega n/k$. We have: $P(J) \leq (1 - J/n)^k \leq e^{-kJ/n} \leq e^{-\omega}$. Let $\omega = 2 \log n$, the contribution to E from $\omega n/k \leq J \leq n$ is then:

$$\sum_{J=\omega n/k}^{n} JP(J) \leq n^2 e^{-2 \log n} = 1$$

Similarly, if $\omega = 3 \log n$ then, with high probability the number of non-follower agents is never bigger than $(3 \log n) \, n/k$ when the leader toggles its phase. Thus for $\omega = (2 \log n) \, n/k$, we have:

$$E \leq 1 + [(2 \log n) \, n/k] \sum_{J \leq (2 \log n) \, n/k} P(J) = O((\log n) \, n/k)$$

As for the expected period, for any k a phase completes in $O(kn)$ interactions with the leader. So the length of the phase is $O(n^2 k)$ with high probability.

Second Approach. To reduce even more the space complexity, we propose in the sequel, two population protocols that solve the SS-OSC problem and that use, in addition to the leader, another agent that we call *marked agent* and that we denote by M. Recall that the SS-LE protocol proposed in [7] not only elects a leader, but also provides a kind of identification, i.e., each agent a_i has unique state $C(i)$ such that $C(i) \in \{0, 1, \ldots, n - 1\}$. Hence, we can assume that the leader is the agent $a_i \in A$ such that $C(a_i) = 0$ and the marked agent is the agent $a_j \in A$ such that $C(a_j) = 1$. Thus, no other run of the leader election protocol is performed.

First Solution. The idea of the first solution is as follows: at each time the leader interacts with the marked agent, the leader's counter is incremented. On another hand, when the leader interacts with a non-follower agent, the non-follower agent updates its state to become a follower. When the leader's counter value reaches its maximum, i.e., after $(k + 1)$ interactions with the marked agent, the leader toggles its phase and re-initializes its counter value. The formal description of the first solution is given in Protocol 4.

Protocol 4. Self-stabilizing stochastic oscillator with central control using the marked agent trick without re-initialization

---

$(C(\text{Leader}), C(\neg \text{Leader})) \rightarrow \delta(C(\text{Leader}), C(\neg \text{Leader}))$

1. $(L_0,\text{i}), 0 \rightarrow (L_0,\text{i}), 0$ if $i < k$
2. $(L_0,\text{i}), 1 \rightarrow (L_0,\text{i}), 0$ if $i < k$
3. $(L_0,\text{i}), M \rightarrow (L_0,\text{i+1}), M$ if $i < k$
4. $(L_0,\text{k}), M \rightarrow (L_1,0), M$
5. $(L_1,\text{i}), 0 \rightarrow (L_1,\text{i}), 1$ if $i < k$
6. $(L_1,\text{i}), 1 \rightarrow (L_1,\text{i}), 1$ if $i < k$
7. $(L_1,\text{i}), M \rightarrow (L_1,\text{i+1}), M$ if $i < k$
8. $(L_1,\text{k}), M \rightarrow (L_0,0), M$

Let $\mathcal{X}$ (respectively $\mathcal{X}(i, i + 1)$) be the number of interactions to reach the maximum value of the leader's counter (respectively to the number of interactions in order for the leader's counter to be incremented from i to $i + 1$), we have: $\mathcal{X} = \sum_{i=0}^{k} \mathcal{X}(i, i + 1)$. Recall that the leader's counter is only incremented when the leader interacts with the marked agent, that is, $\mathcal{X}(i, i + 1)$ has a geometric distribution of parameter p: $P(\mathcal{X}(i, i+1) = m) = (1-p)^{m-1}p$, where p is the probability to get an interaction between the leader and the marked agent. Note that $p = \frac{2}{n(n-1)}$. The expected number of interactions to increment the leader's counter from i to $i + 1$ is

$$E[\mathcal{X}(i, i+1)] = \frac{1}{p} = \frac{n(n-1)}{2}.$$

Using the linearity of the expectations, we obtain $E[\mathcal{X}] = (k + 1) \frac{n(n-1)}{2}$. So after $E[\mathcal{X}]$ average interactions, the leader updates its phase to initiate the next phase of the oscillation.

Assume without loss of generality that the leader's phase is equal to 0. Let us now determine the expected amplitude ι_a which represents the expected number of non-follower agents that become followers before the leader's counter reaches its maximum value. Let $A_b(t)$ refers to the number of non-follower agents at time t. The expected number of non-follower agents at time $t + 1$ ($A_b(t + 1)$) is given by: $A_b(t+1) = A_b(t) - \frac{2 \cdot A_b(t)}{n(n-1)}$. That is, at time $(t+1)$, the number of non-follower agents either remains the same or decreases when there is an interaction between the leader and a non-follower agent. Approximately we have:

$$\frac{dA_b(t)}{dt} = -\frac{2}{n(n-1)} A_b(t), \text{ hence, } A_b(t) = A_b(0) \ e^{-\left(\frac{2t}{n(n-1)}\right)}$$

Recall that we know the expected number of interactions before reaching the amplitude. By replacing t by $E[\mathcal{X}]$, we obtain the expected number of non-follower agents when the amplitude is reached. That is:

$$A_a(E[\mathcal{X}]) = n - A_b(0) \ e^{-(k+1)}$$

We observe that if $k = log(n)$, $A_a(E[\mathcal{X}]) = n$.

Second Solution. We present in the sequel, a variation of Protocol 4 aiming at solving the SS-OSC problem with $k \in O(1)$ (recall that k is the maximum value of the leader's counter). The idea of the solution is similar to the one used in Protocol 4 except that, when the leader interacts with either a follower or a non-follower agent, it re-initializes its counter, that is, the leader, needs to interact $(k+1)$ consecutive times with the marked agent in order to toggle its phase. The system can be represented by a Markov chain as shown in Figure 1, where p is the probability to get an interaction between the leader and the marked agent, q is the probability to get an interaction between the leader and either a follower or a non-follower and $M = 1 - (p+q)$ (interactions that do not include the leader).

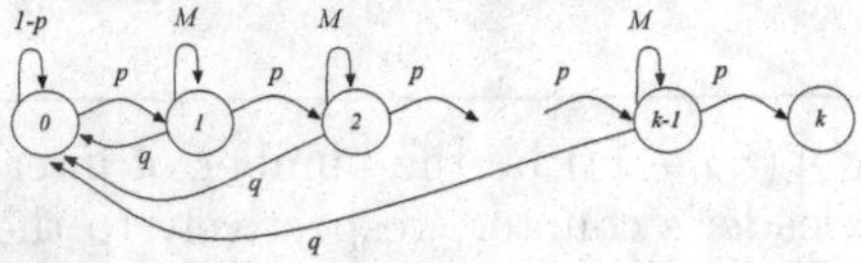

Fig. 1. Corresponding Markov Chain

The average number of interactions I_k, for the leader to toggle its phase, can be computed using the first step analysis. We obtain:

$$I_k = \frac{n(n-1)}{2} \left(\frac{(n-1)^k - 1}{n-2}\right) \quad (k > 1).$$

Assume that $(i - 1)$ non-follower agents have already updated their phase to become followers. Let compute the probability, P_{Next-i}, that a new non-follower agent changes its phase to become a follower before the switch of phase is performed by the leader i.e., before the $(k+1)$ consecutive interactions between the leader and the marked agent. We have:

$$P_{Next-i} = P_{b_i} \cdot \left(\sum_{j=0}^{k-1}(P_M^j)\right) \cdot \sum_{g \geq 0}\left(P_{w_i} \cdot \sum_{j=0}^{k-1}(P_M^j)\right)^g$$

Probability	Probability of an interaction	Value
P_M	(Leader, Marked agent)	$\frac{1}{(n-1)}$
P_{b_i}	(Leader, non-follower agent)	$\frac{B-i+1}{(n-1)}$
P_{w_i}	(Leader, follower agent)	$\frac{n-B+i-3}{(n-1)}$

Let $Z = \sum_{j=0}^{k-1} P_M^j$ and $Z' = \sum_{g \geq 0}(Z \cdot P_{w_i})^g$. Both Z and Z' are geometric series of common ration (P_M) and $(Z \cdot P_{w_i})$ respectively. Hence:

$$Z = (1 - P_M^k)/(1 - P_M) \text{ and } Z' = (1 - (Z \cdot P_{w_i})^m)/(1 - Z \cdot P_{w_i})$$

For a large population of agents, $P_M^k \simeq 0$ even if $k \in O(1)$. In the same manner, since, $(Z \cdot P_{w_i}) < 0$ and $m \rightarrow \infty$, $(Z \cdot P_{w_i})^m = 0$. Thus, $P_{Next-i} \simeq 1$. That is, all the non-follower agents become followers before reaching the maximum value of the leader's counter. Hence, $\iota_a \simeq n$

5   Conclusion

In this paper, we have considered the PPs model and have addressed the problem of autonomously generating oscillatory executions. We have considered the problem using deterministic protocols and have shown that, under a deterministic scheduler, $\Omega(n)$ states are necessary to solve the SS-OSC problem. This result emphasizes somehow the impact and the importance of randomization in biological systems and chemical reactions in creating self-oscillations. We have then proposed some protocols that solve the problem assuming a probabilistic scheduler. This is a preliminary work as several open questions arise: (i) All the proposed solutions in this paper, assume a central control, that is, the agents first need to elect a leader in order to create the desired oscillatory behavior. This is really costly especially for these kinds of systems, since the number of agents is usually huge. Thus, the problem of designing protocols that solve the SS-OSC problem in a decentralized way remains open. The main challenge is to achieve the self-stabilizing oscillatory behavior using a number of states that is independent from any global parameter of the system. Observe that when decentralized solutions are considered, it is impossible to achieve the oscillatory behavior as defined in this paper as, during the increasing phase (respectively, the decreasing phase) of an oscillation, the number of agents whose state is in the set S can decrease (respectively, increase) before (respectively, after) reaching the amplitude. However, there is a scaling effect that ensures that if we consider the global behavior of the population, by zooming out and ignoring the small fluctuations due to the agents that may toggle their phase before (respectively, after) reaching the amplitude of the oscillation, the population could display an oscillatory behavior. (ii) We have recently addressed the SS-OSC problem in a slightly different setting in which we assume that the population is synchronous i.e., each agent is part of an interaction at each instant t. We were able to implement a self-synchronized clock and use it to design primitive oscillators. The number of states used to solve the problem does not depend on the size of the population however, it does depends on the period of the oscillator. Hence, it would be also interesting to investigate the impact of the degree of synchrony on the SS-OSC problem. Finally, (iii) it would be challenging to simulate, as for the *Fourier Transform*, in a self-stabilizing way, any periodic behavior of a given population using a finite number of deterministic oscillators. We were able to do so in a recent investigation assuming synchronous populations. Extending the investigation taking in account different level of synchrony seems to be interesting direction to investigate.

References

1. Angluin, D., Aspnes, J., Chan, M., Fischer, M.J., Jiang, H., Peralta, R.: Stably computable properties of network graphs. In: Prasanna, V.K., Iyengar, S.S., Spirakis, P.G., Welsh, M. (eds.) DCOSS 2005. LNCS, vol. 3560, pp. 63–74. Springer, Heidelberg (2005)
2. Angluin, D., Aspnes, J., Diamadi, Z., Fischer, M.J., Peralta, R.: Computation in networks of passively mobile finite-state sensors. In: PODC, pp. 290–299 (2004)
3. Angluin, D., Aspnes, J., Eisenstat, D.: Fast computation by population protocols with a leader. Distributed Computing 21(3), 183–199 (2008)
4. Angluin, D., Aspnes, J., Fischer, M.J., Jiang, H.: Self-stabilizing population protocols. TAAS 3(4) (2008)
5. Beauquier, J., Burman, J.: Self-stabilizing synchronization in mobile sensor networks with covering. In: Rajaraman, R., Moscibroda, T., Dunkels, A., Scaglione, A. (eds.) DCOSS 2010. LNCS, vol. 6131, pp. 362–378. Springer, Heidelberg (2010)
6. Beauquier, J., Burman, J.: Self-stabilizing mutual exclusion and group mutual exclusion for population protocols with covering. In: Fernàndez Anta, A., Lipari, G., Roy, M. (eds.) OPODIS 2011. LNCS, vol. 7109, pp. 235–250. Springer, Heidelberg (2011)
7. Cai, S., Izumi, T., Wada, K.: How to prove impossibility under global fairness: On space complexity of self-stabilizing leader election on a population protocol model. Theory Comput. Syst. 50(3), 433–445 (2012)
8. Kinpara, K., Izumi, T., Izumi, T., Wada, K.: Improving space complexity of self-stabilizing counting on mobile sensor networks. In: Lu, C., Masuzawa, T., Mosbah, M. (eds.) OPODIS 2010. LNCS, vol. 6490, pp. 504–515. Springer, Heidelberg (2010)
9. Murata, S., Konagaya, A., Kobayashi, S., Saito, H., Hagiya, M.: Molecular robotics: A new paradigm for artifacts. New Generation Computing 31(1), 27–45 (2013)

Towards a Universal Approach for the Finite Departure Problem in Overlay Networks

Andreas Koutsopoulos, Christian Scheideler, and Thim Strothmann[(✉)]

Department of Computer Science, University of Paderborn, Paderborn, Germany
{koutsopo,scheidel,thim}@mail.upb.de

Abstract. A fundamental problem for overlay networks is to *safely* exclude leaving nodes, i.e., the nodes requesting to leave the overlay network are excluded from it without affecting its connectivity. There are a number of studies for safe node exclusion if the overlay is in a well-defined state, but almost no formal results are known for the case in which the overlay network is in an arbitrary initial state, i.e., when looking for a *self-stabilizing* solution for excluding leaving nodes. We study this problem in two variants: the *Finite Departure Problem* (*FDP*) and the *Finite Sleep Problem* (*FSP*). In the *FDP* the leaving nodes have to irrevocably decide when it is safe to leave the network, whereas in the *FSP*, this leaving decision does not have to be final: the nodes may resume computation when woken up by an incoming message. We are the first to present a self-stabilizing protocol for the *FDP* and the *FSP* that can be combined with a large class of overlay maintenance protocols so that these are then guaranteed to safely exclude leaving nodes from the system from any initial state while operating as specified for the staying nodes. In order to formally define the properties these overlay maintenance protocols have to satisfy, we identify four basic primitives for manipulating edges in an overlay network that might be of independent interest.

1 Introduction

Any distributed system must be based on some overlay network that specifies which nodes can directly send messages to which other nodes in the system. For distributed systems across the Internet, this is achieved by the nodes storing IP addresses of other nodes in that system, and in this case a node is said to be able to directly send a message to another node whenever it knows its IP address. A basic prerequisite for an overlay network which allows all pairs of nodes to exchange information is that it is connected, and a fundamental problem for overlay networks is to *preserve* connectivity while nodes are leaving, i.e., the nodes requesting to leave the overlay network are eventually excluded from it without disconnecting any staying nodes. Since due to permanent or transient failures a distributed system may rarely be in an ideal state, it would be desirable to find *self-stabilizing* protocols for the exclusion of leaving nodes, i.e., from *any* initial state connectivity is preserved. While this seems to be a fundamental problem, only recently first solutions were found.

© Springer International Publishing Switzerland 2015
A. Pelc and A.A. Schwarzmann (Eds.): SSS 2015, LNCS 9212, pp. 201–216, 2015.
DOI: 10.1007/978-3-319-21741-3_14

Foreback et al. [15] proposed to study this problem in two variants: the *Finite Departure Problem (FDP)* and the *Finite Sleep Problem (FSP)*. In the *FDP* the leaving nodes have to irrevocably decide when it is safe to leave the network, whereas in the *FSP*, this leaving decision does not have to be final: the nodes may resume computation when woken up by an incoming message. On the negative side, Foreback et al. showed that there is no self-stabilizing local-control protocol for the *FDP*. But if an oracle is available, then an appropriate local-control protocol can be constructed. Moreover, a variant of that protocol can solve the *FSP* without using an oracle. However, these protocols require that there is a fixed total order on the nodes (e.g., their names or IP addresses do not change), and they only work for a specific overlay maintenance protocol that aims at organizing the nodes in a sorted list.

In this paper, we present a self-stabilizing protocol for the *FDP* that can extend a large class of overlay maintenance protocols so that they are then guaranteed to eventually exclude the leaving nodes without risking disconnection and while the overlay maintenance protocol is operating as specified for the staying nodes. As a by-product, we present a set of four basic primitives for the manipulation of edges in overlay networks that are safe and universal in a sense that connectivity is preserved and that, in principle, one can get from any weakly connected graph to any other weakly connected graph. This might be of independent interest as we expect our insights to simplify the design and analysis of overlay maintenance protocols in the future.

1.1   Model

We consider a distributed system consisting of a fixed set of processes in which each process has a unique reference (like its IP address). We refer to processes and their references interchangeably. The system is controlled by a protocol that specifies the variables and actions that are available in each process. In addition to the protocol-based variables there is a system-based variable for each process called *channel* whose values are sets of messages. We denote the channel of process u as $u.Ch$ and $u.Ch$ contains all incoming messages to u. Its message capacity is unbounded and messages never get lost. A process can add a message to $u.Ch$ if it knows u (resp. its reference). Besides these channels there are no further communication means, so only point-to-point communication is possible.

A process u has a variable $mode(u) \in \{$leaving, staying$\}$ that is read-only. If this variable is set to **leaving**, the process is *leaving*; the process is *staying* if the variable is set to **staying**.

There are two types of actions. The first type of action has the form of a standard procedure $\langle label\rangle(\langle parameters\rangle) : \langle command\rangle$, where *label* is the unique name of that action, *parameters* specifies the parameter list of the action, and *command* specifies the statements to be executed when calling that action. Such actions can be called remotely. In fact, we assume that every message must be of the form $\langle label\rangle(\langle parameters\rangle)$ where *label* specifies the action to be called in the receiving process and *parameters* contains the parameters to be passed to that action call. All other messages will be ignored by the processes. Apart from being triggered by messages, these actions may also be called locally by the process, which causes their immediate execution. The second type of action has the form $\langle label \rangle : \langle guard \rangle \longrightarrow \langle command \rangle$, where *label* and *command* are defined as above and *guard* is a predicate over local variables. We call an action whose guard is simply **true** a *timeout* action.

There are three special commands that are important for the study of our finite departure problem. Whenever a process u wants to send a message to a process whose reference is stored in variable v, it executes $v \leftarrow label(parameters)$, which asks the process referenced by v to execute action *label* with parameter list *parameters*. In addition, there are **exit** and **sleep**. If a process executes **exit** it enters a designated *exit state*. We call such a process *gone*. If a process executes **sleep**, it enters a *sleep state*. Such a process is *asleep*. If a process never wakes up again, it is called *permanently asleep*. A process that is neither gone nor asleep is called *awake*. See Figure 1 for the corresponding state graph for a process.

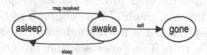

Fig. 1. The state graph for a process in our model

The *system state* is an assignment of a value to every variable of each process and messages to each channel. An action in some process p is *enabled* in some system state if its guard evaluates to **true** and p is awake, or there is a message in $p.Ch$ requesting to call it and p is awake or asleep. In the latter case, p becomes awake again as soon as the corresponding message is processed (in which case it is removed from $p.Ch$). The action is *disabled* otherwise. Hence, while a gone process never wakes up again, an asleep process may wake up again when processing an appropriate message.

A *computation* is an infinite fair sequence of system states such that for each state s_i, the next state s_{i+1} is obtained by executing an action that is enabled in s_i. This disallows the overlap of action execution. That is, action execution is *atomic*. We assume *weakly fair action execution* and *fair message receipt*. Weakly fair action execution means that if an action is enabled in all but finitely many states of the computation when the corresponding process is awake, and the process is awake for infinitely many states, then this action is executed infinitely often. Note that unless a process is gone or permanently asleep at some point (i.e., it never wakes up again), its timeout action is executed infinitely often. Fair message receipt means that if the computation contains a state where there is a message in a channel of a process that is not gone and that enables an action in that process, then that action is eventually executed with the parameters of that message, i.e., the message is eventually processed. Besides these fairness assumptions, we place no bounds on message propagation delay or relative process execution speeds, i.e., we allow fully asynchronous computations and non-FIFO message delivery.

We consider protocols that do not manipulate the internals of process references. Specifically, a protocol is *copy-store-send* if the only operations that it executes on process references is copying them, storing them in local memory and sending them in a message. That is, operations on references such as addition, radix computation, hashing, etc. are not used. In a copy-store-send protocol, if a process does not store a reference in its local memory, the process may learn this reference only by receiving it in a message. A copy-store-send protocol cannot introduce new references to the system. It can only operate on the references that are already there.

The overlay network of a set of processes is determined by their knowledge of each other. We say that there is a (directed) *edge* from a to b, denoted by (a, b), if process a stores a reference of b in its local memory or has a message in $a.Ch$ carrying the reference of b. In the former case, the edge is called *explicit* (drawn solid in figures), and in the latter case, the edge is called *implicit* (drawn dashed). The edges form a directed *process (multi-)graph PG*. A *weakly connected component* of a directed graph G is a subgraph of G of maximum size so that for any two processes u and v in that subgraph there is a (not necessarily directed) path from u to v. Two processes that are not in the same weakly connected component are *disconnected*. We call a process p *hibernating* if p is asleep, $p.Ch$ is empty and all processes q that have a directed path to p in PG are also asleep and have an empty $q.Ch$. The following claim was shown in [15].

Claim. For any copy-store-send protocol and any system state of that protocol in which process p is hibernating, p is permanently asleep.

1.2   Problem Statement

A protocol is *self-stabilizing* if it satisfies the following two properties.

Convergence: starting from an arbitrary system state, the protocol is guaranteed to arrive at a legitimate state.

Closure: starting from a legitimate state the protocol remains in legitimate states thereafter.

A self-stabilizing protocol is thus able to recover from transient faults regardless of their nature. Moreover, a self-stabilizing protocol does not have to be initialized as it eventually starts to behave correctly regardless of its initial state. In *topological self-stabilization* we allow self-stabilizing protocols to perform changes to the overlay network, resp. PG. A legitimate state may then include a particular graph topology or a family of graph topologies.

In the following, a process is called *relevant* if it is neither gone nor hibernating. Otherwise we call it *irrelevant*. Since hibernating and gone processes will never execute any action, for the self-stabilization we only consider initial states in which all processes are relevant. We also restrict the initial state to contain only a finite number of messages that can trigger actions, since other messages are ignored by the processes. Finally, we do not allow the presence of references that do not belong to a process in the system. Their handling would require failure/presence detectors which is beyond the scope of this paper. From now on, an initial system state satisfies all of these constraints.

A system state is *legitimate* if (i) every staying process is awake, (ii) every leaving process is either hibernating or gone, and (iii) for each weakly connected component of the initial process graph, the staying processes in that component still form a weakly connected component. Now we are ready to formally state the following two problems.

Finite Departure Problem ($\mathcal{FDP}$): eventually reach a legitimate state for the case that the **sleep** command (and therefore the sleep state) is *not* available (but only **exit**).

Finite Sleep Problem ($\mathcal{FSP}$): eventually reach a legitimate state for the case that the **exit** command (and therefore the gone state) is *not* available (but only **sleep**).

A self-stabilizing solution for these problems must be able to solve these from any initial state and to satisfy the closure property afterwards. Notice that (i) and (ii) can trivially be maintained in a legitimate state, so for the closure property one just needs to ensure that (iii) is also maintained.

A process p can *safely* leave a system if the removal of p and its incident edges from PG does not disconnect any relevant processes. As shown in [15], there is no distributed algorithm within our model that can decide when it is safe for a process p to leave the system. Hence, we need oracles.

1.3   Oracles

An *oracle* $\mathcal{O}$ is a predicate that depends on the current system state and the process calling it. In the context of the $\mathcal{FDP}$, an oracle is supposed to advise a leaving process when it is safe to execute **exit**, thus we restrict our attention to protocols that *only* allow a leaving process to do so if the given oracle is **true** for it. Such a protocol is also said to *rely* on the oracle. Moreover, we restrict our attention to oracles that *only* depend on the current process graph of relevant processes and the calling process, i.e., oracles are of the form $\mathcal{O} \colon \mathcal{PG} \times P \to$ {**true**,**false**} where $\mathcal{PG}$ is the set of process graphs and P is the set of processes.

We define the following oracle that we will use throughout the paper. Oracle $\mathcal{SINGLE}$ evaluates to **true** for a process u if u has edges with at most one other relevant process.

1.4   Related Work

To the best of our knowledge, the results by Foreback et al. [15] were the first attempt to rigorously analyze self-stabilizing process departures for overlay networks. The phenomenon they unearthed about the impossibility to locally decide when it is safe to leave the network is similar to the results of Fisher et al. [14] on the *consensus problem*, which is not solvable in an asynchronous system even if only a single process may crash. However, solutions to the *stabilizing consensus problem*, in which it is not required that each process irrevocably commits to a final value but that eventually they arrive at a common, stable value without being aware of that, are known [3,11]. The impossibility can also be circumvented by the use of specialized oracles known as failure detectors [9].

Due to the popularity of peer-to-peer networks, the research literature on this subject is extensive [2,4,5,8,17,24,28]. While departure algorithms have been proposed in these papers, none of these protocols are self-stabilizing. Cases in which the rate of churn is limited have already been considered [1,18,23]. Kuhn et al. [23] present a solution that organizes nodes into cliques of $\Theta(\log n)$ size that they call super-nodes. Hayes et al. [18] handle limited churn with a topological repair strategy called Forgiving Graph. For the case that the nodes have a sufficient amount of time to react, Saia et al. [26] propose an algorithm that repairs the network after an arbitrary number of deletions. Limited churn has also been studied in the context of adversarial nodes [6,27]. While there is almost no work on self-stabilizing node departures, several self-stabilizing peer-to-peer protocols have already been proposed [10,12,19,20,22,25]. The studied topologies range from simple line and ring structures [16] to skip lists and skip graphs [20,25], expanders [13], Delaunay graphs [21], and a Chord variant [22]. Also a universal algorithm for topological self-stabilization is known [7]. However, none of these provide any means to exclude nodes that want to leave the network in a self-stabilizing manner.

1.5   Our Results

Our main result is a self-stabilizing local-control protocol presented in Section 3 that can solve the $\mathcal{FDP}$ when relying on the $\mathcal{SINGLE}$ oracle. The $\mathcal{SINGLE}$ oracle was chosen for its simplicity, since we expect it to be easily implementable via timeouts in practice. The only interfaces our protocol needs to an underlying communication layer is that it can send a message to a process identified by some reference (by executing $v \leftarrow label(parameters)$ for some variable v holding a reference) and that it can check (via $v = w$) whether two references v and w point to the same or different processes. This has the advantage that the underlying layer is given full flexibility concerning the management of referencing information and that it does not have to pass any of that information (apart from whether two references point to the same process) to the process layer, which might be useful for anonymous networks. Instead, the protocols in [15] require that there is a fixed order on the processes. Also, the protocols in [15] were designed with a fixed topology in mind while this is not the case for our new protocol, which allows it to be easily integrated into existing overlay maintenance protocols, as we will demonstrate in this paper in Section 4. In order to simplify the analysis and formally specify the class of overlay maintenance protocols that can be used in conjunction with our departure protocol, we introduce four basic primitives for manipulating edges in the process graph in Section 2 and prove some fundamental results about them which might be of independent interest. We point out that the solutions in Sections 3 and 4 require the additional constraint that initially there exists at least one staying process per connected component of the overlay network.

2   Preliminaries

An important property for any overlay management protocol is the fact that weak connectivity is never lost by its own actions. Therefore, it is highly desirable that every process only executes primitives that preserve weak connectivity. Here we introduce four primitives for manipulating edges in an overlay network that are safe in a sense that they preserve weak connectivity (as long as there is no fault). This implies that *any* distributed protocol whose actions can be decomposed into these four primitives is guaranteed to preserve weak connectivity. The four primitives are:

Introduction. If a process u has a reference to two processes v and w, u *introduces* w to v if it sends a message to v containing a reference to w while keeping the reference to w.

Delegation. If a process u has a reference to two processes v and w, then u *delegates* w's reference to v if it sends a message to v containing a reference to w and deletes the reference to w.

Fusion. If a process u has two references v and w with $v = w$, then it *fuses* them if it only keeps one of these references.

Reversal. If a process u has a reference to some other process v, then it *reverses* the connection if it sends a reference of itself to v and deletes the reference to v.

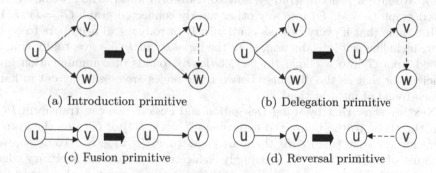

(a) Introduction primitive   (b) Delegation primitive

(c) Fusion primitive   (d) Reversal primitive

Fig. 2. The four primitives in pictures

Note that we assume that u, v, w are pairwise distinct. The only exception is *self-introduction*, a special case of introduction, where u sends a reference of itself to v, but does not delete its reference to v. The four primitives have the advantage that they can be executed locally by every process in a wait-free fashion (as none of the primitives requires any feedback). Also, they just need the ability to check whether two references point to the same process (see Fusion) to be implementable. Other than that, access to the contents of the references is not needed, which is useful. Moreover, it holds:

Lemma 1. *Introduction, Delegation, Fusion, and Reversal preserve weak connectivity.*

Proof. The statement obviously holds for Introduction since only additional edges are introduced. In Delegation an edge (u, w) is deleted, but there still exists a path from u to w via v, so u and w are still in the same weakly connected component. Fusion deletes an edge only if it is superfluous for weak connectivity. The Reversal rule deletes an edge (u, v) but replaces it with an edge (v, u), thereby also preserving weak connectivity.   □

Let $\mathcal{P}$ denote the set of all distributed protocols where all interactions between processes can be decomposed into the four primitives. Not surprisingly, all of the self-stabilizing topology maintenance protocols proposed so far (e.g., [10,12,19,20,22,25]) satisfy this property (as otherwise they would risk disconnection). Lemma 1 implies that any protocol in $\mathcal{P}$ preserves weak connectivity, which was previously shown individually for each cited protocol. Note that the first three primitives even preserve strong connectivity in a sense that for any pair of nodes u, v with a directed path in PG there will always be a directed path from u to v in PG when only allowing these three primitives. We say that a set of primitives is *universal* if the primitives allow one to get from any weakly connected graph $G = (V, E)$ to any other weakly connected graph $G' = (V, E')$ for PG. The set is *weakly universal* if G' is strongly connected.

Theorem 1. *Introduction, Delegation, Fusion, and Reversal are universal.*

Proof. We give a general strategy how to transform an arbitrary weakly connected graph $G = (V, E)$ into any other weakly connected graph $G' = (V, E')$. At first, note that if every process continuously introduces all neighbors to each other, including self-introduction, then the topology of PG is eventually transformed from G into a clique (in fact, $O(\log n)$ rounds of communication are sufficient for that as the distances between the nodes are essentially cut in half in each round of introduction).

Next we show that by using Delegation and Fusion, one can transform PG from the clique to the bidirected extension $G'' = (V, E'')$ of G', i.e., the graph where for any edge $(u, v) \in E'$ there are edges $(u, v), (v, u) \in E''$. To do so, we make use of the fact that G'' is strongly connected. Consider an arbitrary edge (u, w) in PG that is not in E''. Since G'' is strongly connected, there exists a shortest path from u to w in G'' and therefore also in PG (as we first want to keep all edges in G''). Let v_1 be the first neighbor of u along that shortest path. Then u delegates the reference of w to v_1. Now the process v_1 (and all other processes on the shortest path) proceed similar to u by forwarding the reference to w along the shortest path up to the last process v_k, who is a neighbor of w. Process v_k uses Fusion to merge the edge with $(v_k, w) \in E''$. By applying this procedure to all edges not in E'', all that remains is G''.

At last we can use Reversal and Fusion to get from G'' to G'. To do so, every edge (u, v) that is in E'', but not in E' is reversed by u. Then the newly created edge (v, u) is fused with the already existing edge $(v, u) \in E'$.   □

Note that Theorem 1 only shows that *in principle* it is possible to get from any weakly connected graph to any other weakly connected graph. From the proof we can conclude the following corollary.

Corollary 1. *Introduction, Delegation and Fusion are weakly universal.*

Furthermore, Introduction, Delegation, Fusion and Reversal are not only sufficient for universality but also necessary, i.e., by removing one primitive, universality is lost.

Theorem 2. *Introduction, Delegation, Fusion and Reversal are necessary for universality.*

Proof. To prove the lemma, we show that each primitive has a unique function that cannot be replaced by the other primitives. Introduction is the only primitive that can create new edges, so without it, any Graph G' with $|E'| > |E|$ cannot be reached from G. Fusion is the only primitive that reduces the overall number of edges. Delegation is necessary, since by using only Introduction, Fusion and Reversal, a protocol can never locally disconnect two specific processes. Finally, consider an example graph G consisting of two processes u and v and an edge (u, v). Reversal is necessary to reach the goal topology G' that consists solely of the edge (v, u).   □

3   Process Departures

In this section we present a self-stabilizing protocol for the $\mathcal{FDP}$ that only needs to compare references for equality as needed for the four primitives.

Our protocol consists of various actions. In the $present(v)$ action, a reference v is introduced to some process (i.e., the sending of a $present(v)$ message to u, corresponds to Introduction primitive). Moreover, in the $forward(v)$ action, the reference v is delegated to the executing process.

We assume that whenever a process a sends a request to call $present$ or $forward$ containing a reference of a process b to another process c, it automatically sends some relevant information it knows about b along with it. In this section the only relevant information is the *mode* of b, which we denote as $a.mode(b)$ (i.e., a's knowledge of b's mode), which can be **staying** or **leaving**. Note that since we aim at a self-stabilizing protocol, $a.mode(b)$ might be incorrect (i.e., $a.mode(b) \neq mode(b)$) since b might have a different mode than a thinks it has. In this case we say that process a contains invalid (mode) information about process b. A system is in an *invalid* state if there exists at least one relevant process u with invalid information stored in u itself or in some incoming message in $u.Ch$. In both cases we say that u *has invalid information*. If no node has invalid information, the system state is said to be *valid*.

We denote the set of all references a process u stores in its local memory as the neighborhood set $u.N$ of u. Note that $u.N$ is not a variable of u but just a notation we use, which simplifies our protocol description and the proofs. Along with each $v \in u.N$, process u also stores its knowledge of the mode of v, denoted by $u.mode(v)$. Our solution makes use of a special variable called *anchor* whose reference is the only one *not* being in $u.N$ (i.e., it will be treated differently than all other references of v throughout our protocol). The *anchor* will only be used by the leaving nodes, so in a legitimate state, the *anchor* of a staying process is empty, denoted by $\bot$. The anchor of a leaving process v is a reference to some process which, according to the local information of v is a staying process. Therefore, each time v gets a message from a third process w, v forwards w to its anchor by a $forward$ message in the hope of eliminating all references to itself. Each process has a periodically executed *timeout* action. In case a process u is leaving, it sends a $present(u)$ message to its anchor in the *timeout* action (in order to verify it has a staying anchor). If it is staying, it sends a $present(u)$ message to all neighbors (to make other processes aware of it). This is an implementation of our earlier presented *self-introduction* primitive. Periodically executed self-introduction can ensure that invalid information vanishes from the system, as we will show later. Additionally, leaving processes consult $\mathcal{SINGLE}$ in *timeout*, and if it evaluates to true, the process is safe to perform **exit**. The actions of our protocol are presented in Algorithms 1- 3.

Algorithm 1. $u.timeout$

1: **if** $u.anchor \neq \bot$ and $u.mode(anchor) = leaving$ **then**
2: $\quad\quad u \leftarrow present(u.anchor)$ $\hfill \triangleright \diamondsuit$
3: $\quad\quad u.anchor := \bot$
4: **if** $mode(u) = leaving$ **then**
5: $\quad\quad$ **if** $u.N = \emptyset$ **then**
6: $\quad\quad\quad$ **if** $\mathcal{SINGLE}(u)$ **then**
7: $\quad\quad\quad\quad$ **exit**
8: $\quad\quad\quad$ **else**
9: $\quad\quad\quad\quad$ **if** $u.anchor \neq \bot$ **then**
10: $\quad\quad\quad\quad\quad u.anchor \leftarrow present(u)$ $\hfill \triangleright \diamondsuit$
11: $\quad\quad$ **else**
12: $\quad\quad\quad$ **for all** $v \in u.N$ **do**
13: $\quad\quad\quad\quad u \leftarrow forward(v)$ $\hfill \triangleright \diamondsuit$
14: $\quad\quad\quad u.N := \emptyset$
15: **else**
16: $\quad\quad$ **if** $u.anchor \neq \bot$ **then**
17: $\quad\quad\quad u \leftarrow present(u.anchor)$ $\hfill \triangleright \diamondsuit$
18: $\quad\quad\quad u.anchor := \bot$
19: $\quad\quad$ **for all** $v \in u.N$ **do**
20: $\quad\quad\quad$ **if** $u.mode(v) = leaving$ **then**
21: $\quad\quad\quad\quad u.N := u.N \setminus \{v\}$
22: $\quad\quad\quad v \leftarrow present(u)$ $\hfill \triangleright \diamondsuit$ or $\clubsuit$

Algorithm 2. u.present(v)

1: **if** $v = u.anchor$ and $u.mode(v) = leaving$ **then**
2:     $u.anchor := \bot$ ▷ ♠
3: **if** $u.mode(v) = leaving$ **then**
4:     **if** $mode(u) = leaving$ **then**
5:         $v \leftarrow forward(u)$ ▷ ♣
6:     **else**
7:         **if** $v \in u.N$ **then**
8:             $u.N := u.N \setminus \{v\}$
9:         $v \leftarrow forward(u)$ ▷ ♣
10: **else**
11:     **if** $mode(u) = leaving$ **then**
12:         **if** $u.anchor \neq \bot$ **then**
13:             $v \leftarrow forward(u)$ ▷ ♣
14:         **else**
15:             $u.anchor := v$
16:     **else**
17:         $u.N := u.N \cup \{v\}$ ▷ ♠

Algorithm 3. u.forward(v)

1: **if** $v = u.anchor$ and $u.mode(v) = leaving$ **then**
2:     $anchor := \bot$ ▷ ♠
3: **if** $u.mode(v) = leaving$ **then**
4:     **if** $mode(u) = leaving$ **then**
5:         **if** $u.anchor = \bot$ **then**
6:             $v \leftarrow forward(u)$ ▷ ♣
7:         **else**
8:             $u.anchor \leftarrow forward(v)$ ▷ ♡
9:     **else**
10:         **if** $v \in u.N$ **then**
11:             $u.N := u.N \setminus \{v\}$
12:         $v \leftarrow forward(u)$ ▷ ♣
13: **else**
14:     **if** $mode(u) = leaving$ **then**
15:         **if** $u.anchor \neq \bot$ **then**
16:             $u.anchor \leftarrow forward(v)$ ▷ ♡
17:         **else**
18:             $u.anchor := v$
19:     **else**
20:         $u.N := u.N \cup \{v\}$ ▷ ♠

3.1   Correctness Proof

To show that our proposed protocol is a self-stabilizing solution to the $\mathcal{FDP}$, it remains to show two properties.

Safety: The protocol never disconnects any relevant processes.
Liveness: All leaving processes are eventually gone.

Lemma 2. *If a computation of our protocol starts in a state where the subgraph PG of relevant processes is weakly connected, it remains weakly connected in every state of the computation.*

To prove safety we make use of the results from Section 2.

Proof. First of all, note that each relevant process is also awake, since obviously gone processes cannot be relevant. The proof of the lemma relies on the fact that our protocol that the (awake) processes run is a composition of the four primitives presented in Section 2. To illustrate this, the protocol is annotated with the symbols $\Diamond, \heartsuit, \spadesuit, \clubsuit$. Each symbol represents a primitive: $\Diamond$ is (Self-)Introduction, $\heartsuit$ is Delegation, $\spadesuit$ is Fusion and $\clubsuit$ is Reversal. Therefore, we can use the result of Lemma 1 and the fact that $\mathcal{SINGLE}$ preserves weak connectivity in the only case in which we do not use a primitive, (i.e., a process executes **exit**). This proves the lemma.   □

It remains to show that our protocol makes progress such that all leaving processes eventually leave the system. Due to space constraints, we only sketch the proof of Lemma 3.

Lemma 3. *Leaving processes eventually execute the **exit** command, thereby preserving liveness.*

Sketch of Proof: Let Φ_t be a potential function that denotes the amount of invalid information present in the system at some time t, i.e., Φ_t is equal to the number of edges (x, y), either explicit or implicit, such that $mode(y) \neq x.mode(y)$.

The only way Φ_t could increase is if invalid information is copied. In order to do so, a process u has to forward invalid information about process v to another process w, since the information sent about oneself is always valid. The only spots in the pseudocode where this can potentially happen are lines 8 and 16 of the $forward$ action, where u sends $forward(v)$ to $u.anchor$. However, in that case v is not saved by u. So, even if u sends invalid information about v to $u.anchor$, the invalid information is not duplicated in the system. Therefore, $\Phi_t \geq \Phi_{t'}$ for any $t' > t$. To show that the system state is eventually valid, it suffices to show that as long as $\Phi_t > 0$ it holds that for any t there is a $t' > t$ such that $\Phi_{t'} < \Phi_t$.

Let (u, v) be an edge that contains invalid information at time t. We have to show that for every combination of the values of $mode(u)$ and $mode(v)$ the potential drops. Due to page limitations we skip this part of the proof.

The statement of Lemma 3 follows, since we can show that eventually a leaving process which has an edge to or from some staying process u executes

exit. By using this argument inductively we have that eventually all leaving processes execute **exit**.   □

From Lemma 2 and 3 we can conclude the following Theorem.

Theorem 3. *The protocol depicted in Algorithms 1- 3 together with the oracle $\mathcal{SINGLE}$ is a self-stabilizing solution to the $\mathcal{FDP}$.*

4   Embedding in Existing Overlay Protocols

In this section we show how the protocol that was developed in Section 3 can be combined with a large class of distributed overlay protocols. Note that the original protocol does not necessarily have to be self-stabilizing. However, it must satisfy our safety requirement, i.e., no action should disconnect processes. The framework given below solves the $\mathcal{FDP}$ (Section 4.1).

4.1   FDP for Arbitrary Protocols

Consider any protocol $P \in \mathcal{P}$ (i.e., P is based on the four primitives and hence satisfies the safety condition). In order to combine our protocol with P, P has to fulfill two algorithmic requirements. First, P conducts periodic *self-introduction*, i.e., it has a periodically executed (*timeout*) action, in which the executing process introduces itself to all processes in its neighborhood (among other activities). The timeout action of P is called *P-timeout*. Second, P has a *postprocess* action, which is able to handle messages that cannot be delivered, i.e., if a message $v \leftarrow label(parameters)$ cannot be delivered, *postprocess* is able to act accordingly in order to reintegrate the information into the process. We need *postprocess* to handle messages that cannot be delivered because references of leaving processes are in *parameters*. Therefore, we require that *postprocess* uses the *forward* messages of our original protocol to get rid of these references. The exact inner workings of *postprocess* are closely tied to P itself, therefore we do not specify how *postprocess* deals with references of staying processes and other variables that are in *parameters*. Apart from being useful for us to solve the $\mathcal{FDP}$, such a *postprocess* action is also helpful in cases of messages that need to be reintegrated into the process, for example because their delivery failed before. Many known self-stabilizing overlay protocols proposed so far can easily be adapted to satisfy these requirements.

Let P' be the protocol framework that combines P and the already presented protocol to solve the $\mathcal{FDP}$. The idea of P' is to introduce an action *preprocess* that is used every time a process u sends a message $v \leftarrow label(parameters)$ in P. Instead of sending this message directly, u calls its *preprocess(label, parameters)* action. This action saves the message in a message list and verifies the mode of v and each process x in *parameters* by sending a *verify(u)* message to that process. These *verify* messages are resent in timeout, if an answer has not been received yet. Once all processes have answered by a *process(v)* message, u either sends the message $v \leftarrow label(parameters)$ if all processes in *parameters* are staying, otherwise it calls the local *postprocess(parameters)* action. The *postprocess* action makes sure that all *leaving* processes in *parameters* are excluded and that staying processes are reintegrated into P. Note that *preprocess* and *postprocess* can only be called locally. To enhance readability we write $(x_1, \ldots, x_k)$ instead of *parameters* in all algorithms, thereby focusing on the process references of messages in P and leaving out the part of *parameters* which does not contain process references, but just additional information. However, this additional information in *parameters* is not lost by *preprocess* and *postprocess*, but we do not interfere with it.

Another addition is that every process u executing P' is required to maintain an additional variable $u.anchor$, which (in a valid configuration) has the value $\perp$ if u is staying. Moreover, each process maintains a list variable $u.mlist$ which stores all the messages u wants to send. These are sent out once the valid information from the x_i processes arrive by *process* messages. In addition to our earlier protocol the mode information of a reference saved in *mlist* can have the additional value *unknown* to indicate that a *process* message has not been received yet, i.e., the *mode* is not verified. Of course, the mode information the node v stores about itself $(mode(v))$ still can only have either the value *leaving* or *staying*. It remains to specify how leaving nodes react if a *label(parameters)* message of P is received. A leaving node will not execute the corresponding action of P but sends *present* messages to all processes in *parameters* in order to remove possible references to it.

Due to space constraints the framework for constructing the modified protocol P' cannot be presented in this paper. Note that even though we do not present them in a specific algorithm, all actions of P have to adhere to the changes presented in the last paragraph (not only *timeout*). Furthermore, the *present* and *forward* actions from the last section are changed in case a staying process gets a reference from another staying process.

Correctness Proof. We need to show that all leaving processes are eventually gone and, in case P is self-stabilizing, that protocol P' eventually works like P (e.g., reaches the same target topology). The proof of Theorem 4 proceeds analogously to the proofs of Section 3.

Theorem 4. *Let $P \in \mathcal{P}$ be a distributed overlay protocol which solves some distributed problem $\mathcal{DP}$ with the already mentioned requirements. Then there is another protocol P' constructed as described above, such that P' eventually solves $\mathcal{FDP}$. In addition, if P is self-stabilizing, then P' also solves $\mathcal{DP}$.*

Analogous to the results in [15], we can overcome the use of oracles by relaxing the $\mathcal{FDP}$ to the $\mathcal{FSP}$. In this problem a process u can either be asleep or awake. If u is asleep, it does not preform any actions besides waiting for incoming messages. If it is awake, it conducts the desired protocol as usual. Once an asleep process receives a message, it automatically becomes awake again and executes the corresponding actions.

5   Conclusion

We presented a self-stabilizing protocol for the $\mathcal{FDP}$ and the $\mathcal{FSP}$ that can be combined with a large class of overlay maintenance protocols. Additionally, we identified four basic primitives for manipulating edges in an overlay network that preserve weak connectivity and are universal.

In the future we want to investigate stronger safety conditions for overlay networks than just connectivity.

References

1. Albrecht, K., Kuhn, F., Wattenhofer, R.: Dependable Peer-to-Peer Systems Withstanding Dynamic Adversarial Churn. In: Kohlas, J., Meyer, B., Schiper, A. (eds.) Dependable Systems: Software, Computing, Networks. LNCS, vol. 4028, pp. 275–294. Springer, Heidelberg (2006)
2. Andersen, D., Balakrishnan, H., Kaashoek, F., Morris, R.: Resilient overlay networks. In: SOSP, pp. 131–145 (2001)
3. Angluin, D., Fischer, M.J., Jiang, H.: Stabilizing Consensus in Mobile Networks. In: Gibbons, P.B., Abdelzaher, T., Aspnes, J., Rao, R. (eds.) DCOSS 2006. LNCS, vol. 4026, pp. 37–50. Springer, Heidelberg (2006)
4. Aspnes, J., Shah, G.: Skip graphs. ACM Transactions on Algorithms 3(4), 37 (2007)
5. Awerbuch, B., Scheideler, C.: The hyperring: a low-congestion deterministic data structure for distributed environments. In: SODA, pp. 318–327 (2004)
6. Awerbuch, B., Scheideler, C.: Towards a scalable and robust dht. Theory Comput. Syst. 45(2), 234–260 (2009)
7. Berns, A., Ghosh, S., Pemmaraju, S.V.: Building self-stabilizing overlay networks with the transitive closure framework. Theor. Comput. Sci. 512, 2–14 (2013)
8. Bhargava, A., Kothapalli, K., Riley, C., Scheideler, C., Thober, M.: Pagoda: a dynamic overlay network for routing, data management, and multicasting. In: SPAA, pp. 170–179 (2004)
9. Chandra, T.D., Toueg, S.: Unreliable failure detectors for reliable distributed systems. J. ACM 43(2), 225–267 (1996)
10. Clouser, T., Nesterenko, M., Scheideler, C.: Tiara: A self-stabilizing deterministic skip list and skip graph. Theor. Comput. Sci. 428, 18–35 (2012)
11. Doerr, B., Goldberg, LA., Minder, L., Sauerwald, T., Scheideler, C.: Stabilizing consensus with the power of two choices. In: SPAA, pp. 149–158 (2011)
12. Dolev, D., Hoch, E.N., van Renesse, R.: Self-stabilizing and Byzantine-Tolerant Overlay Network. In: Tovar, E., Tsigas, P., Fouchal, H. (eds.) OPODIS 2007. LNCS, vol. 4878, pp. 343–357. Springer, Heidelberg (2007)
13. Dolev, S., Tzachar, N.: Spanders: Distributed spanning expanders. Sci. Comput. Program. 78(5), 544–555 (2013)
14. Fischer, M.J., Lynch, N.A., Paterson, M.S.: Impossibility of distributed consensus with one faulty process. J. ACM 32(2), 374–382 (1985)
15. Foreback, D., Koutsopoulos, A., Nesterenko, M., Scheideler, C., Strothmann, T.: On Stabilizing Departures in Overlay Networks. In: Felber, P., Garg, V. (eds.) SSS 2014. LNCS, vol. 8756, pp. 48–62. Springer, Heidelberg (2014)

16. Gall, D., Jacob, R., Richa, A., Scheideler, C., Schmid, S., Täubig, H.: Time Complexity of Distributed Topological Self-stabilization: The Case of Graph Linearization. In: López-Ortiz, A. (ed.) LATIN 2010. LNCS, vol. 6034, pp. 294–305. Springer, Heidelberg (2010)
17. Harvey, N.J.A., Jones, M.B., Saroiu, S., Theimer, M., Wolman, A.: Skipnet: A scalable overlay network with practical locality properties. In: USENIX Symposium on Internet Technologies and Systems ((2003)
18. Hayes, T.P., Saia, J., Trehan, A.: The forgiving graph: a distributed data structure for low stretch under adversarial attack. Distributed Computing 25(4), 261–278 (2012)
19. Herault, T., Lemarinier, P., Peres, O., Pilard, L., Beauquier, J.: Brief Announcement: Self-stabilizing Spanning Tree Algorithm for Large Scale Systems. In: Datta, A.K., Gradinariu, M. (eds.) SSS 2006. LNCS, vol. 4280, pp. 574–575. Springer, Heidelberg (2006)
20. Jacob, R., Richa, A.W., Scheideler, C., Schmid, S., Täubig, H.: A distributed polylogarithmic time algorithm for self-stabilizing skip graphs. In: PODC, pp. 131–140 (2009)
21. Jacob, R., Ritscher, S., Scheideler, C., Schmid, S.: Towards higher-dimensional topological self-stabilization: A distributed algorithm for delaunay graphs. Theor. Comput. Sci. 457, 137–148 (2012)
22. Kniesburges, S., Koutsopoulos, A., Scheideler, C.: Re-chord: a self-stabilizing chord overlay network. In: SPAA, pp. 235–244 (2011)
23. Kuhn, F., Schmid, S., Wattenhofer, R.: Towards worst-case churn resistant peer-to-peer systems. Distributed Computing 22(4), 249–267 (2010)
24. Malkhi, D., Naor, M., Ratajczak, D.: Viceroy: a scalable and dynamic emulation of the butterfly. In: PODC, pp. 183–192 (2002)
25. Nor, R.M., Nesterenko, M., Scheideler, C.: Corona: A Stabilizing Deterministic Message-Passing Skip List. In: Défago, X., Petit, F., Villain, V. (eds.) SSS 2011. LNCS, vol. 6976, pp. 356–370. Springer, Heidelberg (2011)
26. Saia, J., Trehan, A.: Picking up the pieces: Self-healing in reconfigurable networks. In: IPDPS, pp. 1–12 (2008)
27. Scheideler, C.: How to spread adversarial nodes?: rotate! In: STOC, pp. 704–713 (2005)
28. Stoica, I., Morris, R., Liben-Nowell, D., Karger, D.R., Frans Kaashoek, M., Dabek, F., Balakrishnan, H.: Chord: a scalable peer-to-peer lookup protocol for Internet applications. IEEE/ACM Trans. Netw. 11(1), 17–32 (2003)

Refinement of Probabilistic Stabilizing Programs Using Genetic Algorithms

Ling Zhu$^{(\boxtimes)}$, Jingshu Chen, and Sandeep Kulkarni

Department of Computer Science and Engineering,
Michigan State University, East Lansing, MI 48824, USA
{zhuling,chenji15,sandeep}@cse.msu.edu

Abstract. In this paper, we evaluate the role of genetic algorithms (GAs) for identifying optimal probabilities in probabilistic self-stabilizing algorithms. Although it is known that the use of probabilistic actions is beneficial for reducing the state space requirements and solving problems that are unsolvable in the deterministic manner, identifying the ideal probabilities is often difficult. This is especially the case where several independent probability values need to be selected. We analyze two token ring protocols proposed by Herman –an asymmetric program where one process is distinguished and a symmetric program where all processes are identical (anonymous). We find that for the asymmetric program, unequal probabilities are preferred for smaller rings. Moreover, the size of the ring for which equal probability is desirable increases with the increase in the states available to individual processes. By contrast, unequal probabilities are preferred for the symmetric token ring when the number of processes increases. We also consider the case where the symmetric protocol is modified to allow each process to choose the probabilities independently. We find that making a few processes almost deterministic reduces the expected convergence time. Finally, we note that the analysis in the paper can also be used to identify the increased cost of randomization when compared to a corresponding deterministic solution.

1 Introduction

A stabilizing program [5] ensures that starting from an arbitrary state, the program recovers to its legitimate states. Moreover, after reaching a legitimate state, in the absence of faults, it remains in legitimate states forever. Thus, a stabilizing program ensures that it can recover to its legitimate states from any transient fault. Examples of stabilizing systems include [5,11,12,14,16]. Programs used in [5,14,16] ensure that any computation of the program will inevitably reach the legitimate states, and programs used in [11,12] guarantee that legitimate states will be reached with probability 1.0. In other words, programs in [5,14,16] ensure that any computation starting outside legitimate states cannot stay outside legitimate states forever. By contrast, programs in [11,12] can have computations that stay outside legitimate states forever. However, by assigning probabilities to individual program actions, we can make this probability negligible.

Although programs in [11,12] guarantee convergence to legitimate states with probability 1.0, identifying optimal probability valuesto minimize the expected

© Springer International Publishing Switzerland 2015
A. Pelc and A.A. Schwarzmann (Eds.): SSS 2015, LNCS 9212, pp. 217–232, 2015.
DOI: 10.1007/978-3-319-21741-3_15

convergence is often difficult. If the program involves several independent probabilities, then even a brute force analysis could be impossible.

With this motivation, in this paper, we focus on the problem of identifying ideal probability values that will reduce the expected convergence time using genetic algorithms (GAs). GA is a computation method based on the principles of natural evolution to solve optimization problems. In GA, we begin with a population of programs and identify their objective function that characterizes the level to how they satisfy the program specification and/or minimize the desired objective. Subsequently, the programs of the next generation are generated by selecting elite programs of current population and applying mutation and crossover to evolve new programs. Although the solutions (programs) identified by GA are not always the provably optimal solutions, GA has the potential to find optimal solutions. Moreover, if the same optimal solution survives several generations, it is typically considered as a final optimal solution. GA can substantially reduce the search space and can be effective in the case where the independent probabilities make the brute force search impossible.

In our work, we utilize GA with both single objective and multiple objectives. In cases of multiple objectives, GA finds multiple non-dominating programs (called Pareto-optimal solutions). We utilize the multiple objectives to effectively find best probability values for each size of the underlying network.

We analyze the programs in [11,12] by GA. Of these, the program in [12] is an asymmetric token ring program that has one distinguished process that runs a different set of actions than all other processes. The program in [11] is a symmetric token ring program where all processes are indistinguishable from each other. The main observations of our analysis are as follows:

- For the asymmetric token ring program, when the number of processes is small, the expected convergence time is least with a biased coin. However, as the number of processes increases, an unbiased coin is required to reduce expected convergence time.
- We also consider an extension of the asymmetric token ring program in [12] where we increase the domain of each variable. We find that the number of processes for which unbiased coin is preferred keeps increasing with the domain size of each variable. Specifically, if the domain of variables used by processes is 3 then an unbiased coin is desirable when the number of processes is 6 or larger. By contrast, for a domain size of 4, an unbiased coin is desirable when the number of processes is 11 or larger. Finally, for a domain of size 5, the number of processes for which an unbiased coin is preferred is large; exact number could not be identified due to the state space explosion problem.
- For the symmetric token ring program, we were able to validate a previously known result that when the number of processes is less than or equal to 7, an unbiased coin reduces the expected value of the convergence time. As the number of processes increase, it is desirable that the coin bias is increased. For example, for 15 processes, a coin that produces 0 with 31% probability is ideal.

- We also consider a simple extension of the symmetric token ring program in [11] where each process chooses its probability values independently. Although this violates the pure symmetry (anonymity) of processes, we find that this can reduce the expected convergence time even more. For example, for 5 processes, the expected value of convergence time reduces by more than 5%, and for 3 processes, reduces by 10% when compared with the fully symmetric program. Additionally, in this approach with 5 processes, the best solution identified by GA made 2 of the processes to be lowest probability value and 3 of the processes to be the highest value.

2   Preliminaries

In this section, we recall the definitions of programs, computations and stabilization. These definitions are based on the work in [3,5,6].

A program p is specified in terms of a set of processes. Each process is associated with a set of variables and a set of actions. Each variable is associated with a finite domain. An action is of the form:

$$Action\_name :: \langle guard \rangle \longrightarrow pr_1 \quad \langle statement_1 \rangle,$$
$$pr_2 \quad \langle statement_2 \rangle,$$
$$\dots;$$

where $Action\_name$ is the name given to the action, $pr_1, pr_2 \cdots$ are real numbers in $[0..1]$, guard is a Boolean expression involving program variables (i.e., the union of the process variables) and statement(s) updates one or more variables of the process. Furthermore, the sum of probability values associated with a given action is 1.0. We assume that if a process has multiple actions then the guards corresponding to those actions are disjoint.

A state of the program is obtained by assigning each program variable a value from its domain. The state space of the program is the set of all possible states of the program. A state predicate of program is a subset of its state space.

A transition of a program from state s_0 is obtained as follows. Each process identifies the guard of an action (if any) that is true in state s_0. If such an action exists then it executes one of the corresponding statements based on the given probability values. If no such action exists then the state of that process remains unchanged. The new state of the program is obtained by simultaneous execution of all processes in the program. Finally, this process is continued ad infinitum to obtain a computation of that program. Observe that this execution is in synchronous semantics.

Finally, we say that a program p stabilizes to state predicate S iff (1) if p starts from an arbitrary state it reaches a state in S with probability 1, and (2) if p starts from a state in S then it remains in S forever. Observe that the above definition allows the possibility that the program can stay outside S forever. However, the probability of such a computation can be made as small as possible.

3 An Asymmetric Probabilistic Self-stabilizing Program

In this section, we recall the asymmetric probabilistic self-stabilizing program for a unidirectional ring of processes by Herman [12]. This algorithm is a variant of Dijkstra's K-state token ring program.

This program, say $\mathcal{P}_{\mathcal{A}}$, consists of n processes numbered $0..(n-1)$ that are organized in a ring. The program is asymmetric in the sense that there is a special process (named 0) that runs a different set of actions than all other processes. All other processes run the same program. Each process j maintains the variable $x.j$ whose domain is $\{0, 1, 2\}$. The actions of this program are as follows:

$$
\begin{aligned}
A_0 \quad &:: \quad x.0 == x.(n-1) \quad \longrightarrow \quad \lambda : x.0 := (x.0 + 1) \bmod 3 \\
&\qquad\qquad + \quad 1 - \lambda : \ x.0 := (x.0 + 2) \bmod 3; \\
A_j \ j \neq 0 &:: \quad x.j \neq x.(j-1) \quad \longrightarrow \quad x.j = x.(j-1);
\end{aligned}
$$

In the above actions, A_0 is specifically designed for process 0. When the guard condition $x.0 == x.(n-1)$ is satisfied, process 0 is *privileged*, (respectively, holds a token). Then, with probability λ, process 0 increments its value by 1 in modulo 3 arithmetic. Alternatively, with probability $1 - \lambda$, it increases the value by 2 in modulo 3 arithmetic. The second action is designed for other processes j, $0 < j < n$. When the guard condition $x.j \neq x.(j-1)$ is satisfied, j is *privileged*. Subsequently, process j copies the value of its predecessor.

Observe that if all x values are initialized to 0 then only process 0 has the token. In this state, process 0 can either change its value to 1 or 2. Without loss of generality, consider the case where process 0 changes its value to 1. In this state, only process 1 has the token. Execution of process 1 changes $x.1$ to 1. In this state, process 2 has the token. This execution continues until all x values change to 1. In this state, process 0 can execute again and change $x.0$. The states reached in the execution of this program are the legitimate states of the program. Additionally, as shown in [12], if the program starts in an arbitrary state, with probability 1, it is guaranteed to reach a legitimate state. In other words, although this program can have computations that stay outside legitimate states forever, the probability of such computations can be made smaller than any ϵ, $\epsilon > 0$. Furthermore, after it reaches a legitimate state, its subsequent execution only includes legitimate states.

The above program is a variation of the K-state program by Dijkstra [5] in synchronous semantics. Specifically, in [5], the value of λ is always 1, i.e., process 0 always increments its value by 1. Although this program is often studied in interleaving semantics, it is known to be stabilizing in synchronous semantics as well. And, in this program, any computation is guaranteed to reach a legitimate state and stay there forever. However, to ensure stabilization, it requires that the domain of x be equal to $[0..K-1]$, where $K \geq n$. By contrast, the program in [12], provides probabilistic stabilization even if the domain of x is only $\{0, 1, 2\}$.

The above program can also be easily extended to the case where domain of x is slightly increased. For example, if the domain of x is $\{0, 1, 2, 3\}$ then we need to change the above program so that process 0 increments $x.0$ by 1 with probability λ_1, by 2 with probability λ_2 and by 3 with probability $1 - \lambda_1 - \lambda_2$. We consider these variations in our analysis of this program.

4   A Symmetric Probabilistic Self-stabilizing Program

In this section, we recall the symmetric token ring program in [11]. Similar to the program in Section 3, this program also arranges the processes $0..(n - 1)$ in a ring, where n is odd. However, unlike the asymmetric program in Section, 3, in the symmetric program, all processes execute an identical code and cannot use their ID. In other words, the process IDs are only for understanding the program and not used by processes themselves. The action of the program is as follows:

$$
\begin{aligned}
A_j:\quad & x.j == x.pre \quad \longrightarrow \quad \lambda \quad :: x.j := 0 \\
& \qquad\qquad\qquad\qquad\quad + 1 - \lambda :: x.j := 1; \\
A_j:\quad & x.j \neq x.pre \quad \longrightarrow \quad 1 \quad :: x.j := x.pre
\end{aligned}
$$

where pre denotes the process that comes before process j in the ring. Observe that in the above program, process j is privileged (respectively, process j has the token) iff its value equals that of its predecessor. In this case, it randomly chooses to update its value. In particular, with probability λ, it sets the value to 0. And, with probability $1 - \lambda$, it sets it to 1.

In this program, process j is said to have the token iff $x.j$ is the same as its predecessor. Since the number of processes are odd, it follows that the x values of at least two neighboring processes are equal. In other words, there is at least one process that has the token. Now, consider the case where we have five processes and the x values of processes are $\langle 0, 1, 0, 1, 0 \rangle$. In this state, process 0 has the token since $x.0$ is the same as its predecessor. Process 1 will have the token after the execution of one program step. Furthermore, this program guarantees that with probability 1, the program converges to its legitimate states where exactly one process has the token and this token circulates along the ring.

5   Methodology

5.1   Overall Framework

The overall framework (Figure 1) is as follows: For a given probabilistic program, we determine probabilities need to optimize, then encode these probabilities into genome. GA initializes the population with random created genomes (programs), evaluates programs using a probabilistic model checker - PRISM, and optimizes the program by iterative reproduction (selection, crossover and mutation).

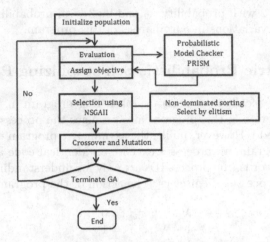

Fig. 1. Overall Framework

5.2   Genetic Algorithm

GA[15,23] is a guided search or optimization technique, inspired by the bio-
logic evolution. The solution (or program) is encoded into artificial chromo-
somes(genomes), and these genomes preserve the problem structure and information during the evolution. The implementation of GA is shown in Figure 1. It
begins with a population of randomly generated genomes(programs), then GA
evaluates generated programs using PRISM and assigns objective values to each
program. After that population for next generation (called offspring) is created
by selecting and recombining the population of current generation (called parent genomes). Iteratively, GA evolves the population that the average objective
values get better until some stopping criterion is reached. The stopping criterion
is either if the number of generation reaches the maximum allowed generation
or the optimal solutions are found.

Genome. In this paper, we optimize a set of probabilities (λs) that maximize
the program performance, and use bit strings to represent these probabilities
with a range of [0.01, 0.99]. Each probability value is obtained by mapping an
7-bit string to an integer value from [1, 99], then divided by 100. The genome, a
representation of solutions to the problem, consists of one or multiple bit strings.

Multi-objective and NSGAII. In GA, objective functions are to evaluate
the quality of the genome, and it is called multi-objective GA if two or three
objectives used in GA. In this paper, one of the objective functions measures
the expected convergence time of the probabilistic programs using PRISM, and
GA is set to minimize this objective. The other objective is the total number
of processes in the ring. By using the multi-objective GA, we can get minimum

expected convergence time for all different sizes of ring from run of GA. Otherwise, if we use single objective, then we need run GA multiple times with each time running for a specific size of ring.

We apply nondominated sorting GA (NSGAII [4]) to implement multi-objective GA. NSGAII is one of the state-of-art methods for multi-objective GA. It preserve all the elites to emphasize the good solutions, at the same time, maintains diversity of the search. It uses nondominated sorting which compares two solutions by the concept of domination. Domination is defined as follows: A solution A dominates B if A is no worse than B in all objectives, and A is strictly better than B in at least one objective. NSGAII sorts the population rank by rank, and nondominated solutions in a generation are the solutions of first rank and considered as best ones in that generation. If nondominated solutions of first rank are removed from the population, then another set of non-dominated solutions are emerged and called solutions of second rank. Within the same rank, the solutions are compared based on the crowding distance, that is, less crowded solution is considered better. Using nondominated sorting and crowding distance, NSGAII quickly converges to the optimum front as well as maintain the diversity among the solutions in the front.

Genetic Operator. We apply single point crossover and bit-flip mutation. In single point crossover, two solutions are combined by taking a part of the gene from one solution and another part from the second solution. This crossover would create a new program that is obtained by combining different probabilities. The mutation operator is a random bit flip in the genome.

6   Experiments

6.1   Experiment Setup

In experiments, we use NSGAII with the population size of 40 (in Section 6.3) and 100 (in Section 6.2). For genetic operator, mutation has the probability ranging from of 0.05 to 0.1, and 0.95 for crossover operator. We set the maximum number of generations to 500. However GA is stopped when the best solution survives more than 50 generations. We also save the objective value of any solution firstly evaluated in our algorithm. In other words, if a solution is preserved in future generations, we do not need to compute its objective function again. Each experiment runs multiple times, and we take the common best programs found in all runs.

6.2   Results of Asymmetric Probabilistic Self-stabilizing Program

This section depicts experimental results for identifying the optimal probability values for the asymmetric probabilistic self-stabilizing token ring program described in Section 3. We consider three variations of this program. The first program, denoted by $Asymmetric_1$, is the same as that shown in Section 3.

The second program, denoted by $Asymmetric_2$, increases the domain of $x.j$ to $\{0, 1, 2, 3\}$. Hence, if $x.0$ equals $x.(n-1)$ then process 0 increases $x.0$ by 1 with probability λ_1, by 2 with probability λ_2, and by 3 with probability $1 - \lambda_1 - \lambda_2$. Likewise, the third program, denoted by $Asymmetric_3$, increases the domain of $x.j$ to $\{0, 1, 2, 3, 4\}$ and introduces three independent probabilities λ_1, λ_2 and λ_3. For each variation, we consider different sizes of the ring.

The goal of GA is to generate the program of each ring, which achieves the best performance, by evolving optimal probabilities. Generated programs contain two objective functions: N (size of the ring) and the expected convergence time for the program. We set GA to maximize N and at the same time minimize expected convergence time. Solving the optimization in the multi-objective manner, we could find the potential optimal probabilities for all rings of different sizes by calling GA once.

Tables 1, 2 and 3 show the optimal probabilities (found by GA) for the three variations mentioned above. In Table 1 for most of rings ($N \geq 6$), the optimal λ found by GA is 0.50. Thus, for $Asymmetric_1$ program, executing two actions with equal probability is most preferable when the size of ring is equal to or greater than 6. However, for a ring smaller than 6 processes, biasing the coin towards one value is preferable. We note that for the case where we have 4 processes, the optimal value of λ identified in Table 1 is 0.22. GA also found another solution where λ is 0.78. This is expected due to symmetry of the solution. In all experiments performed in this section, GA found such symmetric solutions as well. However, for brevity, we only discuss one of them.

Table 1. Optimal Probabilities for *Asymmetric*₁

N	λ	$1 - \lambda$
4	0.22	0.78
5	0.40	0.60
6	0.50	0.50
7	0.50	0.50
8	0.50	0.50
9	0.50	0.50
10	0.50	0.50
11	0.50	0.50
12	0.50	0.50
13	0.50	0.50

Table 2. Optimal Probabilities for *Asymmetric*₂

N	λ_1	λ_2	$1 - \lambda_1 - \lambda_2$
4	0.01	0.01	0.98
5	0.01	0.01	0.98
6	0.01	0.15	0.84
7	0.01	0.20	0.79
8	0.01	0.25	0.74
9	0.09	0.27	0.64
10	0.25	0.33	0.42
11	0.34	0.33	0.33
12	0.34	0.33	0.33
13	0.34	0.33	0.33

Table 2 shows our analysis for $Asymmetric_2$. For $N < 9$, the optimal λ_1 is the minimum value 0.01, whereas λ_3 is very large from 0.74 to 0.98. Thus, the solutions that reduce the expected convergence time heavily prefer the third action (where $x.0$ is increased by 3) over the first two actions. As N increases the three probabilities λ_1, λ_2 and $1 - \lambda_1 - \lambda_2$ are balanced. Also, the optimal value for λ_2 also increases when the size of ring increases. Thus, in both results in Tables 1 and 2, we observe that equal probabilities are preferred as the size of the ring increases. However, unequal probabilities are preferred for smaller rings. Also, the exact size of the ring for which equal probabilities are preferred increases with the size of domain of x.

In Table 3, for $N < 11$, the optimal λ_1 and λ_2 are the minimum value 0.01. As N increases, λ_3 increases slightly and $1 - \lambda_1 - \lambda_2 - \lambda_3$ decreases accordingly. Unlike the previous two cases, for the large size ring $N = 11$, executing all actions with equal chance is not the optimal, and the optimal solutions still prefer executing one actions with high probability. This is anticipated in that the size of the ring where equal probabilities are preferred is expected to be much higher.

To analyze the performance of GA, in Figure 2, we plot the variation of population's average objective value (second objective, expected convergence time) with the generation number. To compare three cases, all the values are normalized here. The figure shows that the optimization of $Asymmetric_1$ reaches the minimum values very quickly at generation 5. Minimum value for $Asymmetric_2$ is reached moderately slower at generation 17. And, the number of generations required for $Asymmetric_3$ is 95. Although the search space for the last case is as large as 8×10^6 (100 possible values for λ_1, λ_2 and λ_3 and 8 values for number of processes), GA effectively finds the optimal probabilities within 100 generations. Hence, the number of solutions discovered is around 8000. When the search space is small, for instance $Asymmetric_1$, GA is not very competent since it still takes 5 generations that explore around half of the search space. Hence, for the small search space, using small size of population is a better choice. In all these three cases, once the minimum is found, the whole population converges to it very quickly.

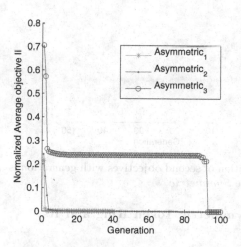

Fig. 2. Variation of second objective with generation number for asymmetric program

Table 3. Optimal Probabilities for $Asymmetric_3$

Ring Size N	λ_1	λ_2	λ_3	$1 - \lambda_1 - \lambda_2 - \lambda_3$
4	0.01	0.01	0.06	0.92
5	0.01	0.01	0.01	0.97
6	0.01	0.01	0.05	0.93
7	0.01	0.01	0.08	0.90
8	0.01	0.01	0.10	0.88
9	0.01	0.01	0.13	0.85
10	0.01	0.01	0.15	0.83
11	0.01	0.01	0.18	0.80

6.3   Optimization Results of Symmetric Probabilistic Self-stabilizing Program

This section depicts experimental results for identifying the optimal probability values for the symmetric probabilistic self-stabilizing token ring program, say *Symmetric*, described in Section 6.2. We consider the cases where the ring size varies from 3 to 15 and where the domain of x variable is $\{0,1\}$. Similar to Section 6.2, we use NSGAII to find ideal probabilities for all different sizes of ring. Thus, the generated programs also contain two objective functions: ring size N and expected convergence time, and GA maximizes the former and minimizes the latter.

Table 4 shows the optimal probabilities of *Symmetric*. For *Symmetric* program, λ and $1 - \lambda$ are symmetric. We observe that for smaller size of ring $N < 9$, the optimal λ found by GA is 0.50, and for $N \geq 9$, biased to one of the action is more desirable. Moreover, as the ring size increases the difference between λ and $1 - \lambda$ increases.

We also plot the variation of average second objective value with the generation number in Figure 3. The figure shows that the optimization of *Symmetric* reaches the minimum values very quickly at generation 6 marked in dotted line. Since the population size is set to 40, the search of GA explores around 28% of the entire search space. The success rate of GA is 100%. Thus, GA is a promising approach for optimizing probabilistic self-stabilizing program.

Table 4. Optimal Probabilities for *Symmetric*

N	λ	$1 - \lambda$
3	0.50	0.50
5	0.50	0.50
7	0.50	0.50
9	0.46	0.54
11	0.37	0.63
13	0.33	0.67
15	0.31	0.69

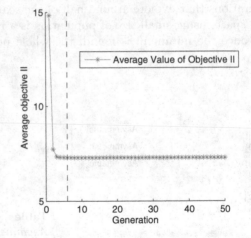

Fig. 3. Variation of second objectives with generation is shown for the *Symmetric*

6.4   An Alternate Program for Symmetric Token Ring and Its Analysis

In the program in Section 4, if a process has the token, it chooses its new value by tossing a coin. An informal example given to describe this program from [11] is as follows:

Imagine seven boys, seated in a circle, each with a coin laying at on one hand. In unison, all boys do the following. Each boy looks at the face of his own coin and that of the boy to his left in the circle; if the two coins show differing faces (head and tail) then he will turn his coin over; otherwise he will toss his coin to obtain a random face. This unison step is repeated ad infinitum. Regardless of the initial faces of the coins, after a finite number of steps (with probability one) only one boy tosses a coin in each step.

The results in Section 6.3 show that for the above program, a biased coin reduces the expected convergence time. In the above program, if x value of process j equals that of $x.(j-1)$ then the new value of $x.j$ does not depend upon the old value of $x.j$. Next, we consider the following variation: When process j tosses a coin then if the coin toss returns *head*, it keeps the old value. On the other hand, if it returns *tail*, it flips the value. In other words, the revised program is as follows:

$$A_j: \quad x.j == x.pre \quad \longrightarrow \quad \lambda \quad :: x.j := x.j$$
$$+1 - \lambda :: x.j := 1 - x.j;$$
$$A_j: \quad x.j \neq x.pre \quad \longrightarrow \quad 1 \quad :: x.j := x.pre$$

Thus, the new program denoted as *Alternative* can be described by the following informal example:

Imagine seven boys, seated in a circle, each with a coin laying at on one hand. In unison, all boys do the following. Each boy looks at the face of his own coin and that of the boy to his left in the circle; if the two coins show differing faces (head and tail) then he will turn his coin over; **otherwise he will flip his coin with probability** $1 - \lambda$. This unison step is repeated ad infinitum. Regardless of the initial faces of the coins, after a finite number of steps (with probability one) only one boy is eligible to flip his coin in each step.

Given the similarity of this program with the program in Section 4, we evaluated this program with GA to identify the optimal values of λ to reduce the expected convergence time. The results are as shown in Table 5. It is surprising that even though these two programs are similar, the ideal value of λ for the above program is 0.5.

7 Evaluating Token Ring Program of Probabilistic Model(s) and Non-probabilistic Model

In this section, we compare the expected convergence time for the asymmetric token-ring program (introduced in Section 3) with the program in [5] in synchronous semantics. Specifically, compared to the program in [5], the program

Table 5. Optimal Probabilities of *Alternative*

Ring Size	λ	$1 - \lambda$
3	0.50	0.50
5	0.50	0.50
7	0.50	0.50
9	0.50	0.50
11	0.50	0.50
13	0.50	0.50

in Section 3 aims to reduce the space requirement of each process while providing probabilistic stabilization (as opposed to deterministic stabilization provided by [5]. In particular, we use the best solutions identified by GA for $Asymmetric_1$, $Asymmetric_2$ and $Asymmetric_3$ with that in [5] that the x value of each process is chosen from domain $0..K-1$, where $K \geq n$, the number of processes in the ring. By contrast, the domain of x values in $Asymmetric_1$, $Asymmetric_2$ and $Asymmetric_3$ is 3, 4 and 5 respectively.

Specifically, Figure 4 plots the number of processes against expected convergence time in terms of steps. For those experiments, we consider the case where the number of processes is in the set $\{4, ..., 11\}$. As expected, average convergence time increases with introduction of randomness. In particular, when $n \geq 6$, the expected convergence time is minimum for the deterministic program and it is maximum for $Asymmetric_1$.

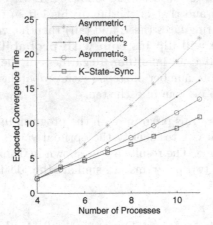

Fig. 4. Expected Convergence Time for the Asymmetric Program

8 Symmetric Token Ring Protocols Using Asymmetric Probabilities

In Section 6.3, the values of λ used by all processes are identical. This captures the intuition of [11] that the processes are anonymous and cannot use their process ID. In this section, we consider the effect of relaxing this so that each process chooses its λ value independently. We denote λ for process j as λ^j. We consider this for ring size of 3 and 5. The optimal probabilities identified by GA are showm in Table 6.

As shown in Table 6, with 3 processes, making one of the processes to be (almost) deterministic is ideal for reducing the convergence time. However, we note that such a solution is unacceptable, since it will (almost) bring the token circulation to halt in some legitimate states. Hence, we performed these experiments again with the constraint that $\lambda \in [0.25..0.75]$. The results are as shown in Table 7. Given the constraint, the optimal solutions require one of the processes to choose the least probability value.

Table 6. Optimal Probabilities of *Symmetric* Using Asymmetric Probabilities With Domain Range [0.01..0.99]

N	λ^1	λ^2	λ^3	λ^4	λ^5	Expected Conv Time
3	0.99	0.01	0.50			0.25250
5	0.99	0.99	0.99	0.01	0.01	1.61997

Table 7. Optimal Probabilities of *Symmetric* Using Asymmetric Probabilities With Domain Range [0.25..0.75]

N	λ^1	λ^2	λ^3	λ^4	λ^5	Expected Conv Time
3	0.75	0.25	0.50			0.30769
5	0.25	0.75	0.25	0.75	0.25	1.83535

We also consider the algorithm in Section 6.4 where each process could choose the value of λ independently. We restrict λ to be in [0.01..0.75] (In this program choosing λ to be very small implies that the process almost always chooses to flip its value. This is acceptable. However, keeping its original value is not acceptable.) The results are as shown in Table 8. One of the interesting observations is that allowing processes to have independent λ reduces the expected convergence time (compared to the *Symmetric*). Moreover, the optimal expected convergence time of *Alternative* using asymmetric probabilities with domain range [0.01..0.75] is better than *Symmetric* using asymmetric probabilities.

Table 8. Optimal Probabilities of *Alternative* Using Asymmetric Probabilities With Domain Range [0.01..0.75]

N	λ^1	λ^2	λ^3	λ^4	λ^5	Expected Conv Time
3	0.75	0.75	0.01			0.26810
5	0.75	0.75	0.01	0.75	0.01	1.21268

9   Related Work

A number of studies have considered Herman's probabilistic stabilizing programs, including [1,7,9,10,17,18,20]. Specifically, most existing work focus on analyzing Herman's probabilistic stabilizing program in terms of expected convergence time and propose an upper bound. Also, some existing work in [1,17] states that expected stabilization time should minimized by the equidistant configuration. Our technique differs from previous work in several ways: First, our technique infers *optimal probabilities* for randomized stabilizing program with respect to ideal expected convergence time. This is not addressed by existing work. Second, Our technique employs GA. The key insight underlying our approach is using evolution-based problem solving technique.

Evolution-based techniques in the context of program synthesis and refinement have been studied in [2,8,19,21]. In [2,8], authors propose an evolutionary approach to automatically repair software bugs. In [21,22], authors introduce evolution based approaches for synthesizing distributed programs. Instead, our work here focuses on refining distributed program, attempting to achieve optimal performance. Similar to our work, [19] investigates the trading-off of non-functional properties of a self-stabilizing program using GA and PRISM. However, our work considers more than one program and shows many interesting observations. Recently, authors in [24] focuses on identifying trade-offs between closure and convergence properties of stabilizing programs. Our work focuses on the approach of identifying optimal probability values to reduce the convergence time.

10   Conclusion

In this paper, we used genetic algorithms (GAs) to analyze the probabilistic stabilizing programs in [11,12]. Although it is well known that randomized algorithms can reduce the state space required to achieve stabilization as well as solve several problems that cannot be solved in a deterministic setting, identifying the optimal probability values for optimum results is often difficult.

For the program in [12], we showed that a biased coin is preferable when the ring size is small. However, unbiased coin is desirable when the ring size is large. Moreover, when the state space of the program is increased, the ring size for which unbiased coin is preferable increases. To the best of our knowledge, this result was not previously known.

For the program in [11], we showed that unbiased coin was preferable when the ring size was small. However, as the ring size increases, a biased coin is desirable. Moreover, as the ring size increases, the level of the bias also increases. This result was previously known [18] by exhaustive analysis. We showed that this result could be identified with GA as well. Moreover, GA did not require analysis of the entire search space.

In [11], when a process chooses a new value, it chooses the value 0 with probability λ and the value 1 with probability $1 - \lambda$. In other words, the new value is independent of the old value. We considered a variation of this problem where the value λ identifies whether the process should keep its current value. We found a surprising result that that with this variation, an unbiased coin is preferable for all ring sizes up to 13.

As expected, when the number of independent probabilities is larger, the corresponding search space is large too. GA is most beneficial in these cases. Particular, for $Asymmetric_3$, GA was able to identify the best solutions by searching less than 0.1% of the search space. However, when the number of independent probabilities are small, GA search covered most of the search space. For example, for $Asymmetric_1$, GA searched for about 65% of the search space.

In our solution, we used PRISM [13] to analyze individual programs. Hence, one bottleneck for the use of GA in this manner is any bottleneck (e.g., state space explosion) associated with PRISM. One future work in this area is to develop algorithms for objective functions that provide a rough estimate of the desired property (expected convergence time in this case) more efficiently. This will allow GA to identify almost optimal solutions quickly. One future work in this area is to identify whether this approach can improve the performance of GA. Another future work in this area is to use parallelization. Since GA provides easy opportunities for parallelization, we anticipate that this will be especially valuable for large programs. We also plan to investigate these algorithms in terms of providing trade-off between token circulation time and time for stabilization. It is anticipated that for the program in [11], an unbiased coin would be preferred for token circulation in legitimate states. However, for certain ring sizes, it is known that a biased coin decreases the convergence time. It will be useful to identify the potential trade-off between these two objectives.

References

1. Annabelle, C.M.: Mcovera. An elementary proof that herman's ring is (n2). Information Processing Letters **94**(2), 79–84 (2005)
2. Arcuri, A., Yao, X.: A novel co-evolutionary approach to automatic software bug fixing. In: IEEE World Congress on Computational Intelligence Evolutionary Computation, pp. 162–168 (2008)
3. Arora, A., Gouda, M.: Closure and convergence: A foundation of fault-tolerant computing. IEEE Trans. Softw. Eng., 19(11), November 1993
4. Deb, K., Pratap, A., Agarwal, S., Meyarivan, T.: A fast and elitist multiobjective genetic algorithm: Nsga-ii. IEEE Transactions on Evolutionary Computation **6**(2), 182–197 (2002)
5. Dijkstra, E.W.: Self-stabilizing systems in spite of distributed control. Commun. ACM **17**(11), 643–644 (1974)
6. Dolev, S.: Self-Stabilization. MIT Press (2000)
7. Feng, Y., Zhang, L.: A tighter bound for the self-stabilization time in herman's algorithm. Inf. Process. Lett. **113**(13), 486–488 (2013)
8. Forrest, S., Nguyen, T., Weimer, W., Goues, C.L.: A genetic programming approach to automated software repair. In: Proceedings of the 11th Annual Conference on Genetic and Evolutionary Computation, New York, NY, USA (2009)

9. Fribourg, L., Messika, S., Picaronny, C.: Coupling and self-stabilization. Distributed Computing **18**(3), 221–232 (2006)
10. Haslegrave, J.: Bounds on herman's algorithm. CoRR, abs/1405.5209 (2014)
11. Herman, T.: Probabilistic self-stabilization. Inf. Process. Lett. **35**(2), 63–67 (1990)
12. Herman, T.: Self-stabilization: Randomness to reduce space. Distributed Computing **6**(2), 95–98 (1992)
13. Hinton, A., Kwiatkowska, M., Norman, G., Parker, D.: PRISM: A Tool for Automatic Verification of Probabilistic Systems. In: Hermanns, H., Palsberg, J. (eds.) TACAS 2006. LNCS, vol. 3920, pp. 441–444. Springer, Heidelberg (2006)
14. Hoepman, J.-H.: Uniform deterministic self-stabilizing ring-orientation on odd-length rings. In: Proceedings of the 8th International Workshop on Distributed Algorithms, WDAG 1994, pp. 265–279 (1994)
15. Holland, J.H.: Adaptation in natural and artificial systems: an introductory analysis with applications to biology, control, and artificial intelligence. U Michigan Press (1975)
16. Huang, S.-T.: Leader election in uniform rings. ACM Trans. Program. Lang. Syst. **15**(3), July 1993
17. Kiefer, S., Murawski, A.S., Ouaknine, J., Wachter, B., Worrell, J.: Three tokens in herman's algorithm. Formal Asp. Comput. **24**(4–6), 671–678 (2012)
18. Kwiatkowska, M.Z., Norman, G., Parker, D.: Probabilistic verification of herman's self-stabilisation algorithm. Formal Asp. Comput. **24**(4–6), 661–670 (2012)
19. Millard, A.G., White, D.R., Clark, J.A.: Searching for Pareto-optimal Randomised Algorithms. In: Fraser, G., Teixeira de Souza, J. (eds.) SSBSE 2012. LNCS, vol. 7515, pp. 183–197. Springer, Heidelberg (2012)
20. Nakata, T.: On the expected time for herman's probabilistic self-stabilizing algorithm. Theor. Comput. Sci. **349**(3), 475–483 (2005)
21. Weise, T., Tang, K.: Evolving distributed algorithms with genetic programming. IEEE Transactions on Evolutionary Computation **16**(2), 242–265 (2012)
22. Weise, T., Zapf, M., Geihs, K.: Rule-based genetic programming. In: Bio-Inspired Models of Network, Information and Computing Systems, Bionetics 2007, 2nd edn. pp. 8–15 (2007)
23. Whitley, D.: A genetic algorithm tutorial. Statistics and Computing **4**(2), 65–85 (1994)
24. Zhu, L., Kulkarni, S.: Using genetic programming to identify tradeoffs in self-stabilizing programs: A case study. In: Proceedings of the 2015 IEEE 35th International Conference on Distributed Computing Systems Workshops, ICDCSW 2015, Columbus, OH, USA (2015)

Avatar: A Time- and Space-Efficient Self-stabilizing Overlay Network

Andrew Berns[✉]

Department of Computer Science, University of Wisconsin-La Crosse,
La Crosse, WI, USA
aberns@uwlax.edu

Abstract. Overlay networks present an interesting challenge for fault-tolerant computing. Many overlay networks operate in dynamic environments (e.g. the Internet), where faults are frequent and widespread, and the number of processes in a system may be quite large. Recently, self-stabilizing overlay networks have been presented as a method for managing this complexity. *Self-stabilizing overlay networks* promise that, starting from any weakly-connected configuration, a correct overlay network will eventually be built. To date, this guarantee has come at a cost: nodes may either have high degree during the algorithm's execution, or the algorithm may take a long time to reach a legal configuration. In this paper, we present the first self-stabilizing overlay network algorithm that does not incur this penalty. Specifically, we (i) present a new locally-checkable overlay network based upon a binary search tree, and (ii) provide a randomized algorithm for self-stabilization that terminates in an expected polylogarithmic number of rounds *and* increases a node's degree by only a polylogarithmic factor in expectation.

1 Introduction

Today's distributed systems are quite different from those only a decade ago. Pervasive network connectivity and an increase in the number of computational devices has ushered in an era of large-scale distributed systems operating in highly-dynamic environments. One type of distributed system that has gained popularity recently is the overlay network. An *overlay network* is a network where communication occurs over *logical* links, where each logical link consists of zero or more *physical* links. The use of logical links allows the design of efficient logical topologies (e.g. topologies with low diameter and/or low degree) irrespective of the physical topology, enabling efficient data structures to be constructed from large systems with arbitrary physical networks.

The dynamic nature of many overlay networks makes fault tolerance extremely important. *Self-stabilization*, first presented by Dijkstra in 1974 [6], is an elegant fault-tolerant paradigm promising that, after *any* memory-corrupting transient fault, the system will eventually recover to a correct configuration. *Self-stabilizing overlay networks* are logical networks that guarantee a correct topology will be restored after any such transient fault.

© Springer International Publishing Switzerland 2015
A. Pelc and A.A. Schwarzmann (Eds.): SSS 2015, LNCS 9212, pp. 233–247, 2015.
DOI: 10.1007/978-3-319-21741-3_16

1.1   Related Work

Many overlay networks include a mechanism to tolerate a subset of possible faults. For instance, CHORD [15] defines a procedure for nodes to join the network efficiently. The FORGIVING GRAPH [9] presents a self-healing overlay network which maintains connectivity while limiting degree increases and stretch despite periodic adversarial node insertions and deletions.

Self-stabilizing overlay networks, however, are a relatively new area of research. In 2007, Onus et al. presented the first silent self-stabilizing overlay network, building a linear topology in linear (in the number of nodes) rounds [14]. The SKIP+ graph, presented in 2009 by Jacob et al. [10], was the first self-stabilizing overlay network with polylogarithmic convergence time. Berns et al. presented a generic framework capable of building any locally-checkable overlay network, and proved that their result was near-optimal in running time [4].

Current self-stabilizing overlay networks have suffered from one of two limitations. First, some self-stabilizing overlay networks require a long time to reach a correct configuration. For instance, RECHORD [11], a self-stabilizing variant of CHORD, requires $\mathcal{O}(n \log n)$ rounds to reach a correct configuration. Other self-stabilizing overlay networks that converge quickly have required a large amount of space. For example, SKIP+ [10] has a polylogarithmic convergence time, but may increase a node's degree to $\mathcal{O}(n)$ during convergence. The Transitive Closure Framework [4] requires $\Theta(n)$ space. To date, no work has achieved efficient convergence in both time and space.

1.2   Contributions

In Section 3, we present AVATAR, a generic locally checkable overlay network, and describe a specific "instance" of the network called AVATAR$_{\text{CBT}}$ which is based upon a binary search tree. Section 4 presents a randomized self-stabilizing algorithm for creating the AVATAR$_{\text{CBT}}$ network, as well as an analysis sketch of the algorithm's performance in both convergence time and space (using a new metric we call the *degree expansion*).

2   Model of Computation

We model the distributed system as an undirected graph $G = (V, E)$, with nodes V representing the processes of the system, and edges E representing the communication links. Each node u is assigned an identifier from the function $id : V \to \mathbb{Z}^+$. We assume each node stores $id(u)$ as immutable data. Where clear from context, we refer to a node u by its identifier $id(u)$.

Each node $u \in V$ has a *local state* $S(u)$ consisting of a set of variables and their values. We assume all nodes have access to a shared immutable random sequence Ψ. A node u can modify the values of its variables using *actions* defined in the *program* of u. All nodes execute the same program. We use a *synchronous* model of computation, where in one *round* each node executes its program and communicates with its neighbors. We use the *message passing* model of communication, where a node u can communicate with a node v in its *neighborhood* $N(u) = \{v \in V : (u,v) \in E\}$ by sending node v (called a *neighbor*) a message. A node can send unique messages to every neighbor in every round. We assume reliable and bounded capacity communication channels where a message is received by a node u at the beginning of round i if and only if it was sent to u by some $v \in N(u)$ in round $(i-1)$.

In the overlay network model, a node's neighborhood is part of its state, allowing a node to change its neighborhood with program actions. In a round i, a node u can delete any subset of edges incident upon it, and add edges to any nodes currently at distance 2 from u. Specifically, let G_i be the configuration in round i. A node u can (i) delete any edge $(u,v) \in E(G_i)$, resulting in $(u,v) \notin E(G_{i+1})$, and (ii) create the edge (u,w) if $(u,v), (v,w) \in E(G_i)$, resulting in $(u,w) \in E(G_{i+1})$. We restrict edge additions to only those nodes at distance 2 to reflect the fact that only nodes at distance 2 share a common neighbor through which they can be "connected". We assume that $v \in N(u) \Leftrightarrow (u,v) \in E$ – that is, every neighbor of u is known, and u has no "false neighbors" in $N(u)$ (this can be achieved with the use of a "heartbeat" message).

Our problem is to take a set of nodes V and create a *legal configuration*, where a legal configuration is defined by some predicate taken over the state of all nodes in V. Since edges are state in an overlay network, the legal configuration predicate often includes the requirement that the topology matches a particular *desired topology* $ON(V) = (V, E)$. The *self-stabilizing overlay network problem* is to design an algorithm $\mathcal{A}$ such that, when executed on nodes V with arbitrary initial state in an arbitrary weakly-connected initial topology, the system eventually reaches a legal configuration. Furthermore, once the network is in a legal configuration, it remains in a legal configuration until an external fault perturbs the system.

Performance of an overlay network algorithm can be measured in terms of both time and space. To analyze the worst-case performance, it is assumed that an *adversary* creates the initial configuration using full knowledge of the nodes and the algorithm they will execute. The adversary does not, however, know the value of the shared random sequence Ψ. The maximum number of rounds required for a legal configuration to be reached, taken over all possible configurations, is the *convergence time* of $\mathcal{A}$. One measure of space complexity is the number of incident edges on a node, as each incident edge requires memory and maintenance (heartbeat messages). We introduce the *degree expansion* as a space complexity measurement. The degree expansion, informally, is the amount a node's degree may grow "unnecessarily" during convergence. For a graph G with node set V, let Δ_G be the maximum degree of nodes in G. For a self-stabilizing algorithm $\mathcal{A}$ executing on G, let $\Delta_{\mathcal{A},G}$ be the maximum degree of any node from V during execution of $\mathcal{A}$ beginning from configuration G. We define degree expansion as follows.

Definition 1. *The* degree expansion of $\mathcal{A}$ on G, *denoted* $DegExp_{\mathcal{A},G}$, *is equal to* $(\Delta_{\mathcal{A},G}/\max(\Delta_G, \Delta_{ON(\lambda)}))$. *Let the* degree expansion of $\mathcal{A}$ *be* $DegExp_{\mathcal{A}} = \max_{G \in \mathcal{G}}(DegExp_{\mathcal{A},G})$

The degree expansion is meant to capture the degree growth of the algorithm while excluding clever initial configurations from the adversary resulting in a high degree increase.

A self-stabilizing overlay network algorithm is *silent* if and only if the algorithm brings the system to a configuration where the messages exchanged between nodes remains fixed until a fault perturbs the system [7]. Traditionally, these messages consist of a node's state. In order for a silent self-stabilizing overlay network algorithm to exist using only this information, the network must be locally checkable. An overlay network is *locally checkable* if and only if each illegal configuration has at least one node (called a *detector*) which detects that the configuration is not legal using only its state and the state of its neighbors, and all legal configurations have no detectors.

3   The AVATAR Network

3.1   AVATAR Specification

One of the challenges with creating silent self-stabilizing overlay network algorithms is designing a locally checkable topology as many previous overlay networks are *not* locally checkable. For instance, SKIP+ [10] was created to have a locally-checkable variant of the SKIP graph [1]. Similarly, the self-stabilizing RECHORD network [11] is a locally-checkable CHORD [15] derivative built using real and virtual nodes. Simplifying this network design task is the motivation for AVATAR. AVATAR easily allows many different topologies to be "simulated" while ensuring local checkability.

AVATAR is based around the idea of network embeddings. A *network embedding* Φ maps the node set of a *guest network* $G_g = (V_g, E_g)$ onto the node set of a *host network* $G_h = (V_h, E_h)$ [13]. The *dilation* of Φ is defined as the maximum distance between any two nodes $\Phi(u), \Phi(v) \in V_h$ such that $(u,v) \in E_g$. The AVATAR network is an overlay network realizing a dilation-1 embedding for a guest network using logical overlay links. To do this *and* ensure local checkability, the (host) overlay edges of AVATAR consist of the successor and predecessor edges from a linearized graph (ensuring host nodes can check which guest nodes map to them) as well as the overlay edges necessary for host nodes of two neighboring guest nodes to be at most distance 1 apart.

Formally, for any $N \in \mathbb{N}$, let $[N]$ be the set of nodes $\{0, 1, \dots, N-1\}$. Let $\mathcal{F}$ be a family of graphs such that, for each $N \in \mathbb{N}$, there is exactly one graph $F_N \in \mathcal{F}$ with node set $[N]$. We use $\mathcal{F}(N)$ to denote F_N. We call $\mathcal{F}$ a *full graph family*, capturing the notion that the family contains exactly one topology for each "full" set of nodes $[N]$ (relative to the identifiers). For any $N \in \mathbb{N}$ and $V \subseteq [N]$, AVATAR$_{\mathcal{F}}(N, V)$ is a network with node set V that realizes a dilation-1 embedding of $F_N \in \mathcal{F}$. The specific embedding is given below. We also show that, when N is known, AVATAR is locally checkable (N can be viewed as an upper bound on the number of nodes in the system).

Definition 2. *Let* $V \subseteq [N]$ *be a node set* $\{u_0, u_1, \ldots, u_{n-1}\}$, *where* $u_i < u_{i+1}$ *for* $0 \le i < n-1$. *Let the* range *of a node* u_i *be* $range(u_i) = [u_i, u_{i+1})$ *for* $0 < i < n-1$. *Let* $range(u_0) = [0, u_1)$ *and* $range(u_{n-1}) = [u_{n-1}, N)$. AVATAR$_{\mathcal{F}}(N, V)$ *is a graph with node set* V *and edge set consisting of two edge types:*

Type 1: $\{(u_i, u_{i+1}) | i = 0, \ldots, n-1\}$
Type 2: $\{(u_i, u_j) | u_i \ne u_j \wedge \exists (a, b) \in E(F_N), a \in range(u_i) \wedge b \in range(u_j)\}$

Theorem 1. *Let* $\mathcal{F}$ *be an arbitrary full graph family, and let* AVATAR$_{\mathcal{F}}(N, V)$ *be an overlay network for an arbitrary* N *and* V, *and let each* $u \in V$ *know* N. AVATAR$_{\mathcal{F}}(N, V)$ *is locally checkable.*

Proof sketch: Note each node can calculate its range using only its neighborhood. Using the state of its neighbors, u can also calculate the range of each neighbor. This information is sufficient for each node u to verify every neighbor $v \in N(u)$ is either from a type 1 or type 2 edge. As all nodes know N and there is exactly one $F_N \in \mathcal{F}$, all nodes can verify their type 1 and type 2 edges correctly map to the given network. Interestingly, AVATAR$_{\mathcal{F}}$ is locally checkable using only $\mathcal{O}(\log n)$ bits from each neighbor: each node need share only (i) its identifier, and (ii) the identifier of its predecessor and successor.

3.2 The Full Graph Family CBT

Our goal is to create a self-stabilizing AVATAR network which stabilizes quickly and maintains low degree during convergence. To this end, we simulate a simple data structure with constant degree and logarithmic diameter: a binary search tree. As we show, an embedding in AVATAR of a binary search tree maintains a low degree and diameter.

Formally, consider the graph family based upon *complete binary search trees*. Below we define the full graph family CBT by defining CBT(N) recursively.

Definition 3. *For* $a \le b$, *let* CBT$[a, b]$ *be a binary tree rooted at* $r = \lfloor (b+a)/2 \rfloor$. *Node* r *'s left cluster is* CBT$[a, r-1]$, *and* r *'s right cluster is* CBT$[r+1, b]$. *If* $a > b$, *then* CBT$[a, b] = \bot$. *We define* CBT$(N) =$ CBT$[0, N-1]$. *Let the* level *of a node* d *in* CBT$[0, N-1]$ *be the distance from* d *to root* $\lfloor N - 1/2 \rfloor$.

Diameter and Maximum Degree of AVATAR$_{\text{CBT}}$. All dilation-1 embeddings preserve the diameter of the guest network, meaning AVATAR$_{\text{CBT}}$ has $\mathcal{O}(\log N)$ diameter. Note a node v in our embedding may have a large $\Phi^{-1}(v)$ – that is, many nodes from the guest network may map to a single host node. Surprisingly, the host nodes for AVATAR$_{\text{CBT}}$ have a small degree *regardless of* Φ^{-1}, as we show below.

Theorem 2. *For any node set $V \subseteq [N]$, the maximum degree of any node $u \in V$ in* AVATAR$_{\text{CBT}}(N, V)$ *is at most* $2 \cdot \log N + 2$.

Proof sketch: Consider $\Phi^{-1}(u)$, the subset of nodes from $[N]$ mapped to node u. Let $[N]_j$ be the set of all nodes at level j of CBT(N). There are at most 2 nodes in $\Phi^{-1}(u) \cap [N]_j$ with a neighbor not in $\Phi^{-1}(u)$ – that is, there are at most 2 edges from the range of a node u to any other node outside this range for a particular level j of the tree. As there are only $\log N + 1$ levels, the total degree of any node in AVATAR$_{\text{CBT}}$ is at most $2 \cdot \log N + 2$.

4   A Self-Stabilizing Algorithm

4.1   Algorithm Overview

At a high level, our self-stabilizing algorithm works on the same principle as Gallager, Humblet, and Spira's algorithm for constructing a minimum-weight spanning tree [8]. The network is organized into disjoint clusters, each with a leader. The cluster leaders coordinate cluster merges until a single cluster remains, at which point the network is in a legal configuration.

Self-stabilizing overlay networks introduce a complication to this pattern. Converging from an arbitrary weakly-connected configuration while limiting a node's degree increase requires coordinated merges, which requires either time (additional rounds) or bandwidth (additional edges). In the overlay network model, we can increase both: we can add edges to the network and add steps to our algorithm. Our algorithm balances these additions using four components, discussed below, to achieve expected polylogarithmic convergence time and degree growth.

1. **Clustering:** As any weakly-connected initial configuration is possible, we must ensure all nodes join a cluster and have a way to efficiently communicate within their cluster. We define a cluster for AVATAR$_{\text{CBT}}$ and present mechanisms for cluster creation and intra-cluster communication.

2. **Matching:** Progress comes from clusters merging, moving towards a single-cluster configuration. However, we will show merging clusters results in an $\mathcal{O}(\log^2 N)$ degree increase for each involved cluster. To control degree growth, we limit a cluster to merge with at most one other cluster at a time. We create a matching to determine which clusters should merge. Using the overlay network model's ability to add edges, we introduce a mechanism to create "sufficiently-many" matchings on *any* topology.

3. **Merging:** Once two clusters are matched they merge together into a single cluster. Merging quickly requires sufficient "bandwidth" (in the form of edges) between two clusters. To limit degree increases, these edges must be created carefully. We present an algorithm for merging two clusters quickly while still limiting the number of additional edges that are created.

4. **Termination Detection:** Finally, to ensure our algorithm is silent, we define a simple mechanism for detecting when the legal configuration has been reached, allowing our algorithm to terminate.

We discuss these components below, providing sketches of the algorithms and analysis. Complete algorithms and analysis can be found in the full version of this work [3].

4.2 Clustering

Defining a Cluster. In the overlay network model, we can create clusters by defining the nodes of the cluster as well as the *topology* of the cluster.

Definition 4. *Let G be a graph with node set V. A CBT cluster is a set of nodes $V' \subseteq V$ in graph G such that $G[V']$, the subgraph of G induced by V', is $\text{AVATAR}_{\text{CBT}}(N, V')$.*

Notice our cluster can be thought of on two levels: on one level, it consists of an N-node guest CBT network, while on the other level, it consists of host nodes V'. We call the root of the guest CBT network the *root* of the cluster. Figure 1 contains the (host) network G with two clusters: T and T'. The two (guest) CBT networks corresponding to these clusters are given in Figure 2.

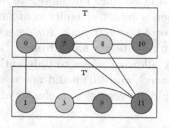

Fig. 1. Host nodes of clusters T (top) and T' (bottom)

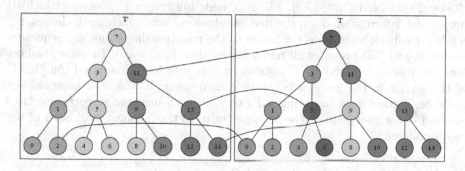

Fig. 2. Guest Nodes for T (right) and T' (left)

To ensure nodes quickly perform the necessary actions to join a cluster, we make our CBT clusters (from here on, simply clusters) locally checkable. To do this, we add three variables to each node: a cluster identifier $cluster_u$ containing the identifier of the host of the root node in the cluster, and a cluster predecessor $clusterPred_u$ and successor $clusterSucc_u$, set to the closest identifiers in the subgraph induced by nodes with the same cluster identifier. Let the *cluster range of u* be the range of u defined by the *cluster* predecessor and successor. We say a set of nodes V' is a valid cluster if and only if (i) the subgraph induced by V' matches $\text{AVATAR}_{\text{CBT}}(N, V')$, and (ii) the legal range in $\text{AVATAR}_{\text{CBT}}(N, V')$ matches the *cluster range* of u in the configuration G.

Like $\text{AVATAR}_{\text{CBT}}(N, V')$, our cluster is locally checkable. The proof follows closely the proof that $\text{AVATAR}_{\text{CBT}}$ itself is locally checkable: nodes in a cluster V' can calculate their cluster range and the cluster range of their cluster neighbors, allowing them to check that their intra-cluster edges are from $\text{AVATAR}_{\text{CBT}}$ (N, V'). Furthermore, if the cluster identifier is invalid, at least one node will detect this. During convergence, there are some cases where a node is not a member of a cluster due to program actions (i.e. merge). Later we show this is also locally checkable.

In the self-stabilizing setting, there is no guarantee that each node begins execution belonging to a valid cluster. Therefore, we define a "reset" operation which a node executes when a subset of faulty configurations are detected. We say that a node u has detected a *reset fault* if u detects (i) it is not a member of a cluster, (ii) it is not in a state reachable from a "legal" merge (as we shall see, merges occur in a way allowing nodes to differentiate fault-induced invalid clusters from merging clusters), and (iii) it did not reset in the previous round. When u detects a reset fault, it "resets" to a cluster of size 1.

Intra-Cluster Communication. Our algorithms require a systematic and reliable means of intra-cluster communication. For this, we use a non-snap-stabilizing variant of the *propagation of information with feedback and cleaning (PFC)* algorithm [5], which we "simulate" on the guest CBT network for a cluster T (denoted $\text{CBT}_T(N)$). The root node initiates a *PFC wave*, which (i) propagates information down the tree level-by-level until reaching the leaves, (ii) sends a feedback wave from the leaves to the root, passing along any requested feedback, and (iii) prepares all nodes for another *PFC* wave. To allow the host network to simulate the *PFC* algorithm, it is sufficient to append the "level" of the sender in the guest network to each message in the host network. For instance, a guest root initiating a *PFC* wave with message m corresponds to the host of the root sending the message $(m, 0)$ to the (at most two) hosts of the root's children.

Analysis of Cluster Creation and Communication

Lemma 1. *Every node u will be a member of a cluster in $\mathcal{O}(\log N)$ rounds.*

Proof sketch: The lemma holds easily for nodes that are members of a cluster initially. Consider a node u that is not a member of a cluster. If a reset fault is detected by u, then u becomes a size-1 cluster in one round. If no reset fault is detected, either (i) u believes it is participating in a merge, or (ii) u believes it is a member of a cluster. For case (i), we will show later that the merge process is locally checkable (that is, if a configuration is reached that is not a valid merge, at least one node detects this), and that every node that detects an invalid cluster from a merge will either complete the merge in $\mathcal{O}(\log N)$ rounds, or reset in $\mathcal{O}(\log N)$ rounds, satisfying our claim. For case (ii), as clusters are locally checkable, there must be a shortest path of nodes $u, v_0, v_1, \ldots, v_k$, with $k = \mathcal{O}(\log N)$, such that all nodes in the path have a cluster identifer matching the identifier of u, and v_k detects a reset fault. When v_k executes a reset, it will cause node v_{k-1} to detect a reset fault in the next round, causing it to reset and v_{k-2} to detect a reset fault, and so on. In this way, the reset will "spread" to u in $\mathcal{O}(\log N)$ rounds, resulting in u executing a reset, satisfying our claim.

Lemma 2. *After $\mathcal{O}(\log N)$ rounds, if a set of nodes $T \subseteq V$ forms a cluster, no node in T will execute a reset action until an external fault perturbs the system.*

Proof sketch: Note that once u is part of a cluster T, no action u executes will cause it to leave cluster T unless it is merging with another cluster T'. If T and T' are merging, they will successfully create a new valid cluster T'', with $V(T) \subseteq V(T'')$. Our lemma's initial "delay" of $\mathcal{O}(\log N)$ rounds handles the case where the initial configuration contains a node which is part of a cluster with a corrupted PFC mechanism. This can only happen in an initial configuration, and it is corrected (either through the PFC mechanism or through resets) in $\mathcal{O}(\log N)$ rounds, confirming our claim.

From this point forward, our analysis shall assume the system is in a "reset-free" configuration consisting of valid clusters and merging clusters.

4.3   Matching

We can add edges during a merge to increase "bandwidth" and thus decrease the time required for the merge. However, we must be careful to limit the resulting degree increase. Therefore, a cluster T can only merge one other cluster at a time. For this, we calculate a matching between clusters. We say that a cluster T has been assigned a *merge partner* T' if and only if the roots of T and T' have been connected by the matching process described below. We say that a cluster T is *matched* if it has been assigned a merge partner, and unmatched otherwise.

We say that the *cluster graph* G_c of G is the graph induced by the clusters in configuration G, where a node v_T in G_c corresponds to a cluster T in G, and an edge $(v_T, v_{T'})$ corresponds to an edge between at least one node $u \in T$ and node $u' \in T'$. Our goal is to find a large matching on the cluster graph. To find this matching, we use a randomized symmetry-breaking technique. "Traditional" matching algorithms, however, are insufficient, as there are topologies where even a maximum matching consists of only a small number of nodes (e.g. a star topology has a maximum matching of a single pair). In these cases, only a small number of merges would occur at a time, resulting in slow convergence. Note, however, that one can identify large matchings on the square of the cluster graph, G_c^2 (the graph resulting from connecting all nodes of distance at-most 2 in G). Since we are in the overlay network model, a matching on G_c^2 can become a (distance-one) matching by adding a single edge between matched clusters. Our matching algorithm creates a matching on G_c^2. We provide a sketch of the matching algorithm in Algorithm 1, and a discussion below.

Our matching algorithm uses two different *roles* selected by the cluster root: *leaders* and *followers*. Leaders connect followers together to form a matching on G_c^2. A cluster root chooses the cluster's role uniformly at random, with the exception of one special case (as discussed below, clusters which are merging become leaders if they were "followed" during their merge). When the root has selected the role of follower (leader), we say that the entire cluster is a follower (leader).

Consider first a follower cluster T. Each node $u \in T$ will check $N(u)$ for a node v such that v is in another cluster T' and v is a potential leader. A *potential leader* is a node which either (i) has the role of leader and is "open" (see below), or (ii) is merging, and thus "available" for followers. A node $u \in T$ will (i) mark one potential leader as "followed" (if one such neighbor exists), (ii) receive at most two edges to potential leaders from its children, and (iii) forward at most one edge incident on a potential leader to u's parent. Eventually, at most two such edges reach the root of the cluster. At this point, the root waits for the selected leader to assign it a merge partner. We define two types of followers: *long followers* and *short followers*. Short followers will only search for a leader for a "short" amount of time ($4 \log N$ rounds), while long followers will search for a (slightly) "longer" time ($24 \log N$). Long and short followers are used to make the scenario where a cluster and all of its neighbors are "stuck" searching for a leader sufficiently rare.

If the root of T has selected the leader role, the root begins by communicating the leader role to all nodes in the cluster. At this point, nodes are considered *open leaders*, and neighboring follower nodes can "follow" these leaders. After this PFC wave completes, the root sends another PFC wave asking nodes in T to (i) become *closed leaders* (no node can select them as a potential leader), and (ii) connect any current followers as merge partners. Nodes in T will connect all followers incident upon them as merge partners, thus creating a matching on G_c^2. If a node $u \in T$ has an odd number of followers, it simply matches as many pairs as possible and forwards the one "extra" follower to u's parent. This guarantees all followers of T will find a merge partner, as the root of T either receives no followers, matches two received followers, or sets the single received follower as the merge partner for T itself. Once this PFC wave completes, the root either (i) begins the merge process with a follower T' (if a merge partner was found), or (ii) randomly selects a new role.

Algorithm Sketch 1. The Matching Algorithm for Cluster T

1. If no role, root r_T selects a role uniformly at random: leader or follower.
2. If r_T is a *leader*:
3. r_T uses PFC to set all nodes as *open leaders*
4.   Upon completion of the wave, r_T uses PFC set all nodes as *closed leader*
5.   Upon completion of the wave, nodes connect all incident followers, and forward to their parent the (at-most-one) unmatched follower
6. r_T matches any received followers
7. r_T either repeats the matching algorithm (if unmatched), or begins merging (if matched)
8. Else
9. r_T selects uniformly at random the role of *long* or *short* follower
10.   Nodes in T search for a leader. Short followers search for $2\,PFC$ waves, while long followers search for $12\,PFC$ waves
11.   If a leader was found r_T waits to be matched with a merge partner
12.   Else T repeats the matching algorithm
13. Endif

Analysis of Matching

Lemma 3. *Consider a cluster T in a configuration G_i. With probability at least $1/4$, all nodes in T will be a potential leader for at least one round in the next $\mathcal{O}(\log N)$ rounds.*

Proof sketch: There are four cases to consider based on the state of T in G_i: T is an open leader, T is a closed leader, T is a follower, and T is merging. If T is an open leader, our claim holds. If T is a closed leader, in $\mathcal{O}(\log N)$ rounds T will either begin a merge (becoming a potential leader) or select the new role of leader with probability $1/2$. If T is a follower, T is a short follower with probability $1/2$, and after $4(\log N + 1) + 4$ rounds T will select a new role of leader with probability $1/2$, or begin a merge (becoming a potential leader). If T is currently merging, then every node will be a potential leader for at least one round during the merging process, which will complete in $\mathcal{O}(\log n)$ rounds.

Lemma 4. *Consider a cluster T in configuration G_i. With probability at least $1/16$, T is assigned a merge partner at least once over $\mathcal{O}(\log N)$ rounds.*

Proof sketch: This proof combines the previous lemma with the fact that a cluster has probability $1/4$ of being a long follower, which will ensure the cluster searches sufficiently long to detect at least one potential leader in a neighboring cluster.

4.4 Merging

After being matched, two clusters can merge. Our merging algorithm adds edges in a systematic fashion to ensure there is enough "bandwidth" for two clusters to merge quickly, yet still limits degree increases. Our merging algorithm can be discussed from two points of view: one which considers two N-node clusters in the guest network merging into a single N-node cluster, and another which considers two clusters in the host network systematically updating their cluster successors and predecessors. Below, we present a discussion from both viewpoints for clarity. Note these are simply different ways of thinking about the same algorithm.

From the point of view of the guest network, merging can be thought of as (i) connecting guest nodes with identical identifiers from the two clusters, beginning with the roots, (ii) determining which of these guest nodes will remain in the new network (using the ranges of their hosts), and (iii) transferring the links from the "deleted" node to the "winning" node (the node remaining in the single merged N-node cluster). The remaining node can then connect its children with the received children from the former root, and these nodes then repeat the "merge" process. This proceeds level-by-level until only a single N-node cluster remains.

From the point of view of the host network, the merge involves (i) connecting the two hosts of two guest nodes with the same identifiers (beginning with the hosts of the root), and then (ii) updating the cluster ranges of these hosts, transferring any links from the "lost range" of one host node to another. Note that initially the hosts of the roots are connected and the cluster ranges of these two hosts overlap. Given the presence of the other host, each host will update their cluster successor or predecessor (if needed), and the host whose cluster range was reduced will transfer any outgoing intra-cluster links to its new successor/predecessor, effectively allowing one host to "take over" the cluster range of another. This change in the cluster range corresponds to the "deleting" of a guest node discussed above. The hosts from the next level in the tree are then connected and the process repeats recursively until all cluster successors, predecessors, and (by implication) Type 2 edges are updated and a new cluster is formed. The merge algorithm is sketched in Algorithm 2.

Algorithm Sketch 2. The Merging Algorithm for Cluster T

    // *Cluster T has been assigned merge partner T'*

1.   Root r_T notifies all nodes of merge partner T' and
            its view of the random sequence Ψ_r

2.   Edges between T and T' are removed if $\Psi_r = \Psi$

3.   Beginning with the roots r_T and $r_{T'}$:

4.   Node r_T updates its range based upon the identifier of $r_{T'}$ (if needed)

5.   Node r_T sends any edges not in its new range to $r_{T'}$,
            and receives edges from $r_{T'}$

6.   Children of r_T and r'_T are connected, and process repeats concurrently

7.   Once process reaches leaves, pass feedback wave to new root

8.   New root $r_{T''}$ sends PFC wave to update nodes in T'' of new cluster identifier.

Note every merge begins with a pre-processing stage which removes all links between merge partners T and T' other than the edge between the roots of

T and T'. To prevent the network from being partitioned, no edge is deleted unless both incident nodes receive from their respective cluster roots a message matching the shared random sequence Ψ. As this sequence is unknown to the adversary, network partitions are prevented with high probability.

Analysis of Merge

Lemma 5. *Consider two clusters T and T' such that T and T' are merge partners. In $\mathcal{O}(\log N)$ rounds, T and T' have formed a single cluster T'' consisting of all nodes in $T \cup T'$.*

Proof sketch: The proof follows from the fact that the merge process requires $\mathcal{O}(\log N)$ rounds of pre-processing, and then resolves at least one level of the guest network in a constant number of rounds. Since there are $\log N + 1$ levels, our lemma holds.

Lemma 6. *The degree of a node $u \in T$ will increase by $\mathcal{O}(\log^2 N)$ during a merge, and will return to within $\mathcal{O}(\log N)$ of its initial degree when the merge is complete.*

Proof sketch: This proof follows from Theorem 2. For any set of nodes T forming AVATAR$_{\text{CBT}}$ (including a cluster), a node $u \in T$ has at most $\mathcal{O}(\log N)$ edges amongst nodes in T. As merging involves transferring the $\mathcal{O}(\log N)$ edges from a contiguous portion of $range(u)$ to some node v at most once per level in the guest network, no node will "take over" more than $\mathcal{O}(\log^2 N)$ edges during a merge. Once the merge is completed, any node in the new cluster T'' has at most $\mathcal{O}(\log N)$ edges in T'', again by Theorem 2.

4.5 Termination Detection

Note the root of a cluster repeatedly executes the matching algorithm. For silent stabilization, the root must know when a legal configuration has been reached so it can cease the matching algorithm. For this, we add a "faulty bit" to the feedback wave sent after a merge has completed. If a node (i) detects the configuration is faulty, or (ii) received a faulty bit of 1 from at least one child, the node sets its faulty bit to 1 and appends this to the feedback message sent to the node's parent. If the root receives a feedback wave without the faulty bit set (i.e. a value of 0), it stops executing the algorithm. If a node u completes this wave with its faulty bit set to 0 and it either (i) detects a faulty configuration, or (ii) detects a neighbor with a faulty bit not equal to 0, u will detect a reset fault. This ensures our algorithm is silent and stabilizing.

Lemma 7. *When our algorithm builds a legal AVATAR$_{\text{CBT}}$ network, the faulty bit will be set to 0, and remain 0 until a transient fault again perturbs the system.*

Proof sketch: Since AVATAR$_{\text{CBT}}$ is locally checkable, a faulty configuration has at least one detector which will set its faulty bit to 1. By similar argument to Lemma 1, in $\mathcal{O}(\log N)$ rounds, all nodes will have their faulty bit set to 1 and begin executing our algorithm. Once the last merge occurs, no node will detect a fault, and all faulty bits will remain 0 until another fault occurs.

4.6 Combined Analysis

Theorem 3. *The algorithm in Section 4 is a self-stabilizing algorithm for the* AVATAR$_{\mathrm{CBT}}$ *network with expected convergence time of* $\mathcal{O}(\log^2 N)$.

Proof sketch: All nodes are members of a cluster in $\mathcal{O}(\log N)$ rounds, at which point the number of clusters will only decrease. Each time a merge occurs, the number of clusters is reduced by 1, and the probability that a cluster merges over a span of $\mathcal{O}(\log N)$ rounds is constant (1/16). In expectation, then, every cluster has merged in $\mathcal{O}(\log N)$ rounds, halving the number of clusters. After $\mathcal{O}(\log^2 N)$ rounds, we are left with a single cluster, which is the legal configuration.

Theorem 4. *The degree expansion of the self-stabilizing* AVATAR$_{\mathrm{CBT}}$ *algorithm from Section 4 is* $\mathcal{O}(\log^2 N)$ *in expectation.*

Proof sketch: A node's degree will increase under only a small number of circumstances. A node will only have $\mathcal{O}(\log N)$ edges to nodes in its cluster (except during merges). During a merge, the degree can increase to at most $\mathcal{O}(\log^2 N)$ (Lemma 6). Each time a cluster selects the leader role, a node in the cluster may have its degree increase by 1. As the algorithm will terminate in $\mathcal{O}(\log^2 N)$ rounds in expectation, there are an expected $\mathcal{O}(\log N)$ such increases. Finally, consider an invalid initial configuration which causes a node u to receive many edges while not in a cluster or merging with another cluster. The only way for a node u to receive additional edges in a round and not execute a reset action is for only a single node to add edges to u. Since no node will send more than $\mathcal{O}(\log N)$ edges in a single round, and u will be in a cluster in $\mathcal{O}(\log N)$ rounds, the degree expansion of our algorithm is $\mathcal{O}(\log^2 N)$.

5 Discussion and Future Work

As it is based on a binary tree, AVATAR$_{\mathrm{CBT}}$ has poor load balancing properties. However, it can be useful as an intermediate step in creating other topologies using a mechanism we call *network scaffolding*. In this approach, AVATAR$_{\mathrm{CBT}}$ is used as an intermediate topology from which another network is built (much like a scaffold is used for construction). Our technique has already been successful in building a self-stabilizing CHORD network with polylogarithmic convergence time and degree expansion [2].

To build on this work, we would like to remove the requirement that all nodes know N, perhaps using a self-stabilizing protocol. We also are examining how much state nodes must continuously exchange to guarantee local checkability with *mutable* state, unlike immutable proof labels [12]. Reducing this exchanged state can reduce the maintenance for correct configurations. We are also investigating bounds for the degree expansion to determine how efficient this algorithm is in this self-stabilizing overlay network setting.

Acknowledgments: I would like to thank my advisors, Dr. Sriram V. Pemmaraju and Dr. Sukumar Ghosh, for their guidance and discussions on this paper.

References

1. Aspnes, J., Shah, G.: Skip graphs. In: SODA 2003: Proceedings of the Fourteenth Annual ACM-SIAM Symposium on Discrete Algorithms, pp. 384–393. Society for Industrial and Applied Mathematics, Philadelphia (2003)
2. Berns, A.: Self-Stabilizing Overlay Networks. Ph.D. thesis, University of Iowa (December 2012)
3. Berns, A.: Avatar: A Time- and Space-Efficient Self-Stabilizing Overlay Network (2015). 1506.0168
4. Berns, A., Ghosh, S., Pemmaraju, S.V.: Building self-stabilizing overlay networks with the transitive closure framework. Theor. Comput. Sci. **512**, 2–14 (2013). http://dx.doi.org/10.1016/j.tcs.2013.02.021
5. Bui, A., Datta, A.K., Petit, F., Villain, V.: State-optimal snap-stabilizing pif in tree networks. In: Workshop on Self-stabilizing Systems, ICDCS 1999, pp. 78–85. IEEE Computer Society, Washington, DC (1999). http://dl.acm.org/citation.cfm?id=647271.721996
6. Dijkstra, E.W.: Self-stabilizing systems in spite of distributed control. Commun. ACM **17**(11), 643–644 (1974)
7. Dolev, S.: Self-stabilization. MIT Press, Cambridge (2000)
8. Gallager, R.G., Humblet, P.A., Spira, P.M.: A distributed algorithm for minimum-weight spanning trees. ACM Trans. Program. Lang. Syst. **5**(1), 66–77 (1983). http://doi.acm.org/10.1145/357195.357200
9. Hayes, T., Saia, J., Trehan, A.: The forgiving graph: a distributed data structure for low stretch under adversarial attack. Distributed Computing **25**(4), 261–278 (2012). http://dx.doi.org/10.1007/s00446-012-0160-1
10. Jacob, R., Richa, A., Scheideler, C., Schmid, S., Täubig, H.: A distributed poly-logarithmic time algorithm for self-stabilizing skip graphs. In: PODC 2009: Proceedings of the 28th ACM Symposium on Principles of Distributed Computing, pp. 131–140. ACM, New York (2009)
11. Kniesburges, S., Koutsopoulos, A., Scheideler, C.: Re-chord: a self-stabilizing chord overlay network. In: Proceedings of the 23rd ACM Symposium on Parallelism in Algorithms and Architectures, SPAA 2011, pp. 235–244. ACM, New York (2011). http://doi.acm.org/10.1145/1989493.1989527
12. Korman, A., Kutten, S., Peleg, D.: Proof labeling schemes. In: Proceedings of the Twenty-fourth Annual ACM Symposium on Principles of Distributed Computing, PODC 2005, pp. 9–18. ACM, New York (2005). http://doi.acm.org/10.1145/1073814.1073817
13. Leighton, F.T.: Introduction to parallel algorithms and architectures: array, trees, hypercubes. Morgan Kaufmann Publishers Inc., San Francisco (1992)
14. Onus, M., Richa, A.W., Scheideler, C.: Linearization: Locally self-stabilizing sorting in graphs. In: ALENEX. SIAM (2007)
15. Stoica, I., Morris, R., Karger, D., Kaashoek, M.F., Balakrishnan, H.: Chord: A scalable peer-to-peer lookup service for internet applications. SIGCOMM Comput. Commun. Rev. **31**(4), 149–160 (2001)

Self-stabilizing Virtual Synchrony

Shlomi Dolev[1], Chryssis Georgiou[2],
Ioannis Marcoullis[2(✉)], and Elad M. Schiller[3]

[1] Department of Computer Science, Ben-Gurion University of the Negev,
Beersheba, Israel
dolev@cs.bgu.ac.il
[2] Department of Computer Science, University of Cyprus, Nicosia, Cyprus
{chryssis,imarco01}@cs.ucy.ac.cy
[3] Department of Engineering and Computer Science,
Chalmers University of Technology, Gothenburg, Sweden
elad@chalmers.se

Abstract. Virtual synchrony (VS) is an important abstraction that is
proven to be extremely useful when implemented over asynchronous, typically large, message-passing distributed systems. Fault tolerant design
is critical for the success of such implementations since large distributed
systems can be highly available as long as they do not depend on the
full operational status of every system participant. Self-stabilizing systems can tolerate transient faults that drive the system to an arbitrary
unpredictable configuration. Such systems automatically regain consistency from any such configuration, and then produce the desired system
behavior ensuring it for practically infinite number of successive steps,
e.g., 2^{64} steps.

We present a new multi-purpose self-stabilizing counter algorithm
establishing an efficient practically unbounded counter, that can directly
yield a self-stabilizing Multiple-Writer Multiple-Reader (MWMR) register emulation. We use our counter algorithm, together with a self-
stabilizing group membership and a self-stabilizing multicast service to
devise the *first* practically stabilizing VS algorithm and a self-stabilizing
VS-based emulation of state machine replication (SMR). As we base the
SMR implementation on VS, rather than consensus, the system progresses in more extreme asynchronous settings in relation to consensus-
based SMR.

1 Introduction

Virtual Synchrony (VS) has been proven to be very important in the scope of
fault-tolerant distributed systems [4]. The VS property ensures that two or more
processors that participate in two consecutive communicating groups should
have delivered the same messages. Systems that support the VS abstraction
are designed to operate in the presence of fail-stop failures of a minority of the

The work of the first author is partially supported by the Rita Altura Trust Chair
in Computer Sciences, and the Israel Science Foundation (grant 428/11). The work
of the second and third authors is supported by the University of Cyprus.

© Springer International Publishing Switzerland 2015
A. Pelc and A.A. Schwarzmann (Eds.): SSS 2015, LNCS 9212, pp. 248–264, 2015.
DOI: 10.1007/978-3-319-21741-3_17

participants. Such a design fits large computer clusters, data-centers and cloud computing, where at any given time some of the processing units are nonoperational. Systems that cannot tolerate such failures degrade their functionality and availability to the degree of unuseful systems.

Group communication systems that realize the VS abstraction provide services, such as *group membership* and *reliable group multicast*. The group membership service is responsible for providing the current *group view* of the recently live and connected group members, i.e., a processor set and a unique *view identifier*, which is a sequence number of the view installation. The reliable group multicast allows the service clients to exchange messages with the group members as if it was a single communication endpoint with a single network address and to which messages are delivered in an atomic fashion, thus any message is either delivered to all recently live and connected group members prior to the next message, or is not delivered to any member. The challenges related to VS consist of the need to maintain atomic message delivery in the presence of asynchrony and crash failures. VS facilitates the implementation of a replicated state machine [4] that is more efficient than classical consensus-based implementations that start every multicast round with an agreement on the set of recently live and connected processors. It is also usually easier to implement [4]. To the best of our knowledge, no *self-stabilizing virtual synchrony* solution exists.

Transient violations of design assumptions can lead a system to an arbitrary state. For example, the assumption that error detection ensures the arrival of correct messages and the discarding of corrupted messages, might be violated since error detection is a probabilistic mechanism that may not detect a corrupt message. As a result, the message can be regarded as legitimate, driving the system to an arbitrary state after which, availability and functionality may be damaged forever, requiring human intervention. In the presence of transient faults, large multicomputer systems providing VS-based services, can prove hard to manage and control. One key problem, not restricted to virtually synchronous systems, is catering for counters (such as view identifiers) reaching an arbitrary value. How can we deal with the fact that transient faults may force counters to wrap around to the zero value and violate important system assumptions and correctness invariants, such as ordering of events? A self-stabilizing algorithm [7] can automatically recover from such unexpected failures, possibly as part of after-disaster recovery or even after benign temporal violation of the assumptions made in the design of the system. We tackle this issue in our work.

Contributions. We present the first self-stabilizing virtual synchrony solution. Specifically, we provide a self-stabilizing counter algorithm using bounded memory and communication bandwidth, and yet (many writers) can increment the counter for an unbounded number of times in the presence of processor crashes and unbounded communication delays. Our counter algorithm is modular with a simple interface for increasing and reading the counter, as well as providing the identifier of the processor that has incremented it. At the heart of our counter algorithm is the underlying labeling algorithm which extends the label scheme of Alon et al. [1] to support multiple writers, whilst the algorithm specifies how the processors exchange their label information in the asynchronous system and how they maintain proper label bookkeeping so as to "discover" the greatest label and discard all obsolete ones. An immediate application of our counter algorithm is a self-stabilizing MWMR register emulation. Our self-stabilizing counter, using the self-stabilizing reliable multicast and membership services yields our self-stabilizing VS solution, which leads to a self-stabilizing VS-based State Machine Replication (SMR) implementation. A full version of this paper can be found in [11].

Related Work. Lamport was the first to introduce SMR, presenting it as an example in [12]. Schneider [14] gave a more generalized approach to the design and implementation of SMR protocols. Group communication services can implement SMR by providing reliable multicast that guarantees VS [3]. Birman et al. were the first to present VS and a series of improvements in the efficiency of ordering protocols [5]. Birman gives a concise account of the evolution of the VS model for SMR in [4].

Research during the last recent decades resulted in an extensive literature on ways to implement VS and SMR, as well as industrial construction of such systems. A recent research line on (practically) self-stabilizing versions of replicated state machines [1,6,9,10] obtains self-stabilizing replicated state machines in shared memory as well as synchronized and asynchronous message passing systems.

The bounded labeling scheme and the use of practically unbounded sequence numbers proposed in [1], allow the creation of self-stabilizing bounded-size solutions to the never-exhausted counter problem in the restricted case of a single writer. In [6] a self-stabilizing version of Paxos was developed that led to a self-stabilizing consensus-based SMR implementation. To this end, a labeling scheme extending the one of [1] to allow multiple writers. Extracting this scheme for other uses does not seem intuitive. We present a simpler and significantly more communication efficient self-stabilizing (bounded-size never-exhausted) counter that also supports many writers, where a single label rather than a vector of labels needs to be communicated. Our solution is *highly modular* and can be easily used in any similar setting requiring such counters.

Practically-stabilizing VS and self-stabilizing VS are identical when VS is defined by the behaviour of classical VS algorithms that use (bounded) counters. These algorithms preserve the VS requirements as long as the counters do not reach their upper bound. In our setting, if a counter reaches the upper bound due to a transient fault our self-stabilizing/practically-stabilizing solution introduces a new epoch with new sequence numbers. It, thus, converges to act exactly as the non-stabilizing VS (for the same number of steps) as an initialized non-stabilizing VS algorithm.

2   System Settings

We consider an asynchronous message passing system that includes a set P of n communicating processors; we refer to the processor with identifier i, as p_i. We assume that up to a minority of processors may become inactive. The system runs on top of a stabilizing data-link layer that provides reliable FIFO communication over unreliable bounded capacity channels [8] and reference therein. The network topology is of a fully connected graph where every two processors exchange (low-level messages called) *packets* to enable a reliable delivery of (high level) *messages*. When no confusion is possible we use the term messages for packets.

The communication links have bounded capacity, thus the number of packets in every given instance is bounded by a constant. When processor p_i sends a packet, π, to processor p_j, the operation *send* inserts a copy of π into the FIFO queue representing the communication channel from p_i to p_j, while respecting the capacity of the channel, possibly omitting the new packet or one of the already sent packets. Packets are retransmitted until more than the total capacity acknowledgments arrive. Acknowledgments are sent only when a packet arrives (not spontaneously). When p_j receives π from p_i, π is dequeued. We assume that packets can be spontaneously omitted (lost) from the channel, however, a packet that is sent infinitely often is received infinitely often.

Over this data-link, the two connected processors can constantly exchange a "token". Specifically, the sender (possibly the processor with the highest identifier among the two) constantly sends packet π_1 until it receives enough acknowledgments (more than the capacity). Then, it constantly sends packet π_2, and so on and so forth. This assures that the receiver has received packet π_1 before the sender starts sending packet π_2. This can be viewed as a token exchange. We use the abstraction of the token carrying messages back and forth between any two communication entities and use it to implement a reliable multicast procedure, and a failure detector in Section 4.

The code of self-stabilizing algorithms usually consists of a do forever loop that contains communication operations with the neighbors and validation that the system is in a consistent state as part of the transition decision. An *iteration* of the algorithm starts in the loop's first line and ends at the last (regardless of whether it enters branches).

Every processor p_i executes a program that is a sequence of *(atomic) steps*, where a step starts with local computations and ends with a single communication operation, which is either *send* or *receive* of a packet. For ease of description, we assume the interleaving model, where steps are executed atomically, a single step at any given time. An input event can be either the receipt of a packet or a periodic timer triggering p_i to (re)send. Note that the system is asynchronous thus rate of the timer is totally unknown.

A *(system) configuration* is a tuple of the form $(s_1, s_2, \cdots, s_n)$, where s_i is the state of p_i (including the values of all the variables and all messages in transit to p_i). Each algorithm step can change the processor's state. An *execution (or run)* $R = c_0, a_0, c_1, a_1, \ldots$ is an alternating sequence of system configurations c_x and steps a_x, such that each configuration c_{x+1}, except the initial configuration c_0, is obtained from the preceding configuration c_x by the execution of the step a_x. A *practically infinite execution* [6] is an execution with many steps (and iterations), where "many" is defined to be proportional to the time it takes to execute a step and the life-span time of a system.

We define the system's task by a set of executions called *legal executions* (*LE*) in which the task's requirements hold, we use the term *safe configuration* for any configuration in *LE*. An algorithm is *self-stabilizing* with relation to the task *LE* when every (unbounded) execution of the algorithm reaches a safe configuration with relation to the algorithm and the task. An algorithm is *practically stabilizing* with relation to the task *LE* if in any practically infinite execution a safe configuration is reached.

The *VS property* requires that any two processors sharing the same sequence of views, ought to *deliver* identical message sets in these views. A legal execution of VS is defined in terms of input/output sequences of the system with the environment. When a majority of processors are continuously active, every external input (and only the external inputs) should be atomically accepted and processed by this majority. Note that in executions lacking a majority, there is no delivery and processing guarantee, but still any delivery and processing is due to a received environment input.

3   Self-stabilizing Labeling Scheme and Counter Increment

In this section we first present the self-stabilizing labeling algorithm for multiple writers and extend this result to obtain self-stabilizing practically unbounded counters.

3.1   Labeling Algorithm for Concurrent Label Creations

Bounded Labeling Scheme. We build on the labeling scheme of Alon et al. [1] to support wait-free multi-writer systems. The *labels* (also called *epochs*) allow the system to stabilize, since once a label is established, the integer counter related to this label is considered to be practically infinite. We extend the label structure of [1] by including the epoch creator's (writer's) identity to break symmetry, to determine the most recent epoch, even when two or more creators concurrently create a new label.

Specifically, we consider the set of integers $D = [1, k^2 + 1]$. A *label* (or *epoch*) is a triple $\langle lCreator, sting, Antistings \rangle$, where $lCreator$ is the identity of the processor that established (created) the label, $Antistings \subset D$ with $|Antistings| = k$, and $sting \in D$. Given two labels ℓ_i, ℓ_j, we define the relation $\ell_i \prec_{lb} \ell_j \equiv (\ell_i.lCreator < \ell_j.lCreator) \vee (\ell_i.lCreator = \ell_j.lCreator \wedge ((\ell_i.sting \in \ell_j.Antistings) \wedge (\ell_j.sting \notin \ell_i.Antistings)))$; we use $=_{lb}$ for label identity. Note that $\prec_{lb}$ does not define a total order. For example, when $\ell_i.lCreator = \ell_j.lCreator$ and $(\ell_i.sting \notin \ell_j.Antistings)$ and $(\ell_j.sting \notin \ell_i.Antisting)$ these labels are *incomparable*. We say that a label ℓ **cancels** another label ℓ', if either they are incomparable or they have the same $lCreator$ but ℓ is greater than ℓ' (with respect to $sting$ and $Antistings$).

Function $nextLabel()$ (Algorithm 1) accepts a set of labels as input and returns a new label, greater than all of the input labels. It has the same functionality as the function $Next_b()$ of [1], but it additionally considers the label creator. It builds a new $Antistings$ set from the stings of all the labels it has as

Algorithm 1. The *nextLabel*() function; code for p_i

1 For any non-empty set $X \subseteq D$, function $pick(d, X)$ returns d arbitrary elements of X;
   input   : $S = \langle \ell_1, \ell_2 \ldots, \ell_k \rangle$ set of k labels.
   output   : $\langle i, newSting, newAntistings \rangle$
2 **let** $newAntistings = \{\ell_j.sting : \ell_j \in S\}$;
3 $newAntistings \leftarrow newAntistings \cup pick(k - |newAntistings|, D \setminus newAntistings)$;
4 **return** $\langle i, pick(1, D \setminus (newAntistings \cup \{\cup_{\ell_j \in S} \ell_j.Antistings\})), newAntistings \rangle$;

input, and chooses a *sting* that is in none of the *Antistings* of the input labels. In this way it ensures that the new label is greater than any of the input. Note that the function takes k *Antistings* of k labels, implying at most k^2 integers, thus the choice of $|D| = k^2 + 1$ ensures the existence of an integer to be used as the *sting*, which is not part of *Antistings* of the input labels.

Each processor p_i is required to "clean up" the system from obsolete labels of which p_i appears to be the creator (for example, such labels could be present in the system's initial arbitrary state). To achieve this, p_i maintains a bounded FIFO history of such labels that it has recently learned while communicating with the other processors, and creates a greater label by passing the labels in its queue to *nextLabel*(); call this new label p_i's *local maximal label*. Performing the above tasks is aimed at having each processor learn the *globally maximal label*, that is, the label in the system that is the greatest among the local maximal ones and *adopt* it. Unfortunately, when some processors are not active, finding a global maximal becomes challenging, since these processors will not "clean up" their local labels. Active processors have to do this indirectly without knowing which processors are inactive. Note that this is not a concern in [1], since the sole writer is responsible of "cleaning" obsolete labels as long as it is active; once the single writer becomes inactive nothing can be done with respect to new label creation.

Let us explain why obsolete labels from inactive processors are problematic when they are not cleaned (canceled). Consider a system starting in a state that includes a cycle of labels $\ell_1 \prec_{lb} \ell_2 \prec_{lb} \ell_3 \prec_{lb} \ell_1$, all of the same creator, say p_x. If p_x is active, it eventually learns about these labels and creates a label greater than them all. But if p_x is inactive, the system's asynchronous nature may cause a repeated cyclic label adoption, especially when p_x has the greatest processor identifier, since the identifier is used to break symmetry. Say that an active processor learns and adopts ℓ_1 as its global maximal label. Then, it learns about ℓ_2 and hence adopts it, while forgetting about ℓ_1. Then, learning of ℓ_3 it adopts it. Lastly, it learns about ℓ_1, and as it is greater than ℓ_3, it adopts ℓ_1 once more, as the greatest in the system; this can continue indefinitely.

As a solution, each processor maintains a bounded queue for each other processor, where a label with $lCreator = j$, is stored in the queue corresponding to processor p_j. Obsolete labels eventually accumulate in these bounded FIFO queues and are never again adopted, ending cyclic adoptions. We show that given a majority of active processors and any initial state, the system eventually converges to a global maximal label.

The Labeling Algorithm. The algorithm specifies how the processors exchange their label information in the asynchronous system and how they maintain proper label bookkeeping so as to "discover" their greatest label and cancel all obsolete ones. As we will be using pairs of labels with the *same* label creator, for the ease of presentation, we will be referring to these two variables as the *(label) pair.* The first label in a pair is called *ml*. The second label is called *cl* and it is either $\perp$, or equal to a label that cancels *ml* (i.e., *cl* indicates whether *ml* is an obsolete label or not).

The Processor's State: Each processor stores an array of label pairs, $max_i[]$, where $max_i[i]$ refers to p_i's maximal label pair and $max_i[j]$ is the most recent label that p_i knows about p_j's pair. Processor p_i also stores the pairs of the most-recently-used labels in the array of queues $storedLabels_i[]$. The j-th entry refers to the queue with pairs from p_j's domain, i.e., created by p_j. The algorithm makes sure that $storedLabels_i[j]$ includes only label pairs with unique *ml* from p_j's domain and that at most one of them is *legitimate*, i.e., not canceled.

Information Exchange Between Processors: Processor p_i takes a step whenever it receives two pairs $\langle sentMax, lastSent \rangle$ from some other processor, say p_j. We note that in a legal execution p_j's pair includes both $sentMax$, which refers to p_j's maximal label pair $max_j[j]$, and $lastSent$, which refers to a recent label pair that p_j received from p_i about p_i's maximal label, $max_j[i]$ (line 16).

Whenever p_i receives a pair $\langle sentMax, lastSent \rangle$ from p_j, p_i stores the arriving $sentMax$ in $max_i[j]$ (line 19). Note that in a legal execution the arriving $sentMax$ is always legitimate. However, when p_j acknowledges p_i's label, it is possible that p_j needs to inform p_i of a label from p_i's domain that cancels p_i's maximal label, *ml* in $max_i[i]$. It does so by sending to p_i a label that cancels *ml* and thus it would be the case, $lastSent$ will have a $lastSent.cl$, that is not $\perp$. Specifically, it contains a label that p_j knows such that $lastSent.cl \not\preceq_{lb} lastSent.ml$, i.e., $lastSent.cl$ is either greater or incomparable to $lastSent.ml$. In case this $lastSent.ml$ still refers to p_i's maximal label, p_i must cancel $max_i[i]$ by assigning it with $lastSent$ (and thus $max_i[i].cl = lastSent.cl$) as in line 20. Lines 21 to 28 show how p_i processes the two pairs received.

Label Processing: Having received a new pair message $\langle sentMax, lastSent \rangle$ from some p_j, processor p_i starts a step by removing *stale* information, i.e., misplaced or doubly represented labels (line 9) in the label storage. When stale information exists, the algorithm empties the entire storage. Processor p_i then tests whether the arriving two pairs are already included in the label storage ($storedLabels[]$), otherwise it includes them (line 22). Based on the new pairs added to the label store, the algorithm determines whether it is possible to cancel a non-canceled label pair (which may well be a newly added pair). In this case, the algorithm updates the canceling field of any label pair lp (line 23) with the canceling label of a label pair lp' such that $lp'.ml \not\preceq_{lb} lp.ml$ (line 23). It is implied that since the two pairs belong to the same storage queue, they have the same creator identity. Line 24 checks whether any pair of the $max_i[]$ array can cancel a record in the label storage, and line 25 removes any canceled

---

Algorithm 2. Self-Stabilizing Labeling Algorithm; code for p_i

---

1 **Variables:**
2 $max[n]$ of $\langle ml, cl \rangle$: $max[i]$ is p_i's largest label pair, $max[j]$ refers to p_j's label pair (canceled when $max[j].cl \neq \perp$).
3 $storedLabels[n]$: an array of queues of the most-recently-used label pairs, where $storedLabels[j]$ holds the labels created by $p_j \in P$. For $p_j \in (P \setminus \{p_i\})$, $storedLabels[j]$'s queue size is limited to $(n+m)$ w.r.t. label pairs, where $n = |P|$ is the number of processors in the system and m is the maximum number of label pairs that can be in transit in the system. The $storedLabels[i]$'s queue size is limited to $(n(n^2 + m))$ pairs. The operator $add(\ell)$ adds lp to the front of the queue, and $emptyAllQueues()$ clears all $storedLabels[]$ queues. We use $lp.remove()$ for removing the record $lp \in storedLabels[]$. Note that an element is brought to the queue front every time this element is accessed in the queue.
4 **Notation:** Let y and y' be two records that include the field x. We denote $y =_x y' \equiv (y.x = y'.x)$
5 **Macros:**
6 $legit(lp) = (lp = \langle \bullet, \perp \rangle)$
7 $labels(lp) :$ **return** $(storedLabels[lp.ml.lCreator])$
8 $double(j, lp) = (\exists lp' \in storedLabels[j] : ((lp \neq lp') \wedge ((lp =_{ml} lp') \vee (legit(lp) \wedge legit(lp')))))$
9 $staleInfo() = (\exists p_j \in P, lp \in storedLabels[j] : (lp \neq_{lCreator} j) \vee double(j, lp))$
10 $recordDoesntExist(j) = (\langle max[j].ml, \bullet \rangle \notin labels(max[j]))$
11 $notgeq(j, lp) = $ **if** $(\exists lp' \in storedLabels[j] : (lp'.ml \npreceq_{lb} lp.ml))$ **then return**$(lp'.ml)$ **else return**$(\perp)$
12 $canceled(lp) = $ **if** $(\exists lp' \in labels(lp) : ((lp' =_{ml} lp) \wedge \neg legit(lp')))$ **then return**(lp') **else return**$(\perp)$
13 $needsUpdate(j) = (\neg legit(max[j]) \wedge \langle max[j].ml, \perp \rangle \in labels(max[j]))$
14 $legitLabels() = \{max[j].ml : \exists p_j \in P \wedge legit(max[j])\}$
15 $useOwnLabel() = $ **if** $(\exists lp \in storedLabels[i] : legit(lp))$ **then** $max[i] \leftarrow lp$ **else** $storedLabels[i].add(max[i] \leftarrow \langle nextLabel(), \perp \rangle)$ // For every $lp \in storedLabels[i]$, we pass in $nextLabel()$ both $lp.ml$ and $lp.cl$.
16 **upon** $transmitReady(p_j \in P \setminus \{p_i\})$ **do transmit**$(\langle max[i], max[j] \rangle)$
17 **upon** $receive(\langle sentMax, lastSent \rangle)$ **from** p_j
18 **begin**
19      $max[j] \leftarrow sentMax;$
20   **if** $\neg legit(lastSent) \wedge max[i] =_{ml} lastSent$ **then** $max[i] \leftarrow lastSent;$
21   **if** $staleInfo()$ **then** $storedLabels.emptyAllQueues();$
22   **foreach** $p_j \in P : recordDoesntExist(j)$ **do** $labels(max[j]).add(max[j]);$
23   **foreach** $p_j \in P, lp \in storedLabels[j] : (legit(lp) \wedge (notgeq(j, lp) \neq \perp))$ **do** $lp.cl \leftarrow notgeq(j, lp);$
24   **foreach** $p_j \in P, lp \in labels(max[j]) : (\neg legit(max[j]) \wedge (max[j] =_{ml} lp) \wedge legit(lp))$ **do** $lp \leftarrow max[j];$
25   **foreach** $p_j \in P, lp \in storedLabels[j] : double(j, lp)$ **do** $lp.remove();$
26   **foreach** $p_j \in P : (legit(max[j]) \wedge (canceled(max[j]) \neq \perp))$ **do** $max[j] \leftarrow canceled(max[j]);$
27   **if** $legitLabels() \neq \emptyset$ **then** $max[i] \leftarrow \langle \max_{\preceq_{lb}}(legitLabels()), \perp \rangle;$
28   **else** $useOwnLabel();$

---

records that share the same ml. The test also considers the case in which the above update may cancel any arriving label in $max[j]$ and updates this entry accordingly based on stored pairs (line 26).

After this series of tests and updates, the algorithm is ready to decide upon a maximal label based on its local information. This is the $\preceq_{lb}$-greatest legit label pair among all the ones in $max_i[]$ (line 26). When no such legit label exists, p_i request a legit label in its own label storage, $storedLabels_i[i]$, and if one does not exist, will create a new one if needed (line 28). This is done by passing the labels in the $storedLabel_i[i]$ queue to the $nextLabel()$ function. Note that the returned label is coupled with a $\perp$ and the resulting label pair is added to both $max_i[i]$ and $storedLabel_i[i]$.

Correctness Proof Outline. Consider an execution R of Algorithm 2 that may start in an arbitrary configuration. We first show some basic facts, such as: (1) stale information is removed, i.e., $storedLabels_i[j]$ includes only unique copies of p_j's labels, and at most one legitimate and (2) p_i either adopts or creates the $\preceq_{lb}$-greatest legitimate local label. We then bound on the number of adoptions, first in the absence of label creations and then in their presence.

Lemma 1. *Let $p_i, p_j \in P$, be two processors. Suppose that p_j has stopped adding labels to the system configuration (the else part of line 28), and sending (line 16) these labels during R. Processor p_i adopts (line 27) at most $(n + m)$ label pairs, $lp_j : (lp_j =_{lCreator} j)$, from p_j's unknown domain ($lp_j \notin labels_i(lp_j)$), where m is the maximum number of label pairs that can be in transit in the system.*

Lemma 2. *Let $p_i \in P$ be a processor. Let $L_i = lp_{i_0}, lp_{i_1}, \ldots$ be the sequence of legitimate label pairs (i.e., $lp_{i_k}.cl = \bot$), $\ell_{i_k} =_{lCreator} i$, from p_i's domain, which p_i stores in $max_i[i]$ over time, where $k \in \mathcal{N}$. It holds that $|L_i| \leq n(n^2 + m)$.*

Active processors can now be shown to eventually stop adopting or creating labels. We show that incomparable label pairs eventually disappear from the system and thus no new labels are adopted or created, which then implies the existence of a global maximal label. Combining all the above, we deduce that starting from any initial configuration, the system eventually reaches a configuration in which there is a global maximal label.

Theorem 1. *Suppose that there exists at least one processor, $p_u \in P$ with unknown identity, that takes practically infinite number of steps in R. Within a bounded number of steps, there is a legitimate label pair $\ell_{\max}$, such that for any processor $p_i \in P$ (that takes a practically infinite number of steps in R), it holds that p_i has that label pair $max_i[i] = \ell_{\max}$ when naming its (local) maximal label, $max_i[i].ml$. Moreover, for any processor $p_j \in P$ (that takes a practically infinite number of steps in R), it holds that $((max_i[j] \preceq_{lb} \ell_{\max}) \wedge ((\forall \ell \in storedLabels_i[j] : legit(\ell)) \Rightarrow (\ell \preceq_{lb} \ell_{\max})))$.*

Proof Sketch. For any processor in the system which may take any (bounded or practically infinite) number of steps in R, we know that there is a bounded number of label pairs, $L_i = lp_{i_0}, lp_{i_1}, \ldots$, that processor $p_i \in P$ adds to the system configuration (the else part of line 28), where $lp_{i_k} =_{lCreator} i$ (Lemma 2). Thus, by the pigeonhole principle, we know that within a bounded number of steps in R, there is a period during which p_u takes a practically infinite number of steps in R whilst (all processors) p_i do not add any label pair, $lp_{i_k} =_{lCreator} i$, to the system configuration (the else part of line 28). During this period, we know that for any processor $p_j \in P$ that takes any number of (bounded or practically infinite) steps in R, and processor $p_k \in P$ that adopts labels in R (line 27), $lp_j : (lp_j =_{lCreator} j)$, from p_j's unknown domain ($lp_j \notin labels_k(lp_j)$), it holds that p_k adopts such labels (line 27) only a bounded number of times in R (Lemma 1). Again, by the pigeonhole principle, there is a period during which p_u takes practically infinite steps in R where neither p_i adds a label, $lp_{i_k} =_{lCreator} i$, to the system (line 28), nor p_k adopts labels (line 27), $lp_j : (lp_j =_{lCreator} j)$, from p_j's unknown domain ($lp_j \notin labels_k(lp_j)$). Consequently, whilst p_u takes practically infinite steps, all processors (that take practically infinite steps in R) name the same $\preceq_{lb}$-greatest legitimate label as the theorem statement specifies. ∎

3.2   Increment Counter Algorithm

In this subsection, we explain how we can enhance the labeling scheme presented in the previous subsection to obtain a practically self-stabilizing counter increment algorithm supporting multiple writers. To do so, we extend the labeling scheme to handle *counters*. A counter cnt is a triplet $\langle lbl, seqn, wid \rangle$, where lbl is an epoch label as defined in the previous subsection, the sequence number $seqn$ is an integer ranging from 0 to 2^b, where b is large enough, say $b = 64$, and wid is the identifier of the processor that last incremented the counter's sequence number, i.e., wid is the counter writer. Then, given two counters cnt_i, cnt_j we define the relation $cnt_i \prec_{ct} cnt_j \equiv (cnt_i.lbl \prec_{lb} cnt_j.lbl) \vee ((cnt_i.lbl = cnt_j.lbl) \wedge (cnt_i.seqn < cnt_j.seqn)) \vee ((cnt_i.lbl = cnt_j.lbl) \wedge (cnt_i.seqn = cnt_j.seqn) \wedge (cnt_i.wid < cnt_j.wid))$. When the labels of the two counters are incomparable, the counters are also incomparable.

The relation $\prec_{ct}$ defines a total order (as required by practically unbounded counters) only when processors share a globally maximum label. In this case, processors can increment a shared counter even when attempting to do so concurrently. Note that by the correctness of the labeling algorithm, starting from any initial state, we eventually reach a configuration where the active processors adopt the same maximal label. Thus, the system stabilizes to use a global maximal label, and so the pair of the sequence number and the identifier of the processor who created this sequence number can be used as an unbounded counter, as used, for example, in MWMR register implementations [13].

Let us highlight the main issues one needs to consider when dealing with counters rather than labels. Recall that in the labeling algorithm each processor p_i maintained two main structures of pairs of labels: array $max[]$ that stored the local maximal labels of each other processor (based on the message exchange) and $storedLabels[]$, an array of queues of label pairs that each processor maintains in an attempt to clean up obsolete labels created by itself or other processors. These structures now need to contain counters instead of just labels (and these structures are called $maxC[]$ and $storedCnts[]$). However, each label can now yield many different counters. In order to avoid increasing the size of these queues (with respect to the number of elements stored), we only keep the highest sequence number observed for each label (breaking ties with $wids$).

If there are corrupt counters in the system (from the initial arbitrary state), then they can only force a change of label if their sequence number is *exhausted* (i.e., $seqn \geq 2^b$). Exhausted counters are treated by the algorithm in a similarly to canceled labels in the labeling algorithm; an exhausted counter cnt_i in a counter pair $\langle cnt_i, cnt_j \rangle$ is canceled, by setting $cnt_i.lbl = cnt_j.lbl$ (i.e., the counter's own label cancels it) and hence making the counter non-legit (thus it cannot be used as a local maximal counter in $maxC_i[i]$). This cannot increase the number of labels that are created due to the initially corrupted ones, as the total capacity of the links in the system still corresponds to m.

Another issue worth mentioning is that the system might revert back to a previous legit label x, in case the current maximal label y is canceled. Label x might have been used before to create counters, so it is required to store the last sequence number written. If x is legit the system should not propose a new label and instead revert to it. Otherwise the queues might grow with no bound. But as mentioned above, each processor stores only the maximal sequence number learned for each label, inside $storedCnts[]$ (i.e., the counter with the maximal $(seqn, wid)$ to the corresponding lbl).

Algorithm Description: To increment the counter, a processor p_i first sends a request to all other processors querying the counter they consider as the global maximum and awaits for responses from a majority. In a procedure similar to the labeling algorithm, p_i (eventually) finds the maximal epoch label and the maximal sequence number for this label. In other words, it collects counters and finds the one(s) with the largest global label; there can be more than one such counter. In this case, it returns the one with the highest sequence number, breaking symmetry with the $wids$. It then checks whether this maximal sequence number is *exhausted*, i.e., if it is equal or greater than 2^b. If so, it proceeds to find a new maximal label until it finds one that is not exhausted and uses the maximal sequence number it knows for this epoch label, incrementing it by one, and setting its own identifier as the writer of this new sequence number. It then sends the new counter to all processors, awaiting for acknowledgment from a majority. This is, in spirit, similar to the two-phase write operation of MWMR register implementations, focusing on the sequence number rather than on an associated value [13].

When a processor p_i establishes a new label ℓ as the global maximum, it sets the corresponding counter $cnt = \langle \ell, 0, i \rangle$; in this case, the label creator identifier and the sequence number writer identifier is i. When there is an already established maximal label ℓ in the system and processor p_i wants to increment the counter, it increases the corresponding (to ℓ) maximal sequence number found ($maxseqn$) by one, and sets the counter $cnt = \langle \ell, maxseqn + 1, i \rangle$; in this case, the label creator identifier and the sequence number writer identifier need not be the same, i.e., if p_i was not the creator of label ℓ. From the above, we have the following correctness result:

Theorem 2. *Given an execution of the counter increment algorithm in which up to a minority of processors may become inactive, starting from an arbitrary configuration, the algorithm eventually ensures that counters increment monotonically.*

Having a self-stabilizing counter increment algorithm, we can implement a self-stabilizing MWMR register emulation. Each counter is associated with a value and the counter increment procedure essentially becomes a write operation: once the writer finds a maximal counter, it increments and associates it with the value to be written. It then communicates this to a majority of processors. The read operation is similar: the reader queries all processors about the maximum counter they are aware of, and waits for a majority to respond. If it does not receive such a counter, it returns $\perp$ so the read has to be repeated; i.e., the system has yet to converge to a maximal label. If a maximal counter exists, it sends this together with the associated value to all the processors, and once it is acknowledged by a majority, it returns the counter with the associated value. The second phase is a standard requirement to preserve the register's consistency [2,13].

4 Virtually Synchronous Stabilizing Replicated State Machine

In this section, we present our practically stabilizing VS algorithm that emulates SMR.

4.1 Preliminaries

As already mentioned, group communication systems providing the VS property implement two main services: a membership service and a reliable multicast service, whilst they assume there is access to an unbounded counter to use as unique view identifiers. We provide these services in a coordinator-based solution, considering a *primary-group* implementation [5]. To assign view identifiers, we use our counter increment algorithm. Specifically, a counter defines a view identifier, and the counter's writer identifier is that of the view's coordinator. This defines a simple interface with the counter algorithm, which provides an identical output. The output of the coordinator's failure detector defines the set of view members; this helps to maintain a consistent membership among the group members, despite inaccuracies between the various failure detectors. Pairing the coordinator's member set with the counter we obtain a *view*. The coordinator is also responsible for the consistency of the multicast mechanism within the group. We first suggest a possible implementation of a failure detector (to provide membership) and of a reliable multicast service over the self-stabilizing FIFO data link given in Section 2.

Failure Detector Implementation: Every processor p, maintains a heartbeat integer counter for every other processor q. Whenever p receives the token from q over their data link, p resets q's counter value to zero and increments all the integer counters associated with the other processors by one, up to a predefined threshold value W. Once the heartbeat counter value of a processor q reaches W, the failure detector of p considers q as inactive. In other words, the failure detector at p considers processor q to be active, if and only if the heartbeat associated with q is strictly less than W. This is essentially the failure detector implementation mentioned in [6]. Note that for the correctness of our VS algorithm, we require a weaker failure detector. Specifically, we require that at least one processor is not suspected, for sufficiently long time, only by a majority of the processors, as opposed to an eventually perfect failure detector that ensures that after a certain time, no active processor suspects any other active processor.

Reliable Multicast Implementation: We use the coordinator, some processor say p_ℓ, to exchange messages (by multicasting) within the group. The coordinator requests, collects and combines input from the group members, and then it multicasts the updated information. Specifically, when p_ℓ decides to collect inputs, it waits for the token to arrive from each group participant. Whenever a token arrives from a participant, p_ℓ uses the token to send the request for input to that participant, and waits the token to return with some input (possibly $\bot$, when the participant does not have a new input). Once p_ℓ receives an input from a certain participant with respect to this multicast invocation, the corresponding token will not carry any new requests to receive input from the same participant; of course, the tokens continue to move back and forth. When all inputs are received, p_ℓ combines them and again uses the token to carry the updated information. The coordinator can then proceed to the next round of input collection.

4.2   Self-stabilizing Virtually Synchrony and SMR Algorithm

We now present our self-stabilizing virtual synchrony and SMR algorithm. The guarantees for VS hold under the assumption that a *primary partition* exists as defined below.

Definition 1 (Primary partition). *We say that the output of the (local) failure detectors in execution R includes a* primary partition *when it includes a supporting majority of processors, $P_{maj} \subseteq P$, that (mutually) never suspect at least one processor, i.e., $\exists p_\ell \in P$ for which $|P_{maj}| > \lfloor n/2 \rfloor$ and $(p_i \in (P_{maj} \cap FD_\ell)) \iff (p_\ell \in (P_{maj} \cap FD_i))$ in every $c \in R$, where FD_x returns the set of processors that according to x's failure detector are active.*

Note that Definition 1, allows for more than one such processor p_ℓ; in this case, it is not necessary for these processors to have the *same* supporting majority.

Algorithm Outline. Each participant maintains a replica $rep[]$ of the state machine. We bound the memory used to store the history of the replica by only keeping the encapsulated influence of the history represented by the current state of the replica (variable *state*). Each participant also maintains the last delivered (composite) message, $msg[n]$, ensuring common reliable multicast, in case the coordinator becomes inactive before ensuring delivery by all members of the group.

The existence of coordinator p_ℓ is in the heart of Algorithm 3. The algorithm determines p_ℓ's availability and acts towards finding a new coordinator when no valid coordinator exists (lines 5 to 9). The pseudocode details the coordinator-side (lines 10 to 16) and the follower-side (lines 17 to 22) actions and how the two sides exchange messages. Lines 1–3 define the processor's state and interfaces.

Determining Coordinator Availability: The algorithm takes an agile approach for multicasting with atomic delivery guarantees. Namely, a new view is installed whenever the coordinator sees a change to its local failure detector, $failureDetector()$, which p_i stores in FD_i (line 5). Nevertheless, we might reach a configuration without a view coordinator as a result of an arbitrary initial configuration, or of a coordinator becoming inactive. Using the failure detector heartbeat exchange, processors can detect such initially corrupted states. Each

Algorithm 3. Self-stabilizing automaton replication using VS, code for proc. p_i

---

1 **Constants:** PCE (periodic consistency enforcement) number of rounds between global state check;

2 **Interfaces:** $fetch()$ next multicast message, $apply(state, msg)$ applies the step msg to $state$ (while producing side effects), $synchState(replica)$ returns a replica consolidated state, $synchMsgs(replica)$ returns a consolidated array of last delivered messages, $failureDetector()$ returns a vector of processor pairs $\langle pid, crdID \rangle$, $inc()$ returns a counter from the increment counter algorithm;

3 **Variables:** $rep[n] = \langle view = \langle ID, set \rangle, status \in \{\text{Multicast, Propose, Install}\}, (multicast\ round\ number)\ rnd, (replica)\ state, (last\ delivered\ messages)\ msg[n]\ (to\ the\ state\ machine), (last\ fetched)\ input\ (to\ the\ state\ machine), propV = \langle ID, set \rangle, (no\ coordinator\ alive)\ noCrd, (recently\ live\ and\ connected\ component)\ FD \rangle$: an array of state replica of the state machine, where $rep[i]$ refers to the one that processor p_i maintains. A local variable $FDin$ stores the $failureDetector()$ output. FD is an alias for $\{FDin.pid\}$, i.e. the set of processors that the failure detector considers as active. Let $crd(j) = \{FDin.crdID : FDin.pid = j\}$, i.e. the id of p_j's local coordinator, or $\perp$ if none.

4 **Do forever begin**

5   let $FDin = failureDetector()$;

6   let $seemCrd = \{p_\ell = rep[\ell].propV.ID.wid \in FD : (|rep[\ell].propV.set| > \lfloor n/2 \rfloor) \wedge (|rep[\ell].FD| > \lfloor n/2 \rfloor) \wedge (p_\ell \in rep[\ell].propV.set) \wedge (p_k \in rep[\ell].propV.set \leftrightarrow p_\ell \in rep[k].FD) \wedge ((rep[\ell].status = \text{Multicast}) \rightarrow rep[\ell].(view = propV)) \wedge crdID(\ell) = \ell\}$;

7   let $valCrd = \{p_\ell \in seemCrd : (\forall p_k \in seemCrd : rep[k].propV.ID \preceq_{ct} rep[\ell].propV.ID)\}$;

8     $noCrd \leftarrow (|valCrd| \neq 1)$;

9   **if** $(|FD| > \lfloor n/2 \rfloor) \wedge ((((|valCrd| \neq 1) \wedge (|\{p_k \in FD : p_i \in rep[k].FD \wedge rep[k].noCrd\}| > \lfloor n/2 \rfloor)) \vee ((valCrd = \{p_i\}) \wedge (FD \neq propV.set)))$ **then** $(status, propV) \leftarrow (\text{Propose}, \langle inc(), FD \rangle)$;

10   **else if** $(valCrd = \{p_i\}) \wedge (\forall p_j \in view.set : rep[j].(view, status, rnd) = (view, status, rnd)) \vee ((status \neq \text{Multicast}) \wedge (\forall p_j \in propV.set : rep[j].(propV, status) = (propV, \text{Propose}))$ **then**

11   **if** $status = \text{Multicast}$ **then**

12          $apply(state, msg)$; $input \leftarrow fetch()$;

13   **foreach** $p_j \in P$ **do if** $p_j \in view.set$ **then** $msg[j] \leftarrow rep[j].input$ **else** $msg[j] \leftarrow \perp$;

14          $rnd \leftarrow rnd + 1$;

15   **else if** $status = \text{Propose}$ **then** $(state, status, msg) \leftarrow (synchState(rep), \text{Install}, synchMsgs(rep))$;

16   **else if** $status = \text{Install}$ **then** $(view, status, rnd) \leftarrow (propV, \text{Multicast}, 0)$;

17   **else if** $valCrd = \{p_\ell\} \wedge \ell \neq i \wedge ((rep[\ell].rnd = 0 \vee rnd < rep[\ell].rnd \vee rep[\ell].(view \neq propV))$ **then**

18   **if** $rep[\ell].status = \text{Multicast}$ **then**

19   **if** $rep[\ell].state = \perp$ **then** $rep[\ell].state \leftarrow state$ /* PCE optimization, line 25 */;

20          $rep[i] \leftarrow rep[\ell]$; $apply(state, rep[\ell].msg)$; /* for the sake of side-effects */

21          $input \leftarrow fetch()$;

22   **else if** $rep[\ell].status = \text{Install}$ **then** $rep[i] \leftarrow rep[\ell]$;

23   **else if** $rep[\ell].status = \text{Propose}$ **then** $(status, propV) \leftarrow rep[\ell].(status, propV)$;

24   let $m = rep[i]$ /* sending messages: all to coordinator and coordinator to all */ ;

25   **if** $status = \text{Multicast} \wedge rnd(\bmod\ PCE) \neq 0$ **then** $m.state \leftarrow \perp$ /* PCE optimization, line 19 */ ;

26   let $sendSet = (seemCrd \cup \{p_k \in propV.set : valCrd = \{p_i\}\} \cup \{p_k \in FD : noCrd \vee (status = \text{Propose})\})$

27   **foreach** $p_j \in sendSet$ **do** $send(m)$;

---

28 **Upon Message Arrival** m from p_j **do** $rep[j] \leftarrow m$;

---

participant that detects that it has no coordinator, seeks for potential candidates based on the exchanged information.

Processor p_i can see the set of processors, $seemCrd_i$, that each *seems* to be the view coordinator, because p_i stored a message from $p_\ell \in FD_i$ in which $p_\ell = rep[\ell].propV.ID.wid$. Note that p_i cannot consider p_ℓ as a (seemly) coordinator unless the conditions in line 6 hold. Intuitively, such a processor must be active according to p_i's failure detector, and there is a majority of processors that also think so. Note that all these are based on local knowledge, which due to asynchrony might not be up to date. The next step is for p_i to consider the processor in $seemCrd_i$ with the $\preceq_{ct}$-greatest view identifier (line 7) as the valid coordinator. Here, set $valCrd_i$ is either a singleton or empty (line 8). If p_i considers some processor p_ℓ as a valid coordinator, it waits to hear from p_ℓ (or learn that it is not active). We call p_i a *follower* of p_ℓ. If there is no such processor, p_i will only propose a new view if its failure detector indicates that there exists a supportive majority of active processors that are also without a valid coordinator (line 9). If such a majority exists, p_i acquires a counter from the counter increment algorithm and proposes a new view, with the counter as the view ID, and the set of processors that appear active according to its failure detector as the group membership.

As we show, if p_i's view is accepted from *all* the processors in the view, then it proceeds to install the view, unless another processor who has obtained a higher counter does so. In a transition from one view to the next, there can be several processors attempting to become the coordinator (namely, those who according to their knowledge have a supporting majority). Still, by exploiting the intersection property of the supporting majorities we prove that each of these processors will propose a view at most once, and out of these, one view will be installed (i.e., we do not have never-ending attempts for new views to be installed). To satisfy the VS property, no new multicast message is delivered to a new view, before the coordinator of this new view has collected all the participants' last delivered messages (of their prior views) and has resent the messages appearing not to have been delivered uniformly.

The Coordinator-Side: Processor p_i is aware of its valid coordinatorship if $(valCrd_i = \{p_i\})$ (line 10). During a normal Multicast round, p_i observes the round end, when for every view member p_j it holds that $(rep_i[j].(view, status, rnd) = (view_i, status_i, rnd_i))$. Depending on its $status$, the coordinator p_i proceeds once it observes a successful round conclusion. At the end of a normal Multicast round, the coordinator increments the round number after aggregating the followers' input (line 11). The coordinator continues from the end of a Propose round to an Install round after using the most recently received replicas and the last delivered messages of each processor to install a synchronized state of the emulated automaton (line 15). After a successful Install round (line 16), the coordinator proceeds to a Multicast round after installing the proposed view and the first round number.

As part of the multicast procedure, the coordinator (line 13), collects inputs (possibly $\perp$) received from the environment and ensures that all group members apply these inputs to the replica producing possible side-effects. The processors need to apply one input at a time, maybe in an agreed upon sequential order, say from the input of the first processor to the last. Alternatively, the coordinator may request one input at a time in a round-robin fashion and multicast it.

The Follower-Side: Processor p_i considers p_ℓ as its coordinator when ($valCrd_i$ $= \{p_\ell\}$) and $i \neq \ell$ (line 17). It has to act upon merely new messages, i.e., the first message round when installing a new view ($rep[\ell].rnd = 0$), the first time a message arrives ($rnd < rep[\ell].rnd$) or a new view is proposed ($rep[\ell].(view \neq propV)$). During normal Multicast rounds (line 18) the follower p_i applies the aggregated message of this round to its current automaton state so that it produces the needed side-effects before adopting the coordinator's replica (line 22). Once a processor does not have a coordinator, and while in a Propose round, p_i does not overwrite its round number, and so the coordinator can know the last round number that p_i delivered a message during the latest installed view. Both the coordinator and the followers periodically send their current replica (line 27) and store the replicas received (line 28). As an optimization, during normal Multicast rounds, processors transmit their full replica state every PCE rounds, where PCE is a predefined constant.

Correctness Outline. We show that starting from an arbitrary state in an execution R of Algorithm 3 and once the primary partition property (Definition 1) holds throughout R, we reach a configuration $c \in R$ where some processor p_ℓ proposes a view including a majority of processors and this view is accepted by all its members. We then prove that a coordinator without a supporting majority stops being the coordinator. Then we show that when there is no coordinator, a processor with a supporting majority eventually proposes a view. All such processors propose at most once, leading to a unique coordinator. We conclude by proving that any execution suffix in R that begins from such a configuration c will preserve the VS property and implement SMR.

Lemma 3. *If the conditions of Definition 1 hold throughout an execution R of Algorithm 3, then starting from an arbitrary configuration, the system reaches a configuration in which any processor p_ℓ with a supporting majority may propose itself as the coordinator at most once. As a consequence, the system reaches a configuration in which one of these processors is the global coordinator until the end of the execution.*

Then we show the main result:

Theorem 3. *Starting from any configuration, an execution R of Algorithm 3 satisfying Definition 1, emulates automaton replication preserving the VS property.*

Proof Sketch. We consider a finite prefix R' of R with an arbitrary configuration c, and a primary partition (as per Definition 1) and assume that this prefix is sufficiently long for Lemma 3 to hold. I.e., we reach a safe configuration in which there exists a global coordinator for a majority of processors. By careful consideration of the code and the way the coordinated multicast steps take place we argue the claim of the theorem. ∎

5   Conclusion

We have presented the first self-stabilizing algorithm that guarantees VS, and used it to obtain a self-stabilizing VS-based SMR emulation; within this emulation, the system progresses in more extreme asynchronous executions compared to consensus-based SMRs. A key component of the VS algorithm is a novel modular self-stabilizing counter algorithm, that establishes an efficient practical unbounded counter, which in turn can be directly used to implement a self-stabilizing MWMR register emulation.

References

1. Alon, N., Attiya, H., Dolev, S., Dubois, S., Potop-Butucaru, M., Tixeuil, S.: Practically stabilizing SWMR atomic memory in message-passing systems. Journal of Computer and System Sciences (2015)
2. Attiya, H., Bar-Noy, A., Dolev, D.: Sharing memory robustly in message-passing systems. J. ACM **42**(1), 124–142 (1995)
3. Bartoli, A.: Implementing a replicated service with group communication. Journal of Systems Architecture **50**(8), 493–519 (2004)
4. Birman, K.: A history of the virtual synchrony replication model. In: Charron-Bost, B., Pedone, F., Schiper, A. (eds.) Replication. LNCS, vol. 5959, pp. 91–120. Springer, Heidelberg (2010)
5. Birman, K., Van Renesse, R.: Reliable distributed computing with the Isis toolkit. Wiley-IEEE Computer society press, Los Alamitos (1994)
6. Blanchard, P., Dolev, S., Beauquier, J., Delaët, S.: Practically self-stabilizing paxos replicated state-machine. In: Noubir, G., Raynal, M. (eds.) NETYS 2014. LNCS, vol. 8593, pp. 99–121. Springer, Heidelberg (2014)
7. Dolev, S.: Self-Stabilization. MIT press (2000)
8. Dolev, S., Hanemann, A., Schiller, E.M., Sharma, S.: Self-stabilizing end-to-end communication in (bounded capacity, omitting, duplicating and non-FIFO) dynamic networks. In: Richa, A.W., Scheideler, C. (eds.) SSS 2012. LNCS, vol. 7596, pp. 133–147. Springer, Heidelberg (2012)
9. Dolev, S., Kat, R.I., Schiller, E.M.: When consensus meets self-stabilization. Journal of Computer and System Sciences **76**(8), 884–900 (2010)
10. Dolev, S., Lahiani, L., Lynch, N.A., Nolte, T.: Self-stabilizing mobile node location management and message routing. In: Tixeuil, S., Herman, T. (eds.) SSS 2005. LNCS, vol. 3764, pp. 96–112. Springer, Heidelberg (2005)
11. Dolev, S., Georgiou, C., Marcoullis, I., Schiller, E.: Practically Stabilizing Virtual Synchrony. CoRR abs/1502.05183 (2015)
12. Lamport, L.: Time, clocks, and the ordering of events in a distributed system. Commun. ACM **21**(7), 558–565 (1978)
13. Lynch, N.A., Shvartsman, A.A.: Robust emulation of shared memory using dynamic quorum-acknowledged broadcasts. In: Proc. of FTC 1997, pp. 272–281 (1997)
14. Schneider, F.B.: Implementing fault-tolerant services using the state machine approach: A tutorial. ACM Comput. Surv. **22**(4), 299–319 (1990)

Brief Announcements

Two-Phase Non-repudiation Protocols

Muqeet Ali, Rezwana Reaz, and Mohamed G. Gouda

Department of Computer Science, University of Texas at Austin,
Austin, Texas 78712, USA
{muqeet,rezwana,gouda}@cs.utexas.edu

Abstract. In this paper, we identify a rich class of non-repudiation protocols, called *two-phase protocols*, and discuss how to formally specify and verify the correctness of these protocols. We also point out some advantages that these protocols have over non-repudiation protocols that are not two-phase.

Keywords: Non-repudiation · Trusted third party · Deterministic execution · Synchronized clocks

1 Introduction

A non-repudiation protocol from party S to party R performs two tasks. First, the protocol enables party S to send to party R some text x along with a proof (that can convince a judge) that x was indeed sent by S. Second, the protocol enables party R to receive text x from S and to send to S a proof (that can convince a judge) that x was indeed received by R. Only one of two outcomes is possible when the execution of a non-repudiation protocol from S to R terminates. The first outcome is that both S and R obtain their required proofs. The second outcome is that neither S nor R obtains its required proof.

Non-repudiation protocols can support several important applications over the Internet. Examples of these applications are certified email [1], cloud storage [2], electronic billing [3], and meter reading in smart grids [4].

Examples of non-repudiation protocols are presented in [5–7].

2 Two-Phase Protocols

A non-repudiation protocol from party S to party R is called two-phase iff execution of the protocol by parties S and R proceeds in two phases. In the first phase, the party (S or R) recognizes that it has not yet received its complete proof and so it continues to execute the protocol as specified. In the second phase, the party (S or R) recognizes that it has already received its complete proof and so it refrains from sending any more messages specified by the protocol because these messages only help the other party complete its proof. In other words, the two parties S and R in any two-phase protocol will always act in their own self-interests during execution of the protocol.

© Springer International Publishing Switzerland 2015
A. Pelc and A.A. Schwarzmann (Eds.): SSS 2015, LNCS 9212, pp. 267–268, 2015.
DOI: 10.1007/978-3-319-21741-3

Two-phase nonrepudiation protocols have the following advantages over non-repudiation protocols that are not two-phase:

(a) Execution of a two-phase protocol is inherently deterministic, whereas execution of a protocol that is not two-phase is usually non-deterministic.
(b) The participating parties of a two-phase protocol do not need to have synchronized clocks, whereas parties of a protocol that is not two-phase need to have synchronized clocks.
(c) It follows from (a) and (b) above that specifying and verifying the correctness of a two-phase protocol are easier than specifying and verifying the correctness of a comparable protocol that is not two-phase.

One more advantage of two-phase protocols is that the exchanged messages in these protocols are of two types only: send-proof messages and receive-proof messages.

3   Security Analysis

We analyzed the security of some two-phase protocols and showed that these protocols can be designed to defend against four security attacks: (1) malicious parties, (2) message loss, (3) collusion attacks, and (4) replay attacks.

Acknowledgement. Research of M.G. Gouda is supported by NSF Award 1440035.

References

1. Oppliger, R.: Providing certified mail services on the internet, vol. 5, pp. 16–22. IEEE (2007)
2. Feng, J., Chen, Y.: A fair non-repudiation framework for data integrity in cloud storage services, vol. 2, pp. 20–47. Inderscience (2013)
3. Zhou, J., Lam, K.Y.: Undeniable billing in mobile communication. In: Proceedings of the 4th Annual ACM/IEEE International Conference on Mobile Computing and Networking, pp. 284–290. ACM (1998)
4. Xiao, Z., Xiao, Y., Du, D.C.: Non-repudiation in neighborhood area networks for smart grid, vol. 51, pp. 18–26. IEEE (2013)
5. Zhou, J., Gollman, D.: A fair non-repudiation protocol. In: 1996 IEEE Symposium on Security and Privacy, pp. 55–61. IEEE Computer Society (1996)
6. Markowitch, O., Roggeman, Y.: Probabilistic non-repudiation without trusted third party. In: Second Conference on Security in Communication Networks, Amalfi, Italy (1999)
7. Kremer, S., Markowitch, O.: A multi-party non-repudiation protocol. In: Qing, S., Eloff, J.H.P. (eds.) Information Security for Global Information Infrastructures, IFIP, vol. 47, pp. 271–280. Springer, Heidelberg (2000)

Secure and Private Bidding Protocol for Incentive-Based Demand-Response System of Smart Grid

Mohammad Shahriar Rahman, Anirban Basu, and Shinsaku Kiyomoto

KDDI R&D Labs, 2-1-15 Ohara, Fujimino, Saitama, Japan
{mohammad,basu,kiyomoto}@kddilabs.jp

Abstract. DR-DB (Demand Response-Demand Bidding) is one kind of incentive-based DR, where certain incentives are awarded to consumers who participate in DR events. Security and privacy of DR-DB bidding system are of paramount importance as consumer data are involved in it. In this brief announcement, we propose a secure and private bidding protocol for incentive-based demand-response system using cryptographic primitives. To the best of our knowledge, our proposed secure and private protocol is the first work in this area.

1 Introduction

As consumers' information is an integral part of incentive-based demand-response systems, securing the data communication and protecting data privacy are crucial. One of the primary security objectives is to ensure that entities participating in the DR protocol and the protocol messages generated by them provide authenticity and integrity. From the viewpoint of privacy, it is required that no untrusted entity should be able to link multiple bids to a specific consumer since being able to do so would reveal private information of that consumer. Moreover, bids accessible by the untrusted entities can be used to infer bidders' private information. We emphasize that, along with authenticity, integrity, and privacy, the following properties must be achieved by an incentive-based demand-response system: (Anonymity) no unauthorized entity shall be able to identify the bidder during the bidding; (Untraceability) the winning bidder should not be traceable at the end of the bidding by untrusted entities, but its legitimacy should be verifiable; (No Impersonation) no one shall participate in the bidding with the identity of another bidder; (Unforgeability) no one should be able to falsify a valid bidding price; (Non-repudiation) bidders cannot deny their bid after the winning bidder has been announced; (Public Verifiability) anyone can verify the validity of the bids; (Single Registration) a bidder needs to register only once, and then can participate in all biddings; (Easy Revocation) registration manager should be able to revoke a bidder easily; (Incentive Allocation) the winner should be able to claim the incentive without revealing his identity and no other entity should be able to impersonate the winner.

© Springer International Publishing Switzerland 2015
A. Pelc and A.A. Schwarzmann (Eds.): SSS 2015, LNCS 9212, pp. 269–271, 2015.
DOI: 10.1007/978-3-319-21741-3

There are three entities in the proposed system: energy supplier as Registration Manager (RM), DR service provider as Bidding Manager (BM) and consumers as bidders. We assume honest-but-curious model for RM and BM. All other participating entities or outsiders are assumed to be malicious. El-Gamal public key encryption [1] and Schnorr's signature scheme [2] are used for encryption and signature purposes, respectively. Our proposed protocol achieves the aforementioned security and privacy properties assuming the hardness of solving discrete logarithm problem.

2 Proposed Approach

Pre-processing: BM and RM create bulletin boards where they can post necessary information. These boards are read-only for all other entities. Also, RM generates public parameters for the protocol, its own private-public key pair and signing-verification key pair. Similarly, BM generates its public key. AM and BM jointly create a bulletin board for the winning bidder.

Bidder Registration: Each bidder generates the necessary keys along with registration key to register himself with the RM for bidding. The bidder also performs some computations to generate other parameters that are useful for bidding. These parameters and the registration key are encrypted using RM's public key and sent to the RM.

Bidding Key Generation: RM broadcasts a signed request to all the registered bidders. Upon receiving and verifying the request, all the bidders send their necessary information (encrypted) for generating the bidding key to RM. RM generates the bidding keys and posts them in its bulletin board. Each bidder also computes its bidding key and keeps it with him.

Bidding Setup: Using the parameters posted in RM's bulletin board, BM generates bidding certificate for each bidder and posts the certificates in its bulletin board.

Bidding: Each bidder generates its bid, encrypts the bid information and signs the encrypted bid. He writes his bidding certificate, encrypted bid and its signature on BM's bulletin board. BM verifies all the signatures coming from the bidders and decrypts the encrypted files to get all the bids. BM then announces the highest bid publicly to continue the current bidding round.

Bid Verification: Anyone can verify bid's validity using verifiable computations.

Winner Announcement: At the end of a bidding session, BM announces the winning bidder's information on the winner's own bulletin board. Anyone can check and verify the winning bid.

Incentive Claim: After the bidding ends, the winner can claim the incentive by placing a zero-knowledge proof to the RM.

References

1. El Gamal, T.: A public key cryptosystem and a signature scheme based on discrete logarithms. IEEE Trans. Inf. Theor. **31**(4), 469–472 (1985)
2. Schnorr, C.P.: Efficient identification and signatures for smart cards. In: Quisquater, J.-J., Vandewalle, V. (eds.) EUROCRYPT 1989. LNCS, vol. 435, pp. 239–252 (1990)

Brief Announcement: Meta-MapReduce
A Technique for Reducing Communication
in MapReduce Computations

Foto Afrati[1], Shlomi Dolev[2], Shantanu Sharma[2], and Jeffrey D. Ullman[3]

[1] National Technical University of Athens, Athens, Greece
[2] Ben-Gurion University of the Negev, Beer-Sheva, Israel
[3] Stanford University, Stanford, USA

The federation of cloud and big data activities is the next challenge where MapReduce should be modified to avoid (big) data migration across remote (cloud) sites. This is exactly our scope of research, where only the very essential data for obtaining the result is transmitted, reducing communication, processing and preserving data privacy as much as possible. We propose *an algorithmic technique for MapReduce algorithms*, called *Meta-MapReduce*, that *decreases the communication cost by allowing us to process and move metadata to clouds and from the map to reduce phases*. Details are given below:

Locality of Data. Input data to a MapReduce job, on one hand, may exist at the same site where mappers and reducers reside. However, ensuring an identical location of data and mappers-reducers cannot always be guaranteed. On the other hand, it may be possible that a user has a single local machine and wants to enlist a public cloud to help data processing. Consequently, in both the cases, it is required to move data to the location of mappers-reducers. In order to motivate and demonstrate the impact of different locations of data and mappers-reducers, we consider a real example, as: *Amazon Elastic MapReduce*. Amazon Elastic MapReduce (EMR) processes data that is stored in Amazon Simple Storage Service (S3), where the locations of EMR and S3 are not identical. Hence, it is required to move data from S3 to the location of EMR. However, moving all data from S3 to EMR is not efficient if only small specific part of it is needed for the final output.

Communication Cost. The *communication cost* dominates the performance of a MapReduce algorithm and is the sum of the total amount of data that is required to move from the location of users or data (*e.g.*, S3) to the location of mappers (*e.g.*, EMR) and from the map phase to the reduce phase in each round of a MapReduce job. In this paper, we are interested in *minimizing the data transferred* in order to avoid communication and memory overhead, as well as to protect data privacy as much as possible. If *few* inputs are required to compute

More details appear in the technical report 15-04, Department of Computer Science, Ben-Gurion University of the Negev, Israel, 2015. Supported by the project Handling Uncertainty in Data Intensive Applications, co-financed by the European Union (European Social Fund) and Greek national funds, through the Operational Program "Education and Lifelong Learning," under the program THALES, Orange Labs, Rita Altura trust chair in computer science, the Lynne and William Frankel Center for Computer Science, and the Israeli Science Foundation (grant number 428/11).

© Springer International Publishing Switzerland 2015
A. Pelc and A.A. Schwarzmann (Eds.): SSS 2015, LNCS 9212, pp. 272–274, 2015.
DOI: 10.1007/978-3-319-21741-3

the final output, then it is not communication efficient to move all the inputs to the site of mappers-reducers, and then, the copies of same inputs to the reduce phase.

Meta-MapReduce. We provide a new *algorithmic* approach for MapReduce algorithms, Meta-MapReduce, that decreases the communication cost significantly. Meta-MapReduce (M-MR) regards the locality of data and mappers-reducers and avoids the movement of data that does not participate in the final output. Particularly, *M-MR provides a way to compute the desired output using metadata*[1] (which is much smaller than the original input data) and avoids to upload all data (either because it takes too long or for privacy reasons). It should be noted that we are enhancing MapReduce and not creating entirely a new framework for large-scale data processing; thus, M-MR is *implementable* in state-of-the art MapReduce systems such as Spark or modern Hadoop. In addition, M-MR also allows us to protect data privacy as much as possible in the case of an *honest-but-curious* adversary by not sending all the inputs. Nevertheless, by the auditing process, a *malicious* adversary can be detected. Moreover, in some settings auditing enforces participants to be honest-but-curious rather than malicious, as malicious actions can be discovered and imply punishing actions.

Having the same scenario of locality of input data, in the standard MapReduce, users send their data to the site of mappers before the computation begins. However, in M-MR, users send metadata to the site of mappers, instead of original data.

An Example of Equijoin of Two Relations $X(A, B)$ and $Y(B, C)$. We present an example to show the impact of different locations of data and mappers-reducers on the communication cost involved in a MapReduce job. *Problem statement*: The join of relations $X(A, B)$ and $Y(B, C)$, where the joining attribute is B, provides output tuples $\langle a, b, c \rangle$, where (a, b) is in A and (b, c) is in C. In the equijoin of $X(A, B)$ and $Y(B, C)$, all tuples of both the relations with an identical value of the attribute B should appear together at the same reducer for providing the final output tuples. In Fig. 1, two relations $X(A, B)$ and $Y(B, C)$

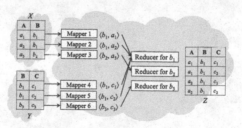

Fig. 1. Equijoin of two relations.

---

[1] The term metadata is used in a different manner, and it represents a small subset, which varies according to tasks, of the dataset.

are shown, and *we consider that the size of all the B values is very small as compared to the size of values of the attributes A and C*.

Communication Cost Analysis: In Fig. 1, the communication cost for joining of the relations X and Y is the sum of the sizes of all three tuples of each relation that are required to move from the location of the user to the location of mappers, and then, from the map phase to the reduce phase. Consider that each tuple is of unit size, and hence, the total communication cost is 12 for obtaining the final output. Using M-MR, where values of the attribute B work as metadata, there is no need to send tuples having values b_2 and b_3 to the location of computation. Thus, a solution to the problem of equijoin has only 4 units cost plus a constant cost for moving metadata.

Table 1. The communication cost for joining of relations using Meta-MapReduce.

Problems	Communication cost	
	using Meta-MapReduce	using MapReduce
Join of two relations	$2nc + h(c + w)$	$4nw$
Skewed Values of the Joining Attribute	$2nc + rh(c + w)$	$2nw(1 + r)$
Join of two relations by hashing the joining attribute	$6n \cdot \log m + h(c + w)$	$4nw$
Join of k relations by hashing the joining attributes	$3knp \cdot \log m + h(c + w)$	$2knw$
n: # tuples in each relations, c: the maximum size of a value of the joining attribute, r: the replication rate, h: # tuples that actually join, w is the maximum required memory for a tuple, p: the maximum number of dominating attributes in a relation, and m: the maximal number of tuples in all given relations.		

Brief Announcement:
Vehicle to Vehicle Authentication

Shlomi Dolev[1], Łukasz Krzywiecki[2], Nisha Panwar[1], and Michael Segal[3]

[1] Department of Computer Science, Ben-Gurion University of the Negev,
Beersheba, Israel
{dolev, panwar}@cs.bgu.ac.il
[2] Institute of Mathematics and Computer Science,
Wroclaw University of Technology, Wrocław, Poland
lukasz.krzywiecki@pwr.wroc.pl
[3] Department of Communication Systems Engineering,
Ben-Gurion University of the Negev, Beersheba, Israel
segal@cse.bgu.ac.il

Vehicle Authentication. In recent future, vehicles will establish a spontaneous connection over a wireless radio channel, coordinating actions and information. Vehicles will exchange warning messages over the wireless radio channel through Dedicated Short Range Communication (IEEE 1609) over the Wireless Access in Vehicular Environment (802.11p). Unfortunately, the wireless communication among vehicles is vulnerable to security threats that may lead to very serious safety hazards. Therefore, the warning messages being exchanged must incorporate an authentic factor such that recipient is willing to verify and accept the message in a timely manner.

Our Contribution. (*i*) Coupling fixed and non-fixed vehicle attributes with the public key, (*ii*) Optical out-of-band communication channel, (*iii*) Adaptation with existing authentication protocols, (*iv*) Verification.

Previous Work. Vehicles utilize wireless communication standard, i.e., IEEE 802.11p Wireless Access in Vehicular Environment (WAVE) based on IEEE 1609 Dedicated Short Range Communication (DSRC). Raya and Haubaux proposed a Public Key Infrastructure (PKI) based vehicle security scheme, however, an active adversary may launch an impersonation attack. Moreover, roadside infrastructure is required to provide the most updated Certificate Revocation List (CRL). Our scheme removes the active participation of roadside units as well as the regional authorities.

Problem Statement. Every vehicles public key is signed by the authorities and can be verified by the receiver, still, an impersonation attack among the

S. Dolev and N. Panwar—Partially supported by the Rita Altura Trust Chair in Computer Sciences, Lynne and William Frankel Center for Computer Sciences, Israel Science Foundation (grant 428/11), the Israeli Internet Association, and the Ministry of Science and Technology, Infrastructure Research in the Field of Advanced Computing and Cyber Security.
Ł. Krzywiecki—Partially supported by fundings from Polish National Science Center (decision number DEC-2013/09/B/ST6/02251).

© Springer International Publishing Switzerland 2015
A. Pelc and A.A. Schwarzmann (Eds.): SSS 2015, LNCS 9212, pp. 275–277, 2015.
DOI: 10.1007/978-3-319-21741-3

moving vehicles is possible. Accordingly, the scenario starts when a vehicle v_1 tries to securely communicate with v_2 and requests for the public key of v_2. Vehicle v_3 pretends to be v_2 and answers v_1 with v_3 public key instead of v_2. Then v_3 concurrently asks v_2 for its public key. Vehicle v_1 is fooled to establish a private key with v_3 instead of v_2, and v_2 is fooled to establish a private key with v_3 instead of v_1. Vehicle v_3 conveys messages from v_1 to v_2 and back decrypting and re-encrypting with the appropriate established keys. In this way, v_3 can find the appropriate moment to change information and cause hazardous actions to v_1 and v_2.

System Model. (*i*) Light Amplification by Stimulated Emission of Radiation (LASER), (*ii*) LIght Detection And Ranging (LIDAR), (*iii*) Autocollimator, (*iv*) Physically Unclonable Function(PUF).

Proposed Scheme. The proposed approaches for the vehicle to vehicle authentication are summarized as below:

Basic Scheme[1]. We propose to certify both the public key and out-of-band senseable static attributes to enable mutual authentication of the communicating vehicles. Vehicle owners are bound to preprocess a certificate (periodically, possibly during the annual inspection procedure) that signs monolithically both a public key and a list of fixed unchangeable attributes (e.g., license number, brand and color) of the vehicle (extending ISO 3779 and 3780 standards). With such a scheme the vehicle can verify (say by using a camera) that the public key belongs to the specific vehicle to which the connection should be established (rather than a public key of a standing by adversary).

Intermediate Scheme[2]. We consider the case of multiple malicious vehicles with identical visual static attributes. Apparently, dynamic attributes (e.g., location and direction) can uniquely define a vehicle and can be utilized to resolve the true identity of vehicles. However, unlike static attributes, dynamic attributes cannot be signed by a trusted authority beforehand. We propose an approach to verify the coupling between non-certified dynamic attributes and certified static attributes via an auxiliary laser communication channel.

Sophisticated Scheme[3]. At last, we propose to use, the optical Physically Unclonable Function (PUF) to ensure that response from the receiving vehicle is spontaneous, rather than an answer forwarded from another vehicle. Vehicles utilize an out-of-band optical communication channel in order to exchange the PUF stimulated optical challenge and corresponding response from the sender and receiver, respectively.

---

[1] An extended description of these results can be found in ASCOMS/SAFECOMP 2013.

[2] An extended description of these results can be found in the proceedings of 13th IEEE International Symposium on Network Computing and Applications 2014.

[3] See Technical Report 15-02 of the Department of Computer Science, Ben-Gurion University of the Negev, Israel, 2015.

Claims. We provide an extended proof of the proposed scheme using Spi calculus and BAN Logic, respectively. Our proposed approach adapts the security construction of the conventional Transport Layer Security (TLS) protocol and satisfy two crucial security properties, i.e., (i) Authentication: No active or passive adversary would be able to intercept the communication between sender and receiver and (ii) Secrecy: No active or passive adversary would be able to reveal neither the secret session messages nor the secret key.

Brief Announcement: Data Stabilization Enforcement via ACTIVE MONITORING the Cloud Infrastructure Consistency Case

Alexander Binun[2], Thierry Coupaye[1], Shlomi Dolev[2],
Mohammed Kassi-Lahlou[1], Marc Lacoste[1], Alex Palesandro[1],
Aurélien Wailly[1], Reuven Yagel[2,3], and Leonid Yankulin[2]

[1] Orange Labs, Paris, France
[2] Department of Computer Science, Ben-Gurion University of the Negev,
Beersheba, Israel
[3] Department of Software Engineering, Azrieli – Jerusalem College of Engineering,
Jerusalem, Israel

Introduction. For any system, protection against faults or attacks has long been viewed as a long, endless series of steps where each new counter-measure is introduced to mitigate an upcoming attack or failure, until the next unexpected event occurs. This is particularly the case for cloud systems, where the field of cloud dependability rapidly expands as the reaches of security and safety impacts core cloud features. For example, the expectations from resource sharing, elasticity, or virtualization grow ever deeper and broader to an initially unsuspecting researcher or engineer. What if threats and failures were evolving faster than defense mechanisms? What if stacking so many counter-measures mechanisms was simply not fast enough? We take the approach to admit that faults or attacks will occur no matter what. Instead, focus should be put on graceful recovery. Research on self-stabilizing systems seems particularly promising to allow building self-stabilizing clouds that will converge into and remain in a stable state. But how to build such clouds? We leverage on the initial research addressing the single host layer, in the hypervisor [2]. We aim at stabilizing the following distributed cloud components: monitoring, networking, distributed computation and scheduling mechanisms. Locally, stabilization applies to the hypervisor, to its relevant low layers (e.g. OS drivers) down to the hardware. We stabilize also the computing and the networking components of the cloud. The communication part will enable remote distributed monitoring. Monitoring includes various assertions and actions for detecting and correcting corrupted states. The monitoring facility can be reconfigured and performed through the network. Infrastructure integrity violations are treated by (a) including the relevant self-stabilization components into the hypervisor and by (b) ensuring that the networking infrastructure is functioning and nodes can continue collaborating in spite of faults even in the orchestration level, e.g., loss of synchrony.

Prototyping a Self-Stabilizing Cloud Infrastructure. We focus on OpenStack due to its prominence as an open cloud computation platform. OpenStack

Partially supported by Orange Labs, Rita Altura Trust chair in computer science, the Lynne and William Frankel Center for Computer Science, and the Israeli Science Foundation (grant number 428/11).

A. Pelc and A.A. Schwarzmann (Eds.): SSS 2015, LNCS 9212, pp. 278–279, 2015.
DOI: 10.1007/978-3-319-21741-3

exposes full-fledged IaaS functionality, thus allowing conducting real-life experiments. For each type of resource (storage, networking etc.), the OpenStack specification defines interfaces to cooperate with the relevant resource management services.

Database Active Monitoring. A current state of an OpenStack instance is maintained in the internal database (usually MySQL) and is accessible on demand from the hosts that running the cloud. Depending on its role within the cloud, each host may run *agents* that incorporate certain duties of *cloud services* (modules that implement one of the cloud functions on premises). Agents receive partial information concerning the cloud current state by issuing Web API requests to their services and receiving responses via a messaging queue. At any moment of time, an instance is aware of the recent state of the cloud. In case of data inconsistency that is a result of malicious attack, human mistake or software/hardware malfunction, the cloud state can be inconsistent. We introduce *active monitoring* for detecting internal database instance, and enforce data consistency in a provable self-stabilizing manner (rather than, e.g., intrusion detection based techniques [1]). Active monitoring verifies the data held by each participant by repeatedly querying and examining the source for the data, refreshing the data to gain global consistency by distributed independent updates. In the worst case, active monitoring may imply the need of global assignment of a consistent distributed state (usually the initial one).

On the (correct) Behavior of the Active Monitor. Active distributed monitoring relies on the correct functioning of monitoring agents that should run at every relevant host. We ensure the existence and correct functioning of these agents [2]. Another possible problem is de-synchronization of the current state information of the cloud that was received by different agents that run at the same host or at different hosts. The information can get out of synchronization due to an error while being transferred via a messaging queue or due to a memory corruption. It can also be caused by more recent changes to the cloud state. For example, a network agent has to be aware of VM instances connected to the local network that, not necessarily, run on the same hypervisor as the one that the agent is deployed to. In case of a notification failure, the local network image that is stored within the agent is compromised. We propose an algorithm that is based on enforcing self-stabilization of each of the distributed agents [2], that eventually bring the distributed agents and the distributed database to a consistent state within the cloud.

References

1. Liu, P., Jing, J., Luenam, P., Wang, Y., Li, L., Ingsriswang, S.: The design and implementation of a self-healing database system. J. Intell. Inf. Syst **23**(3), 247–269 (2004)
2. Binun, A., Bloch, M., Dolev, S., Kahil, R.M., Menuhin, B., Yagel, R., Coupaye, T., Lacoste, M., Wailly, A.: Self-stabilizing virtual machine hypervisor architecture for resilient cloud. In: SERVICES 2014, pp. 200–207 (2014)

Self-adjusting Skip Graphs

Sukumar Ghosh and Sikder Rezwanul Huq

The University of Iowa, Iowa, USA
{sukumar-ghosh,sikderrezwanul-huq}@uiowa.edu

Abstract. We present a self-adjusting algorithm for skip graphs that performs topological adaptation to an unknown communication pattern σ. Our algorithm is fully decentralized, conforms to $\mathcal{CONGEST}$ model, and requires $O(\log n)$ memory for each node, where n is the total number of nodes. We derive a lower bound of *amortized* cost for any algorithm that follows our model. We analyze our algorithm and show that the cost is at most a logarithmic factor more than the derived lower bound.

1 Introduction

A Skip Graph [1] $G = (V, E)$ is a useful form of peer-to-peer communication topology that guarantees $O(\log n)$ worst-case communication time between arbitrary pairs of nodes, where $n = |V|$. In practice, however, what matters is the *total time* taken by a sequence of communication requests where each request involves a source-destination pair. Self-adjustment is an attractive tool to reduce the *amortized* times of the sequence of communications. In general, amortized costs in dynamically adjusting topologies are not much worse than their static counterparts, and can lead to significant performance gains when the communication pattern is skewed. This paper proposes an algorithm for the self-adjustment of the topology of a Skip Graph with no *a priori* knowledge of the future communication pattern, and analyze the performance of the self-adjustment protocol.

2 The Model and Definitions

Let $\mathcal{S}$ be the family of all Skip Graphs where each topology $G(V, E) \in \mathcal{S}$ is a skip graph. We denote the base level as level 0 and the top level as level h, where h is the height of corresponding skip graph. A linked list at any level i gets split into two mutually exclusive linked lists (0-list and 1-list) at level $i+1$. Each node x has a unique *membership vector* $m(x)$ where i^{th} bit of $m(x)$ determines node x's linked list at level $i + 1$.

We say a Skip Graph satisfies the *a-balance* property if there exists a positive integer a, such that among any $a+1$ consecutive nodes in any linked list at level i, at most a nodes can step up to a single linked list at level $i + 1$. This property ensures that the length of the search path between any pair of nodes is at most $a \log n$.

© Springer International Publishing Switzerland 2015
A. Pelc and A.A. Schwarzmann (Eds.): SSS 2015, LNCS 9212, pp. 280–281, 2015.
DOI: 10.1007/978-3-319-21741-3

Let $\sigma = (\sigma_0, \sigma_1, ..., \sigma_{m-1})$ be an online access sequence consisting of m sequential communication requests, $\sigma_t = (u, v) \in V \times V$ denotes a routing request from source u to destination v. Let u_i is the source and v_i is the destination specified by communication request σ_i at time i. We construct a communication graph G with the nodes that communicated (either as source or destination) in the time period starting from the last time u_i and v_i communicated, and ending at time i. We draw an edge between any pair of nodes in G if they communicated in this time period. The *working-set number* $t_i(\sigma_i)$ for request σ_i is the number of distinct nodes in G that has a path from either u_i or v_i.

A self-adjusting algorithm transforms the skip graph $S \in \mathcal{S}$ to another skip graph $S' \in \mathcal{S}$ after each communication request. Our self-adjusting skip graph model enforces following constraints: (1) any two communicating node must move to a linked list of size two in the transformed topology (2) the a-balance property can never be violated (3) A node can have $O(\log n)$ memory (4) The height of the skip graph can never exceed $O(\log n)$.

3 Dynamic Skip Graph Algorithm (DSG)

We propose a self-adjusting algorithm DSG for skip graphs that dynamically performs local transformation (by partially reconstructing the network) upon a communication request and conforms to the self-adjusting skip graph model. Every node belongs to a group at each level and holds a *group-id* and a *timestamp* for each of the levels. We propose a routing algorithm ROUTING for skip graphs which is optimized for algorithm DSG. Upon a communication request from node u to node v, routing is first done by using the algorithm ROUTING. Then each node $x \in l_\alpha$, s.t. l_α is the smallest common linked list containing u and v, computes a priority $p(x)$ by using their group-ids and timestamps. We design a distributed approximate median finding algorithm for our skip graph model that finds an approximate median priority in expected logarithmic time. Let l_α be a linked list at level α. Then starting at level α, nodes $x \in l_\alpha$ initiates the approximate median finding algorithm AMF to compute a median priority. Nodes with a priority lower than the median priority move to the 0-list at the level $\alpha + 1$ and change $m(x)$ accordingly. Nodes with priorities higher than the median similarly move to the 1-list. With some exceptions this process continues recursively and parallelly for levels higher than α until all nodes $x \in l_\alpha$ become singleton at some level.

Theorem 1. *At any time i, given that any two nodes u and v communicated earlier, the cost for routing from u to v in the skip graph at time i is $O(\log t_i(u, v))$.*

Theorem 2. *The cost for algorithm DSG is at most logarithmic factor of the optimal algorithm.*

References

1. Aspnes, J., Shah, G.: Skip graphs. In: Fourteenth Annual ACM-SIAM Symposium on Discrete Algorithms, Baltimore, MD, USA, 12–14 January 2003, pp. 384–393 (2003)

A Framework for Containing the Degree Growth in Topological Self-stabilization

Thamer Alsulaiman[1], Andrew Berns[2], and Sukumar Ghosh[1]

[1] University of Iowa, Iowa, USA
{thamer-alsulaiman,sukumar-ghosh}@uiowa.edu
[2] University of Wisconsin-La Crosse, La Crosse, USA
aberns@uwlax.edu

1 Introduction

Overlay networks are built with logical links over one or more physical edges of a network. Logical links can be added or removed via program actions. Overlay networks mostly operate in fragile environments, and without central supervision. Bad configurations may be caused by node or link failures, by a node *join* or a node *leave*, or deliberate actions of nodes trying to derive undue performance benefits for themselves. Such adversarial actions may alter the network topology in an arbitrary manner. Topological self-stabilization takes a walk through the space of all networks defined by a given set of nodes, starting from a source network that is illegal and ending up at a target network that is legal. In the rest of the paper, we work under the assumption that the corrupted topology remains connected. We propose a framework that caps the degree growth to sublinear bounds while generating the target topology. As an illustration of the proposed technique, we present a self-stabilizing algorithm for building a heap.

2 The Main Idea

Background. The network topology $G = (V, E)$ is an undirected connected graph, where nodes have unique, positive identifiers. Each node $i \in V$ maintains a neighbor set $N(i)$ as a part of its local state, along with, maybe, other variables to help node i reach its goal. We assume a synchronous message-passing model. The efficiency of the detection of illegal topologies largely depends on the distribution of the detectors in the network. For overlay networks that are not locally checkable, there may not be a single detector even if the topology is illegal.

Given a faulty topology $G = (V, E)$, the *detector diameter* $D(G)$ for the given class of networks is the maximum hop distance in G between any node in V and its closest detector. The task of notifying every non-detector is time-efficient when the detector diameter is small.

Now, consider an instance of a computation where the topology transitions are represented by the sequence $G, G_1, G_2, \ldots, G_f$, here G is the initial topology and G_f is the final legal topology. Maintaining large degrees, even for an interim period, is challenging for the nodes of any overlay network. This is why we

© Springer International Publishing Switzerland 2015
A. Pelc and A.A. Schwarzmann (Eds.): SSS 2015, LNCS 9212, pp. 282–283, 2015.
DOI: 10.1007/978-3-319-21741-3

would prefer the computation to steer the topology of the given network through the space of all "low degree" topologies with n nodes. The following definition quantifies the degree growth parameter:

Definition 1. *Consider a topological self-stabilization algorithm $\mathcal{A}$ that transforms a given initial topology G into a legal topology G_f. Let δ_{max} be the largest of all the node degrees between G and G_f. Then the degree growth of $\mathcal{A}$ is contained, if in none of the intermediate configurations, the degree of any node exceeds $\delta_{max} + f(n)$, where $f(n)$ is sublinear.*

The Framework. Our framework consists of three components. The first component uses a predicate DETECT to notify every process that the current configuration is not a legal one. The second component builds an interim LINEAR topology out of the given topology G. The third and the final component is a subroutine REPAIR that transforms the linear topology into a legal topology of the desired class.

The LINEAR network consists of all the nodes of a graph connected in the total order of their identifiers. We adopt the Pure Linearization algorithm from [2], since it caps the degree growth during stabilization. In [2], the degree of a node can increase by at most two in each round. We observe that the degree cannot keep increasing monotonically till the end – at some point the degree growth tapers off. See Theorem 1.

The REPAIR procedure starts after the linearization is over. The node with the largest id acts as the *leader*, and uses the linear chain to collect the identifiers of all the nodes in $O(n)$ rounds. Thereafter, the leader locally computes the legal topology, i.e. the ideal neighbor set $Nbr(i)$ for each node i, and disseminates them to every node i using the same linear pipeline. Each node i connects with the neighbor set $Nbr(i)$, which concludes the REPAIR phase.

Theorem 1. *For any locally checkable topology, and using the proposed framework, the stabilization time is $O(n)$ rounds. And, for a given node, the degree growth using the Pure Linearization algorithm is bounded by $O(\delta + \sqrt{n})$, where δ is the initial degree of the node.*

Using the proposed framework, we illustrate how a binary max-heap topology can be stabilized in (On) rounds while containing the degree growth. This topology is not locally checkable, but we add an extra variable per node to make it locally checkable. We demonstrate that the detector diameter of the heap topology is $O(\log n)$. Note that without the degree cap, the heap can be stabilized in $O(\log n)$ rounds using the transitive closure framework [1].

References

1. Berns, A., Ghosh, S., Pemmaraju, S.V.: Building self-stabilizing overlay networks with the transitive closure framework. Theor. Comput. Sci. **512**, 2–14 (2013)
2. Onus, M., Richa, A.W., Scheideler, C.: Linearization: locally self-stabilizing sorting in graphs. In: Proceedings of the Nine Workshop on Algorithm Engineering and Experiments, ALENEX 2007, New Orleans, Louisiana, USA, 6 January 2007

Stabilizing Breach-Free Sensor Barriers

Jorge A. Cobb[1] and Chin-Tser Huang[2]

[1] Department of Computer Science, The University of Texas at Dallas,
Richardson, USA
`cobb@utdallas.edu`
[2] Department of Computer Science and Engineering,
University of South Carolina at Columbia, Columbia, USA
`huangct@cse.sc.edu`

1 Contribution

A wireless sensor network (WSN) consists of a geographical area populated with a large number of sensors nodes, where each sensor has a limited battery lifetime. The type of coverage provided by the sensors is classified into full or partial coverage. In full coverage, the entire area is covered at all times by the sensors, and any event within the area is immediately detected [3]. On the other hand, in partial coverage, the area has some regions not covered by the sensors [7].

One form of partial coverage is barrier coverage [6]. A barrier is a subset of sensors that divide the area of interest into two regions, such that it is impossible to move from one of the regions to the other without being detected by at least one of the sensors. Figure 1(a) highlights a subset of sensors that provide barrier coverage to the area.

In the specific case of intrusion detection, only one barrier needs to be active at any moment in time; the remaining barriers can remain asleep in order to conserve energy. When a barrier is close to depleting all of its power, another barrier is placed in service. Finding the largest number of sensor barriers is solvable in polynomial-time [6]. Consider the example in Fig. 1(b) with four barriers, B_1 through B_4. If we use the barriers in a sequential wakeup-sleep cycle, the users are protected for a total of four times the average lifetime of a sensor.

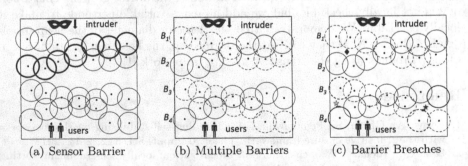

(a) Sensor Barrier   (b) Multiple Barriers   (c) Barrier Breaches

Fig. 1. Sensor Barriers

© Springer International Publishing Switzerland 2015
A. Pelc and A.A. Schwarzmann (Eds.): SSS 2015, LNCS 9212, pp. 284–285, 2015.
DOI: 10.1007/978-3-319-21741-3

Sensor barriers are susceptible to a problem, known as a *barrier-breach*, in which it is possible for an intruder to cross an area during the time that one barrier is being replaced by another [4,5]. The existence of a barrier-breach is dependent not on the structure of an individual sensor barrier, but on the relative shape of two consecutive sensor barriers, which can be illustrated as follows.

Consider Fig. 1(c), where specific points in the plane have been highlighted. The order in which the barriers are scheduled makes a significant difference, in particular, for barriers B_1 and B_2. If B_2 is scheduled first, followed by B_1, then an intruder could move to the point highlighted by a diamond, and after B_2 is turned off, the intruder is free to cross the entire area. Also, only one of B_3 and B_4 is of use. To see this, suppose that we activate B_3 first. In this case, the intruder can move to the location of marked by the black star. Then, when B_4 is activated and B_3 deactivated, the intruder can reach the users undetected. The situation is similar if B_4 is activated first, and the intruder moves to the location of the grey star.

The complexity of obtaining the largest number of breach-free sensor barriers is an open problem. Thus, heuristics have been presented in [4,5]. In [2], we presented a heuristic which outperforms those of [4,5]. This heuristic, as well as those in [4,5], are centralized. In our latest work [1], we transform the heuristic we presented in [2] into a fully distributed solution, where the sensor nodes organize themselves into breach-free barriers. In addition to being distributed, our solution is stabilizing, i.e., starting from any state, a subsequent state is reached and maintained where the sensors are organized into breach-free barriers.

References

1. Cobb, J.A., Huang, C.T.: Stabilizing breach-free sensor barriers. Technical report, Department of Computer Science, The University of Texas at Dallas, May 2015
2. Cobb, J.A.: Improving the lifetime of non-penetrable barrier coverage in sensor networks. In: International Workshop on Assurance in Distributed Systems and Networks (2015, to appear)
3. Huang, C., Tseng, Y.: The coverage problem in a wireless sensor network. In: ACM International Workshop on Wireless Sensor Networks and Applications (WSNA) (2003)
4. Kim, D., Kim, J., Li, D., Kwon, S.S., Tokuta, A.O.: On sleep-wakeup scheduling of non-penetrable barrier-coverage of wireless sensors. In: Proceedings of the IEEE Global Communications Conference (GLOBECOM 2012), pp. 321–327, December 2012
5. Kim, H.B.: Optimizing Algorithms in Wireless Sensor Networks. Ph.D. thesis, The University of Texas at Dallas, Advisor: J. Cobb, May 2013
6. Kumar, S., Lai, T.H., Posner, M.E., Sinha, P.: Maximizing the lifetime of a barrier of wireless sensors. Mobile Computing, IEEE Transactions on **9**(8), 1161–1172 (Aug 2010)
7. Vu, C., Chen, G., Zhao, Y., Li, Y.: A universal framework for partial coverage in wireless sensor networks. In: 2009 IEEE 28th International Performance Computing and Communications Conference (IPCCC), pp. 1–8, December 2009

Author Index

Printed in the United States
By Bookmasters